Philipp Spitta

JOHANN SEBASTIAN BACH

VOLUME III

PHILIPP SPITTA

JOHANN SEBASTIAN BACH

HIS WORK AND INFLUENCE ON THE
MUSIC OF GERMANY, 1685-1750.

TRANSLATED FROM THE GERMAN BY

CLARA BELL

AND

J. A. FULLER-MAITLAND.

IN THREE VOLUMES

VOL. III

LONDON
NOVELLO & CO., LTD.

NEW YORK
DOVER PUBLICATIONS, INC.

Published in Canada by General Publishing Company, Ltd.,
30 Lesmill Road, Don Mills, Toronto, Ontario.

This Dover edition, first published in 1992, is an unabridged
republication (in three volumes) of the two-volume 1952 Dover
reprint of the Bell and Fuller–Maitland translation originally
published in three volumes by Novello & Company, Ltd., in
1889. The Bibliographical Note that appears in Volume I was
specially prepared for the Dover edition by Saul Novack.

Manufactured in the United States of America
Dover Publications, Inc., 31 East 2nd Street, Mineola, N.Y.
11501

Library of Congress Cataloging-in-Publication Data

Spitta, Philipp, 1841–1894.
    [Johann Sebastian Bach. English]
    Johann Sebastian Bach : his work and influence on the
music of Germany, 1685–1750 / Philipp Spitta ; translated
from the German by Clara Bell and J.A. Fuller-Maitland.
          p.   cm.
    Includes bibliographical references and indexes.
    ISBN 0-486-27412-8 (v. 1 : pbk.). — ISBN 0-486-27413-6
(v. 2 : pbk.). — ISBN 0-486-27414-4 (v. 3 : pbk.)
    1. Bach, Johann Sebastian, 1685–1750. 2. Bach, Johann
Sebastian, 1685–1750—Criticism and interpretation.
3. Composers—Germany—Biography. I. Title.
ML410.B1S713 1992
780'.92—dc20
[B]   92-25199
                                                          CIP
                                                          MN

CONTENTS.

BOOK VI.

The Final Period of Bach's Life and Work.

Philipp Spitta

JOHANN SEBASTIAN BACH

VOLUME III

BOOK VI.

I.

DISPUTES WITH ERNESTI.—THE *COLLEGIUM MUSICUM*,—

THE ORIGIN OF THE *CONCERT*.

GESNER'S successor as rector of the Thomasschule was Johann August Ernesti,[1] who in 1732 had been appointed Conrector. Ernesti, born in 1707, was still very young when he was placed at the head of the school; but he was qualified for the post by his learning and accomplishments, grounded on a thorough knowledge of the authors of antiquity, and by a conspicuous talent for methodical teaching. Under his guidance the school made wonderful progress, and in this respect he was worthy to· succeed Gesner, whom he even excelled in his writings by their lucidity, accuracy, and a high and pure standard of Latinity. On the other hand, he lacked the geniality, the sympathetic kindliness, and the breadth of culture by which Gesner's highly successful work had been carried out, as well as his judgment and delicate tact. Ernesti held the place of Rector till 1759, when he accepted a professorial Chair in the University.

Bach, who was now nearly fifty, was at first on excellent terms with his superior, whose father he might very well have been in point of age. His family continued to increase; in 1733 he had already requested Ernesti to be godfather to one of his sons, and he did so again on the birth of his last son, Johann Christian, in September, 1735. But these friendly relations were not destined to be

---

[1] See Vol. II., p. 261.

of long continuance. In the choir composed of the foundation scholars the prefects filled the office of deputy to the
cantor, and among them the head prefect held a particularly
important place. In 1736 a certain Gottfried Theodor
Krause of Herzberg filled this post. He had been expressly
enjoined by Bach to keep a strict watch over the smaller
boys, and when, in Bach's absence, any disorderly
conduct should arise in church, to meet it with due
punishment. When Krause found that he could no longer
control the ill behaviour of the troop of boys by admonition,
and when, on a certain occasion of a wedding, their mis-
conduct had gone too far, he proposed to flog some of the
worst. They resisted, and finally had a severer dose of the
cane than had been intended. A complaint was laid before
the rector, who was furious with the prefect. Krause's
previous character was blameless; he was on the point
of going to the University, and had taken part in the
school speeches of April 20.[2] In spite of this Ernesti
condemned him to the ignominious punishment of a public
flogging in the presence of the whole school. Bach inter-
posed and took Krause's fault entirely upon himself, but
without success. When a second attempt to obtain re-
mission was angrily rejected by the rector, Krause, to elude
the disgrace that threatened him, took upon himself to quit
the school. His little possessions and singing money, which
had gradually accumulated to thirty thalers and which was
in the rector's hands, Ernesti withheld, but he had to restore
them by order of the Council (dated July 31) whom Krause
petitioned for redress.

Bach felt himself aggrieved in the person of his prefect,
and the proceeding implanted in his heart a dislike to
Ernesti from which evil results were to follow. The school
regulations of 1723 describe it as the duty and right of
the Cantor to compose the four choirs out of the pupils
fitted for each, and select the choir prefects. In this last
choice he was to obtain the consent of the Superintendent,

---

[2] See Ernesti's school report for April 20, 1736, p. 15, in the Library of the
Thomasschule.

and the rector had to give his approval to the composition of the choirs, though he had no right to any initiative. Traditional custom allowed the cantor even wider control, and left him all but unlimited mastery in all matters relating to the choir; here, as in many other cases, the old practice survived in spite of the new regulations. When Gottfried Krause had refused to submit to the ignominious punishment to which he was condemned, the rector had suspended him from his office, and at the same time had, on his own authority, promoted the second prefect, Johann Gottlob Krause of Grossdeuben[3] to fill his place *pro tem.* But the cantor had for a long time past disapproved of this individual, and had not concealed the fact. On the twenty-second Sunday after Trinity (Nov. 6) of the previous year, Magister Abraham Krügel, of Collmen near Colditz, had been married to the daughter of pastor Wendt of that place. Ernesti and Bach had been invited, and as they were returning home together in the evening the conversation fell on the new appointments to the post of prefect which were always made before the Christmas perambulations. Johann Krause had a right to one from his age and place in the school, but Bach hesitated and said he had always been "a disreputable dog." Ernesti admitted this, but still opined that he could not well be passed over, since he was distinguished for his talents, and seemed to have improved in morals, if only he possessed sufficient musical knowledge. Certain pecuniary benefits were attached to the place of prefect; Krause might be able in this way to release himself from his debts, and thus the school would be spared a discreditable report. In musical matters Bach considered him sufficiently competent, at any rate as a lower prefect, so he was made fourth, third, and finally second prefect; and even his temporary promotion to be first prefect Bach had agreed to, though the rector's independent action annoyed him. However, at the end of a few weeks, he was convinced that Krause was not equal to this responsible and onerous position; he therefore set him down again to be

---

[3] See Vol. II., p. 240

second prefect and gave the more competent Samuel Küttler (or Kittler) of Bellgern[4] the first place, and communicated both nominations in writing to the rector. Ernesti did not like it, but he yielded ; not so Krause himself. He complained to the rector, and was referred by him to the cantor. Now Bach's vexation and wrath blazed out. He let himself be provoked into answering that the rector had shoved him into the place of first prefect on his own authority, and he, the cantor, turned him out again to show the rector who was master here. And he repeated this in the rector's room, to his face. Ernesti thought he ought not to submit to such a mode of proceeding, and, fortified by the Superintendent, he required Bach, in writing, to reinstate Krause. Bach must have seen that he had gone too far ; he showed himself disposed to an amiable accommodation, and even promised to yield to Ernesti's demands. But, at the very next practice, Krause behaved so badly that this was impossible. On July 20 he went on a journey, and did not return till August 1. Ernesti, who was expecting Krause's re-appointment—and it would seem that Bach's conduct justified him in this—became impatient, and when Bach still took no action he wrote to him on Saturday, August 11, a letter categorically stating that if Bach did not at once do what was required of him he himself would re-instate the prefect on Sunday morning early. Bach remained silent. Ernesti carried out his threat and allowed Krause himself to inform Bach of the fact.

It was before Matins ; Bach went at once to Deyling, the Superintendent, and laid the matter before him, and Deyling promised, after making enquiries, to do his best to settle the dispute. Meanwhile the service had begun. Bach fetched Küttler, who, as second prefect, had gone by the rector's order to the Church of St. Nicholas, took him into St. Thomas' and turned out Krause in the middle of the hymn, stating, without any grounds, that he was authorised by the Superintendent. Ernesti saw the proceeding, and after church he also told his story to the Superintendent, whom

---

4 See Vol. II., p. 240.

he won over to his side. This he reported to Bach, who retorted with growing indignation that he would not retract a word in the matter, let it cost what it might, and that he had besides laid a complaint in writing before the Council. Before the beginning of Vespers the rector made his appearance in the organ choir and publicly prohibited the boys, under penalty of the severest punishment, to carry out Bach's orders regarding the prefects. When Bach came and found Krause again in the first prefect's place he once more turned him out with much vehemence ; but now, the foundation boys having been intimidated by the rector's threats, there was no one to lead the motett, and Bach's pupil Krebs, who had been at the University since 1735, and who happened to be present, at his master's request undertook to direct it. The result was a second appeal from the Cantor, who felt himself deeply aggrieved with regard both to his authority and his self-respect. When that same evening Küttler came to table, Bach angrily sent him away, because he had obeyed the rector and not the cantor.[5]

On the following Sunday, Aug. 19, these irritating proceedings were repeated ; Bach would not allow the prefect nominated by the rector to direct and lead the singing, and not one of the other scholars dared to take his place. Bach had to make up his mind to conduct the motett himself, contrary to custom ; and a University student once more led it. On this Bach addressed a third appeal to the Council. He represented that if things went on thus, public scandal and disorder must continue to increase, and that if the Council did not at once look into the matter he would hardly be able to maintain his authority over the scholars. Meanwhile Ernesti was also required to give his account of the affair, in which he ingeniously tried to justify himself and cast all the blame on the cantor. But no interference of the Council followed, notwithstanding the pressing need of it.

Bach now tried other means. His application for a Court title, forwarded to Dresden under the date of July 27, 1733,

---

[5] Bach must have been the School Inspector for these weeks, and must have had to eat with the foundation scholars.

had remained unanswered, the reason no doubt being the political confusion at the beginning of the reign of August III., and his absence from Saxony for nearly two years (Nov. 3, 1734—Aug. 7, 1736). Since then Bach had endeavoured to please the Court by several festival performances, the times were quieter and a repetition of his suit seemed to promise a better issue. His talents as an artist had not been sufficient to secure him from an unworthy, nay, an ignominious position; but certain dignity conferred by the Court might avail to release him from it. On Sept. 27, 1736, he renewed his petition, and since the King was to be in Leipzig for a short time after Sept. 29, it might be conferred on him then and there. But Bach was not even yet immediately successful, and greatly annoyed by this unendurable state of affairs, in November he had drawn up a fourth appeal addressed to the consistory of Leipzig, when the appointment he coveted reached him:—

"*Decret* | Vor Johann Sebastian Bach, as Composer to the King's Court band.

"Whereas His Kingly Majesty of Poland and Serene Highness the Electoral Prince of Saxony has been graciously pleased to grant to Johann Sebastian Bach—at his humble petition presented to His Majesty, and by reason of his good skill—the *Predicate* of Composer to the Court band; this present decree is issued under his Kingly Majesty's most gracious personal signature and Royal Seal. Prepared and given at Dresden, Nov. 19, 1736."

The transmission of the patent was undertaken by the Russian Ambassador to the Royal and Electoral Court, who received it on Nov. 28. His name was Baron von Kayserling, and we shall meet with him again presently.

However, the confidence which Bach had felt in the happy results of his title was disappointed. The contest with Ernesti did not cease, and the Council still showed no signs of intervening. Thus the appeal drawn up in November, but not forwarded, had to be presented on Feb. 12, 1737. Six days previously the Council had indeed made up its mind to issue a letter to accommodate matters, but it lay by for two months, only reaching Ernesti on April 6, Bach on the 10th, and Deyling on the 20th. Nor had the Council taken any particular pains to get at the kernel of the matter in dispute. It selected the simplest issue and pronounced both parties in the wrong; Johann Krause was left first prefect, " his term at the school ending at Easter." Easter fell on April 21, thus the decision had now no practical importance; still Ernesti had conquered so far as Krause was concerned, since Bach was no longer in a position to deprive the incompetent prefect of his post.

He was not disposed, however, to rest content with the decision of the Council. Immediately after Bach's statement of Feb. 12, the Consistory had enjoined the Council and the Superintendent to investigate the matter and to adjust it without delay, as also to arrange that divine service should be performed without hindrance or interruptions. Deyling, however, took Ernesti's part and he certainly would do nothing to give the order in Council a different character to that which it ultimately possessed. Bach's relations to Deyling at that time were of course highly strained, as we may see from the following circumstance. On a certain Wednesday, April 10, in the Church of St. Nicholas, the scholar from St. Thomas' whose duty it was to lead the singing pitched the communion-hymn after the usual sermon by the Superintendent so low that the congregation could not sing with it ; but instead of speaking privately to Bach on the subject, as would have befitted its trifling character, Deyling laid a complaint before the Council through the sacristan. The Council at once summoned the cantor, charged him to enquire into the matter, reprove the leader, and for the future to appoint a fit person to do the duty. Thus Bach was once more set down.

But, on Aug. 21, Bach laid the following facts before the Consistory: "The rector had publicly, and in the presence of the assembled first class, threatened with suspension and the loss of all the singing money due to them, each and all of the scholars who should obey Bach's orders." This he regarded as an injury to the position he held and as a personal indignity, for which he was entitled to demand equally personal satisfaction. Moreover, he disputed the authority of the School Regulations of 1723, on which the decision of the Council was based. These lacked the necessary ratification of the Consistory; and for this reason their validity had already been denied by the elder Ernesti, Gesner's predecessor, while, in point of fact, in all that related to the rights of the cantor, not they, but the traditions of the place, had always been acted on. More particularly, he disputed the conclusion that it was not within the cantor's power to suspend or to dismiss a scholar from a post he had once held, " seeing that cases must arise when, *in continenti*, some change must be made, without waiting for a long investigation into trifling details of discipline and school management; and such changes in matters relating to music stood within the cantor's province, since otherwise the lads, if they know that nothing can be done to them, will make it impossible for him to govern, and fulfil his office satisfactorily." In the document of Feb. 12, Bach had contested even the " concurrence " of the rector in the appointment of the prefects, under the new School Regulations. This was so far justifiable that the rector was not allowed any positive share in the selection, but only a veto. Still, Bach must clearly have seen that he could not, under these regulations, attain what he desired— perfect independence as cantor in all matters musical.

On Aug. 28 the Consistory announced to Deyling and the Council that Bach had again applied to them and required them to furnish a report of the affair within fourteen days; but though the report was not sent in, they did not trouble themselves any farther, and Bach saw only one way open to him to secure his rights. This was by a petition addressed directly to the King, to whom he appealed Oct. 18; and on Dec. 17 the King called upon the Consistory to settle the complaint of Bach, after enquiring what was due to him. On Feb. 1, 1738, the document was handed to the Consistory, and on Feb. 5 they once more emphatically demanded of Deyling and the Council a report within fourteen days. At the time of the Easter Fair, the King himself came to Leipzig and, as has already been told, Bach on this occasion performed in his honour an "Abend-Musik," which was received with universal approval.   Now, at last, his suit was brought to an issue, which, under the circumstances, we may infer was in every way favourable to him.   The sudden lack of all documentary evidence points to the conclusion that this was brought about by the personal intervention of his Majesty.

The struggle had continued for nearly two years—almost as long as the dispute over his uncle's matrimonial difficulty in Arnstadt sixty years previously.[6]   Both had shown themselves to be genuine sons of their race, and had fought with the utmost determination for their rights.   It is not, however, on this account alone that these unsatisfactory proceedings have here been narrated at full length.[7]   They were, in fact, of decisive importance to a whole section of Bach's existence.   I regard it as a specially happy circumstance that I can point this out and treat it as the background of my picture of the last twelve years of his life.   Johann Friedrich Köhler, Pastor at Taucha, near Leipzig, in 1776 planned a history of the Schools of Leipzig,[8] in which he gave due importance to Bach.   His knowledge of that period he derived for the most part from the oral statements of past scholars of St. Thomas'.   He speaks as follows:—" Bach altogether fell out with Ernesti.   The occasion was this: Ernesti turned off the head prefect Krause, who had too severely punished a lower scholar.   He dismissed him from the school, as he had chosen to leave it, and put in his place another scholar to be chief prefect—a right properly pertaining to the cantor, whose deputy the chief prefect must be.   The person chosen being unfit to lead the church music, Bach selected another.   Thus differences arose between him and Ernesti, and from that time they were enemies.   Bach now began to hate the scholars who devoted themselves to the *humanities* and pursued music

---

[6] See Vol. I., p. 162.

[7] The original documents are inserted at full length in App. B. to Vol. II. of the German edition.

[8] The MS., which was never printed, is in the Public Royal Library at Dresden.

only as a secondary study; and Ernesti was a foe to music. If he came across a scholar who was practising on an instrument, he would say: 'Do you want to be a beer-fiddler?' By his importance in the eyes of Burgomaster Stieglitz, he succeeded in procuring that he, like his predecessor Gesner, should be excused from the duty of inspection, which was handed over to the four under-masters. Now, when it came to cantor Bach's turn, he referred to the example of Ernesti, and came neither to table nor to prayers; and this omission had the most adverse influence on the moral training of the scholars. Since that time, though many persons have held both places, there has been but little harmony between the rector and the cantor."

This quotation gives a clear hint as to the side on which the public opinion was ranged in this contest between the two officials. Bach's vehement nature carried him into various indiscretions; still, on the main point, he was in the right. He would have been still in the right, even if he had had less sound ground for appealing to the old tradition, which had never yet been disputed or abrogated. He could not possibly fulfil his office as he himself wished and as he was required to do, unless he was allowed to manage all the affairs of the choir as he judged proper. This Ernesti must have seen, even if the greatness of his antagonist had never dawned upon his mind, nor the absurdity of employing a musician like Bach to teach a parcel of schoolboys. But though he gave himself an air of treating the question from the standpoint of discipline, he nevertheless presumed to try to prove what none but a musician could decide—that Krause was not incompetent to be head prefect; and when Bach asserted that he could not direct the music, he appealed to the opinion of the scholars. Judgment must be pronounced altogether against Ernesti if we only compare the tone and feeling of the documents on either side. Bach's language is stern and sharp, and strictly to the point; and in his numerous utterances not a word is to be found personal to his opponent. Ernesti proceeds very differently. He not

only takes the opportunity of denouncing Bach to the
Council in general terms as a negligent official, who was,
properly speaking, alone guilty of the misfortunes of the
"unfortunate" Gottfried Krause, and as a haughty musician
who thought it "beneath him" to direct a simple chorale;
he accused him of never having given the prefect a lesson
or rehearsal in conducting, so as to lead him into a snare;
and he charges him with "a lie," because Bach only
mentions the appointment of Johann Krause as prefect in
the New Church, and does not allude to his former place
as fourth prefect in the New Year's singing. He does not
hesitate even to represent Bach as corruptible by bribery,
and says "he could adduce yet other evidence that Bach's
testimony is not always to be depended on, and that he,
for his part, would sooner make a discantist (treble singer)
out of an old specie thaler than out of this boy, who was
no more fit for the place than he himself was." Such
accusations as these no man should utter without proof
on the spot, and in default of this he is a slanderer.

The evil results of the contest must therefore be laid, for
the most part, to Ernesti. All that the Thomasschule owes
to him, as an educational institution, must be remembered
to his honour, but he destroyed the harmonious co-operation
of the different teachers, which had been Gesner's happy
achievement. The most nationally German of all the arts was
looked upon no longer as a means of culture, but as a ground
of contention. And not by him alone; for the rest of the
professors, some of whom had been Ernesti's pupils, followed
their rector's lead, and thus Bach fell more and more into
an isolated and doubtful position. This he bequeathed to
several of his successors, and from Ernesti in the same
way a dull and pretentious aversion to music was handed
down to his; thus a reciprocal dislike became hereditary
on both sides. Bach, to a certain extent excluded from the
school, now fixed his attention more resolutely than ever
on his independent musical occupations. Even before this
he had avoided appearing publicly as cantor, certainly not
out of petty conceit, and now he thought of himself chiefly
as composer to the King and director of music to the

princely courts of Weissenfels and Cöthen[9]—appointments
which gave him occupation as a musician at a distance, and
without interfering with the amount of freedom he desired.
His fellow officials at Leipzig must have felt this very
strongly, and that they should not have been pleased at it is
quite intelligible.   A certain ill-feeling towards him survived
among them even after his death, for at a meeting of the
Council of August 7, 1750, it was announced, with a touch of
irony, that the " Cantor—or rather the Capell-director—
Bach was dead "; and as regards a new appointment to the
post, one of the Council was of opinion that "the school
needed a cantor, and not a Capellmeister, though, of course,
he must understand music."

However, it is but justice to point out that more
occult influences were at work in the division between the
scholar and the artist.   By the beginning of the eighteenth
century music had reached a stage of development which
made its close connection with the school an impossibility;
the new vitality in which even the Protestant schools
of the time were beginning to expand was unequal
to the task of reconciling this difference; it stood in
direct opposition to the vigorous growth which in music was
struggling towards daylight.   For just as music is, in
history, the youngest of the arts, so in the course of each
separate period it comes last in the train.   The musical
art of the eighteenth century has its foundations in the
sixteenth—the era of the renaissance; but it did not
flourish till all the other grand and splendid phenomena of
the period had bloomed and faded—like a last ethereal and
glorified reflection of their dying light.   Indeed, it is only
thus that it seems possible—even with the widest allowance
for the happy characteristics of the German nation—that
music should have survived uninjured the ruin of the
thirty years' war.   It had remained in a slowly rising, yet
irrepressible, condition of development, which was destined
to swell to a triumph only in the following century; while

---

[9] Königlicher Hofcomponist, Capellmeister der Fürstenhöfe Weissenfels
und Cöthen, are his titles.

science and poetry—more nearly allied to it—began in this very century a course towards new and various ends. Different objects were desired, theories gradually ceased to be taken for granted, and at last our very greatest poets and most learned men regarded music with indifference or contempt. It was the beginning of this divergence that we may detect in the quarrel between Ernesti and Bach.

But, irrespective of this, any permanent reciprocal co-operation between music and learning was no longer to be hoped for ; music was growing so mightily both in height and breadth that it must necessarily break through the narrow bounds of the schools if not transplanted into freer soil. Bach was by no means the only artist who had run hard at the fence. As much as thirty years before the relations between a rector and cantor had been the subject of a violent dispute and of extensive discussion. About the year 1703 the rector of the school at Halberstadt, on the occasion of the interment of a distinguished Prussian official, had forbidden the whole body of choral scholars, in the open street, and under threats of expulsion from both the choir and the school, to obey the orders of the cantor, although he had previously desired them to co-operate with him, as was customary. On this, Johann Philipp Bendeler, cantor at Quedlinburg, took occasion to define in a searching discussion the limits of the interdependence of the rector and cantor.[10] In matters musical the pre-eminence rests with the cantor; the rector is no doubt the head of the school, but what has the church music to do with the school ? What can it matter to the cantor to whom his assistants are subordinate, except as regards music ? As to the appointment of the prefects, the rector and cantor must come to an understanding, but the rector must not be able to appoint any prefect against the will of the cantor. " When I am required to perform a

---

[10] " *Directorium* | *musicum*, | oder | Gründl. Erörterung | Dererjenigen | Streit-Fragen, | Welche bisshero hin und wieder zwischen | denen Schul-*Rectoribus* und *Cantoribus* über dem *Directorio Musico movir*et | worden, &c. | Von | Joh. Phil. Bendeler, *Cant.* | zu Quedlinb. | Gedruckt im Jahr 1706. Royal Library at Berlin.

musical *Actus* I announce the fact to the rector and order my class, and then enjoin the scholars each to excuse himself properly for his absence to his master." The cantor is to have the power of excluding any scholar who is unavailable for musical purposes from the church music, from the choir, and from the emolument attached to it ; nor shall he be bound previously to consult with the superiors or with the rector. "Any one who deprives the cantor of this power will become the cause of many sins, and treats the cantor not much better than if he turned him out, with his hands tied, among a swarm of bees, humble-bees, and hornets." "When the scholars ought to come they stay away, when they ought to stay they run away, and so on. And in order that they may be the safer they insinuate themselves in all sorts of ways into the good graces of the rector, slander the cantor, and so forth ; whereby the rector is the more zealous to support them, but the cantor the more moved to think of his own safety." The close of the treatise consists of three judgments on the subject, which all pronounce in favour of Bendeler's views ; they are derived from the Universities of Halle and Helmstädt, and from the Court of Assessors of the Electorate of Saxony at Leipzig. It would be easy, as we read this dissertation, to fancy that it proceeds neither from Halberstadt nor from Quedlinburg, and that it was Bach—not Bendeler—who wrote it.

In fact, there was only too good reason for such squabbles, and a similar one took place at Freiburg during Bach's lifetime. Music was forcing its way to freedom—the freedom of the concert. But, in Germany, the time was not yet come for allowing it such freedom. Bach still stands on the old ground, but already a breath of air from the new land is wafted towards him, and shows its influence on his art. How it pervades his compositions has been shown again and again. Now we shall be able to detect it even in the circumstances of his outward life.

What I have here said is not to be understood as meaning that Bach's art lacked in anything requisite to secure its perennial vitality, or that its full thriving and bloom were checked by any narrowness of its surroundings, particularly in his later years. Once more must it be repeated, the whole course of his life was throughout and thoroughly favourable to him ; the difficulties were never greater than his genius could surmount without injury. When the turn came in Bach's affairs, which is marked by his quarrel with the school authorities, he had already reached the highest mark. As we glance over the whole of his accomplished work we never have the sense of anything having been left unfinished. We cannot conceive of Bach in circumstances such as those by which Handel was surrounded, and his creations promulgated, in London. Bach had developed early and quickly, and naturally came early to a standstill ; at the period when he was writing his Passions, the Christmas Oratorio, and the first two numbers of the B minor Mass, Handel was still far from his goal ; and when Handel was in fact just beginning Bach was ceasing to write. Above all, however, it must be explained that Bach took no direct part in the revolution which gradually made its way in the social life of Leipzig during the fifth decade of the century ; although this very revolution was destined to bring about a change which is indicated in many ways in Bach's works—*i.e.*, the neglect of the Church as the chief centre of music, and the gradual evolution of the independent public *Concert*.

The natural and obvious centre for this was offered by the well-known *Collegia Musica*. At an earlier period these had consisted merely of weekly meetings of musicians of repute, and in this form were tolerably general, at any rate in Saxony. Their objects were, as Kuhnau had once said, "constant practice and improvement in a noble art, and to establish side by side with a pleasing harmony of sounds an equal harmony and agreement of minds, which among people of this stamp was too often lacking."[11] Kuhnau himself, in 1688, was member of such a *Collegium Musicum* in Leipzig.

Then, in the beginning of the eighteenth century, we find the first *Musik-vereine*, musical associations of students,

---

[11] Kuhnau, Der Musicalische Quack-Salber. 1700, p. 12.

notably that founded in 1704 by Telemann, which was
subsequently under the direction of Bach himself, and
which became a very important institution.   The endeavour
to extend the breadth and freedom of musical practice by
their means is conspicuous, particularly as these societies
included not performers only but listeners as well; still
they were for the most part confined to the students of
the Universities, and it was not till after 1740 that we find
the citizens caught in the current.   In 1741 Zehmisch, a
member of the worshipful class of merchants, undertook
to form a new society for giving concerts.[12]   But the preparatory arrangements were long in hand, possibly in
consequence of the first war with Schleswig then in progress; it was not till two years later that the society was
formally called into existence.   "On March 11, 1743, the
grand *Concert* was founded by sixteen persons, both nobles
and citizens; each person being required to pay annually
for its support the sum of twenty thalers—that is to say,
one Louis d'or per quarter; the number of performers was
likewise sixteen selected persons, and the Concert was
given at first at the house of Herr Bergrath Schwaben in
the Grimmische Gasse, but four weeks later, as these
quarters proved to be too small, at that of Herr Gleditzsch,
the bookseller."   The enterprise at once achieved such a
brilliant success that on March 9, 1744, its first anniversary
was celebrated with a solemn festal cantata.[18]   In the
Leipzig address book or directory of 1746 and 1747 it is
thus mentioned among the permanent musical institutions:
"(3) on Thursdays a *Collegium musicum*, under the direction
of the worshipful company of merchants and other persons,
is held from five to eight o'clock at the Three Swans in

---

[12] I am unable to give any more exact information concerning this person
who was so important to the advance of Concert music in Leipzig; I find,
at least, three of this name at that time, two merchants and one *Doctor juris
utriusque*.

[18] I derive this information from the programme of the Gewandhaus concert
of March 9, 1843, a centenary celebration of this foundation.   The authority
there given is the "*Continuatio Annalium Lips. VOGELII, anno* 1743." This
work has not come to light again, however, there is no doubt of the accuracy
of the programme.

the Brühl, where the greatest masters, when they come
hither, are wont to perform; they are fashionably frequented,
and admired with much attention."

This transfer from a private house to a public situation
is sufficient evidence of the rapid progress made by the new
society. It is, in fact, the same which still exists as the
" Gewandhaus Concert," and the very day of the performance remains unaltered, though the hours are slightly
changed. An interruption occurred during the seven years'
war, but the concerts were resumed in 1763 under the
conduct of Joh. Adam Hiller, and again given at the
Three Swans. Zehmisch was still at the head of the
society; in 1768 it was said of him "Who will not, even
in time to come, laud that zeal for the advancement of
music which, for the last seven and twenty years we owe
to our friend, Herr Zehmisch? His indefatigable efforts have
given to the Leipzig Concert a character which has not
merely earned for it the unflattering praises of many
foreign professors and connoisseurs, but has even won it
the honour, three times already, of the most gracious and
illustrious Presence (of the king or princes as audience) in
which honour every member of the society has his share."[14]

The interest in music thus suddenly aroused in the
citizens of Leipzig found expression in other ways. For a
long period fifty gülden (= 43 thlrs. 18 gr.) a year had
been paid as a *beneficium* to the foundation scholars of
St. Thomas', out of the funds of the church of St. Nicholas.
From 1746 the Council caused a similar sum to be paid out
of the treasury of St. Thomas' and twenty-five thlrs. out of
that of the New Church for the maintenance of the Thomasschule, and the advancement of church music.[15] This
source of public support, which had hitherto only yielded
driblets in the cause of music, suddenly began to flow more
freely; in 1745 Bach could venture on his own account to
appoint his pupil Altnikol as bass in the church choir.
When he presented himself to receive his salary, May 19,

---

[14] From a historical explanation of pictures in the collection of Gottfried
Winkler at Leipzig (Hist. Erklärung der Gemälde, &c., Leipzig, Breitkopf, 1768).
[15] Accounts of these churches from 1747.

1747, one of the members of the Council expressed his opinion that for the future Bach ought to give notice of such a step; however, the salary was paid—six thlrs., for assisting as bass singer in the two principal churches, from Michaelmas, 1745, till May 19, 1747.

Under this new aspect of affairs the old students' musical unions lost their importance. Görner, to be sure, held his society together with characteristic tenacity, but Telemann's was visibly dwindling. Bach gave up the direction of it; in 1746 it was conducted by Gerlach; in 1747 by Johann Trier, a student of theology, who must have kept up the society till Bach's death, for he was a good musician, and did not quit Leipzig till 1754. Thus the direction, after having remained for a long period in the hands of famous artists, once more fell into those of the students, as at its beginning, and such a relapse is always a sign of decay. Why Bach withdrew is not known, only that he did so at some time between 1736 and 1746. We may safely guess that he felt no satisfaction in remaining at the head of a musical union which had now fallen into the second rank; however, we find no trace of his having taken any part in the newly-formed concert union of the citizens. His supreme superiority and great fame would have entitled him to no less a position than that of conductor if he had been concerned in it at all; and, as he did not fill this post, we may safely assume that he had—or desired to have—no influence in its formation. It was announced that the greatest "foreign" (to Leipzig) masters would perform at the concerts of the new society, but the greatest master of all, a resident in the town, was not mentioned. In 1744, on the first anniversary of its formation, a grand cantata was performed, but it was not Bach who composed it, but a young student of twenty-eight, Johann Friedrich Doles, who had been living in Leipzig since 1738, and who must have known Bach well, but who followed a quite different path of art, more pleasing to the modern taste. Five years after Bach's death Doles was appointed to his place, and held it till 1789. He, and with him Joh. Adam Hiller, forsook the lines of Bach; and, so far, it is a striking circumstance that his name should have been connected from the first with the " great Concert Union." The aims for which this society strove had found their forecast here and there in Bach's life and works, but they had nothing in common with the essential character of the master.

Bach's illustrious position was, however, firmly rooted in the mind of the inhabitants, and nothing could now shake it. He was the glory of their city; no musician of repute ever visited it without paying his respects to Bach. Pupils streamed to and fro, and to be received by him was a coveted honour. He was always regarded as the first authority on organ building; in 1744 he was required to test the new organ built by Joh. Scheibe in the church of St. John. Although Scheibe's son, the author of the " Kritischer Musicus," had incurred Bach's displeasure, the Cantor was thought impartial enough to try the organ, and he pronounced it faultless; though Agricola frankly says that he put it to the severest tests that any organ had perhaps ever undergone.[16] Two years later Scheibe completed another organ, under a contract, for 500 thlrs., at Zschortau, near Delitzsch, and here Bach again was called in to test it, in the beginning of August, 1746.[17]

Some of Bach's secular compositions seem to have become popular and to have long kept a hold upon the people. In a description of the *Kirmess*[18] at Eutritzsch, near Leipzig, in 1783, we are told " the band of musicians strikes up bravely, beginning with sonatas by Bach and ending with ballads."[19] By this must be meant portions out of orchestra-partitas, for in the parlance of the town and tower musicians, even in the nineteenth century, the word *sonata* retained its original meaning of a single instrumental piece in several parts.[20] At any rate, this notice proves that Bach's name

---

[16] Adlung *Mus. Mech.*, p. 251.

[17] Bach's certificate was, in 1872, in the possession of Herr Clauss (General consul) in Leipzig. Bach received 5 thlrs. 12 gr. for his pains.

[18] The Saint's day of the parish church; a festival known as the "wake" in some parts of England.

[19] *Tableau* von Leipzig im Jahre, 1783. 1784.

[20] " In the performances on wind instruments on the tower, besides the simple chorales, *Sonatas* composed expressly were given on the widely

survived among the people. When the concert-room of the Gewandhaus was finished, in 1781, the painted ceiling (by Oeser) showed the older music expelled by modern music, which took its place, and the art triumphant was represented by a genius with a scroll, on which was inscribed only the name of Bach ; Forkel observes this was the highest panegyric he could receive,[21] and, at any rate, this was the intention ; even that generation, which understood the master's mind less than any before or after it, would not deny him the highest rank and praise, and across a blank gulf of thirty years the mighty name sounded out to command veneration and stir a worthy pride.

Still, even before his death, he had ceased to be the heart of musical vitality in Leipzig ; duly contemplating all the facts, we are forced to conclude that, though still admired, he had ceased to be understood or loved. His fate has this in common with that of Beethoven, who, in his later years, in spite of the undiminished respect of the Vienna public, gradually lost his popularity under the foreign influence of Rossini. But Bach could look down calmly enough on all the bustle of the young world at his feet.

A society for musical science (Societät der Musikalischen Wissenschaften), founded in Leipzig in 1738, made itself a good deal talked about. Its promoter and centre was Lorenz Christoph Mizler, born July 25, 1711, at Wurtemberg ; he had been educated at the Gymnasium at Anspach, and subsequently, with a brief interruption, was a student at Leipzig from April 30, 1731, till 1734. He had been a diligent musician from his boyhood, and at Leipzig he was under Bach's personal teaching—probably through Gesner's good offices—in clavier playing and composition. In 1734 he took the degree of *Magister*, and on June 30 disputed

---

resounding instruments, which all the inhabitants of a village or of a whole town might hear." Ch. C. Rolle, Neue Wahrnehmungen zur Aufnahme der Musik, Berlin, 1784. Friedrich Schneider, a native of Saxony (1786-1853) in his youth composed twelve so-called *Thurmsonaten*, for two trumpets and three trombones. See Kempe, Friedrich Schneider, als Mensch und Künstler. Dessau, 1859.

[21] Musikalische Almanach für Deutschland, 1783. Leipzig: Schwickert.

publicly on a dissertation, "*Quod musica ars sit pars eruditionis philosophicæ.*" He dedicated his essay to four musicians: Mattheson, Bach, Bümler, and Ehrmann—the last, a native of Anspach, had grounded him in the elements of musical knowledge. In his address, dated June 28, he says: " I have derived great profit, most famous Bach, from your instructions in the practice of music, and lament that I can no longer enjoy them."[22] He was in fact leaving Leipzig, and soon addressed himself to other studies in Wittenberg. His dissertation met with a favourable reception from those to whom he had, in the first instance, dedicated it, and this must have been one of his reasons for returning to Leipzig, where, from 1736, he gave a series of lectures on Mathematics, Philosophy, and Music, and began to bring out a critical monthly journal entitled "Neu eröffnete musikalische Bibliothek." Mizler had a friend and patron in the person of Count Lucchesini, a man of musical culture, who was captain of the Sehr regiment of Cuirassiers in service of the Emperor Charles VI., and died a soldier's death in 1739. When, during the Polish war of succession in 1735, the Emperor was hardly pressed by France and her allies, Mizler dedicated to the Count a little facetious Latin treatise, in which he represents the course of the war under the figure of the concord and discord of various musical notes.[23] Lucchesini was the first to assist him in founding the Society, while of the four musical patrons to whom he had dedicated his treatise only one supported him, old Bümler of Anspach. Mattheson was already on bad terms with Mizler, since he found himself " scoffed at in a covert manner" in the latter's Musikalische Bibliothek, and he soon became his implacable opponent. To the real aim of the

---

[22] A second edition of his essay appeared in 1736, with a new preface and under the title, " *Dissertatio quod musica scientia sit et pars eruditionis philosophicæ.*"

[23] " *Lusus ingenii de præsenti bello augustissimi atque invictissimi imperatoris Caroli VI. cum fœderatis hostibus ope tonorum musicorum illustrato.*" The key note C stands for France, the fifth, G, for Spain, the third, E, for Sardinia, the octave C for the Emperor Charles. The first three endeavour by deviations from the original key to lower the octave from C to B; they cannot succeed however; by the help of England, A, they are forced to return to their allegiance.

Society, which was to advance the science of music and reduce it to a system, Mattheson was quite indifferent; all his life through he had taught and acted on his own principles only, and had got on very well. What should he care if the Society should propound the question as to why consecutive fifths or octaves were incorrect? In his treatise on figured bass playing, he says: "Two fifths or two octaves must not occur in succession, for not only is this a fault but it sounds badly," and says no more. Or if Mizler tries to connect thorough-bass with mathematics? " In figured basses the left hand plays the prescribed notes, the right adds concords and discords in such wise that a well sounding harmony may be produced to the honour of God, and the permissible diversion of the mind. Where due heed is not paid to this there is no true music, only a diabolical clang and clatter." So Mattheson dismisses the subject. It was a well known fact that Bach never let the connection between mathematics and music worry him for an instant; Mattheson observes: "He (Bach) certainly and positively no more showed him (Mizler) these hypothetical mathematical principles of composition than the other master (meaning Mattheson himself); that I can warrant."[24] Even the writers of the Necrology state plainly: "Bach never went into a deep theoretical study of music."

Unions such as this Society was intended to be, might have their uses, but their possible results are of value only to the average mind. To the soul of genius they say too much or too little. Besides this, Bach must have been averse to Mizler's personality and projects; Mizler had had a wide education and even, for a man of his position, had sound practical views of music; his industry was untiring, and he knew how to put a good face on things in the eyes of the world. But he was vain and a swaggerer, and, at the best, but a barren soul; the compositions which he was so rash as to publish could only excite a compassionate smile in any true musician. Thus it is easy to understand that Bach should have held aloof from this musical society.

---

[24] Ehrenpforte, p. 231, note.

Mizler keenly felt the implied slur thus cast upon his undertaking. In the bye-laws of the Society, to be sure, it was stated that mere practical musicians[25] could find no place in it, since they were in no position to do anything towards the advancement or extension of scientific music. But men of Bach's stamp were not included in this category; for musicians who were strictly speaking practical, as Telemann and Stölzel, were members of it within two years of its being founded, and Handel—practical if anything—was unanimously elected an honorary member in 1745. Besides, Bach, though he had never written a treatise, was well known as a learned composer. Mizler, who by 1743 was no longer at Leipzig but living with Count Malachowski in Poland, took, in fact, great pains to induce Bach to join; in 1746 he proudly announces that it is possible the Society may soon be increased by the addition of three illustrious members; these were Graun, Bach, and Sorge. Graun in fact joined it in July of that year; Bach was not in such haste, he waited till June, 1747. When once he was a member, however, he fulfilled his duties; he composed for the Society a triple canon in six parts, and the variations upon " Vom Himmel hoch." After his death it was asserted that he would undoubtedly have done much more if the short period during which he was a member—only three years —had not prevented it. This may have been more than mere conjecture, for in later years Bach's proclivity for profound and introspective musical problems grew stronger than ever, and in this Society he would have found for these a small but very competent public.

II.

BACH'S MASSES.—THE MASS IN B MINOR.

In the foreground of a picture of Bach's later labours as a composer stand his Latin masses. Of these he wrote five,

---

[25] In the Musikalischer Staarstecher, Leipzig, 1740 (*The Musical Oculist!* to cure the blind in matters musical), Mizler designates as " practical musicians " those who only sing or play and do not compose; this is probably how it was understood in the laws of the Society.

and the first question must be whether, and in what way, these stood in any connection with the Protestant form of divine service.

The form of worship in the principal churches of Leipzig had remained nearly allied to that of the Catholics, as was also the case in various other places, and I have already fully discussed the subject (Vol. II., p. 263). With the Latin hymns and responses and Latin motetts, the *Magnificat* was also sung in Latin at Vespers on the three great festivals, and we have seen how Bach thus found the opportunity for composing one of his most important works (Vol. II. p. 369). In this way the principal portions of the choral Latin mass maintained their existence and actually the very same places in the service that they had always held: partly, indeed, the German texts that replaced them did the same. However, the *Kyrie, Gloria*, and *Credo* only were retained for all Sundays and Holy days, and even these were not always sung all through. The *Sanctus* was introduced only on the great festivals, and we have no evidence as to the *Agnus Dei;* it does not seem to have been used in the choral form.

The case is different as regards the figured treatment of the sentences of the mass, which was never used in a connected form in the divine service as performed at Leipzig. The introduction of the Protestant Church Cantata had partly displaced and throughout restricted all other part music. Indeed, there was not even space left to perform the whole of the shorter mass, *Kyrie,* and *Gloria.* From the account previously given of the forms of worship at Leipzig we can only find certain evidence of the use of the *Kyrie* on the first day of Advent and the Reformation festival, and of the *Sanctus* on the three great festivals. If any other portion of the mass was sung, it must have been an occasional performance. Christmas offered an obvious opportunity for the use of the *Gloria;* it then took the place of the cantata, and Bach did actually make use, for a Christmas performance, of the *Gloria* from his B minor mass in a somewhat abridged form. If we desire to acquire any further information as to occasional use of parts of the mass, we must derive it from a time later than Bach's; this can be done with considerable

certainty. During the whole eighteenth century the tendency
was towards the limitation or even elimination of the Latin
portions of the liturgy. What the Town Council began in
1702 was still being carried on by Johann Adam Hiller in
1791, although by that time the existence of the Latin hymns
or canticles had left no trace behind.[26] It is very certain
that everything that remained in use at a later date must
have been usual in Bach's time, and probably much more.
Thus, even at a late period, we find the *Agnus* sung at the
communion on the feast of the Visitation, and the *Gloria*
after the motett at evening service on the same day. In
the church of the University—which may be cited on this
occasion because its service grew after and out of those at
St. Nicholas and St. Thomas—during the ecclesiastical year
from 1779-1780—the following parts of the mass were sung:
on Christmas-day the whole *Gloria* from a mass by Gassmann;
on the feast of Epiphany the *Sanctus, Benedictus,* and *Agnus*
from a mass by Haydn; on Jubilate Sunday a *Gloria* by
Hasse; on Trinity Sunday a *Credo* by Haydn; on the
second Sunday during the fair a *Gloria* by Graun. Thus
every part of the mass has its representative excepting the
Kyrie.[27]

Though in the liturgy only a few portions of the mass
were prescribed to be performed in the ornate style, still
even this kept up a certain sense of connection with the
mass as a whole, particularly as it still appeared almost
entire in its original chanted form in public worship. Both
artistic and religious reasons tended to allow its survival, at
any rate, as the *Missa brevis.* Nor could the composition of
a solitary *Kyrie* satisfy the soul of the Christian composer;
for its melancholy sentiment craved the relief of a happy
contrast to follow, the feeling of guilt demanded absolution.[28]
Since on the first Sunday in Advent a *Kyrie* in the elaborate

---

[26] In the preface to Hiller's Four-part Latin and German choral hymns.
Part I., Leipzig, 1791.

[27] Collection of texts for church music in Leipzig in the Royal Library at
Berlin.

[28] They were always spoken of as *Kyrie cum Gloria,* not *et;* this indicated
that the *Gloria* was regarded as supplementary to the *Kyrie.*

style was directed to be sung, and afterwards at Christmas, the *Gloria in excelsis* supplied and expressed the leading sentiment of the festival, it was very natural that the composer should refer the one to the other and unite them in a single composition.   And accordingly, we find that Bach's predecessors, Knüpffer and Kuhnau, composed the "short mass."[29]   So also did Görner and Hoffmann, who for a time was the director of Telemann's musical union; as Hoffman instituted performances in the New Church, though they took place only on the high festivals and during the fair time, we may assume that the *Kyrie* and the *Gloria* were sung in succession during one and the same service. However, something else must have contributed in Bach's case to urge him to the composition of a mass, and to give rise in the first instance to several works of his of this class. This was, in fact, his connection with Dresden, and the interest he thus acquired in Italian and in Catholic church music generally; finally, too, his duty, as composer to the Royal and electoral court, of producing some works for the King from time to time.   Bach's liking for Lotti's music has already been mentioned.   Besides a mass in G minor by this master which Bach copied, at about the middle of the Leipzig period, almost wholly with his own hand,[30] there is also extant a mass in G major, in the Italian style for two choirs (and another choir to supplement them) and with instruments, of which Bach also wrote out the whole of the first twelve pages at some time about 1738.   In this we can perhaps recognise the hand of Lotti, though it is unusually diatonic in style for this master's work: at any rate, it is the composition of an Italian, or of a German who has wholly adopted the Italian style.[31]   But going farther

---

[29] Two masses by Knüpffer are mentioned in Breitkopf's list for the New Year 1764, and one by Kuhnau in his list for Easter, 1769.

[30] The watermark in the paper, M A, indicates a period between 1727 and 1736.

[31] This MS. is in the Library at Berlin.   The title is much worn and has almost disappeared, still *d L* can be traced (*di Lotti ?*).   The watermarks agree with those of the MS. of the Easter oratorio, which gives an approximate date for the writing of it; see App. A. to Vol. II., No. 58.—Schicht erroneously calls the work a mass by Joh. Seb. Bach, published by Breitkopf and Härtel.

back than Lotti, Bach also devoted much attention to
Palestrina, and copied out a grand mass of his in parts
for the singers and the supporting instruments, with
a figured bass.[32] He also wrote out a short mass in
C minor, in full score, by an unknown Italian composer of
his time.[33] A *Magnificat* by Caldara, in C major, exists in
Bach's handwriting[34] and one by Zelenka, in D major,
in that of his son Wilhelm Friedemann.[35] A number of
other settings of the *Magnificat* by anonymous but certainly
Italian composers exist, partly in Bach's writing and in
score, partly in separate parts, which are most of them
written by Anna Magdalena Bach, and supplemented here
and there by additions in her husband's hand.[36]

From this we may conclude that he not merely studied
these works, but had them performed. It even appears
that he introduced into them subjects of his own composition. We have already seen that he extended his
own grand *Magnificat* by inserting four Christmas hymns.
He did the same with a *Magnificat* in D major by another
hand; but, with the exception of " Freut euch und jubilirt,"
the hymns are inserted in different places. In the C minor
mass just alluded to, the *Christe eleison*—a short but very
artistically-written duet with *Basso quasi ostinato* — is his
work. He also collected Latin masses or portions of the
mass by other composers ; for instance, a mass by Wilderer
(Capellmeister to the Elector Palatine), and various others
which were long erroneously supposed to be his own compositions.[37]

---

[32] MS. in the Berlin Library.

[33] MS. in the possession of Messrs. Breitkopf and Härtel, Leipzig.

[34] Berlin Library.

[35] Thomasschule Library.

[36] Berlin Library.

[37] Rust has given a list of these in the preface to B.-G. XI.[1] We must,
however, eliminate from this catalogue the mass in E minor (No. 3)—a work
by Nikolaus Bach which is not in Bach's writing. (See Vol. I. p. 132 and note
293, on p. 574). Breitkopf's List for Easter, 1769, like that for Michaelmas 1761,
mentions, on pp. 12 and 13, six masses by Seb. Bach, of which four are
certainly not genuine. The first must be No. 5 of Rust's Syllabus (C minor
mass, with the interpolated *Christe eleison*); the fourth No. 4 of Rust; the
fifth No. 10 (G major mass for three choruses); the sixth No. 3.

From all this, we can plainly see that Bach directed
his attention to Catholic, and more particularly Italian,
Church music ; and this is all the more noteworthy because
it was not till the period of his own ripest maturity, when he
no longer had any imperative and practical necessity for
studying such pieces. From the time and style of their
composition, it seems probable that his own masses were
for the Court of Dresden, even when we do not know it for
certain, as we do with regard to the two first numbers of
the B minor mass. Of the four shorter masses, two were
written about 1737, when Bach had just been appointed
Court composer ; and we must examine them all in detail.

Bach's shorter masses are in G major, G minor, A major,
and F major. No chronology of them can be given, since
all that is certain is that all four were written after 1730,
and the first and third about 1737. I may, however,
express my own conviction that Bach composed them all
within a short time ; and I arrange them in accordance
with certain internal evidence. The masses in G major
and G minor were not new compositions—they consist
entirely of portions of cantatas written previously.[38] For
this, however, various re-arrangements were necessary,
which—as always with Bach—are highly instructive, and
in many respects admirable. Even without any direct
reason arising from the fresh text and purpose, he has in
many cases given the compositions a richer and freer form ;
but equally unmistakable is the violence he has often done
his own creations by converting them into portions of the
mass. There are among these remodelled pieces some
which are elevated by the process and severed from a
connection with some less dignified theme ; and this commonly occurs when Bach transfers a composition from a
secular to a sacred purpose. There are also re-arrangements
which work back to the original germ of the idea, and under

---

[38] This has already been pointed out by Mosewius (J. S. Bach in seinen
Kirchen-Cantaten und Choralgesängen, p. 11), and after him by M Hauptmann
in his preface to Vol. VIII. of the B.-G., which contains the masses, as far as
the final chorus of the G major mass, which is a re-arrangement of the opening
chorus of the cantata " Wer Dank opfert, der preiset mich."

the new conditions give it quite a new form. Finally, there
are some which are only a vivid reproduction of a piece;
and just as a finished composition may differ each time it
is repeated, varying with the character of the performers
and the feeling, time, place, and surroundings at the
moment, so it has happened that Bach makes a composition
serve with different effect, though with but slight alteration,
under different conditions of feeling. All these modes of
treatment have artistic justification, but none of them
have been used in the masses under discussion, which,
so far as was possible to Bach, are mere mechanical
arrangements. To see with what relentless objectiveness
Bach could sacrifice the noble proportions of his compositions, we need only compare the *Gloria* of the G major
mass with its prototype. The tremendous opening chorus
of the cantata " Herr deine Augen sehen nach dem
Glauben " is also gravely injured, though only in details,
when we find it forced into the mould of a *Kyrie* for the
G minor mass. Other pieces have suffered less reckless
treatment, but no artistic purpose in their transformation
is anywhere to be detected; and even a superficial comparison must result in favour of the cantata forms. There
each piece seems to have sprung from a living inspiration.
It corresponds to the poetical purpose, and adequately fills
its place as part of a whole; but here each gorgeous blossom
is severed from the stem and bound in an ill-assorted
nosegay. In the G minor mass Bach has not even regarded
that necessary contrast between the *Kyrie* and the *Gloria*
which, being based on the nature of the words, had already
become typical. The *Gloria* does not stand out in radiant
contrast of Christmas glory after the passionate and
agitated *Kyrie*, but, on the contrary, continues the same
strain of sad and unfulfilled longing. Even the closing
chorus, though impressive, retains the same gloomy
solemnity.

It is at once evident that Bach cannot have written the
G major and G minor masses for his churches at Leipzig.
As the chanted mass as a whole had no place in the Leipzig
Liturgy, it is impossible to imagine any reason which could

have prompted him to make up two such questionable
pieces out of some of his finest cantatas, and to set them
before the congregation on some special occasion in this
fragmentary and ineffective form.   These masses must have
been intended for some other place, and Dresden at once
occurs to the mind.   If we may assign the G minor mass
to about the same period as the other, Bach may have
intended to make his mark as Court composer by thus
enriching it, and, at the same time, on account of his
immediate difficulties at Leipzig, to keep himself in mind
at Court.   The work, which was evidently written in haste,
indicates lack of time and of the humour for original
production.

We trace this also in parts of the A major mass written in
1737; in this, with the exception of the Aria in F sharp minor,
the *Gloria* can be shown to be put together from portions of
cantatas,[39] and I have no doubt that even this air might be
found to have its original home elsewhere.   Our judgment
of this work can be no more favourable than of the two
former masses.   That no task was too severe for Bach is
sufficiently proved by the first section, where, to make
the original subject serviceable, a four-part chorus had
to be inserted into the instrumental portions, while a solo
for bass voice had to be amplified into a full chorus.
This is accomplished in the most facile manner, but the
glorious poetry of the original composition, to the words
" Friede sei mit euch "—" Peace be with you " (from the
Cantata " Halt im Gedächtniss Jesum Christ ")—is almost
completely destroyed.   The voice solos are rounded off
and extended, often illuminated by masterstrokes, and on
the whole by no means ill-fitted to their purpose; the
final chorus has brilliancy enough, but the characteristic
ardour which gives the fundamental feeling of the original
has been effaced by the accommodation to a new text.
This *Gloria* is cast into still deeper shade from the *Kyrie*

---

[39] Hitherto this has only been established with regard to the Arias for
the soprano and the alto (see Mosewius, *loc. cit.*).   The final chorus, however,
is also a re-arrangement of the opening chorus of the cantata " Erforsche mich
Gott und erfahre mein Herz."

which precedes it. This is not, as in the other two masses, composed as a single number, but divided into the three sections indicated by the sentences; the first gives us the image of a simple and timid soul in fervent supplication; the second section, *Christe eleison*, displays an amalgamation of the freest with the strictest form, achieved with the daring of genius—it is a chorus in canon, but with the character of a recitative.[40] The last section also is in canon, but more strictly worked out as to form. Both are stamped with the sentiment of helpless weakness and a passionate desire for redemption, kept, however, within the limits prescribed by the first section. The style of the canon treatment contributes greatly to this result; since the parts always follow each other at equally wide intervals —of fourths or fifths—the modulation deviates more and more from its starting point, presently to return by an unexpected phrase into the original path. The feeling of a fundamental key is thus entirely eliminated, conspicuously in the last section.[41] There is no piece by Bach in which depth of purpose and sweetness of sound have more closely joined hands. As a whole this mass will be only fully understood when the last of the four, in F major, is discussed.

The conditions are almost the same in the *Gloria*; the final chorus and the arias for alto and soprano may be pointed out as borrowed from other works;[42] and the opening chorus is unquestionably not written for it; its aria-like structure of itself betrays this, the repeated portion having a different text—quite contrary to all tradition and sense of form. The recurrence of the principal theme (the first sixteen bars) no less than five times in the three sections, and of the middle theme (bars 101—118) no less than three times, is also not in Bach's usual manner. We

---

[40] An analogous, but far less artistic, example is the four-part recitative at the close of the Christmas Oratorio " O'er us no more shall fears of Hell " (Novello's 8vo ed., p. 168).

[41] The *Christe* is quoted by Kirnberger—Kunst des reinen Satzes, II., 3, p. 63—as a masterpiece of canon writing, and he observes that " it is quite unlike all church-music previously written because that was generally in the so-called heavy style in which hardly any variety in the dissonances was admitted."

[42] Hauptmann, preface to B.-G. VIII.

seem actually to see the joins in this chorus, though it is externally compact, and is carried rapidly onwards by its animated flow.[43]   The only bass air which remains could not, of course, be an exception among all these borrowed pieces. It is otherwise, however, with the *Kyrie*. Expressive and appropriate fugal movements develop the text in three sections ; a leading theme runs through them, and in the second section comes forward in a form which is the outcome of a free inversion ; in the third section only the second half is thus modified, while the total subject thus obtained is once more answered in perfect inversion.   While this is going on in the three upper parts, the bass voice as *Cantus firmus* sings the *Kyrie eleison! Christe eleison! Kyrie eleison!* of the Litany. As a second *Cantus firmus* the chorale "Christe du Lamm Gottes" is given out by horns and oboes, only the *Amen* is somewhat altered, and in another position, so as to close in the original key.

It was not unusual at that period to introduce a Protestant sacred melody into a setting of the mass.   Ernst Bach had made the attempt with the chorale " Es woll uns Gott genädig sein " (see App. B., II.) ; Zachau, again, with the Easter hymn, " Christ lag in Todesbanden,"[44] Kuhnau with the hymn for Whitsuntide *Veni sancte Spiritus;* an unknown composer with the Advent hymn, *Veni redemptor gentium;* while Telemann adapted the *Kyrie* no less than five times to Protestant hymn tunes, both cheerful and mournful.[45]   A capital piece of music is Nikolaus Bach's E minor mass, in which the *Gloria* is combined with the chorale "Allein Gott in der Höh" (Vol. I., p. 133); here the words of the mass and of the chorale have just such a correspondence of feeling as in Sebastian Bach's mass, but it was only Sebastian himself who could weld them into an organic unity both of form and purpose, because his conception,

---

[43] The original form may be approximately traced in bars 1—28+65—83 as the first and third sections, and 84—118 as the second; only, of course, as to the main material of the music.   Compare this with the construction of the opening chorus of the cantata " Es erhob sich ein Streit," B.-G. II., No. 19.

[44] Chrysander, Händel I., p. 25.

[45] See Breitkopf's Easter list, 1769, and New Year's list, 1764.

even of the Latin words, was strictly Protestant in
character.[46] The *Kyrie* of the F major mass is one of
his profoundest and most impressive pieces, and trans-
cends even that of the A major mass by what I may
designate as a monumental character, which suggests to our
minds that Protestantism is not the reaction from Catholic
church feeling, but rather the outcome of its development
and continuity ; this work, with its Protestant chorale,
could not, of course, have been written for any Catholic congregation. But its abstruse affinities yet remain to be
indicated, and by them the clue to its full comprehension.
The *Cantus firmus* given to the bass voice is not the ordinary
Kyrie Dominicale but the *Kyrie* from the Litany, and of that
the closing and not the opening phrase :—[47]

In the Litany this is immediately preceded by the appeal
to the Redeemer, " O Lamb of God, Thou that takest
away the sins of the world," &c., the very words of the
Cantus firmus; thus Bach has entwined and supported his
setting of the mass with the last two sentences of the
Litany.

There were only two church seasons during which the
Litany was used at Leipzig : Advent and Lent. Since
during Lent, and on the three last Sundays in Advent, no
concerted music was admissible, this composition, from
internal evidence, must have been written for the first
Sunday in Advent; the congregation is expressly prepared
for that humble supplication for redemption which was

---

[46] One of the two MSS.—not in Bach's hand—in which the work exists
gives the chorale to a soprano voice. This was certainly not Bach's intention ;
the characteristic effect here, as in so many of his similar compositions, depends
essentially on the inarticulate delivery of a familiar melody quite apart from the
confusing mixture of German and Latin words.

[47] Comparison shows how Bach has added character to the phrase by the
addition of chromatic and other passing notes.

offered up after the reading of the Epistle, in which they
all took part, and which was to be repeated every Sunday,
till Christmas-tide brought fulfilment to the prayer.

If the *Kyrie* of the F major mass was written for a
Protestant service the *Gloria* must have been also; and here,
undoubtedly, that religious motive of his art which has
been mentioned strongly influenced Bach. The spirit
that has once so thoroughly imbibed the Advent feeling
embodied in the liturgy, as Bach has done in this
composition, must needs allow the fulfilment to crown
the anticipation; he must rise from this depth of dejection
to joy, must gladden the contrite sinner by the gospel of
salvation. He has worked out this line of feeling and has
supplemented the *Kyrie* of the first Sunday in Advent by
the *Gloria*, as the chief musical piece for Christmas-day.
Though the task has not inspired him (since he could
not fail to care more for a Christmas piece with German
words), so that he preferred to put together a *Gloria* from
earlier compositions, it must be admitted that he has here
produced a *Gloria* which is greatly superior to those of the
other short masses, setting aside the diffuseness of the
first chorus. The forced effects of the other three do not
occur in this one; the modified fragments, so far as we can
recognise them, are more carefully selected, particularly the
last chorus, which in its original state is a Christmas chorus:
" For this purpose the Son of God was manifested, that He
might destroy the works of the devil " (I. John iii. 8). This
selection of a text is still farther evidence that the *Gloria*
was intended as a Christmas piece. With the exception
of the abridged opening and a few other small changes,
the Latin chorus is a faithful reproduction of the original
under somewhat different conditions, and the feeling of the
situation also remains entirely the same. This was not
possible with the aria *Quoniam tu solus*, which, after the
elimination of the most picturesque features in the original
state, remains a neutral composition in no respect suited to
its purpose. The *Kyrie* and *Gloria* of the F major mass, as
they now exist, were conceived of as a complete whole;
this is clear from the last word of the *Cantus firmus* delivered

by the bass, which is not *Amen,* as prescribed by church custom, but once more *Eleison.* This could only occur when the artist's conception found its fitting form in closing with the *Kyrie.* At the performance on the first Advent Sunday the *Amen* was indeed sung,[48] but when the idea was continued and carried out by the *Gloria,* the *Amen* was set aside and found its fit place at the end of the whole piece.

If we now glance once more at the A major mass it is evident that it holds an intermediate position between the F major mass, on the one hand, and the G major and G minor masses on the other. It displays no essential affiliation to the Protestant service, but the well considered and loving treatment of the original *Kyrie,* in contrast to the compiled *Gloria,* makes it probable that this *Kyrie* also was originally intended for the Protestant liturgy; it could, certainly, be equally well used in Catholic worship. But whether this *Gloria* arose under the same demand as that of the F major mass, or was merely added in order to complete it for Catholic use, remains an open question; still, its having been produced as a whole, at the same time as the masses in G major and G minor, renders it probable that its purpose was the same.[49]

But all these works—even the F major mass—are but feeble offshoots of a *Kyrie* and *Gloria* which subsequently formed part of the B minor mass—the only grand and complete mass that Bach ever wrote. The earliest trace of this *Kyrie* and *Gloria* we detect in a passage of the *Domine Deus,* which, in the Leipzig form of prayer, deviated from the canonical text of the Catholic liturgy. In the Leipzig service it was sung thus : *Domine Deus rex cœlestis,*

---

[48] As is proved by a MS. copy of the *Kyrie* as a single piece which belonged to Joh. Adam Hiller, and is now in the Berlin Library.

[49] The autograph scores of the G major and A major masses indicate 1737—1738 as the year when they were written, the paper having the same watermark—in part at any rate—as the score of the Easter Oratorio. The original parts of the A major mass, which have lately come into the possession of the Berlin Library have, it is true, the watermark figured in note 48 of App. A. to Vol. II. Still, as the cantata " Herr deine Augen " has been borrowed from, and as all four masses seem to have been written at about the same period, it is easy to imagine that some remains of paper of a former date may have fallen under Bach's hand.

Deus Pater omnipotens. Domine Fili unigenite, Jesu Christe altissime.[50] The word *altissime* is inserted ; it was not used in the Catholic service, and, so far as I can discover, it was so sung nowhere but in Leipzig. In the B minor mass Bach has followed the Leipzig custom; but when he became more familiar with the Catholic mass he left the word out in other works of this class.

When Friedrich August II., the King and Elector, died, Feb. 1, 1733, Bach resolved to show his devotion to his successor and to raise himself in the estimation of the Leipzig functionaries by connecting himself more closely with the Court. He, therefore, composed these two subjects from the mass, and presented them himself in Dresden, July 27, 1733. The dedication that accompanied them is well-known, but must not be omitted here :—

To the most illustrious Prince and Lord, the Lord Friedrich August, King and Prince of Poland and Lithuania, Duke of Saxony, &c., &c., my most gracious Sovereign,

Most illustrious Elector,
Most gracious Lord.

I lay before your Kingly Majesty this trifling work (or proof) of the science which I have been able to attain in music, with the very humble petition that you will be pleased to regard it, not according to the measure of the meanness of the composition, but with a gracious eye, as befits your Majesty's world-famed clemency, and condescend to take me under your Majesty's most mighty protection. For some years, and up to the present time, I have had the direction of the music in the two principal churches in Leipzig; but I have had to suffer, though in all innocence, from one and another vexatious cause—at different times a diminution of the fees connected with this function, and which might be withheld altogether unless your Kingly Majesty will show me grace and confer upon me a *Prædicate* of your Majesty's Court *Capelle*, and will issue your high command to the proper persons for the granting of a patent to that effect. And such a gracious acceding to my most humble petition will bind me by infinite obligations; and I hereby offer myself in most dutiful obedience to prove my indefatigible dilligence in composing church music, as well as in your orchestra, whenever it is your Kingly Majesty's most gracious desire, and to devote my whole powers to your Majesty's service, remaining with constant fidelity your Kingly Majesty's most humble and obedient servant,

Dresden, July 27, 1733.[51]   JOHANN SEBASTIAN BACH.

---

[50] Vopelius, *ob. cit.*, p. 422.

[51] See the preface to the B.-G. edition of the B minor mass, VI., p. xv.

His desire to prove himself serviceable to the Court was the inducement which led Bach to undertake the composition of a complete full mass. The *Kyrie* and *Gloria* were, in this instance, conceived of as a whole from the first, flowed from the same fount, and were cast in the same mould. This is evident even from the scheme of key by which the last subject of the Kyrie is set—not in B minor, but in F sharp minor, to obviate the effect of a full close, and also, as the *Gloria* was to consist of two movements in B minor, to avoid monotony. The fact, too, that the first *Kyrie* is in five parts, and the last only for four, is significant from this point of view.[52] The remaining portions — the *Credo*, *Sanctus*, and *Osanna* to the *Dona*—were written separately and by degrees. It is not quite certain that the *Credo* was written later than the first two portions; if we may trust certain tokens, it may be assigned to as early a date as 1731-32. As, however, the composition of a *Credo* was not obviously necessary under the conditions of the Leipzig liturgy, it is more probable that Bach did not write this portion till the idea of writing a full mass was suggested to him by the magnificent success of the *Kyrie* and *Gloria*. The *Sanctus* was probably written in 1735 ; certainly not sooner, but not later than 1737. Since, then, for the remainder, which consists almost entirely of re-arranged pieces, no great trouble was involved, and as Bach seems to have been anxious to get the work finished, we may consider 1738 as the latest date of Bach's labours on the B minor mass.[53]

There is not the slightest indication that Bach ever presented the last three portions of the B minor mass to the King; and the two first even were never performed in Dresden, if we may derive any inference from the state of the parts as they remain in the Berlin Library. Their

---

[52] The autograph score is a clean copy, which, to judge from the initials M. A. must have been finished, if not actually in 1733, at any rate soon after. The *Kyrie* and *Gloria* are closely connected, for on p. 20, where the *Kyrie* ends, the *Gloria* is at once subjoined; and in the original score they were included together under No. 1.

[53] See App. A., No. 1.

unusual length unfitted them for use in the Catholic church;
and Bach was no doubt well aware of this, and had not
reckoned on any such performance. Still, so thoroughly
practical a musician as he was never wrote anything—and
least of all such a mighty work as this—simply to leave it
buried unheard.   He had intended it for the churches of
St. Nicholas and St. Thomas in Leipzig, and, at any rate,
performed it there—not as a whole, to be sure, but in
detached portions.   This can be proved with regard to the
Gloria and *Sanctus* and each of the following numbers.   Of
the first there is still extant a score copied in 1740, with the
significant note : " On the Feast of the Nativity." [54]   Bach
must, however, have discerned that the whole *Gloria* was
not fitted for the intended Christmas performance ; and he
prepared an arrangement which was limited to the first
and last choruses and the duets between.   The text of the
first chorus remained unchanged ; but he set the words
of the Doxology *Gloria patri et filio et spiritui sancto* to
the duet which ends at bar 74 of the original work.   The
rest of the Doxology—*Sicut erat in principio et nunc et
semper et in sæcula sæculorum.   Amen*—he set to the final
chorus ; and to this end he had to alter the opening bars.
This re-arrangement, however, does not preclude the possibility that Bach should have performed the whole *Gloria*
on occasion, as a piece of ceremonial church music.   The
Sanctus, too, was used as a Christmas piece, and was,
indeed, originally composed for that purpose, though, at
the same time, its grandiose proportions were, no doubt,
determined by the general character of the mass of which
it was destined to form a part.

The *Sanctus* in ornate style, as has already been said,
had a fixed position in the Leipzig liturgy.   At the three
great festivals it was sung at the close of the preface before
the Communion.   Bach wrote many other settings of the
Sanctus for this purpose, one of which has already been

---

[54] " *Festo Nativitatis Christi.   Gloria in excelsis Deo.*" The autograph
belongs to Herr Kammersänger Hauser, of Carlsruhe, who was good enough
to introduce it to my notice. See App. A. of Vol. II., No. 57.

mentioned when speaking of the Christmas festival of 1723 (see Vol. II. p. 369). The most important of them, however, which was also written during the early years at Leipzig, is in D major; it is a piece full of solemn inspiration constructed on attractive and beautiful themes, while an accompaniment of violins hovers seraphically above it.[55] All these compositions are somewhat meagre and only intended as a finish to the preface; the *Osanna* and *Benedictus* are wanting in all. Certainly, the mighty proportions of the *Sanctus* of the B minor mass somewhat outstep the bounds of the traditional liturgy; still it is quite clear that it was originally composed to follow the proper preface at one of the great festivals, from the fact that the *Osanna* and *Benedictus* do not form part of it.[56] Bach had combined this with the *Agnus,* a circumstance which affords an unmistakable hint as to the application of the last four numbers of the mass. It must be remembered that during the Communion service at the great festivals elaborate music was always performed. Here the *Agnus* finds its most natural place, and it can be shown to have held it even at a later date. It only was appropriate to begin the Communion music with the *Osanna* when the *Sanctus* had been previously sung. Thus Bach performed both sections in the course of one service, so that the preface ended with the *Sanctus,* then the Sacramental words were recited, and afterwards, during the distribution of the Lord's Supper, the *Osanna, Benedictus, Agnus,* and *Dona* were sung as a consecutive whole. The *Kyrie* of the B minor mass was

---

[55] B.-G., XI.,[1] p. 81. The *Sanctus* in D minor and that in G major, published in the same volume, are of inferior worth, particularly the latter; that in D minor, notwithstanding its simplicity and brevity, cannot be said to have any characteristic feeling. Two *Sanctus,* in F major and in B major which appear under Bach's name—and seem to have been set down as his original compositions even in Breitkopf's list for Michaelmas 1761—are obviously spurious; on the other hand, there is an eight-part *Sanctus* in D major which I cannot repudiate without further evidence: see Rust's Preface to B.-G., XI.,[1] p. xvii. No. 7 and 8, p. xvi. No. 6.

[56] It is a noteworthy detail that Bach always in the *Sanctus* wrote *Gloria ejus* instead of *Gloria tua;* following the text of the Bible and not that of the Canonical Mass.

too long for the customary service at the festivals of the
Reformation, and the first Sunday in Advent; by itself it
attains the dimensions of a moderately long cantata. But
as the principal anthem it may have been performed on
the Sunday next before Lent, for instance. The feast
of the Trinity, with its dogmatic character and purpose
must have seemed especially suited to the performance of
the *Credo*, and this, as I have before shown, subsequently
became the established custom. But the Saints' days
were also to be considered, because, on those days, after the
Gospel was read, the entire Nicene Creed was sung by the
choir, and the ornate *Credo* was very fitly connected with
this. There were, however, no independent services kept up
for the Saints' days at that time; they were merged into
the nearest Sunday.[57]

Though no portion of the B minor mass may ever
have been performed at Dresden, even in Bach's lifetime
it was not unknown to circles beyond Leipzig. We know
that he sent the *Sanctus* to Count Sporck. Franz Anton
Count von Sporck, born at Lissa, in Bohemia, in 1662, and
at one time Stattholder of that Province, was a man of
superior culture, many-sided interests, and great wealth.
His services to music were conspicuous. He sent native
German artists to be educated in Italy, and was the first
person to introduce the Italian opera into Bohemia. When
the "French horn" was invented in France, he made two
of his servants learn the new instrument, and so introduce
it into Germany. His noble Christian spirit was always
occupied in works of benevolence and undertakings for the
benefit of the world at large. He was a Catholic, but of a
breadth and independence in his religious views far in
advance of his time. He suffered at the hands of the
spiritual authorities, since he would not confess the sole
saving efficacy of the Catholic faith, but admitted the equal
value of the different forms of religion, deeming it sufficient
to seek salvation through Christ, to love God and one's

---

[57] The merging of the Saints' days into the nearest Sundays seems to have
become general in Leipzig by the end of the seventeenth century. See Vopelius,
op. cit. p. 20.

neighbour according to His laws, and that he who did this would be saved, whatever creed he might profess. He founded a printing press at Lissa, by means of which he spread abroad his religious works, some of which were translated into French by his daughters.[58] He had long been connected with the artists and learned professors of Leipzig; Picander dedicated to him, in 1725, the first fruits of his sacred poetry: the Collection of Edifying Thoughts ("Sammlung erbaulicher Gedanken"), and in the dedicatory poem he sings the praise of "pious Count Sporck." Count Sporck died at an advanced age, March 30, 1738, at Lissa.[59] His introduction to Bach's masses must therefore have been one of the latest occurrences of his life.

The mention of this Mecænas of the eighteenth century has led us away from the study of the B minor mass, its essential character, and the spirit in which it is worked out. Though the external suggestion was afforded by the Catholic form of service, Bach wrote the work for the Protestant worship of the churches of St. Thomas and St. Nicholas. He accepted the form established by the Catholic church just as it stood, and adhered to the vein of sentiment which had already become typical for each section of the mass: the absorbed gravity of the *Kyrie*, the jubilant animation of the *Gloria*, the strong confidence of the *Credo*, and solemn grandeur of the *Sanctus;* he even intensified these feelings. In the choruses of the *Credo* a kind of polyphony appears, to which we are unused in Bach's Cantatas; an effect produced by broad and simple phrases of melody, a highly artistic extension of the theme, and elaborate stretto of the *Cantus firmus*, which is borrowed, not from any congregational hymn, but from the priest's chant. We also find in this mass the subdivision of the greater sections into several independent smaller ones, the utilisation of the aria and the duet—all of which had made its way under the

---

[58] Zedler, Universal Lexicon, Vol. 39. Leipzig and Halle, 1744. Also, G. B. Hancken's Weltliche Gedichte. Dresden and Leipzig, 1727, p. 30 and p. 123.—J. Ch. Günther's Gedichte. Breslau and Leipzig, 1735, p. 137.

[59] Gerber, N. L. IV., col. 243.

influence of the Italian opera during the seventeenth century.   Still, Bach could not be false to his own Protestant style.   This, which was founded on the firm basis of German organ music, had, with careful eclecticism, grasped every other form worthy to survive, and now proved itself capable of absorbing that element which distinguishes the B minor mass from all the rest of Bach's church music.   Wherever the Protestant liturgy required it, Bach has deviated from the main lines of the Catholic mass.   Thus the B minor mass is scarcely less essentially Protestant than the rest of Bach's church music, but its roots strike deeper.   Luther's purer creed was born in the lap of the Catholic church, and it was only the ill-founded pretensions of the Mother Church, which had nothing in common with her original constitution, which forced Protestantism to fight for an independent position.   The political exigencies of Princes, and the antagonism of nations and races, roused a hostile fury which led to the most terrible religious war ever waged, and left an enduring bitterness, even late in the eighteenth century.   Nowhere was this bitter spirit stronger or more stubborn, on the Protestant side, than in Saxony, and it was precisely there that the great work of art was destined to be created which showed Protestantism no longer as the antagonist and foe of Catholicism, but as an inevitable outcome and development from it, grown from the same soil.   The B minor mass plainly reveals how immeasurably deeper and broader Bach's church feeling was than that of his age.   In him dwelt the true spirit of the Reformation-epoch, with all its assertiveness and its personal meditative sentiment, but also with its comprehensive and assimilative power. When Luther arose, all the most cultured and honest minds were agreed as to the necessity for the self-examination and reconstruction of the church ; and all the nobler souls, even though they might not go over to Protestantism, were of one mind with Luther in this.   Almost all Germany was at once devoted to the new doctrine, and in the enlightened classes throughout Europe it found numerous adherents.   The reformers themselves were far from purposing a breach with the Catholic church; they accepted the Nicene Creed in the books containing their profession of faith, as well as the *Credo unam sanctam catholicam et apostolicam ecclesiam,* in token of their community of belief with true Catholics. But this lofty conception of the work of reformation had totally vanished within two hundred years. At Bach's time the old warlike spirit still lived in the orthodox, though under restraint, it is true, and the fervent religious sentiment survived in the Pietists; but scarcely any one preserved the sense of the historical continuity and internal connection of Protestantism with the Catholic church. It remained for Music to re-unite all these different currents of thought, and to show them to the world in an immortal work, and that in the same part of the German empire whence the most powerful impetus was first given to the Reformation— a solemnly suggestive fact, but scarcely understood.

At that time the art of music had not yet been fully adapted to mirror all the new ideas of the period. All the Protestant music that attained any importance displays, under merely superficial variations, forms of art which sprang not from contemporary life, but from the later middle ages. It was once more to be proved that, of all the arts, music requires the longest time to become available for the utterance of a new type of culture. Just like Handel's music—nay, like all the music of the eighteenth century—Bach's music is based on the period of the renaissance. It was his vocation to produce the most thoroughly objective—because the latest—the purest and most glorified image of the spirit of the reformed church of that great epoch in his B minor mass.

It is only in certain portions that he shows himself subject to the conditions of the Protestant liturgy; indeed, it is only in the *Sanctus* and *Agnus* that this necessitates any particular form. The *Gloria, Kyrie,* and, above all, the *Credo* are only slightly and more arbitrarily connected with it. The structure of the whole work rested solely on the personal will of Bach, who found in the Protestant form of worship only the ruins of a magnificent liturgical work, which was both capable and worthy to be reconstructed

in the spirit of the Reformation. This, more than anything else, is the free expression of his own powerful
individuality—of an individuality which has drawn all its
nourishment from the life of the church, down to the rock
of its foundation. This mass is more absolutely inseparable
from the Protestant Church of his time than even the
cantatas and Passion music. Though the Passion according to St. Matthew extended to a length which made the
Vesper service of Good Friday seem almost a secondary
object, the connection was real, and, if only for the sake
of the chorales, quite indispensable. In the B minor mass
Bach has refrained from any use of the congregational
hymn, although there were examples at hand for each
portion of the mass. He adopted no Sunday nor holy day,
no church solemnity as its background; and nevertheless
there is no work which more amply satisfies the true spirit
of Protestantism. But when Bach purposed to work down
to the very core of the liturgy, the height of the structure
had to correspond to the depth of the foundations; he
could not let the edifice run up like a spire in the Protestantism of the time; it must over-arch it. In this work the
artist addressed himself with independent Protestant feeling
to the "one holy and universal Christian church"; any one
who yet recognised that, and had cherished its spirit, could
understand his work.

Though, even in the B minor mass, certain portions are
recognisable as remodelled from cantatas, still the nature
and purpose of the whole work at once dismiss any idea
of this having been done for convenience sake, or from
pressing haste; a comparison of the re-arrangements with
the originals shows, too, that Bach carefully selected only
such pieces as agreed in poetic feeling with the words to
which they were to be adapted. In the *Gloria*, the sentence
Gratias agimus tibi propter magnam gloriam tuam was set to
a chorus, of which the original words were "Wir danken
dir Gott "—" We thank Thee, O Lord, we thank Thee, and
proclaim Thy wonders"—(see Vol. II., p. 450). In the same
portion of the mass, the words *Qui tollis peccata mundi*, &c.,
are based on the first portion of the opening chorus of a

cantata, of which the words are "Schauet und sehet"—
"Behold and see, was ever sorrow like unto my sorrow"—
(Vol. II., p. 427). The text of the second chorus of the *Credo*
is: *Patrem omnipotentem, factorem cœli et terræ;* the text of the
original "Gott wie dein Name so ist auch dein Ruhm"—
"God, as Thy Name is, so is Thy glory, even unto the world's
end"—(Vol. II., p. 441). The *Crucifixus* is a revival of the
cantata chorus "Weinen, Klagen, Sorgen"—"Weeping,
anguish, terror, pain, and grief are the Christian's bread of
tears"—(Vol. II., p. 404). All these subjects are precious
gems which, in their new setting, not only sparkle more
brightly in themselves, but add to the magnificence of a
splendid whole. Bach has left nothing wholly unaltered,
though the pieces have not been reconstructed from the
foundations. In many cases some small detail adds to their
characteristic fitness; in the *Crucifixus*, the *tremolo* bass and
the closing modulations; in *Qui tollis,* the muffling of the
sound by the cessation of the supporting wind instrumennts.
The chorus "Gott wie dein Name" really seems to have been
awaiting its conversion into the *Patrem omnipotentem;* the
slight modification in the theme, which was necessitated by
the Latin text, first fully brought out its sinewy structure,
and the rhythm of the words from the mass fit the melody
better than the Bible text.

Besides those already mentioned, there are but two that
are not perfectly new compositions, and these must be
judged somewhat differently. The *Agnus* is founded on the
alto aria in the Ascension oratorio "Ach bleibe doch, mein
liebstes Leben" (Vol. II., p. 593 f.)—but only one long phrase
of it is used, and the remainder is quite a new composition.
The *Osanna* occurs at the beginning of the secular cantata,
"Preise dein Glücke" (Vol. II., p. 631). But even there it
is not in its original place; on the contrary, it bears conspicuous marks of arrangement, and must be more unlike
the true original than the *Osanna,* so that in this instance
nothing can be said as to the connection between the
original and the reproduction.

Among the twenty-six numbers into which the B minor
mass is divided there are six arias and three duets. There

are no recitatives, as they were not admitted into Catholic church-music, and must have seemed unsuited to the grand generalisation of the text in the Protestant service. Five-part writing predominates; it is absent only in the re-arranged choruses and the *Sanctus*, which was originally independent, and in the second *Kyrie*, which may therefore, perhaps, be regarded as a remodelled piece. Bach has rarely written five-part music, and here the influence of Italian church music is unmistakable.

The preference for the chorus-form was required by the nature of the great undertaking, and was also the outcome of the structure of the text, which is nowhere open to subjective treatment; and though solos could not be wholly avoided in so colossal a work, as they were indispensable for the sake of contrast, it is very intelligible that they should assume a less personal character than is usual even with Bach. But the intrinsic contradiction which is inherent in the very nature and idea of *impersonal solo* singing can be removed by the whole work which this subserves. And this is the case in the B minor mass; these arias and duets would have less charm apart from their connection than those even of the cantatas and Passion music, but in the course of the work they adequately fill their place. The duet, *Christe eleison*, conveys something of the trustful and tender feeling of the sinner towards the Divine Mediator, and the introduction of the sub-dominant in the first bar of the symphony suggests it at once. The fervent devotion to the Saviour which impresses us in the *Agnus Dei* is not yet attained; this is prohibited by the juxtaposition of the two choruses. In the course of ideas presented by the text of the *Gloria*—which suggests the proceeding of Christ from God, His deeds and sufferings on earth, and His return to the Father—the aria, *Laudamus te,* is intended as a transition from the lofty rejoicing over the incarnation of the Son of God to the solemn thanksgiving for God's glory. The duet, *Domine,* then enlarges on the mysterious Unity of the Father and Son, on which the possibility of the atonement depends, and ends with the vocation of Christ on earth. This doctrinal aspect is the source whence Bach derived the tone-picture, which cannot be understood but by a reference to it. The violins and violas playing *con sordini* the *pizzicato* in the basses, and the fantastically wandering passages for the flutes have a very mystical effect.

The musical germ which diffuses its life through every portion of the piece is a motive of four notes :—

It is, as it were, the musical symbol of the Unity which this dogma inculcates, and is thus put forward at the very beginning of the piece. The phrases *Domine Deus rex cælestis, Deus Pater omnipotens—Domine Fili unigenite, Jesu Christe altissime,* are not sung straight through as the mass text gives them, but the tenor addresses himself to God the Father, and the soprano, beginning a bar later, to God the Son ; each develops the melody, which proceeds in imitation, by extensions of the motive quoted above, and presently both sing it together in its original form. The way in which the motive constantly recurs, not prolonged to any fuller melody, but isolated, distinct, and stern as a dogma, is unique among Bach's compositions. In bar 42, the descending passage of octaves for the whole body of violins and violas can have none but a symbolical meaning, coming in as it does without any organic sequence, and quite unexpectedly, in a way which is not usual with Bach. Comparing it with the duet, *Et in unum* (in the *Credo*), which resembles it in many respects, we may fancy it intended to suggest the descent of God to assume the form of men.[60]

---

[60] An observation as to the performance of this may find a place here. The first bar for the flute part is thus written by Bach :—

Later on, where the theme recurs, we find, in the second half of the bar, simple semiquavers, phrased in pairs ; thus the dotted mode of notation only indicates that the first is closely joined to the second, and to be accented, and not that it is of less value than the second. A manual of music by J. G. Walther, of 1708, of which I possess the original autograph, says on

No human emotion anywhere finds utterance as yet, for the words do not give rise to it till later, when the contemplative mind is directed to the atoning death of Christ; and if Bach desired to work out the sections of the mass in a variety of subjects, and not merely as music for music's sake, this was the only course that could result in a profound and impressive composition.

Here his theological learning—which the discovery of the catalogue of his theological library proves to have been considerable—stood him in good stead. Doctrinal theology assigns to Christ a three-fold office—as Prophet, High Priest, and King. The text offered no opening for treating the prophetic aspect—only the priestly and the kingly. As, in considering Christ as a priest, there is again a distinction between Atonement and Mediation (*munus satisfactionis* and *intercessionis*), Bach has figured the former by the chorus *Qui tollis*, and the latter by the alto aria *Qui sedes*, but in close connection, for the key is the same in both. The chorus itself at the end delivers the words *Suscipe deprecationem*, preparing for the aria by a half-close; thus the function of intercession, in accordance with the orthodox dogma, appears as a personal outcome of the work of Atonement—an application of it to the individual soul. The bass aria which follows, *Quoniam tu solus sanctus*, thus refers to the kingly office, which is broadly indicated by the dignified form of the principal subject, and by the solemn blast·of two bassoons and a horn added to the organ and bass solo. The purport of the *Credo* is the presentment of the doctrine of the Trinity. Here it was indispensable that the Unity of the Father and the Son should be more strongly insisted on than in the *Gloria*. The duet *Et in unum* does this by the canonic treatment, which is employed

---

this subject: "*Punctus serpens* indicates that notes written as follows should be slurred," *e.g.*:—

Here it is evident that Bach differs as to this mode of performance, and a note in B.-G. XIII.,[1] p. xvi., might be made more exact.

for the instruments as well as the voices. But, to represent
the essential Unity as clearly as possible, Bach treats the
parts in canon on the unison at the beginning of the principal
subject each time, not using the canon on the fourth
below till the second bar; thus both the Unity and the
separate existence of the two Persons are brought out.
The intention is unmistakable, since the musical scheme
allows of the canonic imitation on the fourth below from
the very beginning.[61]

Indeed, much more may be said without over-straining
the idea. Wherever the chief subject is given to the
instruments, Bach makes the last quaver of the first
bar in the leading part *staccato*, and in the second part
legato, thus :—

Now, the object of this effect, which is consistently carried
out all through, can only be to distinguish the parts in
imitation and already in unison by a somewhat different
expression; and so, even here, to suggest a certain distinction of Persons within the Unity. There are yet other
highly significant features. In bars 21, 22, and 66, we again
meet with the passage of hovering descending octaves,
which is not worked episodically; and as it accompanies
the words *et ex patre natum* and *et incarnatus*, and in the
second case is followed by the voices, its purpose is easy
to be understood. To express *descendit de cœlis*, the instruments sink through three octaves on the chord of the
dominant seventh. It was not until later that Bach cast
the words *Et incarnatus est de Spiritu sancto* in a separate
chorus and, as may still be seen, inserted the score of it on
a sheet by itself. Originally these words were included
in the duet, and the division of the text was, consequently,
different. This, however, must not be set aside in judging

---

[61] Mosewius detected the symbolical meaning. See, in Lindner, Zur
Tonkunst, p. 165.

the composition : the startling modulations at the close, which seem to reveal another world, are to be accounted for by supposing that they are intended to embody the miracle of the passage from the Divine into the human state of existence.   By the other and subsequent arrangement of the text Bach greatly obscured this subtle reference; but, by leaving the original distribution of the text standing in the score side by side with the inserted chorus, he, no doubt, meant to indicate that they could be thus sung, even when the choral subject was used.

The last three solo pieces are more full of warmth and sentiment.   The confession of faith in the Holy Ghost, through whose instrumentality the new and holy life is shed upon mankind, is given in a bass aria.   The sentiment of the melody, which flows softly, like a breath of spring, is only fully understood. when we find it again forming the basis of certain Whitsuntide cantatas (as " Erschallet ihr Lieder," "Also hat Gott die Welt geliebt "). The *Benedictus* is delivered by the tenor ; graceful intricacies on a solo violin[62] mingle with the sweet and solemn song, which makes such an impressive effect between the twice-sung *Osanna*—a grandly massive jubilant chorus.   But the human sentiment is uttered in the most fervent manner by the alto in the *Agnus Dei*.   The character of the feeling Bach here intended to express is clearly indicated by his having borrowed the music from the fervid farewell passage in the Ascension oratorio.   But the *Agnus* as a whole was required to be something quite different, because the text demanded that the music should be in two sections.   Only a faint resemblance remains to the original form in three portions ; of the two subjects, each forming a section by itself, the first is newly-invented, and out of the long-drawn lamentation the song is worked out to a pitch of passionate supplication.

The solo songs stand among the choruses like isolated valleys between gigantic heights, serving to relieve the eye that tries to take in the whole composition.   The choruses,

---

[62] Or flute ; the autograph score gives no directions on this point.

indeed, are of a calibre and grandeur which almost crush the small and restless generation of the present day. As throughout the whole work the most essential portions are given to them, a general consideration of the whole is the best way to understand them. The liturgical elements in the mass are four—the consciousness of sin in man (the *Kyrie*), the Atonement through Christ (the *Gloria*), the Christian Church as proceeding from Him (the *Credo*), the memorial supper in which the Church celebrates its union with and in the Founder (the *Sanctus* and subsequent parts). That which in this mass gives artistic connection to the five sections into which the materials are worked out is not the under-current of congregational feeling which is derived from the performance of a solemn function, and which finds its highest union in the Catholic mass. The predominant sentiment in Bach's work is, of course, absolutely free from any such theatrical element. The inherent continuity of the liturgical theme is alone insisted on; it is an ideal and concentrated presentment of the principal factor in the development alike of Christianity and of the individual Christian up to the solemn realisation of the Holy Sacrament. And even this is but half realised, inasmuch as the music belonging to it is conceived of as inseparable from the other portions of the mass, though it is not, and never can be, performed as a part of Divine Service. The communion music, however, marks the culminating point, at which the essential difference from a mere historical picture of Christianity is defined. It is in the intrinsic connection of the various parts, from the religious point of view, and in the profound contemplation of the special bearings of certain portions of the text which this has induced, that we find the source of that deviation from the typical forms of utterance which has already been alluded to when speaking of the prototype offered to Bach by the Catholic mass. A vein of serious meditation was not lacking, even in the Catholic *Kyrie*; but it rather lent itself to the character of an introduction to a solemn ceremony, and as such, under the increasing frivolity of Catholic Church music, it grew more and more vapid. Bach's *Kyrie* goes

at once to the heart of the matter, without second thoughts
of any kind. Man, convicted of sin, cries in his need to
God for mercy; and the unusual proportions of the first
chorus remove every doubt as to the composer's purpose
of representing in it the common supplications of all
Christendom. A fugue, which lasts from twelve to thirteen
minutes, is worked out in 126 bars of slow *tempo*, in
extremely simple passages and modulations upon a mar-
vellously bold theme steeped in sorrow. It may be safely
asserted that a purely personal emotional idea has never
been worked out so persistently and with such unflagging
strength of feeling, while the subordination of the expression
of pain, so acute as to be almost physical, to the powerful
governing will of the artist, is incomparably sublime. This
gives us the key-note of feeling for the whole work; but,
even within the limits of the *Kyrie*, it has its value. The
condition of mankind as craving redemption—of which
the three-fold *Kyrie* is the symbol—is attributed by the
Church to all the generations before Christ. As it is
expressed in the first *Kyrie*, the elect people of God are
crying to the Redeemer from the very first introduction of
sin into the world. As the time of fulfilment draws nearer,
their longing is more urgent and passionate; and to depict
this is the aim of the short, agitated closing cry of *Kyrie*,
almost desperate in some places (see the last nine bars).
The beginning is epic, the close dramatic—if I may be
allowed the terms. A distinct reference in the separate
subjects to the Three-fold Person of God, which is, of
course, intended by the three cries of the text, is not to be
imagined—the position which this portion of the work was
to occupy precludes this. I regard the *Christe* rather as a
lighter musical subject to give relief, which need not exclude
the idea that its softer character was induced by the image
of the loving Saviour, especially when we remember Bach's
way of letting himself be led by incidental suggestions.

At the beginning of the *Gloria* stands the *Hymnus
Angelicus;* the Bible text of the song of the angels on the
night of Christ's birth: Bach has treated it as a chorus,
which was not the custom in the Catholic mass. In the

settings of the *Gloria* in his shorter masses, the first chorus
always has some sentences of the doxology which come
after, besides the words of the angels' hymn. Here Bach
has severed the Bible words from the liturgical amplification
which follows them ; even if we did not know that in later
years he made use of this chorus for Christmas music, we
could not fail to recognise the Christmas feeling that pervades it, and of which there is no trace in the Catholic
Masses. The treatment of the words *Et in terra pax
hominibus bonæ voluntatis* displays a certain resemblance
with the angels' chorus in the Christmas oratorio ; even
the 3-8 time is characteristic of a festival of which Paul
Gerhardt could sing :—

> Dance my heart with triumph springing,
> On this day
> When for joy
> Angels all are singing.

In fact, this measure recurs in several choruses of the
Christmas oratorio and in the cantata " Christen, ätzet
diesen Tag" (Vol. II., pp. 367—369). But the general impression is definitive ; this is less a hymn of rejoicing mankind,
on whom the day of redemption has risen, than an innocent
jubilation, strung, it is true, to the highest conceivable pitch possible to this type of feeling. We must
accustom ourselves to the colossal proportions of the
B minor mass before we can accurately discriminate
between the different characters that stamp each chorus ;
but then we cannot fail to recognise in this chorus the old
blissful Christmas feeling which we have met with so often
and so touchingly in Bach, not least in the happy tranquil
middle subject, from which the development of a flowing
fugue is as natural as it is characteristic, while the joyful
voices combine in the greeting of " Peace." It is not till
we come to the following air that we are led to the
serious presentation of the dogma of the work of Atonement
initiated by the birth of Christ. Here the splendid and
solemn chorus, which originally stood in the Rathswahl
cantata as " Wir danken dir Gott" has found a worthy
place as *Gratias agimus tibi*. The farther course of this

section is to a great extent given to solo singers; only the climax, the atoning death of Christ, is expressly emphasised by the deeply pathetic chorus *Qui tollis peccata mundi*; and at the close we have a triumphant hymn to Christ, Who, having finished His earthly course, sits on the right hand of the Father. The bold onward march of the theme of the fugue, the victorious *Amen* that bursts into the middle of it, and the surge and roll, so characteristic of Bach, bear the impress of Protestantism. Still, the long-drawn harmonies of the chorus, through which it breaks like a flash of light, eclipsing for the moment all the other individual forms, reveal another and more general sphere of ecclesiastical feeling.

In the *Credo* the Church founded on Christ declares its faith in the words of the Nicene Creed. The opening chorus, *Credo in unum Deum*, stands up like an over-arching portal, by which the precincts of the Church are thrown open to us. As the theme for the fugue Bach has chosen the church tone:—

Cre - do   in   u - num   De - um.

Above the five voices the two violins come in, piling up the structure of the fugue, while the *continuo* wanders up and down in a constant movement of crotchets. At the close the bass delivers the theme in augmentation, and at the same time the second soprano and alto give it out in the proper measure, and the first soprano in syncopation; agreeing with this, syncopation occurs also in the violins. As such complicated arrangements occur rarely elsewhere with Bach, the connection here indicated with the poly-phonous church music of the sixteenth century is pretty obvious, and Bach's study of Palestrina thus acquires a peculiar significance. The utilisation of the priests' chant and of the mixolydian mode remove every doubt that the master had intentionally reverted to that period, since there was as yet no question of a severance, but only of a reconstruction of the whole Church. The symbolism of the augmented theme in the bass and the intricacy of the voice

parts above—the immovably rooted unity of the faith—is
thus made clear at once. In the course of the creed the
image of God the Omnipotent is indicated in broad outline,
and a chorus full of brilliancy and of nervous vigour lauds
Him as the Creator of heaven and earth. It falls to the
part of an intermediate movement for solo voices to
announce the mysteries of His Unity with the Son, and
then Christ Himself appears, the incarnate God. The
broad descending intervals of the opening theme represent
His descent to mortality. A maiden fervency breathes
through this quite simple chorus, which is chiefly homophonous, but it fills us with a mysterious thrill, and the
accompaniment—chiefly by means of the bold passing notes
—affects us like a foreboding of deep grief.

At the close the clouds of sorrow gather; then we have a
new scene—Christ crucified. Bach had gradually so
ennobled and inspired the old forms that he could venture
in this place to introduce a *passecaille.* Nothing more
characteristic can be imagined; the theme, which recurs
thirteen times, holds the fancy spellbound in contemplation
of the stupendous scene that is being enacted. The subject,
which is taken from an earlier cantata, seems even there to
be referable to some still more remote inspiration; the bass
theme itself had haunted the musician from his earliest
youth, and here is cast in its final mould as a *passecaille.*
Indeed, this chorus and the cantata " Jesu, der du meine
Seele," which treats the same subject in the form of a
chaconne, indicate the sum total of Bach's development in
a certain direction. It is an aid to a keener comprehension
of the predominant characteristic of this subject in the mass
to consider the two settings in connection; here we have
not a mere infused colour inspired by a general sentiment
of sacred solemnity, still less a histrionic illustration of a
thrilling event. Beneath the words of the narrative the
inner ear may detect a fervent prayer to Jesus—Who once,
through His death redeemed the world—that He will
vouchsafe evermore to fulfil the work of redemption in all
who seek Him. All is pathetic and piteous, but purified from
every trace of egotism. And what the parts have to say

above the bass theme in their excess of chromatic diminished intervals, either alone or in harmony, is as stupendous as the event they are intended to shadow forth. When at last the thematic bass is released from its rigid progression, and the chorus sinks into the deep cool repose of the shadow of the grave, the hearer is left under the sense of a tone-picture by the side of which anything that has ever been written for this portion of the mass is a pale phantom. Even the chorus *Qui tollis* is cast into the shade by this. And so it should be; there the sufferings of Christ were only a factor in the whole work of redemption, which forms the subject of the section in which it occurs; while here we have the poetical image of the very nature of the Son as contrasted with the Father and the Holy Ghost. Originally the chorus *Crucifixus* was intended to suffice for this purpose; afterwards Bach thought this conception inadequately emphasised and made a chorus of the *Incarnatus est* also. Thus he intended to balance the different sections of the mass against each other.

Out of the silence of the tomb, to which we are led by the closing bars of the *Crucifixus*, the chorus triumphantly starts afresh and raises the standard of the Resurrection; a long instrumental symphony is introduced to accustom the mind to the return of the light. Then with renewed vitality the chorus soars up again and rejoices, not in prolonged phrases, but with constant interruption from the instruments; this gives the subject a character which, in spite of all its vigour and of the defiant boldness of the basses, which declare the promise of Christ's coming again, tempers the movement and keeps it down, for yet another climax remains.

The third Person of the Trinity, the Holy Ghost, is revealed through the Church, and the symbol of admission and fellowship in the Church is baptism. Hence a confession of faith in baptism is at the same time a confession of faith in the Holy Ghost. The elaborate choral treatment of the *Confiteor unum baptisma* is founded on this conception, after the belief in the Holy Ghost Himself has been declared in an aria which is musically indispensable. Here again, as

in the first *Credo*, and with the same allusion to the universal
Christian Church, we find the Gregorian chant as follows :—

Con fi - te - or u - num bap - tis - ma in re - mis - si - o - nem pec - ca - to - rum.

But this tune is not fitted to be the theme of a fugal subject,
and one had to be invented. It is not till bar 73 that the
chant first appears in diminution and close imitations between
the bass and alto, and after this in full time by the tenors
alone. This leads up to the full close ; the Church lives
on beyond the grave in the life eternal, where it attains
to perfection. Through a slow succession of marvellous
harmonies, wherein the old world sinks and fades, we are
conducted to the conception of "a new Heaven and a new
earth." Hope in that future life is poured forth in a chorus
full of solemn breadth in spite of its eager confidence.

The fourth portion of the mass, which belongs to the
Lord's Supper, is in two divisions. In the Catholic mass the
Sanctus, *Osanna*, and *Benedictus* form the first, the *Agnus* and
Dona the second. In the absence of any information as
to the Leipzig usages, it has hitherto been customary to
adhere simply to the Catholic custom in all the editions and
performances of the B minor mass, thus ignoring Bach's
express indications.[63] But the peculiar arrangement of the
B minor mass in this place is important and significant
in more respects than one. In the earliest times the Sanctus,
with the introductory preface, was regarded as a thanksgiving
for the beneficence manifested in the creation, of which the
first fruits, generally in the form of bread and wine, had been
previously offered by the members of the congregation in
the *Offertorium*. The addition of the *Osanna* and *Benedictus*
was made when this symbolical thank-offering sank into the
back-ground by the side of the later conception of a symbolic
sacrifice of the Body and Blood of Christ by the hands of
the ministering Priest ; for the *Osanna* and *Benedictus*
point to the coming of the Saviour, and in this place to

---

[63] The oldest edition, by Nägeli and Simrock, is guiltless of this in so far as
it omits all indication of the distribution of the mass in the liturgy.

His presence in the Bread and Wine.   At the Reformation,
however, this conception of the sacrifice was rejected, and thus
the *Osanna* and *Benedictus* lost their meaning as a continuation of the *Sanctus;* and as treated in an elaborate style they
were even omitted in the great churches of Leipzig as early
as in the seventeenth century.[64]   Bach, who intended this
Sanctus, like his others, to be used in the service, restored
the usage of the primitive church ; whether consciously
or unconsciously cannot be known, the fact remains
that here the *Sanctus* is restored to its original form as a
portion of the mass.   To realise the effect of this *Hymnus
seraphicus* (Is. vi. 3) we must connect it with the words of
the preface, which varied, and still varies, according to
the festival.   But the main paragraph was always the
same and very similar to that now used in the Anglican Communion service—"It is very meet, right, due, and of saving
power that we should at all times and in all places give
thanks unto Thee, Holy Lord, Almighty Father, Everlasting
God ; through Christ our Lord, through Whom the Angels
laud Thy Majesty, the Dominions adore and the Powers fear
it.   The Heavens and the Powers of Heaven and the blessed
Seraphim praise Thee with one shout of triumph ; with
them we beseech Thee let our voices reach Thee and say,
entreating and acknowledging Thee : Holy, Holy, Holy," &c.
The overwhelming idea of a hymn of praise in which the
Powers of Heaven and the Angels unite with man may have
prompted the composer not only to replace the *Sanctus* in
the B minor mass but to extend the harmony to six parts.
In fact, we find that the words of Isaiah have determined even
the details of the composition—" I saw the Lord sitting upon
a throne high and lifted up and His train filled the temple.
Above it stood the Seraphims; each one had six wings," &c.
The majestic soaring passages in which the upper and lower
voices seem to respond to each other are certainly suggested
by the last words "and they cried one to another."   In the
bars where the five upper parts hold out in reverberating
harmony against the broad pinion strokes of the violins and

---

[64] As may be gathered from Vopelius, p. 1086.

wooden wind instruments, the blare of trumpets and thunder
of drums, while the bass marches solemnly downwards in
grand octaves, we feel with the prophet that "the posts of
the door moved at the voice of him that cried, and the house
was filled with smoke." After this majestic *Sanctus* follows an
animated setting of *Pleni sunt cœli*, which so far exceeds
any similar movement in the mass in ecstatic jubilation that
we cannot help feeling that till this moment Bach has only
given us the hymns of praise and joy of mortal Christians,
but that here "the morning stars are singing together and
the sons of God shouting for joy" (Job xxxviii. 7).

The second section of the fourth portion of the mass
Bach has begun with the *Osanna* and it closes with the *Dona.*
We might say, as the *Sanctus* can only give expression to
the most universal form of thanksgiving for the mercies of
God, that it constitutes by itself a fourth division, and that
the *Osanna* and what follows form a fifth. But it has been
shown above that they must have been written to be performed in connection, and indeed an internal relationship
can be traced. It is evident that by a division which should
treat the *Osanna* as introductory and the *Dona* as final in an
independent section of the mass this would have a very
different common character from that which would stamp only
the *Agnus* and *Dona* taken together. In this latter case—
as the observant student has long since detected—the
impression cannot be other than unsatisfactory, not only as
regards each of these numbers separately but as to their
connection and their position as finishing the whole mass.
But in point of fact the *Agnus* is only intended to supply a
very effective transition; it lies like a deep and gloomy
lake between lofty heights; the character of the closing
section is not penitent entreaty, not an overwhelming
sympathy with a tragical event, not even the mystical
exaltation of the Lord's Supper—it is joy and thankfulness
and, so far, a reiteration of the feeling of the *Sanctus*, but
brought down to the level of humanity. The double chorus
Osanna has also much more of the character of an introductory chorus than of a finale, and the critic who objects
to the absence of a ritornel may remember that no concerted

church music was ever performed without an organ prelude. Now, whatever might have been the original purpose of the subject employed for the *Osanna*, it cannot be disputed that these crowding and competing strains of rejoicing are admirably well suited to the words of the multitude who accompanied Christ in His entry into Jerusalem. Indeed, from the point of view adopted for this section as a whole, all that seems strange in the *Dona* even, which simply repeats the music of the *Gratias agimus tibi*, disappears. It is not, nor ought it to be, a prayer for peace. As the grouping of the sentences stood, the close could be nothing else than a solemn hymn of thanksgiving. It can hardly, however, be asserted that this mode of treatment has not given rise to a contradiction between the music and the words—though it is but superficial and, in the whole work, unimportant—nor that a finale with a different setting might be quite conceivable. But at any rate the reproach can no longer be raised that the B minor mass has no close of due importance, based on the main line of feeling that pervades the whole.

The B minor mass exhibits in the most absolute manner, and on the grandest scale, the deep and intimate feeling of its creator as a Christian and a member of the Church. The student who desires to enter thoroughly into this chamber of his soul must use the B minor mass as the key; without this we can only guess at the vital powers which Bach brought to bear on all his sacred compositions. When we hear this mass performed under the conditions indispensable to our full comprehension of it, we feel as though the genius of the last two thousand years were soaring above our heads. There is something almost unearthly in the solitary eminence which the B minor mass occupies in history. Even when every available means have been brought to bear on the investigation of the bases of Bach's views of art, and of the processes of his culture and development; on the elements he assimilated from without; on the inspirations he derived from within and from his personal circumstances; when, finally, the universal nature of music comes to our aid in the matter, there still remains a last wonder—the lightning flash of the idea of a mass of such vast proportions—the resuscitation of the spirit of the reformers, as of waters that have been long gathering to a head, nay, the actual resurrection of the genius of primitive Christianity, and all concentrated in the mind of this one artist—as inscrutable as the very secret of life itself. A feeble quiver from this movement is to be noted, indeed, in the following generations of Protestants; down to quite modern times the idea of a musical setting of the mass has had a mysterious power to tempt composers. But even with the best of them —Spohr and Schumann—it was in great part merely an antiquarian and romantic whim ; although Schumann's saying that " it must always be the musician's highest aim to address his powers to sacred music " betrays an evident feeling for the realm whence the fountain head of art must flow. No comprehensive treatment of the abstract conception of a universal Church, in the form of an ideal liturgy, could proceed from the Catholics, since they have not the requisite freedom within the limitations imposed by the Church ; indeed, it has never been attempted.

No one can set Beethoven's Second Mass side by side with Bach's—as it is just now the fashion to do— who does not wilfully shut his eyes to the unmistakable gulf that yawns between what the idea of such a work demands and the spirit in which the execution of the former work is undertaken. In Beethoven's work we cannot but admire the grand individuality of its creator, and the Mass will be understood and loved as long as a hundred other works exist which reveal his genius more purely and fully. But though all of Bach's compositions might be lost, still the B minor mass, even to the remotest future, would bear witness to the artist's greatness with the weight of a divine revelation. There is only one other work that can really be set by the side of it. Handel's " Messiah " has often been compared to Bach's St. Matthew Passion, but this must inevitably lead to an unfair judgment of both these works, which, in reality, have hardly anything in common. The real companion work to the " Messiah " can only be the

B minor mass. The aim fulfilled by both works is the artistic presentment of the essence of Christianity. But the two men apprehended the subject differently ; Handel viewed it from the independent and historical standpoint ; Bach from the more limited doctrinal side. Though the latter was beyond a doubt the most suggestive as regards the depth of the world of feeling to be expressed, still the former afforded an opening for a more intelligible dramatic treatment, which is no less pure in art. As all the musical inspiration of that period was embodied in these two equally sound and gifted artists, and consequently each can only be perfectly understood through the other, in any honest historical review we must refrain from elevating one at the expense of the other. But the German nation may rejoice in boasting that both these incomparable geniuses were her sons.

III.

THE LATER CHORALE CANTATAS.

BACH devoted himself, even in the later years of his life, to the composition of church cantatas. It is only at first indeed that we observe that royal profusion which created such an unlimited wealth of musical forms during the middle of the Leipzig period.[65] He falls gradually back on one particular form of chorale cantata, he becomes more silent, and, when he speaks, it is in the regular typical form. He gives the finishing touches and the final shape to two of his greatest sacred works, the St. John and St. Matthew Passions, "setting his house in order," as it were, till at last he seems to become quite silent as a composer of vocal church music. His life-work is done, and he prepares himself for death.

We can point with certainty to the cantata with which Bach welcomed the New Year, 1735. This year found Europe plunged in war. In Italy the French, Sardinians,

---

[65] Compare Vol. II., pp. 477 and 434 ff.

and Spaniards were fighting against the Austrians, and the French were attacking the Austrian possessions on the Rhine. The petty rulers of Germany were seized with panic, and in the province of Reuss special weekly hours were set apart for prayer for God's mercy "in these fearful and dangerous circumstances of war." Meanwhile, however, peace had been restored in the empire of August III., after the subjugation and amnesty of Poland, and on his arrival in Warsaw the king was able to publish a pacificatory proclamation dated December 16, 1734. We have seen that on October 7, 1734, Bach composed a birthday cantata for the king,[66] in which he was celebrated as the peacemaker. The writer of the text of the New Year Cantata is inspired by the same idea. He views Saxony and Poland as a secure island around which may be seen the troubled waves of strife. While praising the king in this strain, he prays to Christ the Prince of Peace to perform His office. During all the time Bach was at Leipzig, there is only one occasion which will exactly suit the idea of these words, and that is the beginning of the year 1735. In the Silesian war Saxony was directly and essentially implicated; so that the date of the cantata is fixed beyond all doubt.

The work itself contains much that is remarkable. It is founded on vv. 1, 5, 10 of Psalm cxlvi., vv. 1 and 3 of Ebert's hymn "Du Friedefürst, Herr Jesu Christ"—"Lord Jesu Christ, Thou Prince of Peace," and only two sets of verses in madrigal form. Of these last, the second "Jesu, Retter deiner Heerde" can only be considered as partly in madrigal form, for the tenor solo with the bassoon and bass serves as the counterpoint to the chorale melody played by the violins and violas. So that the chorale comes in three times—first, as the second number, sung alone by the soprano with lovely interwoven accompaniments of the violins and basses; secondly, against the tenor solo in sombre colouring, the dominant idea of which must be contained in the second verse of the hymn;

---

[66] See Vol. II., p. 631.

and lastly, as a chorale fantasia for the chorus and all the instruments. The words of the psalm are used with no less frequency. The cantata begins with the words "Praise thou the Lord, O my soul" ("Lobe den Herrn," &c.). The tenth verse of the psalm is set to one of those bass ariosos which approach so nearly to the form of the aria, and which we have already pointed out as being a characteristic innovation of Bach's, in the years that immediately preceded this period.[67]   Verse five is set to a simple tenor recitative; this kind of treatment is one which we have not hitherto met with in Bach, except in the "mysteries" which do not come into comparison with these works, and even there it is but of rare occurrence. In the cantata the words of the Bible and of the chorale strive, as it were, for the mastery.   In this sense it is significant that the first chorus is of very limited extent (only thirty-five bars), and has no thematic development; so that it is not to be regarded as giving the emotional key-note of the whole; and in the final chorus the chorale is not wholly triumphant.   While in most cases the voices that have the counterpoint sing the same words as those of the *Cantus firmus*, they here give out the last word of the Psalm, "Hallelujah"; both elements being thus united.   In the relation thus established lies the individuality of this remarkable work.[68]

To the effect produced by the wars on the Rhine and in Italy is due the composition of the cantata "Wär Gott nicht mit uns diese Zeit"—"If God were not on our side"—which was performed about four weeks later, on the fourth Sunday after Epiphany (January 30, 1735). It is well known that Luther wrote a paraphrase of Psalm cxxiv. in three verses.   This forms the germ of the text, but the second verse is paraphrased in the madrigal style.[69]   The first verse is in the Pachelbel organ

---

[67] See Vol. II., p. 471.

[68] I know the cantata only by a copy in the Royal Library at Berlin.   I know nothing of where the autograph may be.

[69] In B.-G. II., where this cantata is published, the words start on p. 126, "Ja hätt es Gott nicht zugegeben," apparently by a clerical error (for it is

chorale form. The chorus begins in a fugal style with very ingenious answering in contrary motion, the themes thus introduced being then used as counterpoint against the *Cantus firmus*, which is entrusted to the horn and the two oboes. To work out this new form—not technically, for it is clear at the first glance, but figuratively, as it were, realising in it the representation of an inward experience, must have been immensely difficult. When the chorale is only played, it leaves the greatest room for subjective and subsidiary fancies with regard to its meaning; but when a solo or chorus is added, with words and a melody of its own, we find two contrasting elements, one subjective and fleeting, the other objective and permanent, of which, however, the first, as representing fully the Church element, must predominate, elevating and sanctifying the effect of the objective feeling. This crossing and alternation of emotions is in the truest and most characteristic spirit of Bach's romanticism. In the present case, however, as no essential contrast subsists between the instrumental *Cantus firmus* and its vocal counterpoint, Bach allows an objective element to enter into the subjective character of the melody that is played, but not so as to usurp its place. This would hold good, even though the *Cantus firmus* were sung. Bach has taken care to keep it subordinate. Foreshadowings of the form here ventured upon are found as early as the first chorus of the cantata " Es ist nichts gesundes an meinem Leibe," so far, that is to say, that the themes of the vocal fugue are derived from two lines of the chorale which is played.[70] The two arias are very important, the first with its quaint rhythm being most characteristic, while the second, as full of sentiment as of ingenuity, is most elevating, especially

---

nonsense) for " Ja hätte Gott es zugegeben "; the cantata is also published P. No. 1297. By way of exception to his general rule, Bach himself gives the date of this cantata as 1735. The paper on which the parts are written is the same as that containing those of the cantata " Vereinigte Zwietracht," in its form as altered for the king's birthday. The year fits very well for the performance of this music; see Vol. II., p. 628, note 766.

[70] Vol. II., p. 466.

in the second part, by the expression of a firm and valiant faith.

In March, 1735, Bach completed his fiftieth year. That his creative activity remained in undiminished strength is shown by the fact that to no year can so great a number of church cantatas be ascribed, either with absolute certainty or with reasonable probability. No fewer than twenty cantatas seem to have been produced by him in this year; among them, it is true, are several re-modellings of works written at Arnstadt, Weimar, and Cöthen, and the cantata "Komm du süsse Todesstunde"[71] was left entirely unaltered, excepting that it was now to serve, not for the sixteenth Sunday after Trinity, but for the festival of the Purification (February 2). For Easter day (April 10) he had recourse to a work of his earliest youth ("Denn du wirst meine Seele nicht in der Hölle lassen")[72] and, for the Tuesday in Easter week, to an occasional cantata written at Cöthen ("Ein Herz, das seinen Jesum lebend weiss").[73]

The music for the Monday in Easter week[74] owes its pleasing character to the circumstance of its coming between those two last mentioned. Bach had the gift of throwing himself, up to a certain point, into various kinds of styles, whether those of other persons or his own in his earlier phases. Careful comparison will at once show that there is a relation between the occasional cantata "Erfreut euch ihr Herzen" and the same in its remodelled form. A pleasing character, aiming rather at breadth than at depth, is not the only characteristic that is common to both. The first chorus of the earlier composition agrees exactly in its plan with the last chorus of the later work, and even the passages set as duets, especially those of the middle movement, which in the occasional compositions were necessitated by the text, were copied in their setting in the Easter cantata. Both are full of genius and elegance, although they cannot lay claim to a prominent place among

---

[71] See Vol. I., p. 549 ff.
[72] See Vol. I., p. 229 ff.
[73] See Vol. II., p. 619 ff.
[74] B. G. XVI., No. 66.   P. 2145.

Bach's Easter compositions. It will not escape the attentive observer that the last bar but one of the bass recitative is referred to at the beginning of the second part of the aria which follows it. There was possibly some accidental reason for this, and for the somewhat uncalled-for introduction of the same figure in the recitative itself. A leaf, on which is written the first idea of the beginning of the cantata for the Sunday after Ascension day in the same year, also contains the following sketch :—

This may have been the subject he first intended for the bass aria in the second Easter cantata, and when he altered his mind as to the chief subject he may have introduced this as a subsidiary.

Two cantatas for Whitsuntide—"Wer mich liebet, der wird mein Wort halten," and "Also hat Gott die welt geliebt"— were in part only made up from old compositions. The first is built upon the cantata with the same beginning which Bach wrote in Weimar, to a text by Neumeister.[75] Two numbers from this work are introduced ; but the whole cannot be considered as finer than the older work. The arias for tenor and alto have a remarkably undevotional character, being showy and almost secular ; there is no relation between the length of the cantata and its importance.[76] For the arias in "Also hat Gott die welt geliebt" the material was supplied from the much used occasional composition "Was mir behagt, ist nur die muntre Jagd." The cleverness of this recension, which contains the lovely soprano aria "Mein gläubiges Herze"—"My heart ever faithful "— has been pointed out in another place.[77] Each of the arias

---

[75] Vol. I., 511 ff.

[76] B.-G. XVIII., No. 74.

[77] Vol. I., 568 ff. The instrumental working-out of the bass theme, which in the autograph score of the secular cantata is found on the back of the final chorus, does not belong to the soprano aria " Wenn die wollenreichen Heerden," and there is no evidence for supposing that they have any connection. It would seem that Bach at first threw off this working-out on the blank page that remained, when he undertook to alter the cantata for Whitsuntide, intending it for a coda or appendix to the new recension of the work.

is supplemented by a newly composed chorus, the character of which is given by the aria; the soprano aria closes with the opening chorus, a four-part choral aria, the accompaniment to which makes the whole work into a charming sort of sacred Siciliano. The feeling of the bass aria, on the other hand, is carried out in a powerful concluding fugue, surrounded with passages for the trombones.[78] This cantata is as original throughout as it is important. In all five of these remodelled cantatas, however, the chorale plays now no part at all, and now but a subordinate one.

Bach seems to have written a new cantata for every Sunday and holy day which fell between Easter and Whitsuntide in the year 1735, with the single exception, perhaps, of the first Sunday after Easter For the Ascension he wrote two cantatas; a rare occurrence, but then for this festival it was necessary to perform two pieces of concerted music. The disposition of the text is noteworthy. The poet frequently turns back from the well-worn track of madrigal poetry to the simpler hymn verse, thus originating some agreeable forms; and the words of Scripture are used more frequently than usual. The feeling of the text is deeper and purer than the average of those in the earlier cantatas in the madrigal style, and it often rises to real devotional strength. We should like to know whether this signifies that a new poet was employed, or whether Bach, after plainly showing his distaste for Picander's meaningless doggerel, by composing music to the verses of hymns exclusively, succeeded in inspiring the poet with some of his own earnest spirit. The chief part of the Ascension cantata (Himmelfahrts-Cantate) "Gott fähret auf mit Jauchzen"—"God is gone up"—consists, from the soprano aria onwards, of a poem in six verses, neat in form and not devoid of a certain fervour.[79] The first aria of the third Whitsuntide cantata, "Er rufet seine Schafe mit Namen," is set to graceful words cast in the metre of the hymn "Ach Gott und Herr."[80]

---

[78] B.-G. XVI., No. 68.   P. 1287.

[79] B.-G., X., No. 43 p.   P. 1658.   In English, published by Novello.

[80] The autograph score and original parts of the cantata are in the Royal Library at Berlin.

The similar arrangement of the text of the cantatas for the fourth Sunday after Easter (" Es ist euch gut, dass ich hingehe ")[81]—" It is good for you that I should leave you "—for the fifth Sunday after Easter (" Bisher habt ihr nichts gebeten in meinem Namen ")[82]—" Hitherto ye have asked nothing in my name "—for Ascension (" Gott fähret auf"), and for the third day of Whitsuntide (" Er rufet seine Schafe mit Namen")—" He calleth His sheep by His name "—in which a text of Scripture is introduced both at the beginning and in the middle, shows that they are by the same hand.[83] Bach, for his part, who, in remodelling his earlier compositions for these cantatas was somewhat fettered by their original form, has left us a set of new compositions of the rarest beauty. He has here developed a form which he had previously attempted in single instances —namely, a new style of vocal solo setting of Scriptural words—a form in which the addition of concerted instrumental parts to the ordinary arioso with contrapuntal figured bass should bring it nearer to the richer form of aria, while remaining quite distinct from it. We can conceive of nothing which could more perfectly point out both the meaning of the sacred words and the necessity of their personal application than the lovely bass solos with which the compositions for the second Sunday after Easter (" Ich bin ein guter Hirt "),[84] for the fourth Sunday after Easter (" Es ist euch gut, dass ich hingehe "), and for the fifth Sunday after Easter (" Bisher habt ihr nichts gebeten ") begins. The arioso with the mere *basso continuo* is not, however, discarded in these cantatas. Several passages of Scripture are also treated in the pure recitative style, contrary to Bach's general usage in the church cantatas properly so-called. Two of the cantatas begin thus modestly with a recitative of this kind; as also does the cantata for the Sunday after Ascension day (" Sie werden euch in den

---

[81] B.-G., XXIII., No. 108. P. 2148.

[82] B.-G., XX.,[1] No. 87.

[83] The words of the Whitsuntide cantata " Wer mich liebet," in which three Bible texts are introduced, seem to be by the same author.

[84] B.-G., XX.,[1] No. 85. P. 2140.

Bann thun") [85]—" They will cast you out." On the whole, a great freedom of formation, both in outline and detail, characterises these cantatas. A good part of this is due, of course, to the exceptional forms of the texts. As the words were not written with constant regard to the scheme of the Italian aria, the composer had to accommodate himself to them. This gave rise to various ingenious departures from the usual form. The shorter cantata for Ascension ("Auf Christi Himmelfahrt allein")[86]—in which the text is incoherent and generally inferior—offers the original phenomenon of an aria which loses itself in recitative, but yet so far verifies its character that at the conclusion the opening ritornel of the aria is brought in as a close. Many of the solos, for the splendid wealth of melody, the tender expressiveness, the blending of colours, the swing and majestic pathos which they display, are worthy to rank among the very highest of Bach's productions in this kind. The choruses are comparatively few. Chorales are for the most part introduced only as simple closing movements ; the shorter cantata for the Ascension alone begins with a chorale fantasia, and in the music for the second Sunday after Easter such a fantasia occurs in the middle, but the soprano alone takes part in it. And yet where free choruses do occur they are instinct with character and life, and replete with that freedom and boldness of form which characterise true genius.

For the third Sunday after Easter he begins with a chorus, " Ihr werdet weinen und heulen "[87]—" Ye shall weep but the world shall rejoice "—in which the contrasts of tears and joy are depicted with marvellous power, and are at length united in a double fugue; after this there comes a bass recitative, followed by the opening movement developed at greater length and with other words.

The great cantata for Ascension ("Gott fähret auf"), the character of which is in the first three movements rather that of the oratorio, while the rest is more devotional,

[85] Autograph score and original parts in the Royal Library at Berlin.

[86] B.-G. XXVI., No. 128.

[87] B.-G., XXIII., No. 103.   P. 1697.

exhibits a tone-picture of Christ's Ascension full of majestic
and graphic movement, both in outline and in detail; everything presses upward, the form of the different themes as
well as the construction of the fugue, and one important
subject comes crashing in like the blast of a trumpet.
The opening of the choral movement is thoroughly original;
it is a short and solemn instrumental adagio which fore-
shadows the first fugal theme by way of a prelude. When
the allegro is reached, the theme and the counter subject
are developed at first on the instruments, and after the
most complete musical preparation the chorus bursts in with
the clash of trumpets and drums.

In the cantata " Es ist euch gut, dass ich hingehe," all
the middle of the work is usurped by one grand chorus
on the words " Wenn aber jener der Geist der Wahrheit
kommen wird "—" Howbeit when He, the Spirit of truth, is
come, He will guide you into all truth." It comes in
immediately after a *recitativo secco*, and speaks to us in
inspired and overpowering tones, like those of the Apostles
at Pentecost. In the fugal theme which breaks through
every barrier :—

Wenn a - ber je - ner der Geist der Wahr - heit kom - men wird

we seem to feel that "the Lord's word is like a hammer
that breaketh the rock." [88]

There are but few cantatas having their chief choruses
founded on freely invented themes, besides those which
have been mentioned, for during the last period the
chorale cantata is decidedly in the ascendant. In works
which can be confidently assigned to the same date as
those just described, his predilection for new forms, ingeniously wrought out and sharply characterised, is very
evident. The text ordered for the sermon for the Reformation festival of 1735—which was kept on October 30, the

---

[88] In the parts Bach changed the *d* of the first entry into *e*, so that the skip
of a seventh becomes a sixth, probably only in order to facilitate the attack.
We may be allowed to retain the original reading. For the date and watermark, see Appendix A., No. 2.

twenty-first Sunday after Trinity (the proper day, October 31, falling on a Monday)—was Ps. lxxx. 14—19. The words "Look upon it . . . it is burned with fire, it is cut down," were evidently chosen with application to the results of the war in 1735. And in the text of the cantata "Gott der Herr ist Sonn und Schild " the lines—

Denn er will uns ferner schützen,	His protecting hand shall save us,
Ob die Feinde Pfeile schnitzen	Though the foe exult and brave us
Und ein Lästerhund gleich billt—	Raging and blaspheming still—

suggest a vein of feeling that cannot be adequately accounted for by the ordinary character of the Reformation festival. The music too is by no means devoid of martial character. In the duet "Gott, ach Gott," the violins do not content themselves with a contrapuntal accompaniment in Bach's usual manner, but paw the ground like impatient chargers, and burst in upon the voice parts with unrestrained energy. A similarity to the second movement of the cantata "Ein feste Burg" must not be overlooked; and it is worth mentioning that this movement, when it is transferred to the G major Mass, has a quite different accompaniment. One of the chief subjects of the opening chorus too is instinct with martial vigour and the roar of battle. In the construction of this chorus Bach was imbued with the idea of the concerto form, for two strongly contrasted subjects are introduced side by side and alternately. But the most striking and typical feature is the way in which the chorus is crystallised, as it were, on the instrumental form. At first it only affords a background of wide-spread harmony to the second subject, to the words "Gott der Herr ist Sonn und Schild," clearly symbolising that every battle is to be fought in the name of God. This subject is subsequently turned into the theme of a fugue. The elaborate combinations of instruments which are found throughout this great work, down to the rhythm of the drums, cannot be gone into in detail. The poetic meaning of the first subject becomes perfectly clear in the third movement, where it serves as an accompaniment to the chorale "Nun danket alle Gott," sung by the chorus in simple and beautiful harmony.[89]

At the time of the first performance of the Easter oratorio— *i.e.*, 1736—Bach wrote a cantata for the second day of Easter (April 2, 1736); " Bleib bei uns, denn es will Abend werden "—" Bide with us," &c.[90] The Gospel for the day narrates the touching story of the two disciples on the way to Emmaus. In the principal chorus a movement full of deep feeling and yet of mild expression, composed of several subjects most skilfully interwoven, is enclosed between two slow movements, the longing and yet simple character of which is deeply affecting. This kind of triple division, in which the emotion passes from quiet stillness to strongly moved passion, and then back again, is a new phase in Bach's cantata choruses; for the choruses in overture form have nothing in common with these, owing to the totally different character of that form.[91] The chorus is also remarkable for an intensely vivid picture of nature, which has already been noticed.[92] In the middle movement the long-drawn notes " Bleib bei uns " are heard through and above the tangled web of parts, as though distant voices were heard calling across a plain through the twilight. Long dark shadows fall across the landscape at the beginning and end; Bach himself took care that there could be no misunderstanding of his meaning here, for the same effect of tone is used by him in the tenor aria of a secular cantata, where it serves to illustrate the words " Frische Schatten, meine Freude, sehet wie ich schmerzlich scheide "—" Cooling shades, my great delight, see with what regret I quit you."[93] The downward motion of most of the parts suggests the approach of night; and in various passages of the alto aria, which is steeped

---

[89] B.-G., XVIII., No. 79. P. 1013. See Appendix A., No. 2.

[90] B.-G., I., No. 6. P. 1015. See Appendix A. of Vol. II., No. 58; and Appendix No. 2 of this Vol. Published in English by Novello.

[91] Among Bach's solos the aria " Seligster Erquickungstag," from the cantata " Wachet, betet," has this kind of form. See B.-G., XVI., p. 364 ff.

[92] See Vol. II., p. 561.

[93] B.-G., XI.,[2] p. 181.

in noble yearning, the gloom of darkness is represented in a strangely weird manner by means of sequences of tone and harmony. Whether Bach thought that enough had been done in this direction, or from some other cause, the beautiful evening hymn " Ach bleib bei uns, Herr Jesu Christ," which was such an especial favourite for evening services, and which forms the middle movement of the cantata, is rather wanting in depth for a composition of Bach. As in an organ trio, the soprano sings the *Cantus firmus* while the figured bass and a *Violoncello piccolo* have counterpoint upon it. The last-named instrument derives its subject from the first line of the tune, but soon goes off into wonderful leaps, arpeggios, and runs. At the close, where we should expect the return of the same chorale, we find the second verse of " Erhalt uns Herr bei deinem Wort," which was probably suggested by the doctrinal turn now taken by the words of the cantata. At all events, the remainder of the work cannot be compared with the impressive beauty of the first two movements.

The cantatas " Es wartet alles auf dich " (seventh Sunday after Trinity)[94] and " Wer Dank opfert, der preiset mich " (fourteenth Sunday after Trinity)[95] were used for the Masses in G minor and G major, so that they must have been written before the date of these works, and that is about 1737. The Gospel tells of the feeding of the four thousand, and the chief chorus of the first cantata extols the goodness of God, Who nourishes all His creatures with inexhaustible gifts, in the words of the Psalmist (Ps. civ., 27 and 28). The chorus is grandly conceived and splendidly worked out, excepting that, considering the subject, it is curiously gloomy. In the course of the work, which goes on to a general glorifying of God's mercies, this character is not however maintained. On words taken

---

[94] The autograph score and original parts in the Royal Library at Berlin; the original instrumental parts are in the possession of Herr Professor Rudorff of Lichterfelde, near Berlin. I have lately observed that the watermark seems to assign it to July 7, 1732. It is that described in note 48, Appendix A., of Vol. II.

[95] B.-G., II., No. 17. P. 1282.

from the Sermon on the Mount (Matt. vi., 31 and 32) there is developed one of those bass ariosos which so nearly resemble the aria, full of that doctrinal zeal which Bach knows so well how to clothe with beauty. The arias for alto and soprano have a character of waving fulness like ripe cornfields with their golden blessings. There is in them something of that warm and lovely sensuousness which Mozart was the first to bring to perfection. There is a most captivating passage in the soprano aria *Un poco allegro* in 3-8 time, in which the chief subject of the Adagio appears again with altered rhythm. The old-fashioned style of the hymn of praise, "Singen wir aus Herzensgrund," leads us back into the feeling of the principal chorus. The cantata "Wer Dank opfert," also extols the goodness and might of God, but throughout in brighter colouring. The joyful strain of the chief chorus is brought in in a splendid fugue. The middle of the cantata is built on a short passage of Biblical narrative, which suggests a new starting point. The same method is pursued in the Ascension cantata "Gott fähret auf mit Jauchzen."

In the period between 1738—1741 there are three more cantatas with choruses in a free style, which consist more or less of remodelled forms of other works. A composition for St. John's day "Freue dich, erlöste Schaar,"[95*] is to be assigned to June 24, 1738. It is founded on the secular cantata "Angenehmes Wiederau,"[96] and expresses a calm and happy feeling which is less suited to the dogmatic character of the festival than to the time of year at which it is held.

To about the same time, perhaps to the late autumn of 1737, belongs an important work for a marriage ceremony, "Gott ist unsre Zuversicht." All the chief numbers of its second part are taken from the Christmas cantata "Ehre sei Gott in der Höhe."[97] The great opening chorus is very effective and intelligible, and yet full of purpose. The broadly treated melodies of the alto aria are full of a certain enchanting sweetness of a kind which

---

95* B.-G. V., No. 30. P. 1017.

96 See Vol. II., p. 635, and Appendix A., to Vol. II., No. 58.

97 See Vol. II., p. 440.

occurs only in Bach's wedding cantatas. The title which
the work bears, *In diebus nuptiarum*, indicates a great
and solemn ceremonious occasion, very likely the marriage
of some exalted personages. One wedding cantata, which,
however, has only come down to us in an incomplete
state, but which seems to have been a very important and
interesting work, was used by Bach about 1740 or 1741 for
a Whitsuntide cantata " O ewiges Feuer, o Ursprung der
Liebe."[98] It contains two choruses and an alto aria
" Wohl euch ihr auserwählten Seelen "—" Rejoice, ye souls
elect and holy"—between two short recitatives. The re-
arrangement is perceptible in the brevity of the final chorus,
which had not the same position in the wedding cantata ; it
is also conspicuous in the aria, in no part of which can the
original bridal feeling pass unnoticed. For its pure and
ardent atmosphere, its magic charm of tone, its lovely
melodies, it is indisputably fitted to rank at the head of all
Bach's works of this kind, and to be considered an unapproachable model. In the lavish adornment of the first
chorus there is a touch of ardent human love, which, from
Bach's pure ideal nature, is in no way incompatible with
the emotional aspect of Whitsuntide, but which only receives
its full explanation when we understand the original purpose
and object of the chorus.

It has already been pointed out that Bach adapted
instrumental works for his church cantatas, not merely as
symphonies but also as solos.[99] There are indeed two
cantatas in which instrumental movements are turned into
choruses—a Christmas cantata, " Unser Mund sei voll
Lachens,"[100] and a work for the third Sunday after Easter,
" Wir müssen durch viel Trübsal in das Reich Gottes
eingehen."[101] As in the *Gloria* of the Mass in A major, the

---

[98] B.-G., VII., No. 34. P. 1291. In English, " O light everlasting " (Novello).
See Appendix A. to Vol. II., No. 57. I may here remark that, in 1742, owing to the
fortnight's mourning for the death of the widowed Empress Maria Amalia, no
church music was performed on Whitsunday or Trinity Sunday, so that the
cantata " O ewiges Feuer" cannot have been performed in 1742.

[99] See Vol. II., p. 448.

[100] B.-G., XXIII., No. 110. P. 1681.

[101] In a later MS. in the Royal Library at Berlin.

chorus is worked into the fabric of the instrumental piece, without altering it in any essential particular. For the Christmas cantata Bach used the overture of an orchestral suite in D major.[102] We cannot be certain when this suite was written; but a comparison between it and the suites in C major and in B minor makes it probable that Bach wrote it, not in Cöthen, but in Leipzig, where works of this kind were naturally suggested by his post of director of the Musical Society. As we already know three cantatas for Christmas Day written by him between 1723 and 1734, and as he did not enter upon the conductorship of the Musical Society until 1729, it is highly improbable that the cantata " Unser Mund sei voll Lachens " can have been written before 1734.[103] Only the fugal allegro of the overture is transformed, and that with astonishing power, into a chorus, the slow movements forming the symphonies before and after it. Bach adopted a similar method in the cantata " Preise Jerusalem den Herrn," and in the chorale-cantata " In allen meinen Thaten," [104] while elsewhere (" Nun komm der Heiden Heiland," " Höchsterwünschtes Freuden-fest," " O Ewigkeit, du Donnerwort ") he makes the chorus take part in the grave movement.[105] The pompous character of the French overture made it very suitable to a Christmas composition, although it cannot be denied that, by confining the chorus to the allegro movement, he gives that movement a predominance which is foreign to the form from which it is taken. In this cantata we also find the *Virga Jesse floruit* from the *Magnificat* [106] reset to the words "Ehre sei Gott in der Höhe"—"Glory to God in the highest." The rest of the solo numbers, which seem to be entirely new, are of great merit, and, especially in the alto aria, have an earnest and manly character, which we do not find in the earlier Leipzig cantatas. The same may be said of the cantata " Wir müssen durch viel Trübsal in das Reich

---

[102] See Vol. II., p. 141.
[103] See Appendix A. to Vol. II., No. 24.
[104] See Vol. II., pp. 362 f. and 457.　*
[105] See Vol. I., 507, Vol. II., pp. 365 and 421.
[106] See Vol. II., p. 269.

Gottes eingehen." A comparison of the alto aria with organ *obbligato* "Ich will nach dem Himmel zu" with the aria "Willkommen will ich sagen," from the cantata "Wer weiss, wie nahe mir mein Ende,"[107] will make this clear. The arias have many points of resemblance, even in the disposition and accompaniment of the vocal parts; but the ecstatic longing for death is more intense in the later work. As an instrumental section Bach uses for this cantata the same D minor concerto that he had already used for the introduction to the cantata "Ich habe meine Zuversicht" after the Rückpositiv of the organ in St. Thomas's Church was made to be played upon independently.[108] Here, however, only the first movement is used for the symphony; in the adagio the principal chorus is brought in in such a manner that the part for the solo instrument goes on simultaneously and independently, a masterpiece of ingenuity and skill.

Of the four cantatas for Trinity which have been preserved, one still remains to be mentioned, as to the date of which nothing can be asserted with any certainty. As, however, no fewer than three of these cantatas date from the year 1723—1732 ("Höchsterwünschtes Freudenfest," "O heiliges Geist- und Wasserbad," "Gelobet sei der Herr"), it may be presumed to have been written at a later period; and the style of the music favours this presumption. In particular, this is seen in the chief chorus, the characteristic energy of which makes it a worthy companion piece to the choruses "Herr deine Augen sehen nach dem Glauben," "Ihr werdet weinen und heulen," "Gott fähret auf mit Jauchzen," and others. But, with all its musical beauty, the cantata, as a whole, is an inexplicable enigma. The Gospel contains the story of how Nicodemus came to Jesus by night for fear of the Jews. In this the writer of the words sees an instance of weak cowardice, and, accordingly, he begins his poem with the text, "Es ist ein trotzig und verzagt Ding"—"There is a

---

[107] See Vol. II., p. 451.
[108] See Vol. II., p. 446 f.

perverse and cowardly thing in the heart of man." He goes on to say that when the Christian dares not seek Jesus openly a feeling of shame for his own unworthiness takes possession of him. But he may take courage in the hope of salvation through faith. The sequence of ideas must have been as clear to Bach as it is to us ; for that reason it is inexplicable why he set himself in the most distinct opposition to it in his music. He lays the emphasis in the first chorus not on the faint-heartedness but on the resistance of the heart. And it is a Titanic resistance that storms out against heaven in the fearfully energetic theme of the fugue. The number by itself is a masterpiece of the highest order, but its character deprives it of all inner connection with what follows. In strong contrast to this is the first aria, which is in the style of a gavotte. It is charming as a piece of music, but quite unsuited to its text, which treats of the timidity of the Christian in approaching his divine and wondrous Master. Although, as the work goes on, there is more connection between the words and the music, yet a harmonious co-operation of effect is rendered impossible. If the condition of the autograph did not prove it otherwise, we should suspect that the first two numbers were transferred from elsewhere. But as it is, we can do no more than simply point out the discrepancy that exists.[109]

In each of the two cantatas, having their chief choruses in free style, which still remain to be mentioned, as in the compositions for Trinity Sunday and for Christmas-day, just described, we find a text of Scripture in the middle as well as at the beginning : a form of which the frequent recurrence in the cantatas written at this time will have been noticed. " Brich dem Hungrigen dein Brod " —" Give the hungry man thy bread "—is for the first Sunday after Trinity, and " Es ist dir gesagt, Mensch, was gut ist " for the eighth.[110] The resemblance between the two, as regards the musical conception and execution, lies on the surface. The chorus of the first, set to two

---

[109] The autograph score is in the Royal Library at Berlin.
[110] B.-G., VII., No. 39. P. 1295 ; and B.-G., X., No. 45. P. 1016.

beautiful verses of Isaiah (lviii. v. 7, 8), brings out the meaning of that text in the Sermon on the Mount, "Blessed are the merciful, for they shall obtain mercy," and the cantata is fitly concluded with the sixth verse of the paraphrase of the beatitudes.[111] It is an affecting picture of Christian love, softening with tender hand and pitying sympathy the sorrow of the brethren, and obtaining the highest reward. The peculiar accompaniment, allotted to flutes, oboes, and strings, was very likely suggested to Bach by the idea of the breaking of bread. But how little he cared for such trivial realism is seen, as the number goes on, in a passage where the accompaniment is continued to entirely different words. It gives the piece a tender, dreamy tinge, and this was what Bach chiefly wanted. The second part of the cantata opens with the text in Hebrews, xiii. 16: "Wohlzuthun und mitzutheilen," &c.—"To do good and to communicate forget not, for with such sacrifices God is well pleased." This is sung by the bass in the usual way. The two arias have an expression of loving activity and kindliness. The Gospel for the day treats of the rich man and Lazarus.

The second cantata, which is wholly different from this, is a grand Protestant sermon on the duties required of the Christian by God, in order that he may stand before His judgment seat. The whole has a character of severity, and the chief subject of the first chorus is not without a trace of orthodox harshness. But its source is no dead and barren consent to received dogmas; it is a living enthusiasm for a lofty purpose which imbues this elaborate chorus with earnest vigour.

A mighty *torso* of a church cantata is preserved in a double chorus with the richest orchestral accompaniment, on the words from Rev. xii., 10, "Nun ist das Heil," &c.—"Now shall the grace," &c.[112] It must be called a torso, for it seems that in its present form it falls in with no church use whatever. It is too short to lay claim to the title of a

---

[111] "Kommt lasst euch den Herren lehren," ascribed to David Denicke.

[112] B.-G., X., No. 50. P. 1657. In the Bach Choir Magazine with English words.

church cantata in regular form ; it cannot serve as a motett by reason of its concerted accompaniments, and its subject of course would forbid all thought of its being performed during the communion service ; and there is no other occasion for which it would be suitable. It must certainly have formed the opening of a complete cantata for Michaelmas, and it may be assumed to have had an orchestral prelude. The colossal piece, however, by itself, with its ponderous march and its wild cries of victory is an imperishable monument of German art.[113]

There are extremely few solo cantatas remaining which can be assigned to the later Leipzig period. A *Dialogus* between Christ and the Soul, for the second day of Christmas (" Selig ist der Mann, der die Anfechtung erduldet "),[114] belongs to the class of those compositions which represent domestic sacred music rather than church music. It contains no trace whatever of special fitness, and if the intention of the work were not expressly given no one would conceive that it was meant for Christmas. The case is different with a work for the third day of Christmas, " Süsser Trost, mein Jesus kommt."[115] Deeply and thoroughly as Bach had given expression to the ecclesiastical intention of the festival, both in the Christmas Oratorio and in separate arias in earlier cantatas,[116] this work testifies that he had not yet exhausted the subject. The pure happiness of Christmas is here transfigured and glorified. The bright and silvery soprano voice with its simple, sweet, and longdrawn melodies, accompanied by tender waving passages on the oboe, seems to present to us the idea of an angel of peace hovering over the dark city. The middle movement of the first aria differs

---

[113] A cantata is preserved, though only in incomplete parts, which begins with the chorus " Ihr Pforten zu Zion, ihr Wohnungen Jacobs freuet euch "—" Rejoice, ye gates of Zion, and ye dwellings of Jacob." Zion here represents Leipzig, and the occasion for which the music was composed was the election of the Council. No more definite evidence than this of its date can be given. The fragments of this cantata are preserved in the Royal Library at Berlin.

[114] B.-G., XII.,[2] No. 57. P. 1661.

[115] The original parts are in the Royal Library at Berlin.

[116] " Nun komm der Heiden Heiland," see Vol. I., p. 507; " Tritt auf die Glaubensbahn," Vol. I., p. 560.

in time and pace from the rest, a form not unfrequently
employed by Bach in his Leipzig period.[117] The second
aria has a gentle rocking motion, and though wholly
terrestrial is very lovely; the Christmas chorale "Lobt Got
ihr Christen allzugleich" closes the beautiful little work.

Another *Dialogus* composed for the first Sunday after
Epiphany ("Liebster Jesu, mein Verlangen")[118] has a
particular interest for us in the fact that, in the duet "Nun
verschwinden alle Plagen," an idea which he had evolved
in an earlier cantata for the same Sunday after Epiphany
is developed at greater length.[119]

Side by side with this *Dialogus* we must consider a cantata
for the second Sunday after Epiphany, "Meine Seufzer,
meine Thränen."[120] It betokens the poverty of thought and
one-sidedness of view in the sacred poetry of the time
that no lesson could be deduced from the Gospel story
of the marriage in Cana, in which a tone of noble cheer-
fulness is evidently predominant, than this, so endlessly
reiterated, that Jesus helps the despondent sinner in
his need. With more or less variation all the chief
cantata librettists of the period harp on this thought alone.
The three cantatas composed by Bach for this Sunday[121]
are one and all founded on this idea. In the one now
under consideration the feeling of trouble, of "groans
and piteous crying for salvation," is most persistently
brought forward. Until the chorale at the close, hardly
a single ray of sunlight breaks in upon this overclouded
world. Bach never wove a more compact and con-
sistent fabric of tones of mourning than the arias for
bass and tenor. It seems impossible that this combination of deep and spontaneous emotion with the display

---

[117] For instance, in the cantatas "Ihr Menschen, rühmet Gottes Liebe,"
"Es wartet alles auf dich," "Gott ist unsre Zuversicht," "Am Abend aber
desselbigen Sabbaths," "Ach lieben Christen seid getrost," "Ich freue mich in
dir."

[118] B.-G., VII., No. 32. P. 1663.

[119] See Vol. II., 402.

[120] B.-G., II., No. 13.

[121] The others are "Mein Gott, wie lang ach lange" and "Ach Gott, wie
manches Herzeleid" (in A major).

of infinite ingenuity should ever be outdone. Led by his natural artistic feeling, the master gave to the chorale fantasia which separates the two arias a somewhat milder and simpler character. The semiquaver figures on the violins have a breath of coolness, although this conception is not suggested by the words of the chorale, and therefore no real repose is attained. Bach revelled in sorrow, and to him the setting of cantata poems of this kind was a welcome task. But from this work we again see that music was gradually gaining in independence and beginning to free itself from the Church. A work of this kind is certainly not suitable to a service which ought, in accordance with the Gospel, to point the lesson that Christ holds communion with His elect, showering on them His gifts, and rejoicing in the joy of men.

Still, it can seldom be said that Bach's church music does not fulfil its liturgical purpose. Highly suitable, for instance, are the cantatas for the twenty-fifth Sunday after Trinity ("Es reifet euch ein schrecklich Ende") and for the first Sunday after Easter ("Am Abend aber desselbigen Sabbaths"). The first, in spite of the scanty materials employed, is a powerful and affecting work.[122] The second opens with a lovely symphony, which exhibits the form of the first movement of a concerto in ingenious combination with that of the aria in three sections, and must have been adapted from some secular instrumental composition;[123] the beginning of the alto aria seems also to be an adaptation. The duet between the soprano and the tenor is set to a verse of a chorale "Verzage nicht, o Häuflein klein," but only using the words; the music is freely invented. Here Bach again treads the same path which he struck out in the cantatas "Gelobet sei der Herr," "In allen meinen Thaten," and others.[124] Every one of these solo

---

[122] B.-G., XX.,[1] No. 90. The instruments to be used are not given in the autograph score. They can be supplied, however, from Breitkopf's catalogue for Michaelmas, 1761. There it stands in so many words: *à Tromba*, 2 *Violini*, *Viola*, 4 *Voci*, *Basso ed Organo*.

[123] B.-G., X., No. 42. P. 2144. In the autograph score, the symphony and the first part of the aria are written out fair.

[124] See Vol. II., p. 457.

cantatas is divided among different voices, and they all conclude with chorales in four parts. Only in the cantata " Meine Seele rühmt und preiset " does the tenor sing alone, and there is no chorale. It thus belongs to the same class as the vocal compositions " Ich habe genug," " Widerstehe doch der Sünde," and others.[125] I mention it here at the end because, although there is no doubt of its genuineness, as yet there is no documentary evidence for it whatever.[126]

We come now to that form of cantata in which Bach's creative power as applied to sacred music finally expired. It must not, it is true, be forgotten that a portion of his church cantatas has been lost. As among these some would surely be found which were composed at Leipzig, the existing relations between the groups wherein the different forms are represented, would probably be altered were the works to come to light again. But yet it is clear, from the large number of works in the same form and written in the same period, that during the last part of his life Bach adhered to one and the same form with a persistency not elsewhere to be observed even in him. This form is the chorale cantata.

The reader must be again reminded that about 1732 the idea occurred to Bach of setting complete hymns to music ; that is, that for certain verses the proper melody is retained, while other verses are made to serve as texts for recitations and arias without the help of any words but those of the hymn.[127] I called these cantatas works of transition or of digression, lying on or beside the way to higher developments of form. Works of this kind, treated in a different way, also occur, a chorale being taken as the central idea ;

---

[125] See Vol. II., p. 473.

[126] A late MS. copy from the collection of Professor Fischhoff is in the Royal Library at Berlin. I would expressly draw attention to the general fact that all the solo cantatas described above are only assigned to the later Leipzig period on an assumption of probability. For the correctness of this assumption there is one piece of negative evidence—namely, that they bear no outward marks whatever which would oblige them to be assigned to an earlier date— and positive evidence is borne by their ripeness and depth of feeling.

[127] See Vol. II., p. 454 ff.

but its character, as a hymn, is not fully brought out, since sometimes the words and sometimes the tune only is made use of. In a cantata for the nineteenth Sunday after Trinity[128] the chorale occurs only in an instrumental form in the principal chorus. The chorus sings passages of imitation to the words (Rom. vii., 24) " Ich elender Mensch," &c.— " O wretched man that I am," &c. To the instruments is allotted an independent subject, twelve bars long, which is played again and again from the beginning, according to the method which we first became acquainted with in the chorale " Was Gott thut, das ist wohlgethan," from the cantata " Die Elenden sollen essen." [129] Against this subject, the trumpets and oboes play the chorale in canon on the fifth ; at the close the last two lines are repeated by the trumpet alone, so that the form becomes, as it were, a musical interrogation. In order to understand the complete poetic meaning of the chorus it is necessary to know the words which belong to this chorale melody. They run thus :—

> Herr Jesu Christ, ich schrei zu dir
> Aus hochbetrübter Seele,
> Dein Allmacht lass erscheinen mir
> Und mich nicht also quäle.
> Viel grösser ist die Angst und Schmerz,
> So anficht und turbirt mein Herz,
> Als dass ichs kann erzählen.

> Lord Jesu Christ, I cry to Thee,
> When heart and flesh are failing,
> Show Thine Almighty power to me,
> To keep my soul from quailing.
> So great my pain and deadly smart,
> So troubled and distressed my heart,
> That words are unavailing.

The cantata is brought to a close with the 12th verse of the hymn simply set in four parts. In the middle, however, we meet with a second chorale melody ; the fourth verse of " Ach Gott und Herr " is set in four parts, with modulations

---

[128] B.-G., X., No. 48. P. 1699.
[129] See Vol. II., p. 355.

of incredible boldness.   The middle movements, in a madrigal style, stand in no sort of relation to the chorale. Among them the tenor aria is especially interesting in respect of rhythm and modulation.

Another cantata, for the fifteenth Sunday after Trinity, is set to the first verses of Hans Sachs's hymn, " Warum betrübst du dich, mein Herz." [130]   The first two verses, which follow one another almost immediately, are separated by recitatives on words in the free madrigal style, of the same kind as we have noticed in the cantatas "Wer weiss, wie nahe mir mein Ende," " Herr wie du willst, so schicks mit mir," and elsewhere.   Each of the first three lines of the first verse is prefaced by a short tenor arioso on the words of the hymn, and in this method we see the development of the plan begun in the cantatas above-mentioned, which are set to hymns throughout.   The phrases of the arioso portions are formed upon the principal subject on which the instrumental movement is built, which makes it seem as though the whole movement together were to be in the form of a chorale fantasia.   But it is not so, for whenever the chorus enters the instruments are restricted to the simplest accompaniment.   It is also contrary to the nature of the chorale fantasia that each of the first three lines should be played over on the oboe before the voices begin.   The second verse of the chorale is characterised by a certain want of unity and of repose.   It appears first in the simplest four-part setting, while the last two lines have rich thematic counterpoint, and—which is most remarkable —after an inserted recitative they are repeated almost exactly as before.   The third verse forms the close of the work; it is a real chorale fantasia, although the instrumental movement is of a simplicity not very often met with in such cases in Bach.   This, as well as the un-pretending character of the chorale movements which pre-cede this movement, is probably accounted for by the

---

[130] The autograph score is in the Royal Library at Berlin. It is also published in Winterfeld, Ev. Kirchengesang III., Musical Appendix, p. 145 ff.

nature of the Gospel for the day, in which the faithful Christian is exhorted to leave all anxiety for bodily well-being, in childlike confidence, to his heavenly Father, like the birds of the air and the lilies of the field. That which chiefly gives the cantata the character of an imperfect and transitional production, is the subjective and arbitrary treatment of the first verse of the chorale, and the strange arrangement of the whole. A chorale movement at the beginning and at the end, with middle movements in the madrigal style, or three different treatments of chorales at the beginning, in the middle, and at the end respectively, with madrigal interludes, is intelligible; but not a form in which two chorale movements treated in various ways follow consecutively, after which comes a bass aria in madrigal style, the whole closing with a chorale fantasia. The date of this, and of the cantata described before it, cannot be fixed with certainty. The first of the two must, however, have been written before the Mass in G major, for the bass aria appears again in the last-mentioned work as a transferred movement.

Of the chorale cantata, strictly speaking, Bach has only left isolated specimens of the first Leipzig period. The cantatas "O Ewigkeit, du Donnerwort" (F major), "Liebster Gott, wann werd ich sterben," "Wer nur den lieben Gott lässt walten," "Was Gott thut, das ist wohl-gethan" (second composition), and "Es ist das Heil uns kommen her," display the form in its completeness. Nearly trenching on these are "Wachet auf, ruft uns die Stimme," and "Wär Gott nicht mit uns diese Zeit," which dates from the beginning of the last period. The whole body of chorale cantatas may now be presented in a tabulated form:—

1. Ach Gott vom Himmel sieh darein (second Sunday after Trinity).
2. Ach Gott, wie manches Herzeleid (second Sunday after Epiphany).
3. Ach Herr, mich armen Sünder (third Sunday after Trinity).
4. Ach lieben Christen seid getrost (seventeenth Sunday after Trinity).
5. Ach wie flüchtig, ach wie nichtig (twenty-fourth Sunday after Trinity).
6. Allein zu dir, Herr Jesu Christ (thirteenth Sunday after Trinity).
7. Aus tiefer Noth schrei ich zu dir (twenty-first Sunday after Trinity).

8. Christum wir sollen loben schon (second day of Christmas).
9. Christ unser Herr zum Jordan kam (St. John's Day).
10. Das neugeborne Kindelein (Sunday after Christmas).
11. Du Friedefürst, Herr Jesu Christ (twenty-fifth Sunday after Trinity).
12. Erhalt uns Herr bei deinem Wort (sixth Sunday after Trinity).
13. Gelobet seist du, Jesu Christ (Christmas Day).
14. Herr Christ der einig Gottssohn (eighteenth Sunday after Trinity).
15. Herr Gott, dich loben alle wir (Michaelmas Day).
16. Herr Jesu Christ, du höchstes Gut (eleventh Sunday after Trinity).
17. Herr Jesu Christ, wahr' Mensch und Gott (Quinquagesima).
18. Ich freue mich in dir (third day of Christmas).[131]
19. Ich hab in Gottes Herz und Sinn (Septuagesima).
20. Jesu, der du meine Seele (fourteenth Sunday after Trinity).
21. Jesu nun sei gepreiset (New Year's Day).
22. Liebster Immanuel, Herzog der Frommen (Epiphany).
23. Mache dich, mein Geist, bereit (twenty-second Sunday after Trinity).
24. Meinen Jesum lass ich nicht (first Sunday after Epiphany).
25. Meine Seele erhebet den Herren (Visitation of B. V. M.).
26. Mit Fried und Freud ich fahr dahin (Purification of B. V. M.).
27. Nimm von uns Herr, du treuer Gott (tenth Sunday after Trinity).
28. Nun komm, der Heiden Heiland, B minor (first Sunday in Advent).
29. Schmücke dich, o liebe Seele (second Sunday after Trinity).[132]
30. Was frag ich nach der Welt (ninth Sunday after Trinity).
31. Was mein Gott will, das gscheh allzeit (third Sunday after Epiphany).
32. Wie schön leuchtet der Morgenstern (Annunciation of the B. V. M.).
33. Wo Gott der Herr nicht bei uns hält (eighth Sunday after Trinity).
34. Wohl dem, der sich auf seinen Gott (twenty-third Sunday after Trinity).
35. Wo soll ich fliehen hin (nineteenth Sunday after Trinity).

Putting aside numbers 3, 6, 16, 20, 27, 32, 33 and 34, the twenty-seven cantatas which remain belong, as is sufficiently proved by the evidence of the manuscripts, to one and the same limited space of time. The most that can be asserted

---

[131] Compare, on the melody, Appendix A., No. 1. The form there given differs only in unimportant details from that in the cantata. There are differences of greater importance in the form given in König's Harmonische Liederschatz (Frankfort à M. 1738), p. 280 (O stilles Gotteslamm)."

[132] Entered in Breitkopf's catalogue for Michaelmas, 1761, p. 23, as a communion cantata.

as to their dates is that " Du Friedefürst, Herr Jesu Christ,"
is the latest, falling as it does on November 15, 1744. It
would seem, on the other hand, that among the earliest were
the following : " Was frag ich nach der Welt," " Wo soll
ich fliehen hin," " Ich freue mich in dir," and " Jesu nun
sei gepreiset." Of these the first was probably written for
August 7, 1735, the second for October 16, 1735, the third
for December 27, 1735, and the fourth for January 1, 1736.[133]

In these thirty-five cantatas a series of the most beautiful
and the best known Protestant chorales of the sixteenth
and seventeenth centuries is subjected to elaborate musical
treatment. As the subject has hitherto been only lightly
touched upon, it may be well here and now to analyse completely the way in which the chorales were used, and the
nature and character of Bach's chorale cantatas properly so
called.

The particular hymn in its entirety forms the groundwork
of each cantata. In the case of long hymns several verses
are sometimes omitted ; but this neither alters nor impairs
the course of thought, and is in accordance with the ordinary
custom, even in congregational singing, of leaving out some
stanzas for convenience ; but the first and last stanzas always
appear in their exact original form, and combined with the
original melody. In rarer cases one or more of the other
verses appear, as the work goes on, with the original words,
to which the church melody is always retained as an
inseparable adjunct. For the most part the verses of the

---

[133] See Appendix A., No. 3. The autographs of 3, 33, and 34 are not known,
they only exist in later copies. The following have been published after the
originals : 1 B.-G., I., 2, P. 1194; 2 B.-G., I., 3, P. 1195; 4 B.-G., XXIV., 114;
5 B.-G., V.,[1] 26, P. 43; 6 B.-G., VII., 33; 7 B.-G., VII., 38, P. 1694; 8 B.-G.,
XXVI., 121; 9 B.-G., I., 7, P. 1198; 10 B.-G., XXVI., 122; 11 B.-G.,
XXIV., 116; 12 B.-G., XXVI., 126; 13 B.-G., XXII., 91, P. 2147; 14 B.-G.,
XXII., 96, P. 2142; 15 B.-G., XXVI., 130; 16 B.-G., XXIV. 113; 17 B.-G.,
XXVI., 127; 19 B.-G., XXII., 92, P. 2143; 20 B.-G., XVIII., 78, P. 1294;
21 B.-G., X., 41, P. 1656; 22 B.-G., XXVI., 123; 23 B.-G., XXIV., 115, P. 1687;
24 B.-G., XXVI., 124; 25 B.-G., I., 10, P. 1278; 26 B.-G., XXVI., 125; 27
B.-G., XXIII., 101, P. 1678; 28 B.-G., XVI., 62; 30 B.-G., XXII., 94, P. 2146;
31 B. G., XXIV., 111; 32 B.-G., I., 1, P. 1193; 35 B.-G., I., 5, P. 1197. The
autograph score of No. 18 is in the hands of Herr Ernst Mendelssohn-Bartholdy
of Berlin ; that of 29 belongs to Madame Pauline Viardot-Garcia of Paris.

hymn are transformed into poems in the madrigal style, and in this form they serve as the poetic material for the free solos and concerted numbers. The altered text adheres closely to the original words, with the exception of a few abridgments in some places and prolongations in others.[134] The thoughts, and in part even the turns of expression, and individual words, remain the same. The hymn appears, not essentially changed, but as it were beneath a veil. This rule may be applied with more or less strictness to all the cantata texts. For instance, in the cantatas " Ach Gott vom Himmel sieh darein," " Ach Herr, mich armen Sünder," " Erhalt uns Herr bei deinem Wort," " Liebster Immanuel, Herzog der Frommen," " Schmücke dich, o liebe Seele," " Wo soll ich fliehen hin," the recension follows the original text with remarkable exactitude. Elsewhere, as in " Christum wir sollen loben schon," " Mache dich, mein Geist, bereit," " Nimm von uns Herr, du treuer Gott," " Nun komm, der Heiden Heiland," " Wie schön leuchtet der Morgenstern," " Herr Christ der einig Gottssohn," the poet takes greater liberties, sometimes deviating widely from his original.; but by retaining certain striking words he preserves the feeling that it is still a paraphrase. Only exceptionally and in unimportant passages do independent and original insertions occur, as for example, in the bass recitatives in " Ach lieben Christen seid getrost " and " Das neugeborne Kindelein " ; and in the alto recitatives in " Mit Fried und Freud " and " Wohl dem, der sich auf seinen Gott." The alto recitative of the cantata " Du Friedefürst, Herr Jesu Christ " is also set to independent words; this is probably accounted for by the particular character given to the work by the war of 1744.

If the hymn to be used happened to be too short, more words had to be inserted, in order to fill up the requisite number of arias and recitatives. This is done, for instance, in the case of " Meine Seele erhebet den Herren." Frequently, too, in cases of this kind the verses were divided

---

[134] An example of the process as applied to the hymn " Christ unser Herr zum Jordan kam " is given in the German original of the present work, Vol. II., p. 570.

into two portions; the alto aria of the cantata "Ich freue mich in dir" is founded upon the first half of the second verse, and the soprano aria upon the first half of the third, both the second halves being employed for the recitatives which follow the arias. In the cantata "Jesu nun sei gepreiset" all that is in madrigal style—viz., two arias and two recitatives—is founded upon the middle verse. In the cantata "Mit Fried und Freud" the text of the first aria seems to be suggested by the first verse of the hymn, although this has previously been sung through in its original form. And, on the other hand, in the case of hymns consisting of many verses, we meet with combinations of two or more in one number. In "Ach Gott, wie manches Herzeleid," verses 7—10 are taken for the tenor recitative, and in "Mache dich, mein Geist, bereit," verses 3—6 form the groundwork of the bass recitative. The extreme limit in this respect is reached in the cantata "Ach wie flüchtig," where no fewer than seven verses (3—9), each compressed into a single line, are employed for the recitative. It has been already mentioned that omissions are sometimes made; an example occurs in "Ach Gott, wie manches Herzeleid," where after the tenor recitative, verses 11—14, and then verse 17 are omitted, verses 4 and 5 having previously been left out.

A special kind of paraphrase occurs, also, in which the verse of the chorale is interwoven with recitatives. Either the chorale is sung set for one or more voices, and recitatives are inserted between the lines, or else it is played on the instruments, and a solo voice sings a recitative against it. This never occurs either at the beginning or end of a cantata, but is not unfrequently found in the course of it. I would mention, for example, the cantatas "Ach Gott, wie manches Herzeleid," "Aus tiefer noth schrei ich zu dir," "Das neugeborne Kindelein," "Gelobet seist du, Jesu Christ," and "Ich hab in Gottes Herz und Sinn." Here the words of the recitatives stand in no close connection with the chorale verses, but are merely generally suggested by them. Most of these paraphrases are a kind of explanation of the words, but here this is the case in a quite re-

markable degree.   In the unrestricted madrigal form certain
applications which it was thought desirable to introduce were
easily brought in.   Nicolai's hymn, " Wie schön leuchtet der
Morgenstern," was not originally written for the festival of
the Annunciation.   When used for this occasion, it was
fitting that reference should be made to the event ; hence
the mention of the angel Gabriel in the tenor recitative,
which is built upon the second verse of the hymn.   Besides
this, several allusions to the first verse run through the
words, a method which is not peculiar to this cantata.
The words of the tenor aria " Jesus nimmt die Sünder
an," from the cantata " Herr Jesu Christ du höchstes
Gut," enlarge upon the ideas of the fourth verse which
has been previously sung through word for word, and
at the same time refer to the Gospel for the day—the
parable of the pharisee and the publican.   Any one who
carefully studies the. texts of the chorale cantatas, comparing them with the original hymns, will notice that the
poet frequently transposes the subjects, ideas, and words
in a way which is sometimes ingenious and interesting in its
effect, but which often produces the impression of laboured
and mechanical work.

The style of the texts of all these chorale cantatas is so
very much the same that we may assume them all to have
been the work of one poet.   Picander had a great facility for
this kind of work.   It appears frequently in his own poetry,
and the " Erbauliche Gedanken " show that he could
put together very good hymns.   The hymns divided into
regular verses in this collection are for the most part
mere compilations ; he was almost entirely devoid of
originality in this line, but he compiled with such success
that some of his poems have passed into use in the
church.[135]   We can with safety assert him to be the author

---

[135] Koch. (Geschichte des Kirchenlied), V., p. 500 f. (3rd edition) states that
the hymns, " Bedenke, Mensch, die Ewigkeit," " Das ist meine Freude, dass,
indem ich leide," and " Wer weiss, wie nahe mir mein Ende, ob heute nicht
mein jüngster Tag," are still in ordinary use.   The opening lines, which
are almost identical with well-known hymns, sufficiently prove Picander's
plagiarism.

of at least one of the cantata texts. It must be remembered that he had in his time adapted the Michaelmas hymn from "Erbauliche Gedanken" for Bach, for the cantata "Es erhub sich ein Streit."[136] He again made use of the same materials for the Michaelmas cantata, "Herr Gott, dich loben alle wir," by amalgamating the second verse of the hymn with the closing chorale of the cantata poem for the text of the tenor aria.

We cannot be wrong in assuming Bach to have originated the idea of this new style of text-writing, since he could not find a poet after his own heart. It is easily intelligible that Bach would feel a growing aversion to the dull poetry of the ordinary cantata texts of the time. He must soon have discovered, however, that it was impossible to adapt the verses of hymns to recitatives and arias. The resistance which the form of the verse would show to free musical treatment was not the greatest difficulty he had to encounter. To a refined perception, the contrast between the modern form of verse for musical setting and the hymn-verse was very nearly as strong as that between the modern form of verse and the words of Scripture. Whatever could be done from the side of music to bridge over the chasm had certainly been done by the style in which Bach's church music was cast; and now the work had to be completed from the poetical side of the gulf. In the paraphrase in madrigal style he found a form of poetry which solved the problem, and which must be owned to be unsurpassable for its purpose. By its means the connection with the hymn-form was kept up, and a noble and fitting style of thought was rendered possible; at the same time, it lent itself readily to the existing forms of musical expression. In consequence of the rule that the first and last verses, at least, and sometimes some of the middle verses, must remain untouched in words or melody, so as to constitute the groundwork of the whole, the numbers in madrigal form stand towards the whole in the relation of members, of a lighter structure, but of the same substance.

---

[136] Vol. II., p. 408 ff.

In the cantatas written by Bach in early life, on hymns unaltered in form, he had frequently indulged his fancy with playful imitations of the melody. In this respect he now returned to the strict rules of sacred composition. The chorale melody is something sacred and unalterable. It serves as a central point round which the music crystallises, without itself being drawn into the movement and action consequent upon the process of formation. The most that is allowable is to surround and adorn it. The most effective treatment which can be applied is the combination of the melody with a poetic effusion of a more subjective character. The middle parts more especially of the chorale cantatas present to us interesting examples of Bach's adherence to this fundamental principle. In these we not seldom find fragments of poems in madrigal style built upon detached lines of the chorale melody. They are always perfectly clear and definite, and are inserted with admirable art into the free flow of the piece. In only one case that I know of is such a line of a chorale set to new words. In the tenor aria in the cantata " Herr Jesu Christ, du höchstes Gut," in bars 41—43 and 52—55, the last line of the melody comes prominently forward in both cases in an adorned form to the words " dein Sünd ist dir vergeben." It may have been because the text of the aria stands only in a very loose connection with one verse of the hymn—viz., the fourth; and so this reference in the music may be in order to unite it more closely to the hymn. It is, however, observable that the words are not in a free madrigal form, but are taken from the Bible.[137]

As a general rule, the line of the melody is set to the proper words in the particular verse which forms the basis of the poet's madrigal paraphrase. Examples of this occur in the duet from the same cantata. It is founded on the seventh verse of the hymn, and of this the first, third, fifth, and seventh lines are introduced word for word ; [138] these lines are united to the proper fragments

---

[137] Spoken by Christ on various occasions : Matt. ix., 2 ; Luke vii., 48.
[138] The third line, which is not very happy in its original form, receives a slight alteration.

of the melody, which are afterwards prolonged and developed by freely inverted passages. The bass recitative in "Schmücke dich, o liebe Seele" closes in the same way, with the last line of the eighth verse of the hymn brought in almost in its original form ; and the last line of the melody is developed in a florid arioso. As models of ingenuity in expressively adorning a given musical phrase, these melodic fragments may take very high rank. The two opening bars of the alto recitative in the cantata "Ach Herr mich armen Sünder," which begins with the words of the fourth strophe "Ich bin von Seufzen müde," testify to a wonderful genius for manipulating and transforming musical phrases, as well as to an incomparable depth of feeling. Nor are these qualities less prominent in bars 44—47 of the tenor aria in the same cantata, where the voice, instead of going down by the interval of a second, suddenly rises a seventh. The bass recitative in the cantata "Jesu, der du meine Seele" culminates in the latter half of the tenth verse, of which the actual words are retained. The strings have an independent accompaniment throughout, to which the voice sings the last four lines of the melody, varying them so that they become full of fervour and deep devotion.

Often, too, the fragments appear in their natural simplicity. In the duet of the cantata "Nimm von uns Herr" this occurs at the beginning, and again at the repetition of the same portion; and in the alto aria of the cantata "Ach Gott vom Himmel sieh darein" it occurs in bars 55—59. On those who understand it aright it has a peculiarly thrilling effect, when in the midst of strange phrases and passages the well-known tune of the chorale unexpectedly falls upon the ear; it is like the sun breaking through clouds, and flooding the world with light, to give assurance that although the glory was obscured for a while its life-giving influence was yet present. In two instances fragments of this kind are not merely introduced in passing, but as determining the meaning and character of a whole number. In the cantata "Herr Jesu Christ, wahr' Mensch und Gott," there is a bass solo entitled by Bach "Recitativ und Arie." The "Arie" is to be conceived of as beginning at bar 13. The name was probably chosen because of the more concise character of the text, and because a musical phrase from the beginning recurs at the end, though in part, indeed, in another key. In the text, which is in this instance really poetical, the sixth and seventh verses are paraphrased, the first, third, and fourth lines being taken bodily from the sixth verse. The sections of the melody are treated analogously ; for the fourth line the melody appears in florid extension (33—37), for the first and third in a simple form, but frequently repeated and imitated on the instrumental bass. This becomes the leading idea in the whole " Arie," and it is used alternately with phrases of a more animated kind in 6-8 time and freely invented. There is also an " Arie " for bass in the cantata " Nimm von uns Herr, du treuer Gott," set to the fourth verse " Warum willst du so zornig sein " ("Wherefore so wrathful still, O Lord ? "). A prelude of an agitated character seems to betoken anger. Then the bass gives out, *Andante*, the opening line with its proper melody. At the third bar, however, the more animated instrumental movement breaks in, carrying the voice. part onward with it in its course. It is again interrupted by the measured movement of the chorale melody, and it then changes into the relative major. As it must, however, in accordance with the aria form, return to the original key, the instruments take up the chorale melody. The first line is not enough ; the tune in its entirety soars above the agitation of the voices and of the bass part, as though it had been roused by the vocal opening at the beginning, and had waited the opportunity to assert itself as the chief constituent part of the movement. A form which is of frequent occurrence in these cantatas— viz., the combination of the chorale melody on the instruments with vocal recitative on freely invented words, is here united with the aria, with Bach's inexhaustible power, in order to form an entirely new musical entity.

Thus the hearer perceives in the madrigal paraphrases numerous musical allusions to the source of all these apparently free productions. Still, Bach was not in such subjection to this rule as that whenever the poet inserted a verbal allusion to a well-known hymn he should always second it by the use of the proper tune. In the cantatas "Allein zu dir, Herr Jesu Christ," "Herr Gott dich loben alle wir," "Ich freue mich in dir," "Jesu, der du meine Seele," "Mache dich, mein Geist, bereit," and "Wo Gott der Herr nicht bei uns hält," many verbal reminiscences occur which are allowed to pass without their associated melodies being introduced. Just as these transformed poems themselves were an intermediate and transitional form, so Bach remained at liberty to be guided by his judgment either to the purely musical or to the devotional view of the work.

The two chief pillars of the chorale cantata—viz., the first and the last verses—have so far the same general form that the latter always appears in a simple setting, while the former is always worked up into a composition of considerable length. I have before pointed out what must have been the origin of this arrangement, by which the more ornate musical factor is placed first and the simplest last;[139] it bears the plainest testimony to the religious spirit which pervaded Bach's imagination. The circum-stance that the instruments follow the course of the vocal parts simply and without adornment shows also how the whole fulness of the individual life flows at the end piously and humbly back to the source from whence it rose. It is significant, too, that the upper part in which the melody occurs is often strengthened by as many instruments as possible, giving it undue prominence from the purely musical point of view ; a sense of its high symbolic meaning has led the composer to emphasize it strongly. The cases in which any of the instruments have an independent part in the accompaniment of the closing chorale are quite exceptional. In the cantatas "Gelobet seist du, Jesu Christ," "Herr Gott dich loben alle wir," and "Wie schön leuchtet der Morgenstern" the passages on the horns and trumpets serve only to give colouring to the orchestration,[140]

---

[139] See Vol. I., p. 500.

[140] The ascending trumpet passage in the cantata "Herr Gott dich loben alle wir" may possibly be intended to convey the same poetic meaning which

the short and fanfare-like ritornels in "Jesu nun sei gepreiset" refer back to the opening chorus and have no independent importance.

With regard to the great chorale choruses at the beginning of the cantatas, a general survey shows clearly that Bach considered that he had found once for all the musical form best adapted to this purpose. The proclivity to new varieties of form, which is so evident elsewhere, here has nearly disappeared. By far the greater number of these choruses are chorale fantasias. The motett style is only met with in the cantatas "Ach Gott vom Himmel sieh darein," "Aus tiefer Noth schrei ich zu dir," and "Christum wir sollen loben schön." These grandiose movements show to what a height the motett form could rise when transplanted into the new and fertile soil of the Bach cantata.[141] The so-called Pachelbel chorale form is found in its purity only in the cantata "Ach Herr, mich armen Sünder," and there as a matter of course, at this period of Bach's development, with simple counterpoint. He solved the difficulty of keeping to the same motive, and at the same time preluding before each separate line, by working in the contrapuntal motive and the phrase that is to serve as prelude together. The great organ chorale "Jesus Christus unser Heiland" offers a beautiful example of this.[142] Here he rendered the task still more difficult by using the first line in diminution for the counterpoint throughout, in direct and inverse motion. But his prolific fancy was not satisfied; for besides this he introduces the fragments of the melody which are to serve as preludes to each line in constantly different and distant keys.

---

is clearly brought out in the aria which precedes it and in a similarly treated closing chorale in " Es erhub sich ein Streit."

[141] See Vol. II., p. 598, f.—To the list of chorale choruses in motett form should be added the splendid movement published in B.-G., XXIV., No. 118, "O Jesu Christ meins Lebens Licht," which, however, exhibits a more independent treatment of the wind instruments in the accompaniment. It was probably performed in the open air at a funeral ceremony, and afterwards adapted for indoor performance. Its date is about 1737. See Vol. II., App. A., No. 57.

[142] See Vol. I., pp. 607 and 613.

This method of adorning the Pachelbel chorale form with one and the same subject used as counterpoint, makes it a transitional form towards the chorale fantasia.[143] Accordingly we shall not be surprised, in the cantatas "Nun komm der Heiden Heiland," "Wohl dem, der sich auf seinen Gott," and "Wie schön leuchtet der Morgenstern," to meet with forms that are half one thing and half another. In the first case only the opening line, which is identical with the last line, is introduced by a prelude; in the second, an almost independent movement is developed from the first line, only showing its relationship to the Pachelbel form by the fact that before the fifth line a reference is made to the first line; in the last case the relationship is shown by the union of the melody with the pervading motive in the prelude to the *Cantus firmus* of the second and fifth lines.[144] Another hybrid form occurs in "Jesu nun sei gepreiset"; the opening chorus is at the beginning and at the end a chorale fantasia, but in the middle it is partly in frée fantasia form, and partly in that of the motett.

Several longer choruses reveal their origin in the fully-developed Pachelbel form only by the fact that the music by which the *Cantus firmus* is surrounded and upborne takes its subject from the first line of the chorale. In all other respects they belong to the class of free chorale fantasia. In the cantata "Erhalt uns Herr," only the first three notes are thus used as a theme, while in "Was frag ich nach der Welt" and "Wo soll ich fliehen hin," the whole line is employed. This method is employed also in the cantata "Herr Jesu Christ, wahr' Mensch und Gott." Here, however, the ear is attracted by another combination of great subtlety. The cantata is written for Quinquagesima Sunday, which immediately precedes the church

---

[143] See Vol. I., p. 609.

[144] This motive is also connected with the first line of the melody by its two first notes being identical. It is moreover remarkable that the very same motive is also employed in the chief chorus of "Ach Gott, wie manches Herzeleid." I believe the cantata "Wie schön leuchtet der Morgenstern" to have been written immediately after this, so that Bach still had the motive in his head.

season commemorating the Passion. For this reason, while choir and instruments perform the chief subject, the chorale "Christe, du Lamm Gottes" is introduced in a fragmentary way, so that the idea of the Passion dawns on the hearer. This reminds us somewhat of the tenor recitative in the cantata, also for Quinquagesima Sunday, "Du wahrer Gott und Davidssohn."[145] Bach's careful attention to minor details, even in the firmly-fixed form of chorale-fantasia, is no less clearly illustrated in the cantata "Liebster Immanuel." The hymn—written, probably, by Ahasverus Fritsch—and the melody belong to the second half of the seventeenth century. Notwithstanding its beautiful feeling and expressiveness, it has an almost secular and playful character, and the melody is in the form of a sarabande.[146] Bach does not disregard this character, and, accordingly, the music which takes its subject from the first line of the melody is conceived rather in a melodious and homophonic than in an imitative and polyphonic style.

The opening choruses of all the other chorale cantatas are free chorale fantasias. In the course of its transference from the sphere of organ music to that of concerted church music, the style underwent only those changes which were demanded by the alteration in the tone material. The independent musical creation which was to bring out all the sentiment of the chorale was no longer worked out by means of organ-stops, but by Bach's orchestra on the background of the organ. The *Cantus firmus*, which, when played, ran the risk of being drowned by the important part taken by the rest of the instruments, fills, when sung, a higher and more dominating position. The vocal parts of the chorus fill an intermediate place, connecting the chorale and the instrumental portion. Sometimes they support the voice that has the melody (generally the soprano) in simple harmonies, but more often they appear as a factor in the instrumental portion of the work; and it is obvious

---

[145] See Vol. II., pp. 350—353.

[146] This was remarked upon with displeasure, even in Bach's time. See Witt, Neues *Cantional* mit dem *General-Bass*. Gotha and Leipzig (1715). Preface.

that that portion must hold its place in the work as a whole, not merely by richer musical treatment, but by a picturesque use of the means at hand. As a model of an organ chorale treated in this poetic way, the arrangement of the melody " Ach wie flüchtig, ach wie nichtig," from the " Orgelbüchlein," which numbers only ten bars, has been already mentioned."[147]   It may be compared with the first movement (sixty-five bars long) of the cantata on the same chorale. The mode of construction is the same in both, as is also the fundamental form, although, by degrees, the longer work rises to a height which renders it scarcely possible to recognise their common origin. In outline these choruses have almost a stereotyped form. The composer is revealed in them rather as having attained a high plain and walking serenely over it than as striving upwards—the marks of progress are to be seen in the details.

Still, the impulse towards the development of new forms was not yet exhausted. The splendid opening of the cantata " Jesu, der du meine Seele," which is built on the same theme as the *Crucifixus* of the B minor mass, exhibits a chorale-fantasia in the form of a chaconne. In the cantata " Meinen Jesum lass ich nicht," the chorale-fantasia form is combined with that of the instrumental concerto. This last plan is evident, too, in the cantatas " Herr Jesu Christ, du höchstes Gut " and " Was mein Gott will, das g'scheh allzeit," although, in accordance with Bach's refining method, no solo instrument is here opposed to the *tutti*. On the other hand, the cantata " Christ unser Herr zum Jordan kam " has the regular concerto form ; nay, more, it is a *concerto grosso,* the *concertino* consisting of a solo violin and two *oboi d'amore*, while the *tutti* is formed by the violins, tenors, and bass, with the organ. Meanwhile, the chorale chorus, with the *cantus firmus* in the tenor part, keeps on its way, never heeding this mass of sound ; and yet these two elements are homogeneous. It must, however, be admitted, that in this case the forms

---

147 See Vol. I., p. 602.

are intertwined in a rather perplexing way. It is not enough to analyse how this or that element originated and grew, absorbing others in its development, or how some other has met it half-way till a grand unity is the result. A work of art must be estimated as a whole, and followed with lively sympathy. Every form contains, as its soul, a certain general emotion; and this must be understood before the form itself can be properly appreciated. Unless, by the study of the concertos of that time, we make ourselves familiar with the realm of feeling in which these works have their organic being, we can never understand Bach's intention in these combinations. They will appear strange, and even absurd. The characteristic and vigorous spirit of the first movement of a concerto, as understood at that time, appeared to Bach suitable for giving a particular colouring to the chorale-fantasias in these works. But even a perfect comprehension of this will not bring us to the root of the matter. The chorale fantasia, as it appears in the chorale cantatas, is derived from a higher and by no means a simple artistic idea.

If we examine the nature of the chorale cantata, we find it to be nothing less than the perfect poetic and musical development of some particular hymn by means of all the artistic material which Bach had assimilated by a thorough study of the art of his own and former times. The course of his formation shows that he took organ-music, and especially the organ chorale, as his starting point, and that he mastered and appropriated the various forms of art by welding them into the style of the organ—the only sacred style of the time. This was the case both with the instrumental and the vocal forms of musical art; for, closely as the latter forms were connected with the chorale, they remained latent in Bach's organ music. The poetic element, which is essential to the organ chorale, naturally forced its way into the sphere of vocal music as the form was developed. That form aims at expressing the sentiment and feeling of a hymn, as that sentiment appeals to individuals in the congregation; this is attempted with ever-increasing materials of sound, and in ever

larger proportions.   The voice is found necessary for the
melody, in order to keep the overflowing current of individual
emotion within the bounds of sacred feeling.   Thus we have
a vocal and instrumental composition which, however,
exhausts only one verse of the chorale ; the instrumental
portion is based on the chorale as a whole.   One last and
crowning step remained: to change the essentially musical
idea of combination and concord for that of a succession of
parts, according to the sequence of thought suggested
by the poetry, which now took an active share in the
whole; and to subject the chorale, which had been paraphrased, so to speak, as a whole in the purely instrumental
composition, to a detailed treatment of its separate verses.
Thus the chorale fantasia at the beginning became once
more merely a part of the whole ; only, as it were, a single
petal, the perfect flower being the chorale cantata.

Still, the chorale fantasia determines the style of the whole
cantata.   In such a work as the Easter music, " Christ lag
in Todesbanden," which retains the chorale melody for all
the verses—its model in instrumental music being the
chorale " Christ ist erstanden," in the " Orgelbüchlein "—
the highest stage of development is not yet attained.   The
strong individual character, peculiar alike to Protestantism
and to Bach's style, demanded a wider space in order to
attain its full expansion.   This it obtained in the chorale
cantata.   In the recitatives and arias it appears to have
perfect liberty; even the limits assigned to it by the sequence
of thought and expression in the words of the hymn are
enlarged by the transformation into the madrigal form,
and at times seem to vanish altogether.   Often all that
remains is the general emotional character left by the
remembrance of the hymn.   Then, it may be, the feeling
of connection is again aroused by the introduction of a line
of the hymn word for word ; now a fragment of the melody
appears, and now the whole, on some instrument or, perhaps,
in the voice part, although surrounded and intertwined with
recitatives ; and the limits to the emotional character are
once more emphasised.   If now the hearer, having thoroughly
taken in the great chorale chorus which preceded these freer

middle portions of the cantata, is brought up to the same chorale as the end and aim of the work—and the more unadorned its form the more impressive will be its effect— he will feel that not a moment has passed during which he has not been hearing the chorale, either in its material form or in its inner spirit. In the chorale cantata as a whole— as in the chorale fantasia—the parts are treated in the most independent way possible, so that they seem to build up a fabric on their own account, and yet at the right moment they are referred again to their origin by means of the *cantus firmus*.

In the chorale cantata we meet with the last and highest possible development of the organ chorale. That little piece of ten bars on the melody " Ach wie flüchtig, ach wie nichtig " was the germ of which the cantata with that title, with its great chorale fantasia, its simple closing chorale, its recitatives, and its elaborate arias, is the ultimate fruit. The chorale cantata can only be properly understood by one who has made himself perfectly familiar with the nature of the organ chorale ; and both demand that the hymn and its melody should form part of the vital *experience* of the hearer. While, however, in the former case it is only needful to feel the delicate aroma of the general feeling of the hymn, and the recognition of special feelings and details is a secondary requisite, an exact knowledge of the import of each separate verse is indispensable for the cantata. Without this even the words and general arrangement of the "madrigal" text cannot always be understood. We do not see that the consuming flames and foaming billows referred to in the bass aria of the cantata "Ach wie flüchtig " are not to be understood metaphorically, but actually of perils by fire and water, until we compare it with the tenth verse of the hymn. The words in the bass aria of the cantata "Ich hab in Gottes Herz und Sinn," which run thus : "The roaring of the mighty wind leads to the ripening of the grain," point out that the fruits of the field are not brought to perfection without storms and tempests ; this is not made clear unless we know the ninth verse of the hymn. And, which is of greater importance, the character of the music is often suggested by images or ideas not expressed in the inserted words, but only in the original text.   How did Bach come to give that tender idyllic character to the duet in the cantata "Jesu, der du meine Seele," which consists of a prayer for help in sickness and weakness?   The second verse of the hymn runs thus :—

Treulich hast du ja gesuchet	Faithfully Thou, Lord, hast sought
Die verlornen Schäfelein,	All Thy lost and trembling sheep,
Als sie liefen ganz verfluchet	As they ran with fear distraught
In den Höllenpfuhl hinein.	Headlong into Hell so deep.

We have frequently noticed Bach's way of giving force and point to a tedious or digressive cantata text by seizing upon the emotional character of the Sunday or festival. This example shows how, in the chorale cantatas, he composed the music, not so much with regard to the madrigal version or paraphrase as to the original text. All these works are founded on the assumption that the hearer will have constantly before his mind the hymn in its original form.   The church-goer of those days could compare the printed text of the cantata with the version in his hymn book; or he could even dispense with this material aid, since those hymns were in every heart as a possession common to all.   He had sung them times without number in church, had taken them as his guide in daily life, and had drawn consolation and edification from isolated verses under various experiences.   This was the audience to which Bach addressed himself, and such an audience do these compositions still require, for to such alone will they reveal all their meaning and fulness, both in outline and detail.

As we glance backwards from this point over Bach's life, we are struck by the completeness and rounding-off of his artistic development.   His starting-point in early youth was the sacred song of the people, and to it he returns at the end of his career.   He felt that all he could create in the sphere of Church music must have an inherent connection with the chorale and the forms of art conditional to it.   He must have deemed it the noblest goal of his ambition to give his genius that direction which should create a form that displays the chorale in its highest possible stage of artistic development. The chorale cantatas lack, it may be, that profuse variety of form which during the earlier and middle periods of his life calls forth our highest wonder. But the serene mastery over the technical materials of his art, the deep mature earnestness which pervades them, can only be regarded as the fruit of such a superabundant art-life. In considering these works in their unalterable and characteristic grandeur, we seem to be wandering through some still, lofty, Alpine forest in the peaceful evening that closes a brilliant summer day.

IV.

THE CHORALE COLLECTIONS.—THE ECCLESIASTICAL MODES, AND BACH'S RELATIONS TOWARDS THEM.

BACH, while in Leipzig, had made a collection of chorale melodies with figured basses. It comprises all the melodies in ordinary use there, in number about two hundred and forty. In the year 1764 the manuscript was in the possession of the musicseller, Bernhard Christoph Breitkopf, of Leipzig, who offered copies of it for sale at ten thalers each.[148] This important collection is lost.[149] A few fragments of it, however, seems to have been saved. Pupils of Bach who took down copies of his organ chorales appended to them the two-part figured settings from Bach's chorale book, when they could get access to them. Thus, when they played the organ chorale as a prelude, they could afterwards use the melody, as harmonised by their revered master, for accompanying the congregational singing. In this way the figured setting of the melodies " Christ lag in Todesbanden," " Herr Christ der einge Gottssohn," " Jesu meine Freude,"

---

[148] " Bachs, J. S. Vollständiges Choralbuch mit in Noten aufgesetzten Generalbasse an 240 in Leipzig gewöhnlichen Melodien. 10 thl." Breitkopf's catalogue for New Year, 1764, p. 29.

[149] Herr W. Kraukling, of Dresden, possesses a chorale book with figured bass, in small quarto; on the pig-skin cover stand the words : " Sebastian Bachs Choral-Buch." The volume, however, exhibits neither Bach's writing nor, in the writing to the chorales, a single trace of Bach's style or spirit.

"Wer nur den lieben Gott lässt walten," have come down to us.[150] Johann Ludwig Krebs has also handed down to us Bach's figured setting of four Christmas hymns—viz., "Gelobet seist du, Jesu Christ," "*In dulci jubilo*," "Lobt Gott, ihr Christen allzugleich," and "Vom Himmel hoch." The interludes introduced in them show that they were written for the very purpose of accompanying the congregation. The harmonising, which is of rare originality and power, makes us feel how much we have to regret in the loss of the whole chorale book.[151]

A third source, which may possibly contain some fragments of the chorale book, is a collection printed and published in Bach's lifetime. In May, 1735, a student from Zeitz, Christian Friedrich Schemelli, entered the Leipzig University.[152] His father, George Christian Schemelli, "Schloss-Cantor" at Zeitz, occupied himself with the editing of a hymn book with tunes, on the model of Freylinghausen's popular and widely known "Geistreiches Gesangbuch"; but it was to be free from pietistic colouring and sectarian spirit, bringing together whatever was good from any quarter, and containing also the recognised treasures from among the old hymns. At that time Bach was still intimately connected with the students through the medium of the Musical Society. The fact that Bach's name appears as the arranger of the musical portion of the work, which was published in 1736, was probably due to the persuasion of Schemelli's son.[153] Hitherto, so far as we know, Bach had not done any work of this kind. If, however, the

---

[150] These will be found in P. S. V., C. 5 (244), No. 53; in the same volume in the Appendix to No. 7; also in C. 6 (245), No. 16; and same volume, No. 29. What is known as to their origin is given in the preface.

[151] These Christmas chorales are in an organ book by Krebs in the possession of Herr F. A. Roitzsch, of Leipzig (p. 241 f.). Probably the setting of "Jesu der du meine Seele" on p. 253 is also by Bach. The chorale "Gelobet seist du" is given in the Musical Appendix to this volume (4, A.). A comparison of this with the one spoken of in Vol. I., p. 594, will show that it has the same harmonies, and that the interludes are identical.

[152] See the books of the University.

[153] Schemelli, the father, b. 1676, was sixty years old when the book appeared; Schemelli, the son, b. 1712, succeeded him, when he was superannuated, in his office (Archives of the Schlosskirche at Zeitz).

book was to have a success equal to that of Freyling-hausen's, a well-known name was indispensable. The preface therefore duly announced that "the melodies to be found in this musical hymn book are in part newly composed, and in part improved by the addition of figured bass, by Herr Johann Sebastian Bach, Capellmeister to the Grand Duke of Saxony, and *Directore Chori Musici* in Leipzig." In spite of this the book did not meet with great success. A second enlarged edition, which was advertised to appear after the sale of the first, did not appear, although the first edition was only a small one.[154]

It is doubtful whether Bach cared much what became of the book. It was published in Leipzig by Breitkopf, and the name of the engraver, who, by the way, did his work remarkably well both in the title-vignette and in the melodies, is a Leipzig name. But it bears traces of care-lessness in the copies for the plates, and in the supervision of the work. Otherwise, putting aside engravers' errors, it would never have happened that over every hymn that has a melody appended to it the same number appears twice; that above No. 627 there is an engraved title: "*Di S. Bach, D. M. Lips.*," while many of the other melodies—as, for example, 397 and others—were composed by Bach; and that in the case of the hymn " Jesu, meines Glaubens Zier," not only are the two numbers, one engraved and the other printed, set over it, and the melody is in its right place before the hymn, but it is notified again: " N.B.—This melody belongs to No. 119." It is also evident that many hands took part in the preparation of the copies for engraving. Thus it seems very probable that Bach had the greater part of the melodies simply written out from his chorale book. The number of the

---

[154] " Musicalisches | Gesang-Buch, | Darinnen | 954 geistreiche, sowohl alte als neue | Lieder und Arien, mit wohlgesetzten | Melodien, in Discant und Bass | befindlich sind | Vornemlich denen Evangelischen Gemeinen | im Stifte Naumburg-Zeitz gewidmet, | . . . . von | George Christian Schemelli, | Schloss-Cantore daselbst. | . . . Leipzig, 1736. | Verlegts Bernhard Christoph Breit-kopf, Buchdr." | Copies of the work, which has now become scarce, are in Count Stolberg's Library at Wernigerode and in the Royal Library at Berlin.

melodies is sixty-nine. Among these are forty melodies by various composers, dating from the sixteenth, seventeenth, and eighteenth centuries. In the preface we are informed that about two hundred more melodies were ready to be engraved, and that they would be given in a second edition if that were called for. This makes altogether two hundred and forty melodies, exactly the number contained in Bach's chorale book.

In those chorales which still remain to us we have a valuable possession. These melodies, with their slight but animated figured basses, reveal to us, as in a sketch, the art which the master carried out in the elaborate four-part chorale movements. To their publication, also, we are indebted for our knowledge of a series of short original compositions set to hymns which should have a still higher value for us. Since Bach himself wrote a part of the tunes contained in Schemelli's Hymn book, and since a thorough examination of the melodies in use up to that time in the evangelical church shows that forty out of the sixty-nine melodies are by other composers, we have a perfect right to assign the remaining twenty-nine to Bach. We know by documentary evidence that two are by him (" Dir, dir Jehovah will ich singen " and " Vergiss mein nicht, vergiss mein nicht, mein allerliebster Gott "). But the others, at least the majority of them, bear upon them the unmistakable impress of Bach's style.[155] In the case of seven out of the twenty-nine, we have ground for assuming that they were written expressly for Schemelli's Hymn book.[156]   Bach can hardly have intended them as

---

[155] It is to Winterfeld (Ev. Kirchenges III., p. 270 ff.) that we are lastingly indebted for the first thorough investigation of this subject, although he was partly led to wrong results. Since, as I have endeavoured to prove (see Vol. I., p. 369), Bach's having taken any share in Freylinghausen's Hymn book is out of the question, the number of the compositions in Schemelli's Hymn book which may be ascribed to him is considerably diminished. All the melodies contained in that hymn book have been brought out by Breitkopf and Härtel, edited by C. F. Becker. According to this edition the tunes by Bach are Nos. 4, 7, 8, 10, 11, 14, 19. 21, 24, 26, 30, 31, 32, 42, 44, 46, 47, 51, 52, 53, 56, 57, 59, 62, 63, 64, 66, 67, and 68.

[156] Nos. 31, 32, 47, 59, 64, 67, and 68. In preparing the plates for engraving, two different copyists were employed. The above Nos., together with

melodies suitable for public worship. Schemelli's collection, like that of Freylinghausen and others, was intended particularly for domestic devotion, and for this purpose, towards which Bach showed a leaning even in many of his greater sacred compositions, these works written for Schemelli were also intended. After devoting his whole life to the work of chorale arrangement, with an energy which fathomed every hidden quality of the chorale, he must have known what was wanted for a popular hymn for public worship; and he must also have known that his own manner of expressing himself, animated, melodious, and refined by the highest art, lent itself readily to the most subjective expression, but ran counter to the character of congregational use. We must not apply the standard of the church chorale to these melodies of Bach's. They are sacred arias, and the fact of their not having passed into church use—not more than five of them have even been included in any of the later chorale collections—in no way derogates from their value.[157] Their charm, which is all their own, is like that of a pious family circle, musically cultured, and we may delight to fancy that these touching hymns, so delicately worked out in their small limits, were sung, at the master's household devotions, by one or other of the members of his family.

The music-book of Anna Magdalena Bach, made in 1725, which was intended purely for domestic use, actually contains, on p. 115 ff, one of the hymns, Crasselius's "Dir, dir Jehovah will ich singen," and Bach's name is expressly

---

40, 194, and 281, are in the same handwriting. They differ from the rest in the form of the clef and in the use of the brace. The soprano clef exhibits pretty clearly the form most usually employed by Bach at that time. Besides this we may notice a larger and more hasty style of writing the notes, although it is much equalised in the engraving. It is probable that Bach himself wrote out the tunes which he composed specially for Schemelli's Hymn book.

[157] Winterfeld (loc. cit., p. 278 f.) says that in J. B. König's "Harmonische Liederschatz" (Frankfort a. M. 1738), only Nos. 4 and 63 are given without alteration, while to the hymns Nos. 24, 56, and 57 are found mere popular tunes. Here, however, he is mistaken. No. 8 is also found in König unchanged; No. 57 is found in an altered form; and No. 24 with a newly written first part to the tune (p. 490 in König); No. 56 has quite a different tune.

given as the composer.   There are besides several other
pieces of the same kind in it.   A composition, also entered
in Bach's name, to Gerhardt's " Gieb dich zufrieden und
sei stille," surpasses all the others by its lofty and individual
beauty.   Another melody to the same hymn leaves us in
doubt as to its composer ; it is strikingly simple for a
composition of Bach's ; but at all events it is new.[158]
A melody to the hymn " Wie wohl ist mir, o Freund der
Seelen" has a similar character.   Though we must hesitate
to assign these two to Bach without further evidence, the
hymn "Schaffs mit mir Gott nach deinem Willen" shows
plainer tokens, and the compositions "Warum betrübst du
dich und beugest dich zur Erden" and "Gedenke doch, mein
Geist zurücke" show unmistakable marks of his style.[159]
It seems probable that Bach wrote several hymn-tunes
expressly for Schemelli's book ; his pupil Krebs, who was
very intimate with him just about this time, being his
deputy in the Musical Society and also in the Church,[160] has
handed down to us five such hymns, which there is ground
for regarding as Bach's compositions.[161]

After Schemelli's hymn-book had gone forth to the world
to meet with so poor a reception, Bach continued his
work upon it for his own pleasure in a remarkable way.
He added to his copy no fewer than eighty-eight chorales,
written fully out.   At his death the volume came into the
hands of Philipp Emanuel Bach, but has since been lost.[162]
Doubtless, among these, Bach had set many, if not all,
of his own melodies, in four parts.   Of these we are sure
of four—" Dir, dir Jehovah," " Jesu, Jesu, du bist mein,"

---

[158] König gives it at p. 340 of his " Harmonische Liederschatz."

[159] Comp. Vol. II., p. 148 f.   The hymn " Gedenke doch, mein Geist " is
published in Bitter (Vol. I., Musical Supplement).

[160] See p. 7 of this volume.   In the Musical Society he accompanied on
the harpsichord ; see Gerber, Lex. col. 756.

[161] These five hymns with the melodies alone, as well as the hymn "Warum
betrübst du dich" are given in the Musical Appendix to this volume (4, B.).
Further remarks as to their genuineness will be found at App. A., No. 4.

[162] In the printed catalogue of Emanuel Bach's effects (Hamburg, 1790), on
p. 73, it is mentioned among the compositions by Sebastian Bach : " The
Naumburg Hymn-book, containing printed chorales, and also eighty-eight
chorales written out in parts."

" Meines Lebens letzte Zeit," and " So giebst du nun, mein Jesu gute Nacht." [163]

Besides those written for Schemelli, Bach left several other original melodies to hymns, set in four parts, and among them, fortunately, is the splendid one " Gieb dich zufrieden." What was said above of the character of the tunes in one part with a figured bass holds good of these, which we only know in their four-part form, so far as we are justified in assuming them to be of Bach's composition. They are not so much chorales as devotional songs for household use, and as such are, for the most part, full of character and beauty. The fact that two original melodies such as these are introduced in their entirety in the fourth part of the Christmas Oratorio was before adduced as bearing significantly on the character of that work.[164] A similar chorale opens the cantata " Also hat Gott die Welt geliebt,"[165] and another is found at the end of the motett " Komm, Jesu, komm."[166] Among the nine four-part compositions which, besides these, we are more or less justified in attributing to Bach, are found some which approach more nearly to the chorale character. Two of these (" Da der Herr Christ zu Tische sass " and " Herr Jesu Christ, du hast bereit ") were included by Johann Balthasar Reimann in his Hirschberg Chorale Book in 1747.[167] Reimann was with Bach in Leipzig from 1729 to 1740, and, as he himself tells us, was "affectionately received by him and charmed with him."[168] The melody with which Bach prefaces the cantata " Ach ich sehe," written in Weimar, has the character of a chorale. It is,

---

[163] The first is in Anna Magdalena Bach's book, the others in Philipp Emanuel Bach's editions of his father's four-part chorales. (Leipzig, Breitkopf, 1784-1787). In " So giebst du nun, mein Jesu " (No. 206 there), a whole bar is omitted after bar 7.

[164] See Vol. II., p. 586. One of them is set as a chorus, and forms the closing movement of the part, and the other appears with a four-part instrumental accompaniment and with counterpoint in a recitative bass part.

[165] See Vol. II., p. 695.

[166] See Vol. II., p. 605.

[167] As has been remarked by L. Erk, Choralgesänge II., No. 178 and 222.

[168] Mattheson, Ehrenpforte, p. 292.

however, nothing more than a compound produced by the fusion of the melodies " Herr ich habe missgehandelt " and " Jesu, der du meine Seele." [169]

On the whole, Bach can hardly have cared to exhibit his greatness as a church composer in this particular branch of work. When we consider the grand tasks it was his fate to fulfil, his hymn tunes can only be regarded as subsidiary work.

We have evidence that Bach's style of harmonising a chorale melody in four parts had, even in early times, excited the admiration of a large circle. After his death the melodies so treated by him were collected, and, at the New Year of 1764, Breitkopf, of Leipzig, was in possession of a manuscript containing one hundred and fifty chorales in score, copies of which were sold by him. [170] This was, probably, the collection of which Birnstiel, of Berlin, undertook to publish a printed edition in 1765. At the last moment he very wisely thought of getting Emanuel Bach to revise the manuscript. He did this so far that the collection, containing one hundred chorales, received correction from his hand ;

---

[169] See Vol. I., p. 554. I am now thoroughly convinced of Bach being the author of this melody, which occurs nowhere else. Erk (see Choralgesänge II., No. 159) holds it to be merely another version of " Jesu, der du meine Seele." But, to my mind, it betrays an unmistakable connection with " Herr, ich habe missgehandelt " (see Choralgesänge, 1784, No. 35). The remaining hymn-tunes, in four parts, which may be attributed to Bach are " Nicht so traurig, nicht so sehr " (C minor), " Ich bin ja Herr in deiner Macht," " Was betrübst du dich, mein Herze," " Für Freuden lasst uns springen," " Gottlob es geht nunmehr zu Ende," and " O Herzensangst, o Bangigkeit." Winterfeld (op. cit., p. 282 ff) thinks that there are still a number of other hymns which may be assigned to Bach. With regard to the hymns " Ist Gott mein Schild," " Schwing dich auf zu deinem Gott," " O Mensch, schau Jesum Christum an," and " Auf, auf mein Herz und du mein ganzer Sinn," the incorrectness of the assumption that they are by Bach is demonstrated by Erk in his admirable edition of Bach's chorale melodies. In the case of the hymns " Meinen Jesum lass ich nicht," " Das walt Gott Vater und Gott Sohn," and " Herr nun lass in Friede," Winterfeld himself has half recanted his opinion. But the hymns " Dank sei Gott in der Höhe," " O Jesu du mein Bräutigam," and " Alles ist an Gottes Segen," appear in König in forms which show plainly that the reading of both Bach and König are nothing but variations of older original forms.

[170] Breitkopf's Catalogue, New Year, 1764, p. 7 : " Bach, J. S. Capellmeister and Musikdirector in Leipzig, 150 chorales, in 4 parts. 6 Thlr."

but he had nothing to do with the second collection, which appeared in 1769. Not long before his death he arranged a second, a better and more complete, edition, which was published by Breitkopf. It is in four divisions, and contains three hundred and seventy chorales.

These chorales were taken for the most part from Sebastian Bach's concerted church compositions, so that they were intended for voices with instrumental accompaniment. For the convenience of the organ or clavier player, the editor arranged them on two staves. The announcement that the collection was to constitute a complete chorale book was only made in order to increase the number of purchasers. Under the existing circumstances it could not be a chorale book, comprising all the melodies in ordinary use in any particular town or neighbourhood; and if it had been, the various arrangements of one and the same melody would be purposeless. The real purpose of the book was to delight those who knew and loved the art of music, and to provide models for the study of the rising generation of composers. The last object may have been the cause of the son's treading so much as he did in his father's steps; for the chorale played an important part, not only in his own compositions, but also in his course of instruction in composition.

Johann Philipp Kirnberger says with regard to Bach's method of teaching composition, that it led up step by step from the easiest subjects to the most difficult; that among all those known to him it was by far the best; that he always referred back to fundamental principles, and sought to lay bare all the secrets of the world of music.[171] From this it follows that we may regard the scheme of study in Kirnberger's theoretical writings as having been invented and approved by Bach himself, if not the foundation of the method and special points of teaching. Kirnberger's chief work, "Die Kunst des reinen Satzes in der Musik,"[172] stands high as an instruction book for composition. It treats in

---

[171] Kirnberger, Gedanken über die verschiedenen Lehrarten in der Komposition. Berlin, 1782, p. 4 f.

[172] Part I., 1774; Part II. (up to third section), not before 1776—1779.

succession of the scales, the temperament, of intervals, of chords, with their combinations, and of modulations; also of the formation of melodies, and of simple and double counterpoint. The greater part of the work deals with counterpoint; Kirnberger intended to append to this an additional section of instruction in vocal composition, and the character of the dance-forms, and then to conclude with instruction in fugue. His plan, however, was not fully executed. The title ("The Art of pure composition") does not exactly correspond to the contents of the work, which is chiefly intended to cultivate the composer's taste as well as his technical knowledge, by giving especial prominence to the works of Bach. Though in matters of detail it leaves much to be desired as an instruction book, it acquires a special importance as a reflex of Bach's practical teaching, even in its scientific defects, since from these we may infer what the life, variety, and wealth of Bach's personal influence must have been. As a necessary introduction to his school of composition, Kirnberger subsequently published a book of instruction in thorough-bass.[173]

From his twenty-second year, through a space of forty-three years, Bach had had a very large number of pupils in composition. Putting aside the fact that a method of instruction takes a considerable time to form, it is not to be supposed that his teaching was always exactly the same even in his mature life. Friedrich Wilhelm Marpurg, when engaged in a controversy with Kirnberger on some questions concerning the theory of music, seeing that his adversary always quoted Bach, said: "Good God! Why should old Bach be dragged into a discussion in which he would have taken no part if he had been alive? No one will ever be persuaded that he would have expounded the principles of harmony according to the views of Herr Kirnberger. I believe that this great man had more than one method of instruction, and that he always adapted his style to the capacity of each pupil, according as he was more or less gifted by nature, or as he turned out to

---

[173] Grundsätze des Generalbasses als erste Linien zur Composition. 1781.

be pliable or stupid, clever or a mere blockhead. But
I am perfectly well assured that if there still exist any
introductions to harmony in manuscript by this master,
they will nowhere be found to contain certain things which
Herr Kirnberger wants to palm off upon us as Bach's way
of teaching. His celebrated son in Hamburg ought to
know something about it."[174] There is no doubt some truth
in this. And yet Kirnberger was sufficiently intimate with
the elder sons and other pupils of Bach to escape suspicion
of his having built up his system solely on the basis of
what he himself had learnt from Bach. The appeal to
Emanuel Bach turned out ill for Marpurg; for he distinctly
took Kirnberger's side, with the most decisive disapproval
of the polemic tone adopted by Marpurg, and he authorised
Kirnberger to say that Sebastian Bach had in no way shared
Marpurg's opinions of Rameau.[175] And as regards Bach's
writings on the art of composition, they only serve to prove
that the method ascribed to Bach by Kirnberger was really
that of the master.

The short rules of thorough-bass which Bach noted down
for his wife, Anna Magdalena, in her later clavier book are
all that has hitherto been known of his method.[176] There
exists, however, a more elaborate work on thorough-bass
by Bach, which Kirnberger seems to have known nothing
about, for he was of opinion that Bach had written
nothing on the theory of music.[177] It was preserved to
posterity by Johann Peter Kellner; its date is 1738, and
its title is as follows: " Des Königlichen Hoff-*Compositeurs*
und Capellmeisters ingleichen *Directoris Musices* wie auch
Cantoris der Thomas-Schule Herrn *Johann Sebastian Bach*
zu *Leipzig* Vorschriften und Grundsätze zum vierstimmigen

---

[174] Marpurg, Versuch über die musikalische Temperatur, nebst einem An-
hang über den Rameau- und Kirnbergerschen Grundbass (Essay on musical
temperament, with an appendix on the thorough-bass of Rameau and
Kirnberger. 1776, p. 239.)

[175] Kirnberger, Kunst des reinen Satzes. II. 3, p. 188 : " You are at perfect
liberty to say that my late father's principles and my own were opposed to
Rameau."

[176] They are given in Appendix B., XIII.

[177] Gedanken über die verschiedenen Lehrarten, p. 4.

Spielen des *General-Bass* oder *Accompagnement,* für seine *Scholaren* in der Musik." (Principles of thorough-bass, and directions for performing it in four-parts in accompanying, for his scholars in music, by Herr J. S. B., royal court composer, capellmeister, director of the music and cantor of the Thomasschule in Leipzig.) The copy, corrected here and there by Kellner, seems to have been made by a person of only moderate musical education, and from the manuscript made by a pupil of Bach's. The first assumption rests upon the numerous and silly blunders of writing, and the second upon frequent inaccuracies in the four-part writing. Details, such as that of the often recurring word *modus* for *motus,* seem to imply that Bach dictated the text of the manuscript. He may have prepared the work for use in class instruction, which would account for the fact that the basses set in four parts contained in the manuscript have not been corrected by him, or at least not throughout, and thus there remain mistakes.[178]

The instruction in thorough-bass is divided into two portions, a " short instruction in Thorough-bass so-called," and a " complete instruction in Thorough-bass"; the first apparently intended for mere beginners, the second for more advanced pupils. Even this little work testifies to the deep and powerful moral earnestness which pervaded all Bach's artistic activity. " The ultimate end and aim of thorough-bass should only be the glory of God and the recreation of the mind. Where these are not kept in view there can be no real music, only an infernal jingling and bellowing." The book is remarkable for clearness, conciseness, and an admirable methodic progress. In these respects it reveals a considerable gift for tuition, and confirms Kirnberger's statement that Bach used to go step by step from the easiest things to the most difficult. It is important to note that Bach calls thorough-bass the beginning of composition, adding that if any one who is willing to learn can take in thorough-bass and imprint it on his memory, he may be

---

[178] The MS., printed in its entirety in Appendix B., No. XII., is now in the possession of Herr Professor Wagener of Marburg, to whom I hereby offer sincere thanks for his kind permission to publish it.

assured that he has already grasped a great part of the whole art.[179] This shows that when Kirnberger insists on beginning his instructions in composition with thorough-bass, calling it " the first lines of composition," it is quite in accordance with Bach's views. The great importance attached by Bach to a knowledge of thorough-bass, not only for the purpose of accompanying, is confirmed by other evidence. In the instruction book now before us the pupil is led up to the accompaniment of short fugal movements. There can scarcely be any doubt that a collection of sixty-two preludes and fugues which remains to us, written through-out on one stave, with figured basses, and bearing the name of Bach as the composer, served as the continuation of his thorough-bass instructions,[180] and that Bach was accustomed to lead his advanced pupils up to the point of making an *ex tempore* accompaniment, even to independent pieces of music, by means of a figured bass and a few other indications.

However, this work of Bach's on figured bass is not altogether original. In chapters 1 to 9 of the section which is entitled " Gründlicher Unterricht des General Basses," Bach has relied largely on Part I. of Friedrich Erhardt Niedt's Musicalische Handleitung, and in parts the original arguments of Niedt are merely abridged and compressed.

In other places, it is true, the development is differently worked out, particularly in chap. 8, where not a trace of Niedt's hand remains ; the examples of musical notation also are some of them new, and some of Niedt's are rendered more instructive and concise. The whole work is so treated and altered that Bach might well regard it as his own. At the same time, it is interesting to know that Bach was familiar with Niedt's instruction book and found material in it of which he could make use for his own purposes.

In a preparatory instruction book for composition such as this is, it seems evident that Bach, like Kirnberger, should in actual teaching have preferred the method which leads straight on, after treating of intervals, to chords, chord-

---

[179] In Cap. 5 (" Of the Harmonic Triad ").
[180] See Vol. II., p. 98, note 138.

combinations, and modulations, and after that too, not to begin with two-part counterpoint, but with simple counterpoint in four parts. Quite in accordance with Bach's opinion is Kirnberger's statement " It is best to begin with four-part counterpoint, because it is impossible to write good two or three-part counterpoint until one is familiar with that in four parts. For as the harmony must necessarily be incomplete, one who is not thoroughly acquainted with four-part writing cannot decide with certainty what should be left out of the harmony in any given case." [181] This rule is based on the principle that all combinations of notes which can be placed in juxtaposition are to be referred to, or connected with, certain fundamental harmonies— the only principle adopted in musical practice even so early as the seventeenth century. Bach's compositions take it for granted. The boldness and freedom of his part writing, polyphony, and modulation, his way of resolving discords by the interchange of parts, and even his occasional overstepping of all generally held rules of composition, are always limited by this " harmonic " theory, which he developed to such an astounding degree of certainty that he could dare even the boldest flights. At the same time his ear was so delicately trained to follow the parts, even of the most elaborate and complicated pieces of music, that not only would he immediately notice the slightest theoretical mistake while the piece was being performed, but in his own works he would give himself endless trouble in order to obtain the greatest purity of writing. In his thorough-bass instruction book he explains that consecutive fifths and octaves are the greatest errors in composition ; they had indeed always been considered as such, but the composers of the beginning of the seventeenth century, and, in part also, the contemporaries of Bach, are much more lax in practice than himself. His ear was exceedingly sensitive with regard to hidden fifths and octaves, even in the inner parts.[182] As to

---

[181] Kunst des reinen Satzes I., p. 142.

[182] See Vol. II., p. 173 f. (on the G sharp minor prelude of the Wohltemperirte Clavier) and Kirnberger, Kunst des reinen Satzes I., p. 159. Bach is less intolerant of fifths and octaves when they occur in passing notes or in

the reduplication of discords and of the leading note, he imposed the strictest rules both upon himself and upon his pupils. Kirnberger says that, so far as his own observation goes, Bach only doubled the major third in the chord of the dominant in one single case in a four-part composition.[183] We know, also through Kirnberger, that in five-part writing he forbids the reduplication of the superfluous second, the fourth, the diminished fifth, the superfluous sixth, the seventh, and the ninth.[184] In the chord of the sixth with the diminished triad Bach characterised the doubling of the sixth as a mistake, because it sounds badly.[185] And yet all these carefully stated rules of part-writing were only a secondary consideration with him. He could even allow them to be disregarded without his sensitive ear being offended, so long only as the logical sequence of harmonies remained intelligible and not to be mistaken. His infallible certainty of feeling with regard to these points allowed him frequently to venture upon things of such a kind that even Kirnberger is forced to admit that Bach's works demanded a quite peculiar style of performance, exactly suited to his style of writing. The player should know the harmonies perfectly, otherwise many of them can scarcely be listened to.[186]

We cannot suppose that simultaneously with the practical music of the seventeenth century the theoretical branch of the art developed in proportion, for in all times artistic

---

ornaments. But here he availed himself of one single license which had long ago been taken by his predecessors. This subject is thoroughly gone into by J. G. Walther in his instruction book, fol. 116 f.

[183] Grundsätze des Generalbasses, p. 83. The passage referred to occurs in B.-G., III., p, 194, bar 5. Compare Kunst des reinen Satzes, I., addendum to p. 37.

[184] Kunst des reinen Satzes, II. 3, p. 41: "*Regula Joh. Seb. Bachii: In Compositione quinque partibus instructa non sunt duplicandæ* 2♭, 4, 5♭, ♭, 7, *et* 9."

[185] Notwithstanding, this is done in the Thorough-bass instruction book, Cap. 8, Reg. 4, example, bar 1, last crotchet, nor can it be regarded as an uncorrected error on the part of the pupil who made the copy. Kirnberger (Grundsätze des Generalbasses, p. 57, note) interprets this rule, which is too strict if universally applied in this manner, that the reduplication is only to be avoided when the sixth appears as the leading note.

[186] Kunst des reinen Satzes, I., p. 216 f.

instruction has always been considerably in arrear of artistic practice. So much, however, is certain that there were practical musicians even at the beginning of that century who knew that the easiest introduction to the art of composition was the knowledge of thorough-bass. In the year 1624 the Berlin Cantor, Johann Crüger, calls this method, which he himself employed, a well-known one;[187] and although for a time it held less prominence than various other methods which he describes, it is certain that it never died out again, but that, like practical music itself, it waxed stronger and stronger, and, in Germany at least, gradually became the prevailing method.[188] Thus in employing this method Bach did nothing new, for it had been long in use. Of course it had its weak points, and was liable to misuse and superficial treatment in unskilful hands. On this account it was assailed in the year 1725 by Joseph Fux, Capellmeister in Vienna, with his *Gradus ad Parnassum;* in this he begins the course of composition with simple two-part counterpoint, note against note, and, after a thorough working out of the five kinds of simple two, three, and four-part counterpoint, he proceeds gradually to imitation, to fugue in two, three, and four parts; he next treats of double counterpoint, applying the same again to fugue, and concludes with some chapters on the church style and recitative, thorough-bass and harmony remaining unnoticed. This method was really new at that time in certain circles, and Fux designated it as such, nor does he attempt to conceal the reactionary spirit which led him to oppose the increasing arbitrariness and law-

---

[187] Crüger, *Synopsis Musices.* Berlin, 1624, *page* 57: "*Nos incipientibus gratificaturi compendiosissimam illam et facillimam ingrediamur componendi viam, qua nimirum ad Fundamentum prius substratum et positum reliquæ superiores modulationes adjici possint. Hoc enim qui poterit, facillime postmodum melodiæ regali Tenoris et Cantus reliquas adjunget voces.*"

[188] J. G. Walther, in his MS. instruction book of 1708, says, with evident reference to Crüger's *Synopsis:* "And this is the most compendious and the easiest way to compose, by building the other parts up from the bass, taking that as the foundation. . . . Therefore we will keep to this said easy method, and make a beginning of composition with four parts (as that whereon so much depends)."

lessness in music. In fact, it was only a revival and completion of the musical teaching of the sixteenth century, and
refers only to unaccompanied vocal music in the polyphonic
style, and Fux wished this to be regarded as the starting-
point of all musical education.

Almost at the same time, in France, Rameau had made
a first attempt to justify on scientific grounds the practice
of the time, which rested upon the "harmonic" theory,
and to reduce it to a system. His "Treatise on harmony,"
which appeared in 1722, quickly attracted notice even in
Germany; Nikolaus Bach told Schröter about it in 1724,[189]
and, from Emanuel Bach's statement to Kirnberger, we
must conclude that Sebastian Bach was also acquainted
with it. The chief points of Rameau's system — the
determining of the chord by means of the bass, as
well as the inversions arising from the alteration of
the bass note — had of course been long known and
practised, and so far Bach and Rameau were agreed.
But some of the conclusions arrived at by the French-
man in the course of his system were highly disapproved
of by Bach. We cannot with certainty point out the
passages which met with Bach's disapprobation, but we
may assume them to have treated of those opinions with
which Kirnberger waged war.[190] On the other hand, it

---

[189] Schröter, Deutliche Anweisung zum General-Bass, 1772, p. x.

[190] These were chiefly, perhaps, the chord of the 6-5 constructed on the
subdominant with the addition of the major sixth, and stated by Rameau to be
a root-chord, and also the distinction between essential and non-essential
dissonances. Rameau's method of drawing out the fundamental bass of a
connected piece of music—i.e., of pointing out the series of notes to which the
harmonies of a piece are to be referred as to their proper ground-tones—was
applied by Kirnberger to two of Bach's compositions, but not indeed in an
irreproachable manner (Die wahren Grundsätze zum Gebrauch der Harmonie,
p. 55 ff. and 107 ff.). The same thing has been done with the chief autograph
of the French Suites in the case of the Sarabande and the two minuets in the
D minor suite, as well as in Fischhoff's autograph of the Wohltemperirte
Clavier, in the C minor fugue and the D minor prelude. I cannot confidently
affirm that the numbers and letters inserted in the MS. for this purpose are in
Bach's own writing. It is not, however, impossible that Bach himself may
have demonstrated the nature of Rameau's ground bass theory on his own
compositions.

is allowable to conclude that Bach paid full recognition
to the method of Fux. For no other than a pupil
of his own, Mizler, translated, under Bach's very eye, as
it were, the *Gradus ad Parnassum* into German, and when
Mizler, referring to the value of the work, says that it had
been well received by those who really knew what a good
composition was, he must doubtless refer most directly
to Bach.[191]   As a matter of fact, there was much more
sympathy between Bach and Fux than might appear at first.
With regard to the development of the art in Germany,
it must not be thought that up to Bach's time a strictly
contrapuntal method of teaching prevailed and that Bach
introduced a freer style.   A more exact examination of the
German composers, particularly those of the latter half
of the seventeenth century, and among them notably the
organ and clavier masters who were the glory of that
period, will show plainly that the contrary is the case.
Awkwardness in polyphonic vocal writing had much
increased during the century, and even the authorised
freedom of instrumental composers threatened to degenerate
into arbitrary laxity.   Only to a very limited degree can
Bach be said to have inherited from his predecessors
his astounding contrapuntal skill, and the strictness and
purity of his style.   He re-introduced these qualities into
the art, with a leaning, indeed, towards the old classical
models, but following rather the leading of his own genius.
Through him the old approved rules of part-writing again
came to be duly honoured, with such modifications, it is true,
as were rendered necessary by the alteration in the tone
material, and it was Bach who once more taught the organ
and clavier composers to write as a rule in real parts, and
to keep the same number of parts throughout a whole piece.
Hence, notwithstanding his approval of Fux's method, it was
only natural for him to prefer another style of instruction.
That was very well fitted for vocal compositions; for that
alone could it afford a safe groundwork.   With certain limitations it was also useful for violin players and for writers for

---

[191] See the Introduction to Mizler's translation of the *Gradus*. Leipzig, 1742.

the violin; it could not be used for the instruction of writers for the organ or clavier, since it placed the learner in direct opposition to the demands of his instrument. Whether, as a general rule, it is better to begin with vocal or with instrumental composition is not the question here; we are stating historical facts. It cannot be denied that the only method of instruction that can succeed is one which from the first, let the pupil begin where he may, will awaken his individual feeling for art. In true art there is nothing mechanical, there exists no essential antagonism between reproduction and production; the first phrase sung, or the easiest little clavier piece played, is a starting-point in the art of composition, or it may become so. Thus it was quite natural that in Italy, and in those districts of Germany that remained under Italian influence, the old contrapuntal method, revived by Fux, should predominate, since the musical culture of the Italians was mainly based on vocal music, while in Germany, where instrumental music was always more and better performed than vocal music, the other method was of course preferred. From this point of view we can understand the different positions held by fugues in the method of Fux and Bach (or Kirnberger) respectively. Vocal fugue moreover rested on other conditions than those of instrumental fugue, and what Bach made out of the latter might well be regarded as the highest pinnacle of art, to which none but the most thoroughly and diversely cultured of his disciples could possibly attain.[192]

In the case of two pupils of Bach's, Heinrich Nikolaus Gerber and Agricola, we have sufficiently precise information with regard to the method pursued by the master in their instruction to enable us to see the way in which Bach used the instrument with which the pupils were already

---

[192] Bach himself once was heard to call the fugues of an "old and laborious contrapuntist" dry and wooden, and some fugues by a "modern but no less great contrapuntist" pedantic, at least in the form in which they were arranged for the clavier, because the former kept persistently to his chief subject without change, and the latter did not show enough invention in enlivening his theme by means of interludes (Marpurg, Kritische Briefe über die Tonkunst, I., p. 266). It is not known to what composers he alluded.

familiar as the vehicle of instruction in composition suitable in each case. Gerber had, when receiving instruction from Bach, to " study thoroughly " ("durchstudiren ") his (Bach's) Inventions, a set of suites, and the Wohltemperirte Clavier. Then came the practice of thorough-bass, but not extempore; Gerber had to write out a four-part accompaniment to Albinoni's violin solos, from the bass part.[193] Similarly, Agricola was first instructed in clavier and organ-playing, and after that " in the harmonic art."[194] In neither case was the pupil a beginner nor the instruction elementary; these young men were led on by Bach to real composition by means of harmony and the four-part accompaniment to be written on Albinoni's figured basses. For this purpose he also availed himself of chorales. His method of beginning to teach simple counterpoint was to give a chorale melody to be harmonised in four parts. This is rendered certain by what Kirnberger and Emanuel Bach say. The latter asks, alluding to the chorales by his father that he edited, who can dispute the advantage of an education in composition which begins, not with a stiff and pedantic contrapuntal exercise, but with chorales?[195] Kirnberger recommended beginning with four-part counterpoint, and extols the chorales of Bach as models of four-part writing which it would be impossible to surpass, and in which not only all the parts had their own flowing sequence, but one kind of character was preserved in all.[196] He also holds a diligent practice in chorales to be of the highest value, or indeed indispensable, and that

---

[193] Gerber, L. I., col. 492.

[194] Ch. C. Rolle, Neue Wahrnehmungen, p. 93.

[195] Preface to " J. S. Bach's vierstimmige Choralgesänge." The idea in the sentence above quoted is not expressed with sufficient clearness, for it admits of the interpretation that the method alluded to merely substituted the more animated and interesting chorale melodies for the old-fashioned *cantus firmi* which were of the greatest possible simplicity, and which were used for contrapuntal studies, which does not exclude the possibility of this method having begun with two-part counterpoint. And the sentence was in fact understood thus by Vogler (Choralsystem, p. 61). There would have been nothing essentially different in this system, however, and yet Emanuel Bach doubtless intended to indicate something different to Fux's method.

[196] Kunst des reinen Satzes, I., p. 157.

it is prejudice to consider this kind of exercise as superfluous or pedantic, since it forms the true foundation, not only for good writing, but for the art of composing well and expressively for the voice.[197] Thus this method was not to do away with those difficult yet indispensable first studies at the cost of thoroughness, nor was it ever supposed to do so, though there were persons who considered it pedantic, while, on the other hand, those who knew about such things extolled it for its thoroughness.[198] When Kirnberger regards Bach's chorale movements as models of vocal composition, it must not be forgotten that he meant accompanied vocal music, and that he considered the chief aim in such work to be the invention of simple and expressive melodies. They were not intended as models of an *a cappella* movement in several parts, and nothing was farther from Bach's thoughts than that they should be treated so. These chorale movements are treated for the most part with a rich instrumental accompaniment, never without any accompaniment ; they are almost all integral parts of grand and ingeniously elaborate church compositions, and always strictly adhere to the particular feeling prompted by the words ; this is the manner in which they were conceived, and in this way only are they to be judged. Carl Friedrich Fasch, whose opinion (according to Gerber) was that in Bach each separate part was very vocal, but the combinations between the parts were utterly unvocal, that they were beautiful parts, and yet not welded together to a beautiful whole,[199] had not found this standpoint on which to form his opinion. It cannot be denied that the publication of the chorales as separate pieces in four parts, with the announcement that

---

[197] Kunst des reinen Satzes, I., p. 215. Forkel's account of Bach's method of instruction agrees with this, but he drew his information mainly from Kirnberger ; he had opportunities, however, for learning about it from Bach's sons.

[198] Lingke, Die Sitze der musikalischen Haupt-Sätze. Leipzig, 1766. Introduction. He says, alluding to Emanuel Bach's statement quoted above, " It would be difficult to find a more thorough method than this." It was afterwards related of Kirnberger that he made his pupils work at chorales for three years ; see Vogler, Choralsystem, p. 24.

[199] Gerber, N. L., II., col. 86.

they were to form a complete hymn-book, may have given rise to false impressions, and have done harm.   Bach's book was soon taken as a pattern to an undue extent, and in 1790 Abraham Peter Schulz, in discussing the influence of music and of its introduction into schools upon the national culture, was obliged to admit " that in arranging a simple chorale the greatest harmonists of the Bach school sought rather to display their erudition by multiplying unexpected and dissonant progressions—often rendering the melody quite unrecognisable—than to regard that simplicity, which is necessary to render the chorale intelligible to the common people."[200]

In connection with the four-part chorales of Bach there is still another question, equally important as regards the master's attitude towards the music of the past, and the way in which he taught his disciples.   A great part of the chorale melodies set by him date from centuries when the formation of melodies followed other laws than those of our own, or even of Bach's day.   The formation of a passage in accordance with one of the six, or, counting the plagal modes separately, the twelve kinds of octaves, gave rise to very characteristic modulations, and, when set in several parts, to a harmonic accompaniment of corresponding individuality.   Until the middle of the seventeenth century, the feeling for the different characters of the various modes was still kept up to a moderate extent among Protestant musicians.   It then began to die out, and eventually the multiplicity of the church modes gave place to the duality of major and minor.   Though the former continued to exist in name for a time, no definite idea attached to most of them.   Johann Schelle once asked Rosenmüller, whom he so highly admired, what was his opinion with regard to the old musical modes.   Rosenmüller laughingly replied that he only knew the Ionian and Dorian modes.[201]   The amalgamation of those scales which contained the greater

---

[200] Schulz, J. A. P., Gedanken über den Einfluss der Musik auf die Bildung eines Volks, und über deren Einführung in den Schulen der Königlich Dänischen Staaten. Kopenhagen, 1790.

[201] (Fuhrmann), Musicalischer Trichter. 1706. P. 40 f.

third into the C clef was more easy than the concentration
of the Dorian, Phrygian, and Æolic modes, whose triads contained the lesser third, into the minor key.   Werkmeister at
first agreed with Rosenmüller in thinking that the Dorian
mode was the best representative of the minor,[202] but was
afterwards more in favour of the Æolian.[203] Johann Gottfried
Walther took a middle course, for, in the year 1708, he
taught that three modes were in ordinary use at that
time, Dorian, Æolian, and Ionian.[204]   Lastly, Bach recognised only two modes, the Ionian with the greater and
the Æolian with the lesser third.[205]   This gradual process
of simplification is very interesting. The Dorian and
Æolian modes were adapted each to its special purpose.
The Dorian allowed of a perfect cadence on the key-note,
on the fourth, and on the fifth, without overstepping the
limits of the diatonic system (putting aside the raising of
the leading note).   In the Æolian a diatonic cadence on
the fifth was impossible. On the other hand, it had the
more distinct minor character, inasmuch as the triads on
the key-note, on the fourth, and on the fifth, all had the
minor third, while in the Dorian mode the triad on the
fourth has the major third.   Our minor mode appears to be
more strictly a combination of the Dorian and Æolian.
Although the modern two-mode system is firmly established
in Bach, he yet keeps up a close connection with the system
of six modes, by simply taking the Æolian mode for the
minors.   Theoretically there only existed for him one and
the same scale for ascending and descending passages alike,
while Rameau, and Kirnberger, used the scale a b c d e
f♯ g♯ a, in ascending, and Lingke, in order to get over the

---

202 *Harmonologia musica.* 1702. P. 59.

203 Musikalische Paradoxal-Discourse.   1707.   P. 86.

204 MS. Musical Instruction Book, Fol. 152b.

205 Clavier Book of Anna M. Bach.   1725.   P. 123.   " The scale with the
minor third is: 1st, a tone ; 2nd, a whole tone; 3rd, a half; 4th, a whole ;
5th, a whole; 6th, a half; 7th, a whole ; 8th, a whole tone ; from this comes
the following rule : (for the intervals) the 2nd is in both scales major ; the 4th
remains the same in both ; the 5th and 8th are perfect ; and as the 3rd is so are
the 6th and 7th."

anomaly of having two different scales, made up the scale
a b c d e f g♯ a, for both kinds of movement.[206]

Bach's minor scale has no distinctive bearing on his
practice, but it serves to explain his attitude towards
the two opposing systems. When, as organist at Weimar,
he first displayed his full mastery over the chorale,
Mattheson and Buttstedt were disputing about the *raison
d'être* of the ecclesiastical modes, and his success and
achievements served as the tragi-comic death-knell to their
quarrel. When Fux, in his *Gradus*, several years later,
attributed a fundamental importance to the church modes,
the opposition of so eminent a man to the modern reform
could not fail to have a certain effect ; but Fux was thinking
chiefly of Catholic church music. In the Protestant church,
the old system of modes could only find the protection it
deserved through a Protestant musician, and this it found,
in part, through Bach. In the principles of composition, as
in chorale treatment, he had achieved a position where
all contrasts were reconciled ; he kept to the historically
developed and fundamental principle of major and minor
scales, and used the church modes as a kind of subsidiary
keys. He obtained from them the full wealth of modulation
which they afford, but always kept them subordinate to
the simpler radical feeling of major and minor.[207] The
consciousness that the beauty of many of the old chorale
melodies would be much impaired by forcing them to submit
to the laws of modulation prescribed by the " harmonic "
system was to Bach only a secondary consideration. He
felt that the art ideas which had taken form in these
hymns carried in them, by reason of their having been
nurtured for centuries in the bosom of the church, an

---

[206] Lingke, Die Sitze der Musicalischen Haupt-Sätze, p. 16 ff.—Lingke laid
this scale, invented by him, before the Society for Musical Sciences in Leipzig
in 1744, and all the members approved of it (see Mizler, Musikalische Bibliothek,
Vol. III., p 360). Bach had not become a member at that time.

[207] In consequence of this, Kirnberger (Kunst des reinen Sätzes, I., p. 103)
says: " In the music of the present day, we not only have twenty-four different
keys, each with a definite character of its own, but we can retain beside them
the modes of the ancients. Hence arises an immense variety of harmony and
modulation."

inalienable wealth of genuine religious feeling. This he neither could nor would dispense with in forming his own church style.   The system of church modes appears in Bach not as one ingeniously employed for certain subjects ; it came to a new birth in his genius, and finds its place not merely in this or that chorale, but in all his music.   When it seemed suitable he would arrange a chorale strictly in accordance with the rules of its mode ; for example, in the Mixolydian melody " Komm, Gott Schöpfer, heiliger Geist."[208] Generally, however, he used what his pupil Kittel calls the " mixed " style of harmonising,[209] giving now more and now less prominence to the characteristic modulations of a particular mode.   Instances of this are the Dorian chorales " Das alte Jahr vergangen ist," " Erschienen ist der herrlich Tag " ;[210] the Mixolydian " Gelobet seist du, Jesu Christ," "Gott sei gelobet und gebenedeiet," "Nun preiset alle Gottes Barmherzigkeit " ;[211] the Phrygian " Christum wir sollen loben schon," " Erbarm dich mein, o Herre Gott."[212]   It also occurs that melodies belonging to one of the ecclesiastical modes appear quite in modern harmonising ; and, on the other hand, Mixolydian modulations (it may be) are introduced into chorales that do not naturally belong to this mode.   The chorales " Jesu nun sei gepreiset," " Es ist das Heil uns kommen her," and " Vom Himmel hoch da komm ich her," in the cantatas of the same name, and especially the chorale in the middle of the second part of the Christmas oratorio, are examples of this treatment.   For all three are, strictly speaking, Ionian, even the second ; it serves, at any rate, to prove that Bach thought that the closing chorale of that cantata was already more than a century old.   From all this it is evident that Bach had evolved from the church modes a means of expression which he used freely wherever the poetic meaning and the musical sequence seemed to him

---

[208] In the chorales published 1785, No. 187; in Erk's edition, No. 255. Compare Kirnberger, *loc. cit.*, II., 63.

[209] Der angehende praktische Organist.   Section III., p. 37 ff.

[210] Nos. 180, 29, and 30 in Erk.

[211] Nos 41 and 213 in Erk, and No. 222 in the chorales of 1786.

[212] No. 175 in Erk, and No. 33 in the chorales of 1784.

to require it ; and for the same reason he harmonises one of
his favourite melodies, "O Haupt, voll Blut und Wunden,"
now in the Ionian, now in the Phrygian mode. The inexhaustible wealth of harmony, which he exhibits not only
in the chorales but in all his compositions, and generally
without any far-fetched modulations, arises from these two
sources ; a thorough familiarity with the ecclesiastical
modes, and an unfailingly keen and certain appreciation of
the harmonic relations subsisting in the systems of major
and minor.[213]

That Kirnberger understood his great teacher's principles
is shown by his not only having felt moved to comment[214]
upon the harmonic nature of a set of organ chorales in the
third part of the "Clavierübung" which had made their
appearance at the time when he was studying with Bach
in Leipzig, but also by his having recognised a certain
form of modulation in the style of the ecclesiastical
modes, even in fugues in the "Wohltemperirte Clavier"
and in the free portions of the cantatas. In his manuscript
copy of the first part of that collection of fugues he
designates those in C major and C sharp major as Ionian,
those in C minor, E flat minor, and G sharp minor as
Æolian, and those in C sharp minor and F sharp minor
as Dorian. The terzett in the cantata "Aus tiefer Noth"
he assigns to the Æolian mode.[215] This nomenclature can,
of course, only have very limited weight, inasmuch as it
expresses nothing more than a preponderance of those
modulations which are peculiar to this or that mode ; and
more than this Kirnberger certainly did not mean to say.
Strictly speaking, scarcely any connected groups of bars
could be found in these pieces in which the diatonic laws
are not somewhere set aside. But such a depth and variety
of harmony was only attainable by the most comprehensive
use of the means of modulation afforded by the ecclesiastical
modes.

---

[213] Compare with this the beautiful passages devoted to this subject in
Winterfeld, Ev. K., III., p. 299.

[214] MS. in the Amalienbibliothek at Berlin. Inserted in App. B., XII.

[215] His MSS. of both are in the Amalienbibliothek, Nos. 57 and 58.

Bach's connection with the system of church modes is also recognisable in his style of writing key signatures. Thus he signs E in the Dorian mode with two sharps, and, consequently, F in the Dorian mode with three flats, and G in the Dorian mode with one flat ; using, of course, no signature in the case of the Dorian, Phrygian, and Mixolydian when they are used in their original positions. To show how very much the character of the scales had been lost at that time, it may be stated here that Mizler calls the Dorian mode D minor, the Phrygian mode E minor, the Lydian mode F major, &c., without more ado.[216] Bach, however, only selected those signatures when he wanted to give to his work the stamp and character of the particular mode. Where this is not the case, he keeps to the simple major and minor. It often seems, indeed, as though his method of procedure was dictated only by custom, and that Agricola's remark was partially true of him, that many composers of the first half of the eighteenth century indicated the Dorian mode when they probably intended the Æolian.[217] This is more particularly to be understood of Bach's free compositions. In the alto aria of the "Homage" cantata, written at Cöthen,[218] Bach gives the first line the signature of G minor and all the rest that of G in the Dorian mode, to explain which there is no inner reason whatever. But from such things as this we see how, in the search after a comprehensive minor key, musical feeling wavered for a long time between the Æolian and the Dorian modes.[219]

---

[216] Musikalische Bibliothek, I., pp. 30, 31, 34, Notes.

[217] Remarks to Tosi, p. 5.

[218] See Vol. II., p. 619 f.

[219] I cannot close this chapter without mentioning Vogler, who, partly in his own "Choral-System," p. 53 ff., and partly through his pupil, C. M. von Weber (Zwölf Choräle von Sebastian Bach umgearbeitet von Vogler, zergliedert von C. M. von Weber. Leipzig, C. F. Peters), attempted to point out the supposed incorrectness and want of beauty in Bach's four-part chorales. That such a ridiculous procedure should have been possible is partly the fault of the editor, Emanuel Bach. As Vogler knew neither the object, position, arrangement, nor, in many cases, even the words of these chorales, and since they were supposed to constitute a complete chorale book, he must have started with utterly false impressions. He is not to be blamed for not having known Bach's relations towards the ecclesiastical modes, since it required a much more com-

V.

WORKS OF THE LAST (LEIPZIG) PERIOD.—CONCERTOS.—THE
LATER WORKS FOR CLAVIER AND ORGAN.

WHILE Bach, during the first part of his life—that is,
down to the close of the Cöthen period—shows himself
chiefly as an instrumental composer, during the Leipzig
time the sphere of his chief activity is seen to be concerted
church music. A natural progress and growth from the
one period to the other is perceptible ; and, putting aside,
as far as may be, the relative intrinsic importance of the
different provinces of art, the earlier period may be said
to stand to the later in the relation of preparation to
fulfilment. The art which had been applied to instrumental music was not given up, but only found expression
through a higher medium ; since the two-fold importance of
song as a means of expression inevitably introduced a new
and independent element. But since instrumental music
was the true source of Bach's art, it was only natural that
he should continue to draw from it, even in the second
period of his life. The number of his later instrumental
compositions is by no means small, and their character is
that of hardly-won fruits ripened in the prosperous harvest
of his life.

The true artist is in the happiest position when all his
works are "occasional" compositions ; and, conversely, he
will be instinctively prompted to apply his art as often as
possible to the events that are nearest to his own life. Both
these statements hold good in the case of Bach. He was
never greater than when he had to make his music conform
to the requirements of his position and office ; and he always
embraced the opportunity of composing music for a definite
object. From 1729 until 1736 he directed Telemann's Musical

---

prehensive view of the work and historical importance of the master than was
possessed by any one at that time. As regards the supposed want of beauty,
Vogler's remarks reveal that his inability to enter into the genius of Bach's
harmonic and melodic sequences was as great as his so-called "improvements"
are lame and tasteless.

Society. Mention has already been made of the chamber vocal compositions with accompaniment that he wrote for it. There is no doubt that his own instrumental works had been performed there. These, no doubt, were orchestral suites. Those "Bach Sonatas," which the musicians at Eutritzsch performed at the opening of the "Kirmess" (fair), in 1783, were probably works of this kind.[220] It is impossible to say with certainty which of his orchestral suites were composed expressly for the Musical Society, since it is very probable that he was engaged in this form of composition even at Cöthen. In the case of the better known of the two D major suites, it is certain that the original parts prepared for its performance were written between the years 1727 and 1736—just about the time when Bach was director of the Musical Society. The other D major suite seems, judging by its contents, to belong to the Leipzig period.[221]

The music performed by the Society was of various kinds; hence we may assume that violin and clavier concertos by Bach were also performed, though more frequently, perhaps, at Bach's house. As no fewer than five claviers, two violins, three violas, two violoncellos, a viol da gamba, and other stringed instruments were left at his death, it is evident that he was well prepared for concerts at home. Nor was there any lack of talented, or, at least, available pupils for these performances. The most flourishing time in Bach's domestic band was, no doubt, from about 1730 until 1733, since the grown-up sons, Friedemann and Emanuel, were still living in their father's house, Bernhard was already grown up, and Krebs, who had been Sebastian's pupil since 1726, was beginning to display his great talents, not to mention the vocal performances of Anna Magdalena and her step-daughter, Katharina. And we know from Bach's own words what a pleasure it was to him at that time "to get up a vocal and instrumental concert."[222] Whether Bach ever wrote violin concertos expressly for them must remain un-

---

[220] Compare ante, p. 21.
[221] See Vol. II., pp. 141—143, and 661. Vol. III., p. 78.
[222] Compare Vol. II., p. 254.

decided; but it is certain that about this time he had works of this kind performed.[223]

In this branch of art he devoted himself chiefly at Leipzig to the clavier concerto. The sonatas and suites for the violin were subsequently arranged by Bach, either wholly or in part, for the clavier or organ; and the comparison of the arrangement with the original shows that the idea of many of these pieces had its root in the clavier style, rather than in that of the violin.[224] The same thing was done with some of his violin concertos, and the comparison of the two versions gives a precisely similar result. But not only did he arrange the violin concertos in A minor, E major, and D minor for clavier and orchestra, transposing them into G minor, D major, and C minor; he also has left three concertos (D minor, F minor, and C minor) which are evidently re-arrangements of violin concertos, the originals of which are unfortunately lost.[225] A fourth, in E major, bears no undoubted signs which point to a violin concerto as its original, so that we must, for the present, assume it to have been originally written for the clavier. After receiving its first form, the whole of it was used for two church cantatas, and then it was re-arranged for a clavier concerto.[226] A fifth, in D minor, also became part of a church cantata; but the original has been lost, with the exception of a small fragment.[227] The A major

---

[223] The time when he was most engaged in the composition of violin concertos was when he was in Cöthen. See Vol. II., p. 125 f. The fact that the original parts of the A minor concerto and two autograph parts of the D minor concerto bear the water-mark M A only proves with certainty that their performance took place between 1727 and 1736—not that they were written during that time.

[224] See Vol. II., p. 80 ff. and 98.

[225] See Rust's dissertations in the preface to B.-G., XVII. Rust (preface to B.-G., XXI.,[1] p. xiii.) has also completely convinced me that the other concerto of the two in C minor for two claviers originated in a concerto for two violins.

[226] See Vol. II., p. 447 ff.

[227] See Vol. II., p. 446 f. It is very probable that among the cantata-symphonies may be embodied parts of lost violin and clavier concertos. One such symphony, its cantata no longer existing, has been published by Rust among the violin concertos in B.-G., XX.,[1] No. 4. I have alluded, on p. 85 of

concerto stands alone, without any direct connection with other works. The two concertos originally composed for two violins and tutti were also arranged for two claviers.[228] The number of simple clavier concertos is seven, including one which only exists in the church cantata.[229]

In the case of several of these concertos the date of composition can be more definitely asserted. The first of those in D minor was turned to account in two different church cantatas, first for "Ich habe meine Zuversicht," which must have been written for the twenty-first Sunday after Trinity, in 1730 or 1731, and afterwards for the music for the third Sunday after Easter, "Wir müssen durch viel Trübsal in das Reich Gottes eingehen."[230] The other D minor concerto is found in the cantata written apparently in 1731, for the twelfth Sunday after Trinity, "Geist und Seele wird verwirret."[231] The first two movements of the E major concerto are contained in the church composition "Gott soll allein mein Herze haben," and the last in the cantata "Ich geh und suche mit Verlangen"; these two are intended for the eighteenth and twentieth Sundays after Trinity, apparently in the years 1731 or 1732.[232] The original compositions must therefore have been written before these dates. The re-arrangement for two solo instruments of one of the two C minor concertos was made in

---

this volume, to another case of this kind. Forkel (p. 60) says that Bach wrote instrumental pieces to be played during the Communion, and that they were always so arranged as to be instructive to the player, but that most of them have been lost. These may also partly have been arranged movements from instrumental concertos, and partly pieces of the same kind as those which are found at the beginning of the second part of the church cantatas in two sections—compare "Die Elenden sollen essen" and "Die Himmel erzählen die Ehre Gottes."

[228] B.-G., XXI.,[1] Nos. 1 and 3.—P. S. II., C. 10 (257).   Both in C minor.

[229] G minor {B.-G. XVII., No. 7 ; P. S. II., C. 2(249).

D major	,,	,,	3 ;	,, 4(251).
D minor	,,	,,	1 ;	,, 7(254).
F minor	,,	,,	5 ;	,, 3(250).
E major	,,	,,	2 ;	,, 6(253).
A major	,,	,,	4 ;	,, 5(252).

D minor (see B.-G. XVII., p. xx. and vii., No. 35).

[230] See Vol. II., p. 446.   Vol. III., p. 79.

[231] See Vol. II., p. 449.   [232] See Vol. II.. p. 448 f.

the year 1736.[233]   In Bach's later years, when he undertook
the final revision of the most important of his organ chorales,
and gave the final form to the Passions according to St. John
and St. Matthew, he also collected his clavier concertos and
put the finishing touches to them.[234]

In Weimar, as we know, Bach had worked diligently at
the arrangement of violin concertos for the clavier; and in
Leipzig he transcribed a great number of Vivaldi's compositions.   The work was identical, excepting that in the
former case the tutti parts are included in the clavier
arrangement, while here the clavier part simply takes the
place of the violin.   Beside the alteration of those passages
and melodic phrases which were too exclusively fitted for the
violin, and their extension to deeper registers inaccessible to
the violin, he had to add a part for the left hand.   Merely
to allot the figured bass part to the clavier was a make-
shift, of which indeed he availed himself frequently, especially
in the D major concerto and in the middle movement of a
concerto in C minor.   When he undertook a more thorough
remodelling he generally surrounded the figured bass with
more animated passages in the clavier bass, and sometimes
introduced an independent third part between the upper part
and the figured bass, or, when the figured bass stopped,
turned the one part of the solo instrument into a trio.   In
this respect the G minor, and in its last recension the D
minor, concerto underwent especially careful treatment, as
also the first movement of that C minor concerto which
still exists in the original.   As contrasted with stringed instruments, the peculiarity of the clavier is its power of playing
in two parts, or even in three or more parts.   By this, as well
as by quality of tone, the clavier can be brought into sharper
contrast with the tutti than the violin.   Since the time of
Mozart the clavier has come into more and more prominence
as the solo instrument in instrumental concertos; and
nowhere is its style more purely and perfectly displayed than

---

[233] B.-G., XXI.,² No. 3.   See Appendix A. of Vol. II., No. 44.

[234] The autograph, in the Royal Library in Berlin, contains seven of these
and also the fragment of the second D minor concerto.   One of them, however
(in F major), is a *Concerto grosso* with clavier, of which more anon.

in the hostile position, so to speak, which it is made to assume towards the orchestra in works of this class by Mozart and Beethoven. The same thing cannot be asserted of Bach's clavier concertos, even when due allowance is made for the conditions of development afforded by the difference between the harpsichord and the pianoforte. It must be remembered that at that time the clavier formed a part of every concerto, taking the figured bass part. As such it had not only to support the solo instrument, but, in Bach especially, to bind together the different instruments which took part in the tutti to an unity to which it gave the general stamp.[235] It has been stated before that even in Bach's clavier concertos the accompanying harpsichord was employed. Thus there could be no sort of distinct opposition between the tutti and the solo instrument; either externally or internally. Bach of course knew this, and he now attempted rather to let the clavier appear openly in the character which had hitherto been as it were latent in it when treated as the exponent of the figured bass. The musical form which arose from the antagonism of two equally matched forces is preserved, as in the Brandenburg concerto, but the clavier is always predominant. These works are, we may say, clavier compositions cast in concerto forms, which have gained, through the co-operation of the stringed instruments, in tone, parts and colour. Accordingly Bach allows the solo clavier to play during all the tutti portions, or to surround them with figures and passages. He thus deprives himself of even the simplest effect of contrast; sometimes to a surprising extent, as, for instance, in the Andante of the G minor concerto. But his great object was to obtain a predominance of the clavier tone, in which he must have succeeded, if we consider that another harpsichord was added to play the figured bass part, and that the tutti portions were generally very thinly orchestrated. The part filled by this second harpsichord in the way of supporting the harmonies is generally so slight that it could easily have been undertaken by the solo instrument, and, indeed, it

---

[235] Compare Vol. II., p. 108.

seems to me that in the last recensions of the D minor concerto and the G minor concerto it was intended that this alteration should be made.

We shall see that Bach followed out to its extreme consequences the idea of making the clavier the predominant part in a clavier concerto. The germ of this idea may be traced in these compositions, even in their original state as violin concertos. For that Bach undertook their re-arrangement merely because he did not care to write new clavier concertos is an assumption utterly contrary to his character, and is disproved even by the large number of these re-arrangements. No doubt he felt that the style of his violin concertos was so much moulded by his clavier style that their true nature could only be fully brought out in the shape of clavier concertos. It cannot be denied that many details, and notably *cantabile* passages, lose in effect in the clavier arrangement; but as a whole we must regard them as new and higher developments, rather than arrangements.

It is clear that in respect to the form, especially of the first movement—to the relation between the solo instrument and the tutti—to the characteristic qualities of tone in each and in the whole, the Bach clavier concerto and the newer form which originated with Mozart must be judged from different points of view. When we have discovered the right one our enjoyment is perfect.[236] Omitting the three concertos which still exist in the shape of violin concertos, and have already been spoken of,[237] and that D minor concerto which only survives in the cantata "Geist und Seele wird verwirret," those for one clavier in F minor

---

[236] Forkel (p. 57) briefly calls Bach's concertos for a clavier with accompaniment antiquated. That they can never be, so long as they are approached with the right kind of preparation. An artist has a right to demand that his productions be viewed as he intended them to be. Hilgenfeldt (p. 127) was led by Forkel's opinion to ascribe the four clavier concertos, which he knew and called "somewhat in the old French style," to the first part of the Cöthen period, and he is followed by Bitter (II., 292). How utterly without foundation this assumption is, is proved by the fact that among them are included one of the Brandenburg concertos, and one remodelled from the Brandenburg concertos which are known to have been written in 1721.

[237] Vol. II., p. 125 f.

and A major demand attention for their clear and compact form. They are particularly well fitted to elucidate the structure of the older form of concerto. The middle movement of the F minor concerto consists only of a continuous and richly ornamented *cantilena* for the solo instrument, while in the Larghetto of the other the stringed instruments, together with the figured bass, perform a kind of free chaconne, which may be compared to the Adagio of the E major violin concerto (in D major for the clavier); only that the theme lies in the upper part, is used to form interludes, and appears also in an inverted form. The concertos in E major and D minor are of large proportions; the first is characterised by a cheerful activity, with a tender fervour in the Siciliano, and the second by a passionate and touching pathos. The latter is indisputably the most important of all, never ceasing to rivet our at.ention by the mighty swing and deep earnestness of its ibjects, as well as by the ingenuity of their treatment. The allegro movement is rather episodical than thematic, as befits the concerto style; the Adagio is a chaconne, the theme of which remains in the bass, excepting that as the key changes short episodical interludes are continually introduced for the purposes of modulation. The wild, uncontrolled energy, which only comes to rest in the passages of deep lament, scarcely relaxing even at the close from its earnest gravity, gives to the work a character unusual in concertos; for at that time, much more than in later periods, it was usual to use this form for nothing more than an agreeably and lightly moved play of feeling. The C minor concerto for two claviers, based upon a lost composition for the violin, has the same gloomy character, and is rather more elegiac in style. The peculiarity of orchestration in this concerto, which is polyphonic and very full, especially in the first movement, is chiefly due to repeated remodelling. Bach evidently bestowed especial care on the task. In an original concerto for two claviers the relation of these to the strings would have been very different.

Besides the simple concerto there was the *Concerto grosso*, in which the contrasting element to the tutti consisted, not of one, but of several instruments in combination. Bach's concertos for two violins belong to this class, as, of course, do those for two claviers which grew out of them. We must assume a concerto for oboe and violin, which is unfortunately lost, to have been cast in this mould.[238] We know from the Brandenburg concertos how fond Bach was of setting the so-called *Concertino* in a very original way. Thus, in the second concerto, the *Concertino* consists of trumpet, flute, oboe and violin; in the fifth, of flute, violin, and harpsichord; and in the fourth, of violin and two flutes.[239] The last-mentioned concerto was re-arranged by Bach, the key being changed from G major to F major, and the clavier appearing in place of the violin; thus the *Concertino* resembles that of the fifth Brandenburg concerto,"[240] and in both the clavier predominates even over the other solo instruments. A third concerto of the kind also employs flute, violin, and harpsichord as the solo instruments. Its allegro movements are grandly developed from a prelude and fugue for clavier alone, which even in that form were seen to be designed for concerto movements; they have already been spoken of.[241] The middle movement is taken by Bach from an organ sonata in three parts in D minor. There is no tutti part in the movement, for the fourth part, rendered necessary in order to weld the solo instruments together, is not *obbligato*, but serves merely to fill up the harmonies.[242]

If we could determine the chronological sequence of the clavier concertos it would be easier to recognise the different stages by which Bach developed and raised this form. Many impulses of various kinds, from without and

---

[238] Breitkopf's catalogue for New Year, 1764, p. 52: "Bach, *G. S.* I. Concerto, *a Oboe Concert. Violino Conc.* 2 *Violini, Viola, Basso.* 1 thlr." From this it would appear as though Bach had written several oboe concertos.

[239] See Vol. II., pp. 132, 134, and 133.

[240] B.-G., XVII., No. 6, and P. S. II., Cah. 1 (248).

[241] Vol. I., p. 421 f.

[242] According to the MS. sketches, which although not original are yet very trustworthy, the solo clavier in this concerto would seem to have taken the part of the figured bass in addition to its own. It is published in B.-G., XVII., No. 8.

from within, assisted him in the attainment of that
excellence which is perfectly exemplified in the C major
concerto for two claviers, the two concertos for three
claviers, and the so-called Italian concerto. The tradition
that Bach wrote the concertos for three claviers in order to
play them with his elder sons is quite trustworthy.[243] This
was an incitement, which well accorded with his own
inclination, to make the concerto more and more into a
form for clavier alone. At all events the C major concerto
for two claviers preceded them, and if they were composed
by 1733 at latest its date will be probably between 1727 and
1730.[244] Of the two concertos for two claviers which exist
only in an altered form, one, as has been said, is to be
assigned to the year 1736. If the other is to be assigned to
an earlier period, we may assume that Bach was moved,
by the very fact of altering this concerto, to attempt an
original composition of the same kind.[245] But it is easily
conceivable that the mere use of a second harpsichord for
the figured bass would suggest to the composer that it
might be raised from its dependent position to a more
prominent one.[246] For it must be regarded as an indubitable
fact that in the C major concerto no instrument is meant
to play the figured bass part; and even in the older C minor
concerto—to judge from the parts which date from Bach's
time—it was not regarded as indispensable. Finally, it must
not be forgotten that a composition for two claviers was
nothing new. Bach may not have had the form suggested
to him by Hieronymus Pachelbel's Toccata for two claviers,
if indeed he knew of it ; Couperin had written an Allemande
for two claviers which Bach, his great admirer, must
certainly have known.[247]

---

[243] S. F. K. Griepenkerl, in the preface to the D minor concerto for three
claviers; P. S. II., Cah. 11 (258).

[244] The autograph clavier parts have the watermark M A. Published in
B.-G., XXI.,[2] No. 2, and P. S. II., Cah. 9 (256).

[245] Forkel (p. 58) says that the C minor concerto here referred to is " very
old," as compared with that in C major. But he seems only to mean that its
style was antiquated.

[246] A theory with which Rust agrees (B.-G., XXI.,[2] p. vi.).

[247] See Couperin's works, edited by J. Brahms (Denkmäler der Tonkunst, IV.,
p. 160).

Be that as it may, the C major concerto leaves not a moment's doubt as to Bach's conception of this form. There is no longer any idea of strife or opposition between the solo instruments and the tutti; the tutti has nothing to do but supply an accompaniment to the harmony, or to support the passages played on the claviers. In the Adagio it is silent, and in the other movements it could quite well be dispensed with without detriment to the construction of the work. Its use is to give fulness and colour. The few short episodes and polyphonic phrases which it has to itself are apparently accounted for by the fact that Bach could not endure the tedium of writing parts which were not *obbligato*. The working-out falls entirely to the share of the claviers, but with this exception it exactly follows the method prescribed by the concerto form. A tutti phrase (bars 1—12) and a solo-phrase (bars 12—28) come into prominence in the first movement, which is developed out of their different combinations and contrasts in different keys. Within the limits of these two chief groups, however, the solo instruments have concerted passages of a very animated kind among themselves. This movement can thus be called a concerto in a two-fold sense, both because it preserves the form of Vivaldi's concerto style, which proceeds from the contrast between the solo and the tutti, and also because it actually contains a strife or competition between two instruments, although these are of different kinds.[248] The last movement of the concerto generally has a dance character and some kind of three-time, and, as compared with the more pathetic first movement, it must always be gay, light, and brilliant. This requirement is fulfilled by Bach in the C major concerto; but the employment of the fugal form is remarkable. The fugue belongs to the sonata form, or to that of the concerto in the sonata style;[249] it has nothing in common with the strict concerto form, since that originates not in polyphony, but in homophony, and its working-out

---

[248] The opening of the tutti-phrase recalls the opening of the first movement of the cantata " Wer mich liebet." I mention this because even the cantata form is built originally upon that of the concerto. See Vol. I., p. 512.

[249] See Vol. II., p. 136, f.

is not thematic but episodic. Bach often employs a fugue for the last movement, especially where the clavier appears as a solo instrument; this is the case, for instance, in the fifth Brandenburg concerto, in the concerto in A minor for clavier, violin, and flute, and also in the fourth Brandenburg concerto, the violin part of which was re-arranged by Bach for the clavier. There, and in the C major concerto, he succeeded in a most masterly way in suiting the form to the character of the movement, by the style of invention and treatment, especially by means of longer episodes, or even interludes, quite in the free style; and he was led to introduce them by the style of the harpsichord and the organ, which always influenced his imagination.[250] Although the fugal style would appear to afford but little temptation for anything of the kind, Bach contrives in this movement to employ the two claviers in such a manner as to make them appear as two factors of equal importance. By this means, the working-out of the fugues, even putting aside the interludes, is characteristic and especially interesting. The two allegro movements, and, in no less a degree, the delicately woven and melancholy quatuor which serves as an Adagio, reveal a fresh though controlled inventiveness, a feeling of strict moderation, which, when united to the highest perfection of form—for the work corresponds absolutely to the ideal of the concerto—make the work a classic model.[251]

The two concertos for three claviers are constructed upon the same principles. The tutti (if, indeed, this name ought

---

[250] See Vol. I., p. 422.

[251] Rust (B.-G., XXI.,[2] pp. 6—8) holds, on the authority of an older copy which contains only the first movement, and that without orchestral accompaniment, that the first movement was written as a separate work, and that the accompaniment was not added till afterwards. This cannot be gathered from the style of the accompaniment, for I cannot see that of the first movement to be different from that of the last, except in so far as is required by the different form of the two movements. It is not organically necessary either in one movement or the other; it has been already noticed by Forkel (p. 58) that the concerto could very well dispense with the accompaniment of the strings, and that it has a quite good effect without it. It may have even been played in this way at an earlier date. Rust cleverly inferred that Bach probably made no full score of the concerto, but may have written the parts for the stringed instruments separately

to be used any longer) serves, with few exceptions, only to
support and strengthen, the musical development being left
to the claviers.   In the working of these together, indeed,
another method of treatment is to be remarked.   On account
of the requisite response in the parts, it is harder to work
three claviers together than two.   Chiefly for this reason,
as I believe, Bach generally used them all together in the
first movement, and without any opposition between a tutti
phrase and a solo phrase.   The consequent close symphonic
structure in the first movement—which he, not content
with clearly-articulated form and marvellous variety, suc-
ceeds in adorning with endless invention—forms an effective
contrast to the last movement, and one which is thoroughly
justified by the rules of the concerto.   Of the two concertos,
that in D minor is certainly the earlier.[252]   Its character is
delightful and soothing ; still, it lacks that perfect workmanship which makes the strong, grave, majestic concerto in
C major one of the most imposing of all Bach's instrumental
compositions.[253]   In the first two movements of the D minor
concerto the first clavier comes into marked prominence,
and in the charming Siciliano, it predominates exclusively,
the other claviers being used only for accompaniment and
support.   The string quartet takes much the same place as
that held in concerted chamber music by the harpsichord on
which the figured-bass part is played.   In this sphere it
fulfils its task with great discretion and taste.   It should
also be noticed how carefully and circumspectly Bach uses
it to strengthen the real parts of the claviers.   But, even
then, the bass lies for the most part in the clavier parts ; if
the string quartet were entirely omitted, the full and perfect
effect of tone might be affected, but not the organism itself,

---

[252] P. S. II., Cah. 11 (258).

[253] P. S II., Cah. 12 (259).   This work, of which—as also of the D minor
concerto—the autograph is wanting, exists in MS. in D major as well.   In
opposition to Griepenkerl's view, I hold this to be the original key, because
of bar 33 of the Adagio.   The published form contains many errors.   Thus, in
the bar just mentioned, after *f* the violas play again in unison with the violins ;
in bar 48 of the last movement, first clavier, left hand, the fourth beat of the
bar should be *f g*, instead of *f e*.

excepting in a few passages which are not intelligible without the string bass.[254]

The C major concerto allots an equally important part to each of the three claviers; and the string quartet, without overstepping its modest limits, has more independence than in the D minor concerto, or even in the concerto in C major for two claviers. In this case the string parts contain the true and indispensable bass; but it is frequently identical with the clavier bass, or forms a central line for the adornments with which it is surrounded by the latter. In a very limited way, too, the quartet is allowed an independent share in the development of the whole. In the first movement it opposes themes of considerable importance to the subject, which enters in unison on all the claviers. On two occasions the string bass gives out, quite alone, the ponderous, hammer-like subject of the last movement; and in the Adagio we meet once more with a veritable *tutti* contrast, so far as such a device can have place in the Adagio of a concerto. This movement is built, as is frequently done by Bach, upon a *Basso quasi ostinato*, which is seven times repeated in its entirety, but in different keys, and is also dissected and used episodically. To this the strings oppose, four times over, their own contrapuntal passage, while the claviers take up the figured bass part; after which the string quartet resumes the accompaniment. Thus this concerto fulfils all the demands which can be made for independence in each co-operating part, according to its importance to the whole effect; and, in respect to the general feeling of the music, the concerto character is kept up throughout. But it is evident that such rich materials treated in such a polyphonic style must necessarily result in grandeur and gravity. It imparts weight to the stern vigour of the first movement; to the melancholy Adagio a slight feeling of austerity; and the last movement soars far above the cheerful vigour of an ordinary finale. It rises with a broad steady flight above the ponderous theme :—

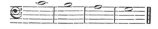

---

[254] Bach must have meant the string bass part for the violoncello. Passages like bars 22 and 116 of the first movement preclude the use of the double-bass.

and spreads to completeness in six parts. Although richly adorned with brilliant passages thoroughly befitting the concerto style, it is almost solemn in its broad, majestic flow.

There also exists a concerto for four claviers, with accompaniment for string quartet (A minor).[255] Forkel[256] considered it an original composition. We now know it to be only an arrangement of a concerto by Vivaldi for four violins. The original is in B minor, and is accompanied by two violas, violoncello, and bass. As in his other arrangements of Vivaldi's concertos, Bach has given the basses greater independence, and worked out the middle parts more richly and fully. He gives the solo instruments more work in counterpoint, and here and there the violin passages display a character more suited to the clavier, he also often adds a fuller accompaniment not unfrequently varied with episodes. But even here the accompaniment is generally used only to fill up and support the harmonies. And yet the work affords new evidence of the master's ingenuity in writing four *obbligato* parts, even in the lightest style. We must assume the arrangement to be about contemporary with the original concertos for three claviers.[257]

At Easter, 1735, Bach published, in the second part of the "Clavierübung," a concerto which, in respect of style, must be admitted to be the maturest of his labours in this form. It is for clavier alone, and composed "in the Italian taste" (nach italiänischem *Gusto*").[258] This description summarises the whole history and character of the Bach instrumental concertos. The concerto was a form of violin music invented by the Italians. Ever since Bach had first taken an active interest in the form, his constant endeavour had been to employ it in the most widely different provinces of music, and we have already seen how he brought it even

---

[255] P. No. 260.

[256] See p. 58 of his work on Bach.

[257] Vivaldi's concerto is to be found in Walsh's *Vivaldi's most celebrated Concertos, opera terza, No. X.* In Roitzsch's edition of Bach's arrangements (P. S. II., Cah. 13) there is a mistake at the beginning. The second violin begins four bars too soon ; and in bar 8, which must then be bar 12, of the second violin part, the third crotchet should be c'', instead of b'.

[258] B.-G., III., p. 139 ff. P. S. I., Cah. 6 (207) No. 1.

into the chief choruses of several chorale cantatas. But
above all he wished, from the first, to turn it to account
for solo music for the organ and clavier. We found that
under the name of Toccata he had written, even in the
first period of his full maturity, pieces for the organ and
clavier which exhibit the concerto form in perfection;
there is a clavier composition of the very earliest period,
with the title of Concerto,[259] and the arrangement of Vivaldi's
concertos ought to count as free compositions for the clavier.
Subsequently, when he wrote real concertos, he clung more
or less to the idea that the prominent part in the work
must always be a single instrument. We have already seen
how, in the case of the clavier concertos with accompaniment,
the clavier gradually gained prominence, while the tutti
sank down into a mere accompaniment and the string bass
to a *basso continuo*. This method is carried furthest in the
concerto in the " Clavierübung." While it is a masterly
composition for the harpsichord, it is, at the same time, a
vivid reflex of a form which was really invented for the violin
and a band of instruments in contrast with it. The influence
of the violin is most easily perceived in the *Andante*. This
influence is what is meant by the words " in the Italian
taste," as also by the phrase " *Alla maniera Italiana*," used
by Bach to describe his earlier clavier variations, in which he
approached the style of treatment most characteristic of the
violin.[260] He was not the only composer of his time to write
a concerto for only one instrument; others had made various
attempts, for the clavier and for the lute. But they were
nothing more than attempts, for only a genius of the
first rank could succeed, and there was but one German
musician capable of uniting two opposing styles with such
harmonious results. This was felt even by Scheibe, who
was by no means an unreserved admirer of Bach. But
every one was obliged at once to allow this clavier concerto

---

[259] See Vol. I., p. 417. A Concerto in G major, for clavier alone, which
bears Sebastian Bach's name in Zelter's handwriting, has lately come to light
in an old MS. in Grasnick's bequest. I cannot, however, accept this dry, stiff
composition for Bach's.

[260] See Vol. I., p. 431.

to be a perfect model of its kind; very few, or indeed hardly any, concertos could be mentioned having such splendid qualities and sound working-out. " It was no less a master of music than Herr Bach, who has made the clavier his especial study, and with whom we can safely venture to compete with any foreign nation, who was to bequeath to us a piece in this form, which should provoke the envy and emulation of all our own great composers, and be vainly imitated by foreigners."[261] The sound working-out consists of clearly grouped and sharply contrasted subjects, which scarcely need the aid of different effects of tone to make them intelligible. Still, a form which is developed on the principle of subjects of different kinds relieving one another in succession, involves a predominance of the homophonic style, and an extension by means of episodes rather than a thematic treatment in many parts. In this way the concerto style resembles that of the modern pianoforte sonata, and Bach's Italian concerto was undoubtedly the classical predecessor of this later form, and may even be regarded as in many respects its prototype. The modern sonata not only took from the concerto the division into three parts, but it found there the Adagio and the last movement fully developed. The first movement is however quite different in the two forms. The sonata movement being the result of a combination of the dance-form with that of the aria in three sections, it could derive nothing from the concerto but the episodic development, and even this had reached its full growth in the aria. The last step towards the attainment of the modern sonata form was not destined to be made by Sebastian Bach, although he was well acquainted with that combined form in two sections, and employed it himself in isolated cases;[262] for this step led downward at first from freedom to narrow and petty limitations; and the master can have felt little impulse in this

---

[261] Critischer Musikus, p. 637 f. Not the great, but the little, German composers strove to emulate Bach, for example, Michael Scheuenstuhl, Stadt-Organist in Hof, who in 1738 published a G minor concerto for clavier alone (Balthasar Schmidt, of Nuremberg).

[262] See Vol. II., p. 60.

direction, particularly at the time of his highest maturity. He left it for his son, Emanuel.

We know that Bach also wrote real clavier sonatas. They are not in the three-movement form, nor are they built upon that of the concerto; their style is that of the Italian violin sonata, and they are merely arrangements for the clavier of violin compositions, some his own and some by other composers.[263] It would have been very surprising if Bach had not transplanted the sonata into the realm of harpsichord music. But his fancy for this form was not of long endurance; in writing in the free style for the clavier he preferred the *Suite*. Bach is not only the last great composer of suites; he is also the greatest, the perfecter of this form in every way; after him there was nothing more to be said in the form of clavier suites, and this accounts for the rapid disappearance of that form from the practical history of the art after 1750. No fewer than twenty-three such works, comprising many movements, have come down to us entire. Of these, six form the collection known as the French suites. Three more appear, so to speak, as the supplement of these; they are very similar to them in character, and in a few MSS. two actually figure among them. One, again, full of unpretentious grace, belongs to the earliest period of Bach's maturity.[264] Here we have only to deal with the remaining thirteen, twelve of which, again, are comprised in two collections of six each.

One of these collections is known by the name of the " English suites." The name refers, even less than in the case of the French suites, to the character of the music. It would be hard to say what material for suites Bach could have found among the English. According to trustworthy tradition they were written for an Englishman of high standing.[265] As to the date of their composition, which

[263] See Vol. II., p. 77 f. and 81 ff.—I am not speaking now of the sonata in Kuhnau's style (see Vol. I., p. 243).

[264] See Vol. I., p. 432.

[265] So says Forkel (p. 56), who must have got it from Bach's sons. In Johann Christian Bach's manuscript of the English suites, above the title of the A major suite, stand the words "*fait pour les Anglois.*"

has hitherto been quite uncertain, so much may now be definitely said, that five of them must have been written, at the latest, by 1727. But apparently they were all written before 1726—*i.e.*, in the first years at Leipzig or the last at Cöthen, for the French suites are certainly older.[266] We have already considered the fundamental form of the clavier suite, its component parts, their meaning and value, and their connection with one another.[267] That Bach thought it needed no further development is evident from the fact that he adheres to it without the least change, not only in the earlier French suites, but now in the English suites, and also in the last six partitas. The four chief parts are the Allemande, Courante, Sarabande, and Gigue. Before the Gigue, came in Bourrées, Minuets, Passepieds, and Gavotte by way of *intermezzi*. The English suites are distinguished from the fanciful and beautiful French ones by their strong, grave, and masculine character. They are in the keys of A major, A minor, G minor, F major, E minor, and D minor; so that the minors preponderate. The richer style of the music demands forms of greater extension. The character of the separate pieces is sharply and distinctly marked, and their feeling intensified by richness of harmony: Bach never wrote sarabandes of such breadth and beauty, or gigues of such wild boldness.[268] In the A major suite he introduces two courantes, and, moreover, furnishes the latter, in Couperin's manner, with two *Doubles;* the sarabande of the D minor suite also has a *Double* of the same kind. These are perfect and complete variations, intended to bring out the character of the pieces they belong to; thus they have their own special place in the development of the whole. On the other hand, the pieces that follow the sarabandes of the A minor and G minor suites are not to be regarded as variations, because they do not, as it were,

---

[266] See App. A., No. 5.

[267] See Vol. II., pp. 84—92.

[268] The gigue in the D minor suite has its prototype in Buxtehude (see my edition of Buxtehude's organ compositions, I., p. 94 f.). Forkel (p. 28) quotes it as an instance of bold harmonic sequences.

deck out the piece that went before in a new musical dress, but merely adorn separate portions of the melody with embellishments.   It was the fashion at that time to embellish simple melodies in performance.   Since, however, for the most part, more was lost than was gained by this practice, Bach, following Couperin's example, wrote out the ornaments in full.   Thus it was not intended that the simple and the adorned sarabandes were to be played in succession, but it was left open to the performer to choose between the two.[269]   The *intermezzi* are in each case two in number ; they belong together, as principal subject and trio. And lastly, the character of the English suites, which strives after what is rich and grand in effect, is revealed in the preludes which are affixed to them, while in the French suites they are entirely dispensed with.   These, which at once lift the hearer into a higher and graver atmosphere, are, one and all, masterpieces of Bach's writing for the clavier.   With the exception of the prelude in A major they are planned on the grandest scale and elaborated with great variety.   The perfect aria-form in three sections is seen in the A minor prelude ; that in G minor is developed on the plan of the first movement of a concerto, and its form is also similar to that of the concerto, but is more fantastic, as is also that of the prelude in F major.   The E minor prelude may be described as a rapid and powerful fugue combined with the aria form ; the same combination is seen in the D minor prelude, but it is preceded by broad passages of broken chords, eminently characteristic of the prelude form.   The whole comprises no fewer than one hundred and ninety-five bars.[270]

The second collection forms the first part of the "Clavier-übung," which Bach himself published in 1731.   The name had been invented by Kuhnau, who in 1689 and 1695 published two works, each consisting of seven clavier suites, under the title of "Clavierübung."[271]   We drew

---

[269] In agreement with this is the fact that Johann Christian Bach left out the ornamented sarabande in his MS. of the G minor suite. The MS., No. 50, in the library of the Princess Amalia of Prussia is also without it.

[270] P. S. I., Cah. 8. (203).   B.-G., XIII.,² p. 3—86.

[271] See Vol. I., p. 237.

attention in another place to the fact that in his church compositions, and also in his earlier clavier works, Bach was influenced in several ways by Kuhnau.[272] In choosing for a collection of clavier suites the same title which had been used by his predecessor for the works that first made him famous as a composer for the clavier—in publishing works of this kind as *Opus I.*, and calling them, in contradistinction to his earlier practice, not suites, but Partitas (*Partien*) like Kuhnau—it is evident that he wished to appear before the world as Kuhnau's successor. He indeed gradually extended the scope of this modest title, which was subsequently made use of by others, such as Vicentius Lübeck, Georg Andreas Sorge, Balthasar Schmidt, Friedrich Gottlob Fleischer, and his pupil Ludwig Krebs. There appeared at Easter, 1735, a second part, containing the Italian concerto already spoken of and another partita. And about 1739 a third part appeared, with a great organ prelude and fugue, a number of organ chorales, and four clavier duets ; and finally, in 1742, the fourth part appeared, with a grand set of variations.[273] The first part, however, was published piecemeal by Bach, so that from 1726 onwards one partita appeared every year until the completion of the work in 1731. As he published it himself, and the engraver's name occurs nowhere, it is possible that Bach may have managed, or at least superintended, the engraving. This supposition receives support from the fact that his son, Emanuel, who at that time resided in his father's house, was occupied with engraving ; his first original composition, a minuet, introducing much crossing of the hands, was engraved by himself, and appeared in 1731.[274] The third part was also published by the author himself ; the other two appeared in Nuremberg, the second published by Christoph Weigel, and the fourth by Balthasar Schmidt.

---

[272] See Vol. II., pp. 369 ff. and 392 f. ; and Vol. I., pp. 236 ff., 243 ff., and 320.
[273] See App. A., No. 6.
[274] See Burney's Musical Tour, III., p. 203. (*Sic* in original ; but ?) We know about the prices from Breitkopf's Catalogue for the new year, 1760 ; Breitkopf received for the whole six partitas (the No. 5 in the Catalogue must be an error) five thalers ; and for the second partita alone, 8 gr.

At that time it was the custom to put opus-numbers to instrumental works only. The "Clavierübung" is, however, universally regarded as the first work published by Bach; the Mühlhaus "Rathswechsel-Cantate," of 1708, was printed but had not yet come out.[275] The fact that Bach only began to publish his compositions at the age of forty-one years, does not mean, of course, that he had hitherto been in any way averse to letting them become known. At that time German music was most widely disseminated by means of transcribed copies. Long before 1726 Bach had become widely known as a composer; even in 1716, in Hamburg, Mattheson spoke with admiration of his compositions for the church and also for the clavier.[276] Even later, and indeed until the beginning of the nineteenth century, the chief part of his works were only known to the musical world in a manuscript form. Besides the four parts of the "Clavierübung," only three other works by Bach appeared in his lifetime; he died as he was preparing a fourth for publication.

The name "German suites" has been given to the six suites of the "Clavierübung" in order to distinguish them from the French and English suites.[277] And not without good reason. Bach's employment of the name "Partita" implies more than a mere imitation of Kuhnau; for the form bore this name in Germany at the end of the seventeenth century, before the influence of the French had become authoritative, and Bach's returning to it showed that although he fully recognised the services rendered by French and Italian musicians to German art the groundwork was still German. The suite is a German form of art, although foreign nations have done much

---

[275] See Vol. I., p. 344.

[276] See Vol. I., p. 393.

[277] Verzeichniss aller . . . Musikalien . . . welche zu Berlin beim . . . J. C. F. Rellstab zu haben sind (1790), p. 67: "Bach, J. S., 6 Partite ou Suites francoises, 4 Thlr.

        — — 6 dito Tedesche   6 Thlr. 12 gr.

        — — 6 dito Anglaises   5 Thlr. 12 gr."

(For this information I am indebted to the kindness of Herr G. Nottebohm of Vienna.)

in assisting its development.[278] It was precisely in the use made of the foreign elements that the German spirit asserted itself most distinctly, and the fact that Bach had a full consciousness of his position with regard to his predecessors is proved by other things besides the choice of the name Partita. The six partitas in the first part of the " Clavierübung " constitute a comprehensive and self-contained work, in which all the elements that bear an important relation to the suite form receive careful and earnest attention. The wealth of structure which they exhibit is quite extraordinary; but yet the outlines of the form as a whole are strictly preserved, a fact which serves to distinguish them from the suites published by Handel in 1720, which are true to their title of Suites only in being free clavier-pieces played one after another.[279]

While in the case of the English suites the external form and arrangement is in each the same, and the invention is almost entirely confined to the treatment of the separate subjects, each partita lays before us a new series, we can hardly say of forms, but rather of artistic types. The Partita in B flat major begins with a Prelude of the kind developed by Bach, which stands as it were on the threshold of the fugal style; there is a real theme, but it is more like a passage than a melody, and its working-out has only time to begin before a section of light episodical work comes in and bears all before it. On the other hand, the partita in C minor opens with a *Sinfonia*. As the name implies, the piece is influenced by Italian art-elements. An Andante in common time, with a richly ornamented upper part, followed by a fugue in 3-4 time, was the usual opening of the Italian violin sonatas. In order, however, to prevent the resemblance to this form being too strong, so as to disturb the unity of the suite, Bach prefaces it with a broad full *Grave* movement. This is in the style of the opening of the French overtures, and thus the prelude-like character of the piece is defined and established. The A minor Partita opens with a *Fantasia*, a two-part piece in the style

---

[278] See Vol. II., p. 72 f..   [279] " *Suites de Pièces pour le Clavecin.*"

of Bach's *Inventions*, only more elaborate. The D major Partita begins with an *Ouverture* in the French style. That in G major is introduced by a *Præambulum*, which is distinguished from the Prelude of the first partita by not being thematically worked out, but consisting of passages and broken chords; as regards the grouping of its sections, it resembles a concerto movement. Lastly, the E minor Partita opens with a *Toccata;* this is considerably simpler even than the toccatas in F sharp minor and C minor;[280] it goes on in one movement without change of time; fantastic passages at the beginning and end form as it were the light husk, the kernel of which is a noble and grave fugue.

It has been remarked farther back that in the hands of the Italians the Courante acquired a special form of its own, so that at the beginning of the eighteenth century the name *Corrente* and *Courante* represented two different types.[281] From the partitas in the "Clavierübung" it appears that Bach regarded them as distinct and of equal importance, as the expression of two nationalities. The first, third, fifth, and sixth partitas have *Correntes*, the second and fourth *Courantes*.[282] The former are in 3-4 and 3-8 time, and in a smooth, rapid style, while the Courantes are impassioned, and yet solid and grave. They alone have the agitated change between two and three time. Usually in Bach the three time predominates, and the displacement of accent occurs only at the close of each section. Cases like that in the French suite in B minor and the isolated suite in E flat major, where the 6-4 time is the principal rhythm, the pure 3-2 time occurring only now and then, are only exceptional; but there the capriciousness with regard to rhythm is carried to such an extent that often the two hands are playing simultaneously in different kinds of time. In this particular the two Courantes in the partitas are in contrast to one another; in the C minor

---

[280] See Vol. II., p. 31 ff.   [281] See Vol. II., p. 85.

[282] In the later editions, and unfortunately even in the B.-G. edition, the title Courante has been given to all, against Bach's express injunction. And in other dances the important distinction which is implied by the use of Italian or French titles has not been regarded by the editors.

Courante 3-2 time predominates; and in the D major 6-4. Yet even there it is marked 3-2 in order to prevent the feeling of the two beats from becoming too strong. The time of the courante was properly neither one nor the other, but a mixture of both. It was a rule that even passages in 6-4 time were to be played in 3-2 time, that is to say that in the case of phrases which were evidently, both by their formations and natural character, in 6-4 time, the remembrance of the 3-2 time was to be kept up by means of occasional 3-2 accentuation.[283] At any rate, it was possible to give to the courante a special character of its own, according to the prominence given to this rhythm or to that, and Bach availed himself of this privilege, showing at the same time that he wished to introduce into the set of partitas all the different forms which this dance was capable of taking.

The *Gigue*, too, underwent a two-fold and divergent development, although not so decisively as in the case of the courante. In the French and German suites the fugal form generally predominated, the theme being treated in inversion in the second section. The Italian *Giga* was homophonous and consequently much lighter in character; it was always in triple time, whether simple or compound.[284] Gigues in fugal style are found in the third, fourth, fifth, and sixth partitas. That in the third (A minor) has no peculiarity in its form; in the fourth (D major) the second part contains, instead of the inversion, a new theme, which serves as counter-subject to the first; yet here the result is not an ordinary double fugue, as in the gigue in the fifth partita, which in other respects resembles it closely.[285]

---

[283] Marpurg, Kritische Briefe über die Tonkunst II., p. 26: " The proper rhythm of the Courantes in the French style, which indeed are strictly to 3-2 time, yet approaches in various places very near to the 6-4 time, in respect of the external form of the measure ; the difference is generally to be marked by playing the 6-4 passages with a 3-2 accent. The late Herr Capellmeister Bach has left us a sufficiency of genuine models of this proper Courante time.''

[284] See Vol. II., p. 89 ff.

[285] In this gigue it is remarkable that in bars 17—19 of the second part he would seem to have formed the idea of a higher compass than was contained in any clavier of that time. The chief subject ought properly to begin on e''',

The gigue in the sixth partita (in E minor) is in direct
contrast to the other three, inasmuch as it dispenses with
triple time.   Bach had already ventured to employ the
two-part *alla breve* time for the gigue, in the French Suite
in D minor.   The dance-form proper is thus abjured ; there
remains only a characteristic piece, full of energy and
passion.   This more general form, however, distilled, as it
were, from the gigue, seemed to the master worthy of being
immortalised in this place as a special type.   Undoubtedly,
too, the gigue served as a model for the last movement of
the second partita (in C minor).   It is in two sections ;
the development is fugal, and in the second part the theme
is inverted.   But both in time (2-4) and general character it
departs so far from the gigue character that Bach does not
use the name, but calls the piece *Capriccio,* as a token that
the piece was created by his own artistic volition.[286]

At the end of the first partita (in B flat major) there is
not a Gigue, but an Italian *Giga.*   The different character of
this piece, which is in a graceful rocking style, is very
obvious.   Bach even draws attention to the relation which
it bears to Italian art by means of the kind of clavier *technique*
which he employs in it.   The crossing of the hands, which
Bach first makes use of in the *Giga* of the B flat major
partita, was a specialty of Domenico Scarlatti's.[287]   That
devices of this kind were beginning to become popular in
Germany about this time is proved by Emanuel Bach's
first work, which appeared in 1731, and was written in his
father's house.   Sebastian Bach also availed himself of this
technical device in a part of the G major partita, and,
again, in the C minor fantasia, which we shall notice

---

but Bach was obliged to begin it an octave lower down.   Such cases are of
rare occurrence in his works, for, as a general rule, he accustomed himself to
keep strictly and steadily within the limits of his instrument.   Two passages of
the same kind occur in the Wohltemperirte Clavier, see Vol. II., p. 163.

[286] The arbitrary skips of tenths in the theme bear a strong resemblance to
the first movement of the Concerto in D minor for two violins.

[287] We do not indeed know that D. Scarlatti had published clavier compositions in print before 1726 ; but there is no doubt that the works of this
master, who was born in 1683, had become widely known in the musical world
by means of manuscript copies.

presently; and in the B flat major prelude, in the second part of the Wohltemperirte Clavier; it then became the fashion for a time among composers, and fell again into disuse about the middle of the century. Subsequently, Emanuel Bach was of opinion that, in many pieces of the kind, the natural position of the hands was preferable to such tricks, but that the crossed position might sometimes be a means of bringing out good and new subjects on the clavier.[288] The latter is the case with the *Giga;* the device of crossing the right hand over the left [? left over right] is not employed only here and there, but the whole piece is to be performed in the same way, and has a peculiar charm of its own.[289]

In other passages in the partitas, also, Bach paid due attention to the different characteristics of the Italian and French styles. The Italians had a tendency to obliterate the distinguishing rhythmic marks of the dance-forms. In order to do this the more effectually, Corelli often merely intimates that a certain piece is to be played in the tempo of this or that dance, and leaves himself free in all other respects. So in the E minor Partita, we find a *Tempo di Gavotta,* while in other respects the piece is more like a *Giga,* or, except for the common time, a *Corrente.* In the partitas in B flat major and D major there are *Menuets;* in that in G major a *Tempo di Minuetto,*[290] a lovely, playful piece with a charming displacement of accent, in which crossing of the hands is employed here and there; but it has nothing more in common with the *Menuet* proper than the 3-4 time. Corelli's free style of treating the *Allemande* seems also to have been noticed by Bach. While, for the most part, his Allemandes flow with extreme smoothness, that of the E minor Partita has a rugged character, which is considerably

---

[288] Versuch über die wahre Art das Clavier zu spielen, I., p. 35 f.

[289] J. A. P. Schulz remarked that this *Giga* must have been haunting Gluck when he wrote the aria *Je t'implore,* in "Iphigenia in Tauris" (see Jahn, Mozart, IV., p. 715). As Marx discovered (Gluck und die Oper I., p. 201), this aria, in essential points, is the same as one in Gluck's opera *Telemacco,* which dated from 1750. It cannot be doubted that the resemblance is no accidental one.

[290] *Minuetta* in the original edition must be a printer's error.

intensified by means of dotted semiquavers. This figure is also found, however, in Corelli's Allemandes,[291] and Bach gave the piece, not the French title, as usual, but the Italian form, *Allemanda*. The partitas contain three other short pieces with Italian titles, which bear no relation to any dance-types ; these are called *Burlesca*, *Scherzo*, and *Aria*. The first two are in the A minor and the third in the D major Partita ; they are free characteristic pieces in dance-form. To balance these there are some in the French style ; in the C minor Partita there is a *Rondeau*, and in the E minor an *Air*. A comparison of the *Air* with the *Aria* shows a distinct difference in style, the latter being more *cantabile*, while the latter is rather in instrumental style.

But even in the pieces which Bach developed independently he exhibits, within the limits of one and the same type, a variety, which perfectly corresponds to the gradual development and modifications carried out by time and nationality. In order to convince ourselves of this we have only to compare the Allemandes of the French and English suites, and afterwards those of the first five partitas. It would seem that Bach wished to test the elasticity of the form to the uttermost in these compositions. It would not be easy to find any pieces more different than the Allemandes in B flat major and D major; and yet full justice is done in each to the requirements of the type. A similar power of variation is displayed in the Sarabandes; but in this case Bach several times does really overstep the limits of the type (in the A minor, G major, and E minor Partitas).[292] Finally, regarding the six partitas as a whole, we see that the differences between them are as marked as the unity which prevails in each by itself. The surest evidence of this is afforded by the introductory pieces, which establish the character of each partita beforehand, while they stand in

---

[291] See the Allemandes on pp. 90 f., 99, 102 f., 110 f., 219 f., of J. Joachim's edition (Denkmäler der Tonkunst III.).

[292] Sarabandes beginning on the up-beat of the bar are found elsewhere only in the orchestral Partie in B minor, the Clavier Sonata in A minor, and the Violin Suite in A major.

complete contrast to one another, and a different title is intentionally given to each.

The contemporary musical world at once appreciated this precious gift. The novelty of the music itself and of the clavier *technique* excited wonder and admiration. To know them perfectly soon became the highest aim of the clavier player, and " he who had learnt to play a few of them could make his fortune."[293] That Bach's contemporaries should recognise the full value of this masterpiece of art was hardly to be expected, and, indeed, it is never confidently asserted that they did.[294] Even Sorge—although in a " dedication " he calls Bach the prince of clavier and organ-players,[295] and recommends his clavier works as models to show how to bring out a good inner part in the left hand, how to treat discords correctly in rapid passages, and how to elaborate the art of improvising—always classes him with Kuhnau, Handel, Mattheson, Walther, and others.[296] Without under-valuing these others, and especially Kuhnau, we now see clearly that the art of harpsichord composition—and that they were designed for that instrument and not for the clavichord is plain from their extensive compass—had attained to the highest conceivable point in these six partitas—a point which no one but Handel, in the suites of 1720, ever reached again. A simple comparison of the works will show that Handel here holds his own. The

---

[293] Forkel, p. 50. Mizler, in an advertisement of the " Wegweiser zu der Kunst, die Orgel recht zu schlagen " (Musikalische Bibliothek I., 5, p. 75), says : " He who cannot finger better than this, will scarcely be able to learn to play the Partitas (Partien) for the clavier by our famous Herr Bach, of Leipzig." The Partita in C minor is considered the easiest (Breitkopf's Catalogue for the New Year, 1760, p. 18 : " the easiest of all ").

[294] Forkel, who considered that " such excellent clavier compositions had never been seen or heard," is no impartial witness to the statements made by Bach's sons, even if they did really tell him that this was the general opinion of Bach's contemporaries.

[295] See his Drittes halbes Dutzend Sonatinas vors Clavier. Nuremberg ; Balthasar Schmidt. The dedication has been reprinted by Schlattener in the Monatschr. für Musikges., 1079, p. 65.

[296] Sorge, Vorgemach der musicalischen Composition. Pt. III. Lobenstein (1747), pp. 338 ff., 404, 416, 425.

difference between them is only a difference of personality;
each hearer, according to his own character, will feel greater
sympathy with the one or with the other.   Handel's suites,
in which a great artist's soul pours out its wealth in free
abundance, are more brilliant and attractive; but Bach's
partitas leave a deeper and more lasting impression, because
he adheres more strictly to the prescribed form.   Viewing
them from the high historical standpoint, Bach must bear
the palm, for he stands out, not only as an individual of
equal greatness with Handel, but as the representative of
the typical form.   Handel, with his Suites, flashed like a
comet through the heaven of art; if they had never been
written or had been lost we should have been deprived of
a brilliant apparition, but there would have been no gap
in the system of co-operating influences.   Bach's partitas
may be called a light-focus, in which alone we see the
brilliancy that might be attained by concentrating the rays
of all the smaller luminaries.[297]

To the cursory observer it might appear surprising that
after Bach had, in the six partitas, said all that was to be
expressed in the suite form, he should return to it in the
second part of the " Clavierübung."   This contains, besides
the before-mentioned Italian concerto, another partita (in
B minor).[298]   But here his purpose was quite different.
He meant to write, not a new clavier suite, but a piece
which should be, as it were, a transference of the orchestral
Partie to the clavier.   The difference between the two
forms has already been discussed.[299]   Bach's intention
betrays itself even in the title " *Ouverture* "; for it was usual
to give the name to the orchestral *Partie* from its opening
piece.   The arrangement of the movements leaves no doubt
of his intention.   There is no Allemande, because, being exclusively a form of clavier music, it had no place in the orchestral

---

[297] Of the editions of the first part of the " Clavierübung," I will only mention
two in this place—viz., P. S. I., Cah. 5 (205, 206), and B.-G., III., p. 46—136.

[298] P. S. I., Cah. 6, No. 2 (208).   B.-G., III., p. 154—170.   A MS. made by Anna
Magdalena Bach, which is preserved in the Royal Library at Berlin, gives
the piece in C minor.   See App. A. to Vol. II., No. 44.

[299] See Vol. II., p. 140 ff.

suite. The Courante, the Sarabande, and the Gigue are all
there, but before the Sarabande are inserted two Gavottes
and two Passepieds, and after it two Bourrées—a series so
numerous that they cannot be called *Intermezzi*, but must
claim to be of equal importance with the other movements.
It was the special privilege of the orchestral suite that it
might have an irregular and arbitrary number of dances,
and this treatment is carried on even beyond the Gigue.
Bach has finished his orchestral suite in B minor with a
Badinerie, and one of the two in D major with a *Réjouissance*.
In this case an *Echo* closes the series; it is in a dance form,
without exhibiting any definite type. It takes its name from
certain imitations of the effect of an echo, which are
especially charming from the fact that the phrases are not
repeated exactly, but with soft, supplementary passing notes,
as if the sound became indistinct in the distant repetition,
as, for instance :—

Bach, of course, had no intention of imitating the orchestral style on the clavier. This would indeed have been
superfluous, for there was so much of his clavier style
in his compositions for the orchestra that when the orchestra
form was transferred to the clavier it prospered quite
naturally. He only requires the hearer to approach this
work in the same frame of mind as that in which he would
listen to an orchestral suite ; just as the Italian concerto
can only have its full effect upon one who knows what
a real concerto of that time was like. Both works have
some intrinsic connection, which may explain why Bach
chose to unite them into a part of the Clavierübung by
themselves. They are reflections on the surface, as it were,
of clavier music, of forms which were invented for a number
of different instruments. An outward bond of union between
them is that, for the proper performance of both, a
harpsichord with two manuals was requisite. As regards
the character of the separate sections of this partita, the
nature of the original model is plainly perceptible. It is

easiest to recognise in the Gigue—for so it must be called, and not a *Giga*—yet how entirely does it differ from the Gigue of the clavier partitas proper and of the English suites. Even those of the French suites are more complicated in their form. The orchestral *partie* adhered more closely than the clavier *partita* to a simple and popular style of Gigue. This is very marked in the Gigue now under notice; it is simpler and more intelligible than even the Gigue of the second French suite, to which it has a strong resemblance in other respects. And the first Bourrée and the second Gavotte have a blunt simplicity about them, which is evidently intentional. Where richer materials are employed there yet remains in the melodies a popular character which is not found in the real clavier partitas. The beautiful and impassioned Sarabande alone seems to look down from inspired heights at the artless gambols of the other pieces.[300]

Bach also wrote three partitas for the lute, which may be briefly mentioned in this place.[301] Under the express title of a composition for the lute we have only one work, in three movements (in E flat major), by him, which however we may regard as a part of the same collection.[302] Strictly speaking, indeed, it is not a partita, but a sonata without a second Adagio and with a prelude in the place of the first. Yet it might pass under this name among other more genuine partitas, provided that Bach really gave it its title. Possibly too the E minor suite, which we have already mentioned in connection with the French suites, may have belonged to the

---

[300] In this place, while referring to Bach's treatment of rhythms and the views of art revealed in it, I might go farther and fulfil a promise half made in Vol. II., p. 175, note 251. But since writing that note, Rudolf Westphal has made renewed researches into the subject, which are shortly to be given to the public, and I believe that their appearance will exempt me from the fulfilment of my promise.

[301] Breitkopf's Michaelmas catalogue, 1761, p. 56: "*Bach, J. S., Direttore della Musica in Lipsia, III. Partite à Liuto solo. Raccolta I.* 2 thlr."

[302] "*Prelude pour le Luth ou Cembal.*" P. S. I., Cah. 3, No. 4. The autograph is in the possession of Henry Huth, Esq., London. There is an independent prelude for lute or clavier transmitted to us by J. P. Kellner, see P. S. I., Cah. 9, No. 16 (200), III.

collection;[303] the low compass within which it is confined makes this supposition very probable.[304]   Bach frequently employed the lute in concerted vocal composition, as, for instance, in the St. John Passion and the Trauerode, and he himself possessed one among his numerous instruments.   It does not follow from this that he played it himself.   The fact of his possessing one is explained when we remember that Bach had an idea of combining the lute with the harpsichord; the result of this was the "Lautenclavicymbel," which Hildebrand was commissioned to build on Bach's own plan in 1740, and of which Bach possessed two specimens.[305] It is possible that the lute-partitas may have been written expressly for this instrument, just as he tested the powers of his *Viola pomposa* by means of a special suite;[306] but he may have been incited to composition for the lute by his intimacy with the Dresden band, which numbered among its members Sylvius Leopold Weiss, the first lute player of his time.[307]   He may also have been personally acquainted with Ernst Gottlieb Baron, who speaks of Bach with admiration.[308]

In the two-part inventions Bach had created a form altogether new to the time.   He proved that he laid great stress on this form by placing four clavier pieces in the form of inventions at the close of the third part of the "Clavierübung," which was intended to contain only organ music.[309] In this case he calls them duets, thus drawing attention to their two-part writing.   All that has previously been said of the Inventions[310] holds good of these, and they are written with the obvious intention of showing that it was possible to display the greatest harmonic richness with perfect distinctness even within the limits of a

---

[303] See Vol. II., p. 160.

[304] Observed before by F. A. Roitzsch, see the preface, P. S. I., Cah. 3, No. 8.

[305] See Vol. II., p. 46 f., and Appendix B, xiv., cap. vi. ?

[306] See Vol. II., p. 100.

[307] Fürstenau, Zur Geschichte der Musik am Sächsischen Hofe, II., p. 126 f.

[308] Baron, Untersuchung des Instruments der Lauten. Nuremburg, 1727, p. 126 f.

[309] P. S. I., Cah. 4, No. 11 (208).   B.-G. III., p. 242—253.

[310] See Vol. II., p. 55 ff.

clavier piece in two parts. In this respect they are really wonderful; but they are not to be regarded as models of strict writing. On the contrary, Bach has made free use of all the license which the "harmonic" system afforded, especially in the use of the interval of the fourth, although Kirnberger was probably justified in asserting that Bach considered the fourth not to be a correct interval in two-part writing.[311] The remark that it is characteristic of these duets that they admit of no third part[312] is obviously beside the mark. For if they are works of art at all they must be capable of expressing all that the composer wished to express, without further filling up. The duets have always been received with surprise rather than with enthusiasm, and this is partly to be understood. The capricious duet in E minor and the more cheerful one in G major are intelligible as continuations of the Inventions; the other two, however, leave behind them an impression that the enormous wealth of harmony, the severity of the ideas and the length of the working-out, are not quite proportionate to the poverty of the material which represents them. They are compositions for those who are connoisseurs of such things, who delight in realising the full harmonic sequences in the bare outlines; they must always be "caviare to the general." The A minor duet looks like a two-part fugue, but the freely-treated sections preponderate to such an extent that it can only be called an elaborate Invention. The theme is capable of an extraordinary variety of harmonies, and notwithstanding all the limitation of means we feel in this duet the free movement of a creative spirit. On the other hand, in the middle section of the F major duet, it is very hard to get rid of a strong scholastic character which pervades it.

Just as the suite-form attains its ultimate development in the partitas, the violin concerto in the Italian concerto, and the invention in the duets, so the ultimate development of the variation form is reached in the fourth part of Bach's

---

[311] See Marpurg, Kirtische Briefe, I., p. 183.
[312] Forkel, p. 51.

" Clavierübung." This part contains an aria with thirty variations for a harpsichord with two manuals.[313] The circumstances which led to the composition of this work will be related presently; here we have only to do with the music itself. The *Variation*, as the oldest form of independent instrumental music, exercised the most diverse influences upon the musical organisms which arose in the sixteenth and seventeenth centuries; on the clavier suite and the chorale arrangement, on the sonata and on music for the violin, but its principal sphere was that of the keyed instruments. The singular manner in which it grew for a long period simultaneously with the suite has been shown before.[314] The chorale variations, or chorale partitas properly so called, flourished however when the difference between clavier and organ music was not sufficiently appreciated. The variation form—*i.e.*, an artistic entity consisting of a theme and a set of alterations or variations upon it—did not belong to the church; and this not only because there was no place for it in divine service, but because it would impair the solemn effect of the chorale melody. Hence it became gradually defined as a form of clavier music, but as such, in spite of its great historical significance, it had few attractions for a man like Bach. Inventive power could only be displayed either in the general outline, in the order of the different variations, or in the finest details of ornamentation. No thorough working out of the theme lay within the scope of a single variation. As regards the extent of the variation, it was strictly confined to the limits of the theme, while the alteration of the theme must consist exclusively of surrounding ornamentation, so that the sequence of harmonies had to remain essentially the same throughout. All this gone, the form had a superficial character, antagonistic to depth and scientific elaboration. It is a significant fact that the variations of Sweelinck, Frescobaldi, or Cornet have the strongest family likeness to those of Mozart, written two hundred years afterwards.

---

[313] P. S. I., Cah. 6, No. 3 (209). B.-G. III., p. 263 ff. The copies of the original edition were sold by Breitkopf in the year 1763 for 2 thlr. 8 gr.

[314] See Vol. II., pp. 74 and 77.

Setting aside Bach's earliest chorale partitas, in which he imitated Böhm, he wrote only one set of variations in the usual style, the variations *alla maniera Italiana*, which we believed ourselves warranted in assigning to the Weimar period.

But he perceived that there existed a kindred form in which the limited and monotonous style of the variation could be avoided. This was the Passacaglio or the Chaconne. The quality which it has in common with the variation is that it consists of a certain number of bars which must remain the same at every repetition, and that the sequence of harmonies must be essentially the same. In practice the Passacaglio or Chaconne is very often confounded with the Variation, the one form passing into the other. The rule that the bass theme is to remain unchanged throughout was not always strictly adhered to; its position and even its notes were altered, and it was resolved into figures; and frequently there was no bass theme at all, but only a number of phrases of four bars each, strung together in the same rhythm, and in triple time.[315] After this Handel tried to combine the Chaconne and the Variation by retaining the upper part throughout as the theme of the variations, supported at first by the bass.[316] Now if a theme in song-form of two sections be given out in the regular way, adhering exactly in the variations, not to the melody but to its bass, then on the one hand the strictly enclosed form of the Chaconne (which consists of either four or eight bars) is enlarged in the best possible way, while on the other hand opportunity is left for the most various combinations in the sphere of the variation form. This is exactly what Bach did.

For the theme he employs a sarabande, which is to be found in the larger clavier book belonging to his wife; it is in her handwriting.[317] As its place in that book is before

---

[315] See the Chaconne and Passacaglio in George Muffat's *Apparatus Musico-Organisticus*.

[316] In the G major Chaconne. Handel Society's edition II., pp. 110—122; Peters, 4 c.

[317] Pp. 76 and 77. It comes between the two divisions of the hymn tune " Bistu bey mir "; she turned over two pages together by mistake, and then

that of the aria " Schlummert ein, ihr matten Augen," from the cantata " Ich habe genug," it is older than that, and must have been written ten years when Bach made it the central point of his great set of variations.[318] It must certainly have been originally written for Anna Magdalena. In giving it this new form he was probably influenced by special motives of a personal kind, with which we are not acquainted; something of this kind may be surmised in the Quodlibet which forms the last variation. If Bach had written the sarabande especially for the variations he would have allowed the bass to be played through quite simply, since the chief part falls to its share, instead of decorating it with passing notes, subsidiary notes, and ornaments, which tend to obscure its outlines. It is most plainly heard in the thirtieth variation, where it runs thus, in the original time:—[319]

When speaking of a set of variations by Johann Christoph Bach, it was remarked that Sebastian may have known of it, because his own variations remind one of it here and there.[320] It is worth noticing that the theme of that set is also a sarabande in G major.

Bach treats the bass of the theme for the most part in Passacaglio style, making it the basis of the harmony even in the variations. As a rule, it comes in to mark the first note of the whole or the half bar. In certain cases it springs up or down an octave, according to the

---

filled up the space with the clavier piece. There is no title; the name *Aria* was not given until Bach used it for variations.

[318] See Vol. II., p. 473 f.

[319] The fundamental form of the first half is given by Kirnberger. Kunst des reinen Satzes II., 2, p. 172 f.

[320] See Vol. I., 128.

requirements of the movement of the piece; but it seldom departs from its course, although here and there a chromatic alteration is found. Sometimes it goes into the inner or upper part in the style of a chaconne, for instance, in variations 18 and 25, but in such a manner that it is always perceptible as the prominent part, and does not remain long in its altered position. The plan of working-out is so consistently adhered to that even in the minor variation 25 the complete bass appears in the major. This is effected by chromatic treatment, which involves very bold and strange harmonic sequences. He had indeed to break through the rule that the significant note of the bass part should always come in at the beginning of the bar. Once, in bar 4 of the second part, he uses *c'* sharp instead of *b;* in bars 9—11 of the first part the bass appears in the tenor register; and in bars 7 and 8 of the second part *b e'* is put for *b* flat *e'* flat.

Above this bass Bach exhibits such a wealth of invention and ingenuity that this work alone would be sufficient to make him immortal. His clavier technique is displayed in its most brilliant light, and in quite a new way, in consequence of the freest and most productive use of the two manuals. Free ideas alternate with those in strict style, clear and almost homophonous sections with polyphonic forms of the greatest possible ingenuity. Thus variation 7 exhibits a gigue, variation 16 a complete overture, variation 25 a richly ornamented Adagio in the style of a violin sonata, variation 26 a sarabande alternately in the left hand and the right, while the other hand plays rapid passages of sextolets of semiquavers. Variation 10 is a fughetta, the theme of which is derived from the ground bass, and which follows the course of the bass up to the end, notwithstanding that its development is perfectly regular. Canons are introduced on every interval, from that of the second to that of the ninth; that on the fifth is in inversion, and moreover its commencement, like that of the canon on the second, is derived from the bass of the theme by diminution. The last variation is a Quodlibet in which two popular songs are combined and worked out in imitation above the bass. And all this is without a trace of constraint. The hardest chains become wreaths of flowers; the whole result is gay and easy, the few variations that are in the minor serving only to intensify the effect of the pervading ground-tone of contentedness.

The question that now presents itself is what part is left to the melody in this elaborate extension of the variation-form. The musical motive of the whole is not the melody but its bass, and the harmonies evolved from it form a framework in which new forms are generated. And yet the effect of the melody is not lost. Setting aside the fact that it fills the hearer with a certain characteristic feeling which serves as a clue to all the variations and accounts for the various changes, it remains as the general design, so to speak, invisible yet everywhere present. The course of harmony which remains in all essential features the same in all the variations, together with separate reminiscences of the melody scattered throughout the work, assists the mental ear in calling up again the outlines of the melody. And indeed the full enjoyment of the variations is dependent upon this. A stronger and more conscious effort is demanded of the hearer in these than in ordinary variations; he must, as it were, project the outlines of the melody into each new musical form; this work is written for cultured hearers or connoisseurs.

The reader who recalls the nature and character of the chorale cantata, as we have described it,[321] will not overlook the near affinity which exists between that form and this set of variations. In both the full melody in its simple form constitutes the end and ultimate goal of the work, in both there are suggestive reminiscences of it in the intermediate sections, and, just as here the bass and the harmony remain essentially the same throughout, so there unceasing reference is made to the hymn which is the basis of the work, though lightly veiled under the madrigal form. This is Bach's contribution to the variation-form, which was an element of the first rank in the development of instrumental music. He

---

[321] See above, pp. 105-6.

lifted it into a high ideal region, giving it an intellectual and inspired form, which, on the incomparably higher level to which Bach had raised instrumental music, was once more worthy of the attention of the most earnest musicians. Although in later times the older variation form has continued to flourish, just because its relations with the origin of instrumental music were of so close a kind, and has borne new fruit in the shape of many delightful creations, yet the best musicians, even down to the latest times, have recognised in Bach's thirty variations the highest model of the form.

We must now return to the Quodlibet which forms the last variation. Musical diversions of this kind, in which even words in different languages were sometimes mixed up, might be performed in two ways. Either a number of well known melodies were sung or played one after another, so that those tunes which had the least inward connection were brought into juxtaposition; if each could be strung on to some unimportant phrase of the words or the music of the preceding one, the joke was all the better. The other method consisted of performing simultaneously several well known melodies with the most incongruous words. This last and more ingenious method was the one chosen by Bach. The words of the two popular songs used are handed down by his pupil Kittel.[322] They run thus:—

Ich bin so lang nicht bei dir gewest,	I long have been away from thee,
Ruck her, ruck her, ruck her;	I'm here, I'm here, I'm here,
Mit einem tumpfen[323] Flederwisch	With such a dull and dowdy prude
Drüber her, drüber her, drüber her.	Out there, out there, out there.

and

Kraut und Rüben	Kail and turnips
Haben mich vertrieben;	Don't suit my digestion;
Hätt mein' Mutter Fleisch gekocht,	If my mother cooked some meat
So wär ich länger blieben.	I'd stay here without question.

---

[322] The information comes to us through Pölchau, who inserted a note to this effect in his copy of the original edition of the variations. This copy is in the Royal Library at Berlin.

[323] Dialect for " Stumpfen."

The melody of the second song, which is sung by the people to this day, is used by Bach in its entirety:—

The lines of the tunes in that Quodlibet were frequently torn from their proper connection and used in fragments, just as it suited. So here the first two bars of the tune are found in the upper part in bars 3 and 4, the last two in the tenor part, bars 7 and 8, and in the upper part at the end; besides this the two first bars are worked out through the whole piece in imitation in the three upper parts. Only the first half of the first tune can be reconstructed from this Quodlibet. It runs thus:—

So far as I have been able to find, this tune is now extinct; the well known tune " Es ist nicht lang, dass g'regnet hat " is identical in metrical structure and almost so in the beginning of the melody. Nor do I find it mentioned in any of the numerous collections of popular songs which have appeared since Herder's time. Only the first line is carefully worked through in its exact form. The second is seen, but not clearly, in bar 2 of the tenor part, but seems not to occur again unless it may be alluded to in bar 10 of the bass part. Of the remaining lines the rhythm alone is employed, especially that of line 3:—

(Tenor, bars 3—4),

(upper part, bars 5—6),

(upper part, bars 8—11).

The fourth line is alluded to in the rhythm of the bass in bars 4—5 :—

and of the upper part in bars 11—12 :—

The Quodlibet formed from these elements is an extraordinary performance, on account of its ingenious construction, but it has a higher interest as throwing light on Bach's artistic personality. In the realm of church music he drew his chief strength from the sacred popular song; and here he shows his intimate sympathy with the secular popular song. For this is the only supposition which can explain his adding such a close to a work on which he had expended his highest ability. This is clearly a trace of that old family spirit of the Bachs, which displayed itself in somewhat rude merriment on the family birthdays, by singing Quodlibets of this kind.[324]

We possess, however, yet another piece of documentary evidence of Bach's interest in popular vocal music, which we will consider, for this reason, here, although as a vocal composition it ought to have been mentioned in another place. On the 30th of August, 1742, the chamberlain (Kammerherr) Carl Heinrich von Dieskau received allegiance as Lord of the Manor (Gutsherr) of Kleinzschocher.[325] As Provost of the district he was inspector of the land, liquor, and income taxes, and of the quarterly tax.[326] We have already seen that in 1743 Picander held the post of receiver of the land and liquor taxes.[327] Whether he was anxious to retain the situation, or to express his thanks to the authorities for allowing him to retain it, his making a *Cantate en burlesque* for the occasion evidently has some

---

[324] See Vol. I., p. 153.

[325] Schwartze, Historische Nachlese zu denen Geschichten der Stadt Leipzig. 1744, p. 231.

[326] See " Das jetzt lebende und *florirende* Leipzig." Years 1736 and 1746.

[327] See Vol. II., p. 340.

connection with the circumstances. The subject of his poetry
was taken from peasant life at Kleinzschocher. He begins
with a chorus sung in the dialect of Upper Saxony, by
peasants who are rejoicing in the holiday which has been
granted them.[328]   After this a couple of peasant sweethearts
are brought in, who praise the new lord of the manor and
his wife, and then make sundry allusions to the receiver
of taxes, to the conscription of recruits, to " Herr Ludwig
and the tax reviser," and end by going into the inn to dance
and make merry.   As the upper classes at that time were
surfeited with French and Italian theatrical representations,
they were naturally pleased, if only for the sake of the
contrast, with a German peasant *Divertissement*.   Not,
however, the representation of healthy, uncultured humanity,
such as was afterwards made the groundwork of Christian
Felix Weisse's opera librettos; they preferred to regard
themselves as cultured and fashionable rulers, governing
an oppressed and unmannerly peasantry.   *Divertissements*
of this kind were got up, not only at the luxurious court
of Dresden, but also in the more simple and sober Weimar,
and in other places.[329]   Picander's burlesque cantata is a
work of this kind.

We need not be surprised that Bach should have felt
impelled to set it to music.   He probably left the ethical
side of the affair quite out of the question ; it gave him
evident pleasure, for once, to compose a secular work in a
popular style almost throughout.   The aristocratic element
appears only in two arias ("Klein Zschocher müsse " and
"Dein Wachsthum sei feste "), the second of which is
taken, not without some violence, from the " Streit zwischen
Phöbus und Pan."   All the rest is confined within the
narrow limits of popular forms.   There is no chorus ; the
first number and the last are only duets, between which the
peasant and his sweetheart alternately sing recitatives and
arias.   The instrumental accompaniment is in the style of a

---

[328] The rest of the poetry is free from dialect, but several provincial ex-
pressions occur, such as Guschel for Mund, Dahlen for Kosen, &c.

[329] See Vol. I., p. 228, note 69.   Fürstenau, Geschichte der Musik am Hofe
zu Dresden.   II., p. 158 f.

village orchestra, consisting only of violin, viola, and bass; a horn is introduced in one passage, but for a special reason. The first number is preceded by an instrumental movement. This is a Quodlibet consisting of seven tunes put together. It begins with a waltz which, however, is not heard in its entirety until the end; on its first appearance it breaks off after seven bars, to make way for a variety of short movements in different rhythms and rates of speed. Many of these sound like genuine popular melodies, especially in this case :—

In the middle occur sixteen bars in sarabande rhythm, the solemnity of which is rendered doubly effective by the use of the unison.   Dance tunes predominate even in the vocal portions of the work.   The opening and closing numbers are bourrées, and the arias " Ach es schmeckt doch gar zu gut " and " Ach Herr Schösser " are polonaises.   On Kirnberger's authority, who lived long in Poland and studied the dance music of the country, the aria " Fünfzig Thaler baares Geld " must be regarded as a mazurka.[330]   The aria " Unser trefflicher " is a sarabande, and the song " Und dass ihrs alle wisst " is a Rüpeltanz (or *Paysanne*).[331]   No distinct type can be recognised in the aria " Das ist galant," but the general character is that of a dance.   All these pieces are short, rough, and merry, but ingeniously worked out ;' witness the delicate way in which in the sarabande the chief subject recurs again and again, yet always in the bass, or in the " Rüpeltanz," the representation of intoxication in the displacements of accent.   The melodic forms are so

---

[330] See Marpurg's Kritische Briefe, II., p. 45.   The words of this song, which in Bach's work vary slightly from those given in Picander (see his Poems, Part V., p. 285), seem to refer to editions made on the occasion of paying allegiance to the lord of the manor.

[331] See Gregorio Lambranzi, Neue und Curieuse Theatralische Tantz-Schul. Nuremberg, 1716, Pt. I., fol. 4.   The words of the *Paysanne* have a genuine rollicking humour about them, and are decidedly too good for Picander.   It seems to me that he has made use of some student song or other, for he was very apt to turn the ideas of other poets to account.

thoroughly popular in style that we may suppose that here and there certain well known melodies must have been running in the composer's head. The supposition receives support from the fact that three popular melodies are used consciously and confessedly in the cantata.

After that, the sweetheart having sung the praises of the new governor in a " genteel " aria, the peasant says, " That is too fine for me, and more fit for the town, we peasants don't sing so softly as that. Listen to the sort of thing that suits me :—

> Ten thousand golden ducats
> Go to the chamberlain every day,
> He drinks his glass of good old wine,
> And on it he flourishes fair and fine.
> Ten thousand golden ducats
> Go to the chamberlain every day.

The melody to which he sings these words is still in popular use in Germany, to the words " Frisch auf zum fröhlichen Jagen." At the time when Bach composed this peasant cantata both the words and the tune had been popular for about eighteen years. The words were written by Gottfried Benjamin Hanke, a Silesian, who lived in Dresden as Clerk of Excise. He wrote them in 1724 for the feast of St. Hubert, for Count Sporck, who was very fond of hunting. The tune is of French origin and belongs to the hunting song " Pour aller à la chasse faut être matineux," which seems also to have served Hanke as a model for his song.[332] About 1730 it was very popular in the Count's dominions in Bohemia, and must have become widely and quickly known in Saxony, if in 1742 it could be called a peasant's tune. It is interesting to notice another

---

[332] See Gottfried Benjamin Hanke's Weltliche Gedichte. Dresden and Leipzig, 1727, p. 144. Poetischer Staar-Stecker, In welchem sowohl Die schlesische Poesie überhaupt, als auch Der Herr v. Lohenstein . . . verthaydiget . . . wird. Breslau and Leipzig, 1730, p. 30. For the information as to its origin we are indebted to Hoffmann von Fallersleben ; see his *Horæ Belgicæ. Pars secunda. Vratislaviæ.* MDCCCXXXIII., p. 100. The words originally began " Auf, auf auf, auf zum Jagen ! Auf in die grüne Heyd !" and numbered twelve verses. In newer collections it is reduced to six verses, and altered in other details. The tune is found in Erk and Irmer, Die deutschen Volkslieder mit ihren Singweisen. Leipzig, 1843. Book I., p. 47.

appearance of Count Sporck in the history of Bach's life. It will be remembered that he was connected with the B minor mass, and that in 1725 Picander dedicated to him the first fruits of his religious poetry.[333] Both the composer and the librettist had a special purpose in introducing the melody; we can now understand why, in this piece alone, a horn should be introduced, there being no opportunity for its use in Picander's words.

The girl replies in a parody of her lover's song as being too "tuneful," and saying that it would make the gentlefolks laugh as much as if she were to sing an old tune—then follows the second popular melody :—

She sings this to words which express hope of a numerous male offspring of the house of Dieskau, which hitherto has been blessed only by daughters. From the character of the tune it may be assumed that it belongs properly to some lullaby or child's song.[334]

A third popular melody is used as an interlude in the first recitative. Its first half comes at the end, and its second half in the middle. When put together and set in the same key, the result is as follows :—

It is evident that the first half is essentially the same as the first half of the tune "Ich bin so lang nicht bei dir gewest," from the Quodlibet in the variations. In that place Bach employed only the rhythm of the second half; we may be certain that this is its original form, for if we compare the words of the recitative in the passage where the interludes (consisting of parts of this tune) occur, with the words in

---

[333] See ante, p. 43.

[334] I have not succeeded in finding any older source of the melody and its original words. Possibly the researches of Herr L. Erk or Herr F. M. Böhme have been more successful.

the popular song which correspond to those parts, a strict connection displays itself in the poetic idea. The ideas suggested in the recitative are expressed in each interlude, and especially in the passage where the first interlude occurs, the wishes of the lovers are explained very plainly. If we assume the composition of the variations and of the peasant cantata to have taken place at the same period, it is easy to understand that it might occur to Bach to bring the same melody into the peasant cantata, as it is of rather later date than the variations.[335]

After this digression, into which we were led by the subject of the Quodlibet in the thirty variations, we return to Bach's clavier compositions, and to the consideration of the fugal works and canons of his later life. And first the Chromatic Fantasia and Fugue. This celebrated work must have been written, at the latest, in 1730,[336] and internal evidence convinces us that it must be assigned to a considerably earlier date; the Fantasia bears a perceptible resemblance to the piece of the same name which precedes the great organ fugue in G minor.[377] This was written before 1725, and we found reason for connecting it with Bach's journey to Hamburg in 1720. Thus it is quite possible, and even probable, when we take into consideration another and an older form of the work which still exists, that the Chromatic Fantasia and Fugue may also date from before the Leipzig period. The effervescent character which pervades both pieces is not in the spirit of the Leipzig productions; and even in his fantasias Bach is not wont to dispense with strict forms, developed either thematically or episodically. Here all is uncontrolled "storm and stress."

---

[335] Compare Appendix A., No. 6. The peasant cantata was first published by Gustav Crantz of Berlin, edited by S. W. Dehn. A second edition appeared published by C. A. Klemm of Leipzig. In 1879 it appeared in the B.-G. edition, xxix., p. 175. There is a tradition, which may be mentioned here, that Bach was the composer of a comic song which was very widely known about the middle of the century, entitled "Ihr Schönen, höret an." I myself do not believe the tune to be by Bach, but I cannot do more than simply state my opinion in this place, leaving the subject, which would branch off into all kinds of different questions, for discussion elsewhere.

[336] P. S. I., ch. 4, No. 1 (207). See App. A., No. 7.

[337] See Vol. II., p. 23 ff.

The bold idea of transplanting the recitative into a clavier-piece had already been embodied in Bach's earlier fantasia in D major ;[338] its germ is found in the works of the northern organists, and its development was assisted by Bach's intimacy with Vivaldi's violin concertos.[339] In the Chromatic Fantasia this idea attained a grand perfection. The piece, in which the boldest feats of modulation are crowded together, has the effect of an emotional *scena*. The fugue worthily carries out the chromatic character and the startling modulations of the piece, and the treatment of the fugue is full of genius, with a mighty demoniacal rush.

Bach wrote another fantasia with a fugue (in C minor) about the year 1738. In composing this work he seems to have been guided by the idea of bringing the technical resource of crossing the hands to bear upon larger forms than those to which it had been applied in the B flat major Partita. As the fantasia is in two sections with repeats—a form nowhere else employed by Bach in pieces of this name—it may be supposed that he was influenced in adopting it by Domenico Scarlatti; and it is interesting to observe the character which the Italian composer's style acquires in Bach's hands. This energetic and brilliant piece is, moreover, the forerunner of Emanuel Bach's sonata form. Bach has only left us the first forty-seven bars of the fugue. We may assume that he finished it, for the autograph is not a sketch, but a fair copy. He must have been prevented by some mischance from writing it out in its entirety. This is doubly to be lamented, since, to judge from the fragment that remains, the fugue must have been a work of especial boldness, and designed on a grand scale.[340]

---

[338] See Vol. I., p. 437.

[339] One of Vivaldi's concertos, which Bach arranged for the organ, has an Adagio in the style of a recitative. See P. S. V., Cah. 8 (247), No. 3 ; and Vol. I., p. 414.

[340] The autograph was discovered in 1876 by Moritz Fürstenau, of Dresden, and it belongs to the musical collection of the King of Saxony. It bears the same watermark as the Easter oratorio : see App. A., of Vol. II., No. 58. Forkel and Griepenkerl have been unfortunate in judging of the work, for they consider that the fugue did not originally belong to the fantasia and that only the first twenty-nine or thirty bars are authentic. Both these opinions are proved false

The irregular proportions which are apparent between the fugue and the fantasia, which in many cases has the character of a prelude, are found in many preludes and fugues of this period. We shall return to this presently.

A third fantasia, with a (double) fugue, is in A minor. By way of fantasia, we have a piece in imitation in strict style. The work has an elevated and steady glow of feeling, and is in every respect so pure and mature in style that it may well have been written in the beginning of the Leipzig period.[341]

Of the many characteristic pieces in fugue form which yet remain to be considered, the most important is a collection which forms a counterpart to the Wohltemperirte Clavier, and, indeed, is known as the second division of that work. Taken in its strict sense, the title conveys a false impression, and it is not at all certain that Bach gave it that title. The loving interest taken by Bach in the first part, and shown in his having transcribed it at least three times, was not bestowed upon its younger brother. We do not possess a single transcript of the second part made by the composer; indeed, there is hardly more than one complete copy in existence.[342] It was certainly finished in 1744; nay, if we may trust one piece of evidence, as early as 1740.[343] I called it a collection. The long-cherished and popular notion that it was only in the first part that Bach incorporated older compositions is certainly an error.

---

by the autograph. Griepenkerl, moreover, believes that the fantasia was written in 1725. See Forkel, p. 56, and Griepenkerl, in the preface to P. S. I., Cah. 9, where both are published—the fantasia as No. 7 (207), and the fugue as No. 18 (212).

[341] The autograph is wanting. Published in P. S. I., Cah. 4, No. 6 (208).

[342] Only one autograph, and that of the A flat major fugue, is at present known. It is in the Royal Library at Berlin. Fragments of a valuable MS. of equal date with this are in the possession of Professor Wagener, of Marburg. They have until now been mistaken for autographs; Kroll even considered them as such (see B.-G. XIV., P. xviii., No. 14A). The rest of this MS. was discovered by Fürstenau in 1876, in the musical collection of the King of Saxony. This makes the MS. complete, with the exception of the prelude and fugue in G major and the fugue in B major.

[343] Schwencke's MS., in the Royal Library at Berlin, gives the date as 1744 (see B.-G. XIV., p. xvi., No. 11). Hilgenfeldt (p. 123) must have had in his hands an autograph, with the date 1740, which was part of Emanuel Bach's bequest.

The C major prelude existed long before 1740. In its original form it contained only seventeen bars, and the fugue was entitled *fughetta*. The prelude was afterwards extended to thirty-four bars; but it did not receive its ultimate form until its third revision.[344]

The G major fugue has also undergone several changes. It was originally in a shorter form, coupled with another prelude, and its counterpoint was of so simple a kind that it must be assigned to the very earliest years of the Weimar period. The next step was to change the prelude, but the new one was not yet the same as that in the " Wohltemperirte Clavier." The fugue itself remained for a time unchanged. Finally, it was revised for the collection, and associated with a third prelude.[345]

The A flat fugue was originally in F major, and only half its present length; it also had another prelude.[346]

The C sharp prelude also bears evident traces of having been an older work, only used again in the Wohltemperirte Clavier. Apparently it was a piece by itself, for the first half alone is in the manner of a prelude, the second being a fughetta of a light and transitory character, it is true, but yet perfectly worked out. It was originally in C major; and its prelude-like portion was so nearly allied to the C major prelude of the first part of the book that Bach could not use it in its original key.[347] But all of the second

---

[344] The prelude appears as a piece of seventeen bars in a clavier book of J. P. Kellner's, bearing the date " 3 Juli, 1726," belonging to Herr Roitzsch, of Leipzig, of which Kroll did not know the existence. Fürstenau's MS. contains it in its second form, together with those numbered 2, 3, 9, 16, and 18 in Kroll, which appear to be connected with it.

[345] The fugue in its original form and the two accompanying preludes are edited by Roitzsch in P. S. I., Cah. 3, Nos. 10 and 11 (214). Of the preludes the second is particularly fine, but it must have appeared too important for the fugue. The first of the two is also given, together with the fugue, by Kellner in the book above mentioned.

[346] P. S. I., Cah. 3, No. 9 (214), and introduction to it.

[347] A MS. of Johann Christoph Bach's still exhibits it in C major. This son of Sebastian was born in 1732; the piece must, therefore, have continued to exist in its old key after the completion of the second part of the Wohltemperirte Clavier, for before its completion the prelude cannot possibly have been written out by Johann Christoph. See B.-G., XIV., p. 243.

part of the Wohltemperirte Clavier that belongs to a later
period must be regarded as having been composed, not so
much with a view to writing a new work to consist of twenty-
four preludes and fugues, as separately and by degrees.   In
the last ten years of his life we find Bach occupied in collecting his most important works, revising them for the last
time, and in many other ways " setting his house in order."
In this way the second part of the Wohltemperirte Clavier
is chiefly to be regarded.   As might be imagined, here and
there pieces were wanting which would make the cycle of
the work complete and proportionate to the first part.   In
these cases, whenever he did not feel inclined to compose
new pieces he availed himself of older works.

These facts leave the value of the whole undiminished.
Bach admitted nothing that was not of equal merit with
the newly composed pieces, or that could not be made
so by revision.   In the first part of the " Wohltemperirte
Clavier " some few pieces are somewhat inferior to the rest.
This cannot be said of the second part.   But, regarded as a
whole, it is not a greater or less degree of genius that
makes the difference between the two parts.   It lies in the
periods of the master's life during which the majority of the
pieces in each were composed.   In the second part, as
compared with the first, are revealed an imagination more
richly saturated with music, a greater grasp and more
developed formative power, and the endeavour to give
the fugue-form more sharply cut outlines and more
characteristic features.   As a whole, the second part, like
the first, is distinguished by a certain general community of
character between the separate pieces.   Compositions like
the great fugue in A minor,[348] which is older, or the chromatic
fantasia and fugue, would never have been included by Bach
in this collection, which was intended to bear that particular
stamp of intensity of expression and contemplativeness which
the clavichord was so well fitted to interpret.[349]

---

[348] See Vol. II., p. 33 f.

[349] Bach, as a rule, adheres to the limited compass of c to c''' in the second
part also ; only in the A flat Prelude the note d''' flat occurs once ; in the B
major Prelude, B occurs twice ; and at the close of the A minor Fugue, A
occurs.   The latter piece has indeed more of the harpsichord character.

Even in the first part of the " Wohltemperirte Clavier "
it was noticeable that several of the preludes were not
coupled to their fugues with such homogeneity as we should
have expected. In Bach the prelude soon grew to a greater
independence than was warranted by its name. Not a few
of the preludes in the first part were independent pieces
as well as the C sharp prelude in the second part;
and indeed after the completion of both parts Bach made,
or intended to make, a collection consisting of preludes
alone.[350] The preludes of the second part, even more than
those of the first, bear the stamp of independent organisms.
In the first part the greater number are nothing more than
an animated development of harmonic sequences. In the
second part, however, it is remarkable that no fewer than
ten preludes have the dance-form in two sections—a form
which occurs only once in the first part—and are short
sonata-movements in Emanuel Bach's meaning of the
word, only for the most part much more polyphonic than
his movements.[351] Others make good their independent
character, if in no other way than by a careful working-out
of an important theme. It has already been remarked that
the B flat minor prelude belongs to the class of three-part
clavier Sinfonien (inventions).[352] It differs in no essential
respect from a fugue; though the theme is accompanied by
counterpoint on its entry, and though later on it is transferred from one part to another (bars 43, 44 and 49, 50),
yet the former instance is hardly different from what happens
in Bach's vocal fugues, when the first entry of the theme is
accompanied with full harmony, and the latter case occurs
also in the G minor fugue (bar 12, in the counter-subject).[353]
The C sharp minor prelude is developed from three suggestive
themes most ingeniously worked out. That which ought to
be the strict purpose of the form—viz., to prepare for the

---

[350] See Vol. II., pp. 165 f., and 666.

[351] Kiruberger has attempted to resolve the first part of the A minor Prelude,
with its characteristic wealth of harmony, into its proper fundamental harmonies; see Die wahren Grundsätze zum Gebrauch der Harmonie. P. 107 ff.

[352] See Vol. II., p. 59.

[353] And also in the F minor Fugue of the first part, bar 19.

most important part of the music which is to follow, and to keep up the interest in that part—is not fulfilled by most of them. They move us too much by their own importance, and each of them exhausts the particular emotion which it expresses. They not only assert themselves as equal to the fugues, but often stand in direct contrast to them. Every one must feel this who will compare the easy grace of the E flat major prelude with the stiff gravity of the fugue, or the devotional aspirations of the E major fugue with the cheerful activity of its prelude.[354]

Of course the relations between them are not fortuitous, nor did they arise simply in arranging the pieces in the collection, but they are Bach's design. From the prelude and fugue a new form in two movements has been developed. It is not entirely strange to us. Not to speak of the fantasia and fugue in C minor, lately spoken of, since that work dates from the last period of Bach's life, an example of the form occurs even in the first part of the "Wohltemperirte Clavier" in the E flat major prelude and fugue; and another example is offered by that prelude and fugue in A minor which was afterwards developed into a concerto.[355] This last instance is particularly instructive, because by his re-arrangement of it Bach has left evidence as to his ideas of the relation between prelude and fugue, and also because the gigue-like style in which the fugue is written is found again in five fugues in the second part of the "Wohltemperirte Clavier" (C sharp minor, F major, G major, G sharp minor, and B minor).[356] Remembering how the fugal gigue was used in the Suites, we may suppose that a similar idea suggested its use in this place. In three cases this is evident. The preludes in C sharp minor, F major, and G sharp minor express a grave, subdued, and in parts a

---

[354] It may be mentioned, by the way, in this place, that S. W. Dehn has discovered a Fugue by Froberger in the Phrygian mode, built upon almost the same theme and with the same counterpoint (see his Analysen dreier Fugen Joh. Seb. Bachs. Leipzig, Peters. 1858. P. 31). As Bach was familiar with Froberger's compositions (see Vol. I., p. 323), the agreement cannot be an accidental one.

[355] See Vol. I., p. 420, and ante, p. 143.

[356] In the first part the G major Fugue is the only one in the gigue style.

resigned mood; the fugues break in upon this repose with a different and lighter feeling.[357] This emotional contrast is also felt in the pairs of pieces in C major, C sharp major, and F minor, where more of the fugues are in gigue form. In the C sharp major set, the allegro end of the dreamy prelude is intended as a connecting link between that and the vivacity of the fugue. As far as the difference of style will allow, we may find analogies to these forms in the two-movement clavier sonatas of Emanuel Bach and of Haydn. Other pairs also stand in opposite contrast; animation is subdued to firmness and repose; sometimes the contrasts are so sharp that no common ground of feeling is to be found for the two. Cases also occur in which the two movements are distinguished only by delicate shades of difference (D major, F sharp major, F sharp minor, B flat minor, &c.), remaining essentially the same in feeling and character. But in all cases—and this must once more be insisted on—the prelude and the fugue are regarded as factors of equal dignity and importance. Instances where the prelude is left to its old function of merely ushering in the fugue are rare, and can scarcely be proved to exist elsewhere than in the pairs in D minor, G minor, and B major.

The artistic skill displayed in the fugues is astounding; and after careful comparison it must be admitted that in this respect the first part is not so finely conceived as the second. The devices of inversion, stretto, and augmentation are used equally often in both. But, on the other hand, in the first part Bach makes very sparing and only occasional use of double counterpoint on the tenth and twelfth,[358] while in the second part it is used with great effect. Although in the B flat major fugue (bars 41 ff. and 80 ff.) it is only introduced incidentally, in the B major fugue counterpoint on the twelfth forms a chief element in the working out (see

---

[357] Kirnberger (Kunst des reinen Satzes II., 1, p. 120) says of the F major Fugue: "In order to perform this Fugue correctly on the clavier, the notes must be struck lightly and with a rapid motion, and without the least pressure."

[358] See the counterpoint on the twelfth in the F sharp major fugue, bars 15, 16 and 32, 33.

bars 36, 43, 54, 94). And an instructive example of the musical wealth which is to be obtained by these artifices, without exaggeration, and without detriment to the sharpest and most characteristic expression, is afforded in the G minor fugue—a piece full of "swing" and determination, as if beaten out with hammers, in which free use is made of double counterpoint on the octave, the twelfth, and the tenth.

Still, if we expect to find in the second part of the "Wohltemperirte Clavier" a model of fugal work in the technical sense we mistake its purpose. That it was never so intended may be concluded from the fact that an equal and not rarely a greater degree of importance is given to the preludes than to the fugues. There is also this difference between the two parts, that in the second the technical treatment is nowhere made prominent. The fugues in C major, D minor, E flat minor, A minor, and B flat minor of the first part, in which the art tends to artifice, find no counterparts in the second part. A comparison between the A minor fugue (of the first part) and the similarly constructed fugue in B flat minor in the second part shows how entirely Bach could eliminate that savour of display which we feel in the older work. The augmentations of the theme which in the C minor and C sharp major fugue of the second part are brought in simultaneously with the themes in their original and inverted forms have, when compared with the same device in the E flat minor (D sharp minor) fugue of the first part, rather a light and purposeless effect. Such combinations are difficult and unusual in instrumental fugues, and are not intelligible unless the theme is quite a short one; the theme of the E flat minor fugue is almost too long, and the effect produced is somewhat over elaborate and erudite. The opportunities offered for ingenious complications increase, of course, in proportion to the number of parts employed; and it is significant that in the first part there are ten fugues in four parts and two in five, while the second contains only nine in four parts, all the rest being in three.[59] Among these last

---

[59] In the C minor fugue the fourth part does not enter until near the end, and then comes in with the augmented subject Bach introduces the same

there is a wonderful triple fugue (F sharp minor), unapproached in ingenuity by the three-part fugues of the
first part ; and yet this ingenuity is perfectly unobtrusive.
Various liberties, too, are taken which would ill befit the
work if they were not intended to prove how gracefully the
strictest writing might be treated.   More than once we
find alterations in the theme in the course of development
(F major, bars 86 and 87; E major, bar 23 ff.; F sharp minor,
bars 54, 55 and 60), or an undue increase in the number
of parts, even in other places than at the close (F major,
bars 86 and 87; G major, bar 60).   These, like the division
of a passage between two parts (G minor, bar 12), or the
daring entry of the answer to the theme on the augmented
fourth, and the long, almost homophonous digressions in the
F sharp major fugue [360]—these are not the remains of that
youthful audacity which characterised Bach's early fugal
compositions.   They prove that his aim now was to create
music which should be full of life and energy and with a
meaning of its own.

One of the highest triumphs of art is so to modify a
form, which, by its limitations, seems adapted only to
convey the most general ideas, as to render it capable
of expressing individual and personal feeling.   It was
this which, even in Bach's lifetime, more than all else,
surprised the musical world in his fugues.   Soon after
Bach's death one writer spoke of their " strange character
that is so different from the ordinary run of fugues."[361]
And another says: " Just at the time when the world (of
music) began to take a new course, when the lighter
kind of melodies became popular, when people were tired
of stiff and harsh harmonies, the late Herr Capellmeister
Bach hit upon a clever idea, and taught us how to
unite a pleasant and flowing melody with the richest

---

effect in the great organ fugue in C major (B.-G., XV., p. 234), the construction
of which in other respects also has a great similarity to that of the C minor
fugue. Apparently, therefore, the dates of both must be near together; and
very possibly the C minor fugue may have been originally written for the organ.

[360] Compare Vol. II., p. 402.

[361] In Marpurg, Kritische Briefe I., p. 192.

harmonies.[362] The fugues in the second part of the "Wohl-temperirte Clavier" are some of the most affecting and characteristic pieces in the whole range of music, and in their own class they are unapproached. The first part has nothing to show that can be compared in this respect with the fugues in D minor, E minor, F minor, G minor, and A minor. But even in the second part of the "Wohl-temperirte Clavier" the great master of fugue has not solved—nor did he wish to solve—exhaustively and once for all the problem of what art in its highest development could do in the fugue form. This task was left till the evening of his life.

There are two works which, from this point of view, present themselves to our notice—the so-called "Musical Offering" (Musikalische Opfer) and "The Art of Fugue" (Kunst der Fuge). The former work is, as it were, the vestibule through which Bach passed to the latter. Without depreciating the value of its several component parts, the Musical Offering, as a whole, must be regarded only as a study by which the master prepared himself for the second and greater work. A part of the work appeared in July, 1747 —two months after Bach played before King Frederick II. at Potsdam. Bach resolved to use the theme set him by the King on that occasion as the basis of a number of thoroughly developed and artistic compositions, since, as he said, his improvisation had not done justice to so expressive a theme. The name "Musical Offering" is derived from its having been dedicated to the king.[363] The

---

[362] Marpurg, Abhandlung von der Fuge, Part II. Berlin, 1754 (in the Dedication). A kind of imitation of the Wohltemperirte Clavier by Gottfried Kirchhoff has come down to us (see Vol., I., p. 521) in his *A.B.C. Musical*, four-and-twenty fugues comprising all the keys. It was a work of similar kind with his "Clavir Ubung, in sich haltend das I. und II. halbe Dutzend Von 24. melodieusen, vollstimmigen und nach modernen Gustu durch den gantzen Circulum Modorum Musicorum gesetzten Præludiis." (Clavier Practice, containing the first and second half-dozen of twenty-four melodious preludes, fully harmonised, and written in accordance with modern taste in the complete circle of musical modes.") Published about 1738 by Balthasar Schmidt, of Nuremberg.

[363] P. S. I., Cah. 12 (219)—an edition in oblong folio by Breitkopf and Härtel. An autograph of the six-part Ricercar is in the Royal Library at

work, which was both composed and engraved piecemeal, contains one fugue in three parts and one in six, eight canons, a
fugue with answer on the fifth in canon form, a sonata in four
movements, and a two-part canon over a free *basso continuo*.
All these are worked out more or less upon the same theme.

Bach gave to both the three-part and the six-part fugue
the name of *Ricercar*. In the case of the second, the name
seems to be accounted for by the fact that it was a hitherto
unheard-of undertaking to write a strict six-part fugue for
clavier alone without pedals. The idea would, probably,
not have occurred to Bach had not King Frederick, on the
occasion of Bach's playing at Potsdam, expressed a wish
to hear an *extempore* six-part fugue played by him. At the
time Bach complied with the king's request, improvising
the fugue upon a fitting theme chosen by himself. In
this work he wished to show that he could also treat the
given theme, although it was not so well adapted for the
purpose, in a six-part fugue. Such a composition, of course,
implies a close interweaving of the parts, more especially
when it is played by two hands alone. If we compare it
with the C sharp minor fugue in the first part of the
"Wohltemperirte Clavier," which contains, not indeed six,
but five *obbligato* parts, and if we notice how much more
intelligible it is than the fugue in the "Musical Offering," it
will appear that Bach has, intentionally, made all the six
parts work together. The mechanical difficulty of the piece
is a second reason for calling it a Ricercar. There are no
other special feats of ingenuity, in the use of counterpoint,
or clever episodical developments. An old-fashioned style,
the effect of which is heightened by the use of the *Tempus
imperfectum*, and which agrees very well with the harmonic
richness, and the bold chromatic treatment running through
the whole work, are the contrasting elements from which
the individual character of this mighty work is developed.[364]

Berlin; it is from Emanuel Bach's effects. As to the original edition, see
App. A., No. 8.

[364] In the original edition Bach had the six-part Ricercar printed in score, in
order to present the intricate interweaving of the parts in a clearer form to the
eye. In the autograph it is brought together on two staves.

The three-part fugue corresponds less to the idea of a Ricercar. It is a simple fugue with moderately extensive digressions, in which, however, only the chromatic portion of the theme undergoes thorough episodical development, and the counterpoint is proportionately less rich. The counter-subjects which are associated with the theme in bars 61—66 are repeated together with it no less than three times; twice, it is true, with double counterpoint in the octave. The passage in bars 38—52 is repeated, almost note for note but in another key, in bars 87—101, and in the same way bars 66—71 are repeated as bars 81—86. Some of the digressions are in themselves rather strange. That sudden triplet figure, which begins at bar 38, giving place after four bars to another digression strongly contrasted with it, ceasing entirely, never to be used in such a way as to account for its strange appearance, must, when viewed from the standpoint of Bach's fugal writing, be regarded as almost anomalous. The case is the same with the digression in bars 42—45, with the passage from bar 108 to the entry of the chromatic quaver-figure, and finally with the close. Without venturing to criticise the master, we believe ourselves fully justified in referring these strange phenomena to the influence of some external circumstances. If we remark how the idea in bar 42 f.—

is repeated again in the first Allegro of the sonata (bars 48 ff. in the flute part, 69 ff. in the violin part, &c.), how the passage in bar 108 onwards is used afterwards to prepare for the Andante, then we must come to the conclusion that Bach intentionally gave to this fugue a light and prelude-like character. There is no evidence to show that while writing it he had any idea of writing the sonata; for at first he offered to the king nothing more than this three-part fugue, the six canons, and the fugue in canon-style. It is probably, however, to be explained by supposing that when he was writing out the work he bethought himself of the fugue which he had improvised at Potsdam, and which had so pleased the king, and that he preserved in it more of the ideas that had occurred to him then than he would have thought permissible under other circumstances. At all events, it seems clear that Bach thought this "Offering" an insufficient one, and so followed up his first gift with a second of more importance, containing the six-part Ricercar, the Sonata, and three more canons.

Bach had five of the canons together with the fugue in canon-style printed on a sheet by themselves and designated by the general title *Canones diversi super Thema Regium.* Besides this he gave them the title of *Regis Jussu Cantio Et Reliqua Canonica Arte Resoluta* (*i.e.*, The theme given by the king's command, together with additions, resolved in canon-style), the initials of the words of the title giving the word *Ricercar.* Above the fourth canon (seventh in Peters), which is in inverted augmentation, Bach inscribed the words (in the dedicatory copy which is still preserved): *Notulis crescentibus crescat Fortuna Regis* (As the notes increase in value, so may the fortune of the king increase). At the fifth (eighth in Peters) an infinite canon, which modulates by ascending a whole tone at every repetition, we find the words *Ascendenteque Modulatione ascendat Gloria Regis* (And with the rising modulation may the glory of the king rise). In this pretty and playful symbolism, which undoubtedly proceeded from the composer himself, may be traced the spirit of the contrapuntists of the Low Countries. The solutions of the canons are indicated by Bach himself. The first (fourth in Peters) is in two parts, and by retrogression (*cancrizans*), the theme lying in the parts that are in canon. The rest are also in two parts, but at the same time they form counterpoint to the theme which is brought in as a *Cantus firmus,* so that the result is a three-part piece. Without any of that dry and unimaginative ingenuity which generally intrudes itself into the domain of canon, these little pieces reveal not only real ingenuity but also true genius and characteristic feeling. Notwithstanding their astounding elaboration, there are very few harsh notes, and those are

only transitory.[365]   A more delightful or interesting little
work of its kind than the canon *per augmentationem, contrario
motu,* written in the French style, certainly does not exist.
The three-part fugue in canon form, too, is a masterpiece
of artifice worked out with playful facility.   Bach has
omitted to say what instrument is to play the uppermost
part with the two clavier parts, but it is apparently a flute.

   The other three canons stand, perhaps from typographical
reasons, one after the three-part fugue and the other two
after that in six parts. (In Peters they are placed before
the other five and numbered 1, 2, and 3.)   The solution of
the last two—one in two parts and the other in four, without
a *Cantus firmus*—is not given by Bach, but are left with
the words " Seek, and ye shall find " (*quærendo invenietis*),
to the ingenuity of the player or reader.   In the four-part
canon the entrances follow each other at the distance of
seven bars ; but the effect of this daring chromatic treatment
verges on the abstruse.[366]   In the two-part canon the bass
as the second part enters, in the strictest contrary motion,
on the second crotchet of the fourth bar.   Moreover, the
canon is so constructed that a correct solution is obtained
by precisely the reverse method—letting the bass begin
with the contrary motion, and the alto follow in direct
motion on the second crotchet of the fourth bar.   And again
the bass may be made to follow on the second crotchet of
the fourteenth bar.   But the first of these three solutions
is the one intended by Bach.[367]

---

[365] Kirnberger solved three of these canons in the Kunst des reinen Satzes II.
3, p. 47 ff.).   In the canon *per motum contrarium* (No. 6 in Peters) bar 3 cannot
possibly be right.   In Bach's dedicatory copy the fourth semiquaver *b* is corrected in red ink to *b* flat, probably by Kirnberger when the copy came into the
possession of Princess Amalie.   Then, however, the *a* before it would have to
be changed into *a* flat ; this would be the most beautiful arrangement, and
thoroughly satisfactory, were it not for the fact that the two naturals of the
original plate receive strong confirmation by the express insertion of the flat
before the last *a* of the bar.

[366] The solution is given by Hilgenfeldt, p. 122.

[367] A MS. of a part of the Musikalisches Opfer, in the Amalienbibliothek,
contains this canon and the first two solutions.   Above the solution which
begins with the bass Kirnberger has written, " This solution is not the one
intended by the author," and above the other " The true solution."   The third
was given by an anonymous writer in the Allgemeine Musikalische Zeitung
for 1806, p. 496, note.

The Sonata, in ordinary four-movement form, displays no less genius, but has, in addition, a warmth and richness of emotional character which the other pieces have not. The Largo is not strictly built upon the theme, but preludes, as it were, upon its characteristic interval of the seventh (see bar 4 in the bass, bars 13 and 14 in the flute and violin, &c.). In the fugal Allegro, however, the theme makes its way gradually into all the parts as a *Cantus firmus*, with very beautiful effect; the proper theme of the fugue itself forms the first countersubject to it, and the second consists of a passage taken from the three-part Ricercar. The expressive Andante is, as it were, a fantasia built chiefly upon ideas taken from the three-part Ricercar, but the beginning of the theme also makes itself distinctly heard in several places. In the final Allegro the theme appears cleverly transformed into 6-8 time, and is developed into an animated fugue.[368] And, as though the composer's powers of combination were quite inexhaustible, he inserts after the sonata yet another canon, this time written out in full. It is in two parts with a figured bass and worked out in strict inversion, the second part coming in first on the fifth above, and afterwards on the fifth below. Quite at the end Bach, by way of a joke, brings in the theme in the figured bass part.

The infinite capacity for combination, the ingenuity, penetrating even to the deepest source of harmony, and the powerful imagination which preserves its full vitality even within the narrowest limitations, make of the " Musikalisches Opfer " a monument of strict writing which will endure for all time. It is not, however, an organic whole, since different instruments are required for the different parts. The first two fugues are clavier music, and some of the canons are intended for the clavier, or at least can be performed upon it. For the other pieces stringed instruments are necessary, and in some their presence is expressly required ; the fugue

---

[368] The figured bass accompaniment to the Sonata has been written out in full, in four parts, by Kirnberger.   The work is published in P. S. III., Cah. 8, No. 3.

in canon style requires a clavier and flute (or violin); the sonata and the final canon are written for clavier, flute, and violin, probably with reference to the fact that King Frederick himself played the flute. The work is simply a group of various pieces composed at different times, and thrown together quite arbitrarily, intended to exhibit one and the same idea under the greatest possible variety of aspects. In this instance, Bach set aside the higher idea of uniting these ingenious component parts into an artistic whole. On that account the Musikalisches Opfer cannot be called anything but a study for a greater work, a half abstract creation, in which the technical points must be chiefly insisted on.

The case is different with the second work, the "Art of Fugue." The idea of creating a great work of art in many parts, but as a perfectly organic whole, from a single theme, by employing all the devices of strict counterpoint, is here fully worked out. By mere chance the master's work has not come down to posterity as he had completed and perfected it. We must assume the main portion of the "Kunst der Fuge" to have been composed in the year 1749. When Bach was intending to have it engraved on copper he revised and completed his manuscript. The greater part had been engraved under his personal supervision, when death overtook him, in the middle of the year 1750. His family were not sufficiently informed of his intention with respect to the manuscript, as it was found amongst the master's effects; his grown-up sons were at a distance, and the task of editing fell into the hands of ignorant people, who put everything on the plates as it came—sketches beside completed movements, original settings beside arrangements, parts that had a connection beside those which had none —in dreadful disorder; and in this state the work was published. But the parts which are to be separated from the mass, as not intended for the complete work, are plainly discernible, although the arrangement designed by Bach for the last part of the work must remain in uncertainty. By mistake or ignorance an older sketch for the tenth piece has crept into the work as published, besides a fugue with

three subjects, on which Bach had been working a short
time before his death, but which has nothing whatever to
do with this work, and lastly, two fugues for two claviers.
Both these last are arrangements of those two three-part
fugues, of which the second is the inversion of the first in all
parts; portions of this are very difficult, nay, impossible, to
play, for the parts often lie so far apart that two simultaneous
notes cannot be reached except by a spring.   In order to
make this "eye music" appreciable by the ear, Bach
arranged the fugues in such a manner that one clavier plays
two parts, while the other takes the third and a free part
added in besides.   A few free additions are also made at
the beginning of each fugue.   The newly added parts give
fresh evidence of Bach's enormous talent in contrivances of
this kind.   The result, however, has but a doubtful value as
a work of art, and was never intended for insertion in the
complete work, since it is a distortion of the idea of writing
a fugue in only real parts, all capable of inversion; while the
introduction of a second clavier radically alters its style and
character.[369]

After the excision of these inorganic elements, we have a
work consisting of fifteen fugues and four canons, on one
and the same theme.   In it we meet with simple, double,
and triple fugues, fugues built upon the theme altered either
in melody or rhythm, fugues with strettos, with the answer
in contrary motion, both in notes of the same value and in
diminution and augmentation, fugues in double counterpoint,
in the octave, tenth, and twelfth, and lastly fugues in which

---

[369] In the present century the " Kunst der Fuge" was first republished by
Nägeli of Zurich, then edited by Czerny, by Peters (P. S. I., Cah. 11—218),
and of late edited by W. Rust (B.-G., XXV.[1]); the last an excellent production,
rich in valuable results of critical labour.   Rust has not ventured to omit the
portions that do not belong to the work.   The relations between the three-part
fugue with its inversion and the fugues for two claviers struck, strange to say,
both him and M. Hauptmann, to whom we owe a fine analysis of the work
(Leipzig, C. F. Peters).   From this relation, however, it is easy to account
for the mistakes to be found in the fugues for two claviers, which Rust
attempts in part to explain away by very bold conjectures; they were overlooked
and left standing when the fourth part was added in, and can indeed be
only due to this.

all three or four parts are in contrary motion to each other, and that in different positions, besides two-part canons in augmented contrary motions, and in the three practicable kinds of double counterpoint. There are forms from the very simplest up to the hardest that is conceivable, such as even Bach himself never produced before in his life. Although it is not certain whether the title " Kunst der Fuge " proceeded from Bach himself, yet the work bears sufficiently plain traces of having been intended to serve an educational purpose. This is proved by the circumstances that the work is written in score, and that the pieces are not called fugues, but " counterpoints," with direct reference to the school. Still, to regard it merely as an instruction book in fugue, with examples, and not as a genuine work of art, would be to misapprehend its nature. The mere idea of imparting instruction awoke Bach's artistic inspiration. Never had he done more excellent work than when he undertook to aid, by his example, in the advancement of the disciples of art. In the " Orgelbüchlein," in the Inventions and Sinfonias, and in the first part of the "Wohltemperirte Clavier," this purpose is avowed with dignified simplicity. The practical and educational purpose and the free artistic ideal are so inseparable here, at the highest point of their development, that there is scarcely a trace of any compromise, or sacrifice of the highest demands of the one factor, in favour of the other. From both points of view we have before us a perfect work.

Whoever seeks instruction in it will confine himself to studying the separate portions. He will perceive the incomparable capability for combining parts, and that almost miraculous wealth and variety of harmony, which will make him feel that Bach has exhausted all the possibilities of harmony, and that after him there is no more to be said in that province of art. Our view of the work as an artistic creation must include it as a whole and rest upon the impressions which it produces as a whole. It differs essentially from both parts of the " Wohltemperirte Clavier,' and from the Inventions and Sinfonias, by the earnestness of its emotional character. There is a greater uniformity

in the characters of the parts, and a more contemplative
nature suggests itself to the hearer even in the first fugue,
which seems like the solemn repose of a winter's night.
Even the theme, which has been unjustly designated as
practicable for musical purposes, but insignificant in itself, is
steeped in this feeling.

The inner development of the work is in a sequence of
grand, majestic groups.   The first group consists of the four
fugues already mentioned.   Even in this group we can
clearly trace a progressive development.   The second fugue
contrasts with the first by its somewhat more animated
counterpoint; the third has the theme altered by inversion,
and here the theme reveals a deep and yearning character of
its own.   It is continued in the fourth fugue on broader lines,
rising from bar 61 onwards to a striking degree of power.

The second group consists of the fifth, sixth, and seventh
fugues.   In contrast to the first group the second is worked
out on a modified form of the theme, the effect depending
chiefly on the rhythm, and it exhibits the theme in different
kinds of time, combined with itself in double counterpoint.
The animation thus produced is increased by Bach in the
sixth fugue by the use of the rhythms of the French overture
style, and in the seventh fugue, which introduces the theme
in its natural time, and diminished and augmented simultaneously, the animation verges on restlessness.   The
progressive development of the second group lies chiefly in
these external qualities.

In the third group (fugues 8—11) external and internal
elements combine to attain the climax.   The principal
subject is now associated with independent and contrasting
themes.   The eighth fugue begins at once with a subject of
this kind, which glides in with stealthy, snake-like windings,
and is full of peculiar individuality both in rhythm and in
melody.   After it has been thoroughly worked out, a second
and very agitated theme, not less important in rhythm and
melody, accompanies it.   A double fugue is thus produced,
in which the strange little taps, as it were, in the second
theme, increase to hammer beats, and the animated movement to violence of unrest; and it is not till the original

quiet movement has been restored that the chief subject enters and is treated fugally. But dissevered as it is by crotchet rests, it also conveys an impression of inward agitation. The other themes now join in with it, and they work together to produce a progressive intensity of effect in a triple fugue in three parts and containing 188 bars. The four-part fugue which follows has only one counter-subject which, owing to its being treated in counterpoint at the twelfth, does duty for two, although it cannot of course appear in two places simultaneously. Setting out with a mighty spring the counter-subject goes on without stop or stay, while against it the chief subject goes grandly and solemnly on in augmentation. In the tenth fugue, which is written in counterpoint at the tenth, there is again only one counter-subject. Its mild and flowing character is felt as a repose after what has gone before, and it prepares us for the full appreciation of the last fugue, in which the three themes of the eighth fugue are worked out again, but in four parts, which intensifies their expression to the last degree and entirely exhausts their harmonic capabilities. This concise and cyclic group reveals the master in that gloomy grandeur which we seek in vain in any other composer. It also shows, in the plainest way, how firm his purpose was to create this work on the truest principles of art.

The fourth group consists of the last two pairs of fugues. From a technical point of view they exhibit Bach on a dizzy pinnacle of eminence. At a height where existence would be an impossibility to others, he breathes with ease and freedom. The formal limits to which he subjects himself, in his case serve only to give to the pieces their true artistic character. The solemn repose of the opening returns upon us, but sublimated to a feeling which is best expressed by the words "a cold grandeur."[370] Bach's last intention with respect to the arrangement and order of the pieces, we only know up to the eleventh fugue. But it may be confidently assumed that of the last two pairs, those in three parts were intended to precede those in

---

[370] Hauptmann, Erläuterungen zur Kunst der Fuge, p. 10.

four.[371]   How he intended the four canons to be associated
with the fugues—whether they were to be inserted after
the third group, or only added on to the whole as an
important appendix—must be left in impenetrable mystery,
owing to the master's premature death.   To us it appears
scarcely credible that Bach could have intended to interrupt
the sequence of the grand structure revealed to us in these
fugues by inserting a number of stricter forms, which,
though very clever and ingenious, suffer from the same
disproportion of idea and material that we have already
noticed in the case of two of the clavier duets, and which
are therefore not well fitted to intensify the harmonic effect
of the fugue-sequence.

The two parts of the "Wohltemperirte Clavier" must be
considered as a whole, although each separate fugue, either
with or without its prelude, gives us a feeling of pleasurable
satisfaction.   Bach himself regarded them as one, for he
would sometimes feel impelled to play them from beginning
to end at one sitting.[372]   In a much higher degree then must
the "Kunst der Fuge" be regarded as a self-contained
unity; and not only because the same theme is the subject
of all the fugues.   The result of this need only have been
a method of treatment which would have shown off each
fugue by itself; no one would look for any inner connection
between Schumann's fugues on the name "Bach."   But in
the "Kunst der Fuge" the separate parts bear a relation
to one another, and only through one another can they
be perfectly understood.   The effect of a piece written in
double counterpoint depends upon the hearer's realizing
the two different registers in which the contrasting
subjects are placed, as a unity, and, at the same time, a
duality; and the meaning of the separate fugues in this
work can only be seen in the right light when the different
modifications undergone by the theme, the various counter-
subjects, and the organic entities resulting from their
association are compared, not only with the original form
of the theme and the simplest fugal form built upon that,

[371] This opinion is shared by Rust, see B.-G., XXV.,[1] p. 28.
[372] Gerber, N. L., col. 492.

but also with one another.   By this is meant an emotional, not an intellectual comparison; indeed, to apply this to the work before us requires special musical culture.   But —to take an instance—in the seventh fugue, where the theme is worked in direct and contrary motion, and in the natural, diminished, and augmented forms, it will scarcely be possible so much as to understand the relations of the parts to each other, unless the ear has been prepared for the task by the combinations that have gone before, and has become thoroughly familiar with the chief subjects.   This preparation alone will enable us to see the full justification of such ingeniously intricate forms.   In reality this last work of Bach's is a single gigantic fugue in fifteen sections.   Hence it may be traced to a single idea, in a much stricter sense than was the case with the two parts of the " Wohltemperirte Clavier."   Hence, too, each section necessarily leaves an impression of incompleteness, and this in great part accounts for the fact that no single fugue of this wonderful composition has taken such firm hold on posterity as even the lightest of the more pleasing fugues of the " Wohltemperirte Clavier." Few, perhaps, have the ability and the inclination to understand it as a whole.   The obscure state in which it has hitherto lain has rendered this task all the harder, and it has thus come about that a composition of incomparable perfection and depth of feeling, although it has always been mentioned with especial reverence as being Bach's last great work, has never yet formed part of the life of the German nation.

The engraving of the original edition was clumsy and full of mistakes.[373]   Emanuel Bach undertook the publica-

---

[373] Rust supposes J. G. Schübler, of Zella, near Suhl, to have been the engraver.   The monogram on p. 25, in which A is the principal letter, seems to contradict this supposition.   Rust's researches, however, have made it certain that it was not done by any of Bach's sons, as has hitherto been generally supposed.   And there is nothing to show that Bach's sons took part, even indirectly, in any supervision of the engraving.   The note in the first supplement of the Berlin autograph (see B.-G., XXV.,[1] p. 115), which may have given rise to such a supposition, is, I am convinced, not by Emanuel Bach's hand.

tion, but his expectations of a large and rapid sale were disappointed. He therefore lowered the price from five thalers to four, and commissioned F. W. Marpurg, of Berlin, to write a longer preface, in place of the short notice which had preceded the work in explanation of its supposed incompleteness. Thus provided, the " Kunst der Fuge " was brought out at the Leipzig Book Fair, at Easter, 1752. But even then its success was very moderate. In the autumn of 1756 Emanuel Bach, having sold no more than about thirty copies, gave up the attempt, and offered the copperplates for sale " at a low price."[374] In the year 1760, Breitkopf was again selling it for a Louis d'or (=5 thalers) a copy.[375] In spite of the slight reception of the work, the few who became acquainted with it were competent judges, and they appreciated it at its real value. Among the first purchasers was Mattheson, who, to the end of his life, took an eager interest in all new works of importance. " Joh. Sebast. Bach's ' Art of Fugue,' " he writes, "a practical and splendid (praktisches und prächtiges) work of seventy plates in folio, will at once amaze all the French and Italian fugue-makers ; provided only that they can understand them rightly—I will not say play them. Let every one, whether a German or a foreigner, lay out his Louis d'or on this treasure! Germany is and remains without doubt the true land of organ music and of fugues ! "[376]

Bach's creative activity did not rest even after the completion of the " Kunst der Fuge." He now took in hand the composition of a clavier fugue on the grandest scale, in

---

[374] The conclusions drawn by Rust, from the supposed preparation of two editions of the " Kunst der Fuge," as to its reception by the public are untenable. For he has overlooked the fact that Forkel, whose opinion he attacks, is here speaking, not on the authority of oral tradition, but from a printed source of information of a trustworthy kind—namely, Emanuel Bach's own statement, made September 14, 1756, given in Marpurg's Historisch-Kritische Beyträge II., p. 575 f. The title and the preface are the only new portions of the so-called second edition.

[375] Breitkopf's New Year Catalogue, 1760, p. 7.

[376] Mattheson's Philologisches Tresespiel. Hamburg, 1752, p. 98. The book was published, as appears from its dedication and preface, at Easter, 1752, and thus must have been written in 1751.

which the last of the three themes is on the letters of his own name. He only wrote 239 bars of this work; at least no more have come down to us, and Emanuel Bach states that his father died while engaged upon it. It is the same fugue that has, by misunderstanding, crept into the original edition of the " Kunst der Fuge."[377] As the fragment only reaches down to the beginning of the combination of all three themes, it probably contains only about three-quarters of the work as originally conceived; from this we can see on what colossal dimensions the fugue was planned. The emotional character, as in the " Kunst der Fuge," is devotional and grave; showing that this must have been Bach's general range of feeling at the time.

Notwithstanding the long line of musical ancestors on which Bach could pride himself, it remained for him to discover that the name of the family could be expressed in musical notes.[378] Subsequently the musical phrase thus generated, which has great melodic individuality and harmonic value, has been used, times without number, for fugues and canons by Bach's sons and pupils, and by later musicians, down to our own time. A well known prelude and fugue in B flat major on the name Bach, ascribed for a long time, as a matter of course, to Bach himself, is now generally considered spurious.[379] We have indeed no manuscript evidence in the case, and there are several other fugues upon the same theme, which have sometimes been considered as Sebastian Bach's. Forkel once asked Friedemann Bach what was the real truth of the case. He answered that his father was not a buffoon, but had only used his name as the theme of a fugue in the " Kunst der Fuge."[380] This sounds very decisive, but it is inaccurate in a double sense. As regards the " Kunst der Fuge" we now know that the piece mentioned by Friedemann has no place in it; and we know from Walther that Sebastian

---

[377] It is found on p. 93 of the B.-G. edition.

[378] It will be remembered that B flat is called B by the Germans, and B natural H (Tr.)

[379] P. S. II., Cah. 4, Appendix.

[380] The story was told by Forkel to Griepenkerl and by him to Roitzsch.

must have written a composition on his name long before this. In the short article upon Sebastian Bach in his Lexicon, he says : " The Bach family must have come from Hungary, and all who have borne the name, so far as can be known, have been attached to music; which may perhaps arise from the fact that even the letters b′ a′ c″ h′ (b′ ♭ a′ c″ b′ ♮) are melodic in their arrangement. (This was first remarked by Herr Bach of Leipzig)." No one can believe that Bach could rest satisfied with the mère observation and not at once use so practicable a phrase as a theme. Walther's lexicon appeared in 1732 ; but his knowledge of Bach's composition was almost entirely confined to the old times of intimacy at Weimar, and more especially to the first half of that period.[381] From internal evidence the fugue in question must date from the first ten years or so of the eighteenth century. If Bach were not its composer, we are confronted with the strange fact that we possess a fugue, and that a very fine one, by an unknown master, while the authentic work of the most celebrated master of fugue has been lost. In my opinion there is no substantial internal evidence against its genuineness, as long as we admit that the fugue is a youthful work. The prelude is formed on the model of the French overture-form, which Bach used frequently as early as the Weimar period. Passages analogous to that in bars 8 ff, &c., occur in the prelude to the great organ fugue in D major.[382] The working-out of the fugal theme is throughout in Bach's style ; the phrases in the second bar occur again in the theme of the B minor fugue in the first part of the " Wohltemperirte Clavier" ; and in the " Kleine harmonische Labyrinth," they are even found with the same counter-point.[383] Passages in thirds, ascending at each repetition, are of quite common use in the compositions of that time, for which Kuhnau's clavier music was the standard ; the

---

[381] See Vol. I., p. 396.

[382] P. S. V., Cah. 4 (243), No. 3.

[383] See Vol. II., p. 43. I do not forget that this amount of evidence is not sufficient to decide the authenticity of the work. But there is not enough evidence on the other side to allow of its rejection.

interruption, for the sake of effect, near the end, is a peculiarity of the style of the Northern masters, from whose influence Bach had not yet freed himself. The whole piece with its youthful freshness and happy playfulness agrees well with the character of Bach's earlier Weimar compositions. Of the other anonymous fugues on the name " Bach," the greater part bear evident marks of their not being by Bach himself. One alone :—

has an old-fashioned air about it, reminding us of Buxtehude's great C major fugue.[384] On this account it may possibly be by Bach, and would in that case have been written before the other, about 1707. If the one mentioned by Walther be one of these, as I assume, it must certainly have been the former, not the latter; as may be seen from his writing down the notes as b′a′c″h′, and not bac′h.

The reader will now expect that Bach's organ compositions should again come under our notice. If in Leipzig Bach's labours in the other branches of instrumental music did not diminish, how much less would they cease in the sphere of organ music, his oldest and most particular domain. Moreover, organ music stands in the closest relation to cantatas, Passions, motetts, and masses, since, like them, it is devoted to the service of the church, and a faculty chiefly exerted in the domain of church music must inevitably recur to the organ. In fact, the concerted works, and the organ works written in Leipzig, have much in common. In the first period, when a great freedom and variety of form prevailed in the cantatas, independent forms also preponderated in the organ compositions. In the second period the chorale cantata came distinctly into the foreground,

---

[384] No. XVII. of the first Vol. of my edition of Buxtehude. The anonymous fugue above cited is from Schelble's bequest; I owe my acquaintance with it to Herr Roitzsch.

and at the same time in instrumental composition the master devoted himself principally to the organ chorale.

On the whole, however, the number of organ works written at Leipzig is not large as compared with those written at Weimar, and they are less remarkable for number and variety than for fulness of import. Of the organ works completed by Bach in Leipzig, many must have originated at an earlier period. Two preludes and fugues in C minor and F major give evidence, in their second portions, of dating from the period of his earlier maturity; probably, too, these are not the original preludes.[385] The preludes which Bach added later are so grand as almost to force the fugues into the background. No exact date can be given for these or for the gigantic F major toccata—for this belongs to the same category—or for the C minor prelude, consisting of harmonic and fugal sections worked out in the form of *tutti* and *solo*. And we must also be content to assign the noble toccata and fugue in D minor (called Doric) in general terms to Bach's central period.[386] A prelude and fugue in G major was completed in 1724 or 1725, and a similar work in C major about 1730.[387] The schemes of these, however, point back to a time before the Leipzig period. When, in Weimar and Cöthen, Bach was working into his art the forms of the Italian chamber music, the idea occurred to him of creating an organ-form in three movements analogous to the Italian concerto. He carried this idea into execution only once, however, as we must assume, in Weimar;[388] he does not seem to have found the form of the first movement of a concerto productive enough for an organ piece. It appears once again in the above-mentioned C minor prelude, although in a very much modified form; but the form

---

[385] The fugues have already been noticed in Vol. I., p. 590 f.

[386] P. S. V., Cah. 3 (242), No. 3.   B.-G., XV., p. 136 ff.

[387] P. S. V., Cah. 2 (241), Nos. 2 and 1.   B.-G., XV., p. 169 ff. and 212 ff. The date is inferred from the condition of the autographs. That of the work in G major has the same authoritative signs of date as the older portions of the Whitsuntide Cantata, "Erschallet ihr Lieder," see App. A. to Vol. II., No. 31. That of the work in C major has M A. See App. A. to Vol. II., No. 44. As to the gradual alterations which the works have undergone, see Rust's preface to B.-G., XV.   [388] See Vol I., p. 421 f.

which chiefly asserts itself is that of the prelude, worked
thematically. Nevertheless, Bach attempted, in the works
quoted in G major and C major, to adhere at least to the
triple form of the concerto by inserting, between the prelude
and the fugue, middle sections in three parts and of a quieter
character. This experiment leads us to assume that both
works may have been conceived at the same time; finally,
however, he abolished the middle sections, perceiving that
his idea could be realised in another way. Thus two pairs
of movements remain, which may be said to hold the happy
medium in the highest sense, like the toccata and fugue in
D minor; they are mature in their form, and nowhere
overstep a delightful moderation. A festal character, common
to both, develops in the C major work into a feeling of
devotion, and in the other into one of rejoicing. The theme
of the G major fugue, which was used in the minor in the
Cantata "Ich hatte viel Bekümmerniss," has a rhythm
which generates a free motive in the prelude.

The composition of the famous A minor fugue, in which
science and effect are united in the most perfect manner,
also extends apparently over two periods of his life.[389] The
first conception of the prelude, which, as compared with
Bach's later style, seems to consist only of passages, may,
from certain characteristic reminiscences of the school
of Buxtehude (see bars 22 ff. and 33 ff.), be referred
to a moderately early time. Only four great preludes and
fugues are to be regarded as the immediate fruits of the
Leipzig period; they are in C major, B minor, E minor,
and E flat major, four stupendous creations, in which are
embodied the highest qualities that Bach could put into
this branch of art.[390] The C major fugue, with its lovely

---

[389] P. S. V., Cah. 2 (241), No. 8. B.-G., XV., p. 189 ff. See also the
preface.

[390] P. S. V., Cah. 2 (241), Nos. 7, 10, 9, and Cah. 3 (242), No. 1. B.-G.,
XV., pp. 228, 199, 236 ff., and III., pp. 173 and 254 ff. The first three, together
with the fugues in A minor (P. S. V., Cah. 2 (241), No. 8), C major (Ibid.,
Cah. 2 (241), No. 1), and C minor (Ibid., Cah. 2 (241), No. 6), are known as the
six great preludes and fugues. As they exist united together in one MS. it is
possible that Bach may have collected them into one work during the last
years of his life.

structure in five parts, rising from the broad foundations of the prelude—like Bach's own artistic greatness from the great middle class of the German people — has a fellow in the C minor fugue in the second part of the "Wohltemperirte Clavier." The latter work is, indeed, in a more unpretending style; but the ingenious interweavings of the theme in direct and contrary motion, and more especially the late entry of the lowest part in augmentation, have the same grand and majestic character as the C major fugue effect.

In the prelude and fugue in B minor he strikes a chord of deep elegiac feeling such as we find nowhere else in the organ works. The prelude, with its firm and close texture, leads us into a labyrinth of romantic harmony, such as has never been constructed by any more modern composer. The fugue is in a vein of quiet melancholy. Bach's power of embodying this feeling in an organ piece in the strictest style, and of keeping it up throughout a work of the longest proportions, would alone secure him imperishable fame. In contrast to this work, in the prelude and fugue in E minor, the whole energy and vitality of the master are displayed. It is a composition not sufficiently described by its present title; it should be called an organ symphony in two movements to give an adequate idea of its grandeur and power. The prelude numbers 137 bars, while the fugue is extended to 231. It is the longest of Bach's organ fugues. The theme is of the greatest possible boldness, and yet, like the rest of the work, in the highest degree dignified. Its date must be between 1727 and 1736.[391]

The prelude and fugue in E flat major, which were published in the third part of the Clavierübung about 1739, belong to the first years of the last period of his life. They form the beginning and the end respectively of that collection which was properly intended to contain only organ chorales. Although so widely separated in position

---

[391] According to the mark M A in the original MS., which is autograph as far as bar 20 (inclusive) of the fugue. (The splendid autograph of the prelude and fugue in B minor, in the possession of Sir Herbert Oakeley, bears the water-mark M A, thus showing that it belongs to the same period as the work in E minor.—Tr.)

they have an inward connection, which may be seen in the quiet stateliness common to both, and also in the fact that both are in five parts, besides which Forkel expressly testifies to their connection on the authority of Bach's sons.[392] The elaborately-constructed prelude belongs to the toccata class. And yet, in the portions which are not fugal, there is an individual character which reminds us of the clavier music of Emanuel Bach and of Haydn.[393] The fugue, on the other hand, exhibits in a remarkable degree the Buxtehude form in several sections;[394] in the second and third of these the theme undergoes hardly more than a change in rhythm alone, but its new counterpoints give it quite another aspect. This work may be most fitly called central or intermediate, for it points towards a period yet to come, and at the same time refers to one already past.[395]

That form in three movements which Bach vainly attempted to produce as long as he tried to insert a contrasting middle movement between the prelude and the fugue, he discovered in the six so-called organ sonatas. These are compositions in which the forms of the Italian chamber sonata, as developed by Bach, and of the instrumental concerto, appear united. They form a companion work to the six violin sonatas with clavier obbligato, adhering to the three-part form with even greater strictness, for in the violin sonatas we here and there find chords in the figured bass. In the organ sonatas two manuals take each a part, the third being allotted to the pedal. Bach produced this form under the influence of his chamber music, and it holds a central position between the style of organ and chamber music ; it is accordingly best suited to an instrument which

---

[392] See Griepenkerl's preface to P. S. V., Cah. 3 (242), No. 1.

[393] Compare Vol. II., p. 121.

[394] Compare Vol. I., p. 324 f.

[395] A beautiful five-part fantasia with fugue in C minor is unfortunately preserved only in a fragmentary condition, inasmuch as the fugue only reaches to bar 27. Griepenkerl's supposition, which I followed in Vol. I., p. 590, that the fantasia belonged originally to the fugue in P. S. V., Cah. 2 (241), No. 6, can scarcely be held, now that the autograph has come to light. The autograph, in a large powerful style of writing, on fine strong paper, was formerly in the possession of Professor Wagener, of Marburg, and is now in the Royal Library at Berlin.

would give expression to this medium character. That
instrument is the pedal clavier with two manuals. The
original MSS. distinctly state them to be for that instrument, and the title of "Organ Sonatas" now in use is,
strictly speaking, incorrect. In his organ music proper,
Bach turned to account much of his chamber music. But
he took care not to transfer the forms without alteration,
and in their entirety. We possess neither genuine organ
sonatas by him nor organ concertos. In contrast to Handel,
he never ceased to regard the organ as devoted to the service
of the church.

These six sonatas were intended to complete the education
of his eldest son, Wilhelm Friedemann, as an organist.[396]
They were produced gradually ; the first movement of the D
minor sonata dates from about 1722 ; the Adagio and
Vivace of the E minor sonata belonged originally to the
church cantata " Die Himmel erzählen," of the year 1723 ;
the last movement of the same sonata and the Largo of the
C major sonata must have been middle movements inserted
between the preludes and fugues in G major and C major
respectively, and therefore date from the Cöthen or the
Weimar period. The whole collection must have been
completed between 1727 and 1733, since in the latter year
Friedemann Bach was appointed organist in Dresden ; we
may with more exactitude put the completion of the work
soon after 1727.[397] It is easiest to understand these sonatas
if we take them up after the six violin sonatas already
mentioned. Fully equal to them in wealth of ideas, in
interesting working-out, in masterly treatment of the three-
part writing, and in sharpness of contrast between each
other, they have a limited individuality consequent on the

---

[396] Forkel, p. 60.

[397] Both the existing original MSS. bear the sign M A. See Appendix A.,
No. 34. Only one of these is autograph ; the other was written as far as
to page 48 inclusive, by Friedemann Bach, and from that point by Anna
Magdalena, Sebastian having only put in a few additions. For the rest see
the preface to B.-G., XV., in which Vol. the sonatas are published, and
P. S. V., Cah 1 (240), with Griepenkerl's preface.

more limited powers of expression of the organ tone-material.[398]

The first, second, and fourth parts of the " Clavierübung " contained works which, each in its way, must be regarded as the highest of its kind, and (for the most part) complete in itself. This is equally true of the third part, which contains the greatest number and the most important of the chorale arrangements made by Bach in the last period of his life.[399]   We are forced to regard the twenty-one choral pieces of the third part as a whole, to which unity is lent by one poetic idea. The root of the work consists of twelve arrangements of the so-called " Catechism Hymns." For each of the five chief divisions of the Lutheran catechism, and also for confession, one of the finest and best known chorales is chosen ; the first is " Dies sind die heilgen zehn Gebot " ("These ten are God's most holy laws "); the second, " Wir glauben all an einen Gott " ("We all believe in one Lord God "); the third, " Vater unser im Himmelreich" (" Our Father which art in Heaven "); the fourth, " Christ unser Herr zum Jordan kam " ("When Christ our Lord to Jordan came "); for confession we have " Aus tiefer Noth schrei ich zu dir " (" From deep distress to Thee I cry "); and for the Holy Communion, " Jesus Christus unser Heiland " (" Jesus Christ our Lord and Saviour "). Each is twice treated, first with pedals and then *manualiter* alone. These are preceded by a two-fold

---

[398] Forkel, p. 60, speaks of yet more sonatas written by Bach, in addition to these six. There are, however, no more extant, except two separate three-part movements in D minor and C minor, which are not complete. The first is found in P. S. V., Cah. 4 (243), No. 14, and the second is in a MS. in the Royal Library at Berlin, containing an Adagio and a fragment of an Allegro. Forkel was probably thinking of the *Pastorale* for two manuals and pedals, which, together with three short clavier pieces which follow, but apparently do not belong to it, has been published by Griepenkerl, on Forkel's authority, as one continuous whole (P. S. V., Cah. 1 (240), No. 3). The *Pastorale* itself, which, as it now stands, begins in F major and ends very unsatisfactorily in A minor, is certainly only a fragment.

[399] B.-G., III., pp. 184-241. The original edition, which appeared in 1739, or at latest, at Easter, 1740, cost 3 thalers ; see Mizler, Musikalische Bibliothek, II., p. 156. Kirnberger's remarks on these chorale arrangements (see ante p. 133) will be found in Appendix B., XIV.

arrangement of " Kyrie Gott Vater in Ewigkeit " (" Father of Heaven, have mercy "); and a threefold one of " Allein Gott in der Höh sei Ehr " (" To God alone be glory "). These two chorales — German versions of the *Kyrie* and *Gloria* of the mass—have here a peculiar importance as being substituted in the Lutheran church for the two first numbers of the mass, and sung at the beginning of the service in Leipzig.

The task of glorifying in music the doctrines of Lutheran christianity which Bach undertook in this set of chorales, he regarded as an act of worship, at the beginning of which he addressed himself to the Triune God in the same hymns of prayer and praise as those sung every Sunday by the congregation. And the fact that the chorale " Allein Gott in der Höh sei Ehr " is treated three times has an ecclesiastical and dogmatic reference. For this hymn is sung in praise of the Trinity, to whom also the prayer of the *Kyrie* is addressed; but in the *Kyrie* the three different melodies require as many different treatments, while in " Allein Gott in der Höh sei Ehr " all the verses were to be sung to the same melody. I have said before that the organ chorale of Pachelbel appears as a kind of ideal act of service in a purely instrumental form.[400] It is the same artistic idea which in the organ chorale, as treated by Bach, became so grand and inspiring. It led on to the chorale fantasia, which, by the introduction of the *Cantus firmus*, is transferred to vocal music; and its ultimate outcome is the chorale cantata, the last and highest development of the Pachelbel organ chorale. It has evidently influenced the character of the set of chorales in the third part of the " Clavierübung," in so far as its character may be viewed as a whole. The different parts of this work have indeed no connection whatever in a musical sense, and their poetical connection is only indirect, depending upon an idea derived from without. Bach had long recognised the fact that the ideal of that form could not be completely carried out in instrumental music, and he proved most conclusively that he recognised it, at

---

[400] See Vol. I., p. 112 f.

the very time when he wrote those organ chorales. But he could not abandon the plan once formed, and all the less so as his intention was to sum up here the whole of his life's work.

Bach has here employed the pure form of the chorale fantasia only for the first arrangements of the melodies "Dies sind die heilgen zehn Gebot," "Christ unser Herr zum Jordan kam," and "Jesus Christus unser Heiland." These grand pieces are at the same time eloquent witnesses to his depth of nature, both as a poet and as a composer. Bach always deduced the emotional character of his organ chorales from the whole hymn, and not from its first verse alone. In this way he generally obtained from the poem some leading thought, which seemed to him of particular importance, and in accordance with which he gave to the composition a poetic and musical character of its own. We must follow out his method in detail in order to be sure that we have grasped his meaning. In the hymn for the Holy Communion, "Jesus Christus unser Heiland," the counterpoint, with its broad, ponderous progressions, may, to the superficial observer, seem unsuitable to the character of the hymn. The attentive reader of the words will, however, soon find the passage which gave rise to this characteristic musical phrase. The fifth verse runs thus :—

Du sollt gläuben und nicht wanken,	Hold it true, nor ever waver,
Dass ein Speise sei der Kranken,	That a feast of sweetest savour
Den'n ihr Herz von Sünden schwer,	Granted is to hearts distressed,
Und für Angst ist betrübet sehr.	With their load of guilt oppressed.

Faith, lively and immovable, together with the solemnity of a consciousness of sin, are the two elements which constitute the emotional groundwork of the piece. A comparison with the no less grand earlier arrangement of the same chorale, or with the mystic composition of "Schmücke dich, o liebe Seele,"[401] gives new insight not only into Bach's wealth of imagination, but into his personal character, by revealing the subjective element in the organ chorales. Again, when in the arrangement of the chorale "Christ

---

[401] See Vol. I., pp. 613 ff. and 617.

unser Herr zum Jordan kam " an unceasing figure of flowing
semiquavers makes itself heard, it needs no skilled critic of
Bach's works to find in this an image of the river Jordan.
Bach's real meaning, however, will not reveal itself
thoroughly to him until he has read the whole poem to the
last verse, in which the water of baptism is brought before
the believing christian as a symbol of the atoning Blood
of Christ. In the five-part organ chorale " Dies sind die
heilgen zehn Gebot," the *Cantus firmus* brought in in canon
on the octave sheds a light on the poetic meaning. The idea
of bondage to the law, which is thus suggested, is one which
we have met with before in the cantata " Du sollst Gott
deinen Herrn lieben," although there it was not so fully
elaborated. In the composition of the organ chorale Bach
certainly had the cantata chorus in his mind, as I have
already argued.[402]

Of more frequent occurrence are those less free forms
—intermediate between the chorale fantasia and a form
approaching nearly to the Pachelbel type—which arise when
a motive or theme, derived only from the first line of the
melody, pervades the whole piece. I will first mention
the longer arrangement of " Vater unser im Himmelreich."
Here the melody appears against three parts in counterpoint in canon on the octave. Bach may have intended
by this to symbolize the believing, childlike obedience with
which the Christian appropriates the prayer prescribed by
Christ Himself. The counterpoints with their peculiar
movement seem to have a specially importunate character.[403]
To the same category belong the two three-part arrangements of " Allein Gott in der Höh," in the second of which,
however, the *Cantus firmus* is brought out alternately in
different parts, and here and there in canon or with a
repetition of the same line. And lastly, the first arrangement of the *Kyrie* in three sections, the majestic structure
of which culminates in a grand five-part composition.

---

[402] See Vol. II., p. 431.

[403] In the way in which certain similar phrases are to be played compare
ante, p. 49, note 60.

As may be imagined, the pure Pachelbel type, to which Bach was so much indebted in his organ chorales, could not be absent from so exhaustive a work as this. It appears in the penitential hymn "Aus tiefer Noth schrei ich zu dir," both in the four-part arrangement for manuals alone and in the six-part arrangement for manuals and double pedals. It is significant of Bach's manner of feeling that he should choose this particular chorale for the crowning point of his work. For it cannot be questioned that this chorale is its crowning point, from the ingenuity of the part-writing, the wealth and nobility of the harmonies, and the executive power which it requires. Even the northern masters had never ventured to write two parts for the pedals throughout, though they had first introduced the two-part treatment of the pedals, and Bach did both Pachelbel and them full justice in this piece. And not in this piece only; in the fughetta on " Dies sind die heilgen zehn Gebot " we recognise the spirit of Buxtehude, although it has received new birth from Bach's genius. The manner in which the ideals of Bach's youth appear again in this last great work for the organ is characteristic of his art and of his nature. We also feel the influence of Georg Böhm, Bach's favourite model during his " apprenticeship " at Lüneburg; the *Basso quasi ostinato* in the organ chorale " Wir glauben all an einen Gott " points clearly to his style. The piece is a fugue on the first line of the melody, and has nothing whatever to do with the bass. And this makes the reference to Böhm quite clear ; for it was not Bach's usual method to write fugues in which the pedal-part neither took any share in the working-out of the fugue nor brought out any *Cantus firmus*, but only repeated from time to time a short, independent phrase.[404] Lastly, that the organ chorale should not be absent in that simplest form, which Bach had elaborated at Weimar and subsequently established by the most splendid examples in the " Orgelbüchlein," he incorporated in the collection the beautiful second arrangement of the " Vater unser."

---

[404] Compare Vol. I., p. 213.

Still he wished to increase the scope of the collection. Not content with producing organ chorales in the most widely different forms, he went back to their original germ and found room even for real chorale preludes, a form that he had never had anything to do with, except, perhaps, in his earliest youth.[405] The organ chorale differs from the chorale prelude in this, that it is an independent work of art, requiring only a previous acquaintance with the melody, while the chorale prelude is nothing more than a preparatory piece, having its central point of interest not in itself, but in the congregational hymn that is to follow it. Accordingly, the treatment of the melody is quite different; the hymn-tune is only referred to, and must never appear entire in the organ piece. Now the second arrangement of " Kyrie Gott Vater in Ewigkeit " in this collection is pre-eminently of this kind; only the first three notes of the chorale are treated in all three parts. In the second arrangement of the baptismal hymn the whole of the first line of the tune is introduced, but no more. But in order to appreciate the almost immeasurable difference between the old chorale prelude and that of Bach, compare the works of this kind composed by Johann Christoph Bach with those just mentioned.[406]

An independent species of chorale prelude is the chorale fugue. And this form, too, had been scarcely touched by Bach during his riper years until now.[407] The third part of the " Clavierübung " contains five such pieces; they are upon the melodies " Allein Gott in der Höh," " Dies sind die heilgen zehn Gebot," " Wir glauben all," and " Jesus Christus unser Heiland." With the exception of the first the fugue theme in each is derived from the first line only. Three of them are fughettas, thrown off with masterly ease, and full of sharply defined character; the smaller work on " Wir glauben all " is in the French style, and the first and most important one is in Buxtehude's manner. The fugue on " Jesus Christus unser Heiland," with which the collec-

---

[405] See Vol. I., p. 219.   [406] See Vol. I., p. 100 ff.
[407] Compare Vol. I., p. 605 f.

tion closes, has very brilliant strettos, and, finally, a combination of the theme in its natural form and in augmentation. The great fugue on "Wir glauben all" has been
already spoken of. In it two form-ideas are united, that of
Böhm's chorale with that of the prelude.

Let it now be decided whether the chorale collection in
the "Clavierübung" may rightly be called a comprehensive
and self-contained work. With its completion Bach considered his life-work practically over as regards the treatment of the organ chorale. From that time until his death
he collected and arranged his older works,[408] but created
very little that was new. One of the works collected and
arranged by him at this time is that set of six chorales for
two manuals and pedals, which he had published between
1746 and 1750 by Johann Georg Schübler, of Zella St. Blasii,
near Suhl. They are taken from cantatas written at Leipzig,
as can be proved in the case of all but one, which can form
no exception to the rest ; and, to be rightly appreciated, they
must be studied from this point of view.[409]

On the other hand, we have an original composition in the
"canonischen Veränderungen" (variations in canon), upon
the Christmas hymn "Vom Himmel hoch da komm ich
her," which appeared, published by Balthasar Schmidt, of
Nuremberg, elegantly engraved.[410] According to a tradition,
which we have no reason to doubt, Bach wrote them for the
Leipzig Musical Society, which he joined in June, 1747.[411]
They were, however, written and even engraved a year
before he joined the Society.[412] From the title, "Variations,'
it would be easy to draw a false conclusion as to their form.
It is, however, valuable, as it teaches us the purpose that
Bach had in view in the work. About the year 1700 the
name "Variation" was also used for "Partita," which last
word originally betokened the separate portions of a collective composition, consisting of pieces in the same key,

---

[408] See Vol. I., p. 655 f.
[409] B.-G., XXV.[2], II.   See App. A., No. 9.
[410] P. S. V., Cah. 5 (244).   Abth. II., No. 4.
[411] See ante, p. 25.
[412] See App. A., No. 10.

and was afterwards used for the collective composition itself.
So carelessly were the two names used that not unfrequently the first "Partita" of a set of variations—*i.e.*,
the theme itself—was called the first variation. Now we
know the chorale partita to have been a form adopted
by Bach in his youth from Böhm's model.[413] Its superficial
and secular nature could no longer satisfy him, and in
the chorale collection of the "Clavierübung" there is
no reference to it. But the feeling that he must complete
his task in the most perfect way possible seems to have
given him no rest. The "Variations" upon the Christmas
hymn are *partitas*. This is evident from the fact that
the work begins at once with the so-called first variation;
this is proper to the partita form, and is of frequent
occurrence, in Pachelbel, for example, whereas a true
variation without a given theme is an impossibility.[414] Thus,
this work is to be compared with the youthful works
"Christ, der du bist der helle Tag," "O Gott du frommer
Gott," and "Sei gegrüsset, Jesu gütig."[415] The same
immense advance will then be perceived as in the case of
the chorale preludes.

The strict variation-form, which keeps exactly to the length
and construction of the theme, was not adhered to in the
chorale partitas, though it played an important part in them.
In the partitas upon the Christmas hymn Bach quite
abandoned it, and with it the adornment of the melody by
means of figures more suitable to the clavier style. He
also abjured the too secular disruption of the theme by
episodes, after the confused method of Böhm, who brings
in the theme now here and now there, setting in motion
a varying number of parts. Bach's are true organ chorales,
of the type which predominates in the "Orgelbüchlein,"
and what unites them into a whole is the style of canon
treatment which is common to all. In the first four partitas

---

[413] See Vol. I., p. 210 ff.

[414] Kirnberger (Kunst des reinen Satzes, II., 2, p. 173) seems to have quite
misunderstood the form; he was misled by the term "Variation," and by the
fact that in the majority of the partitas the *Cantus firmus* lies in the bass.

[415] See Vol. I., p. 604.

the canon lies in the parts that have the counterpoint—a form
with which we became acquainted in the " Musikalisches
Opfer." The imitation follows in the octave, the fifth and
the seventh, and in the octave with augmentation. But
Bach set himself a more complicated task, not merely
deriving the counterpoint from the melody, but in the third
partita interweaving between the *Cantus firmus* and the two
parts in canon a very *Cantabile* melody, freely invented.
In the last partita, which properly consists of four complete
workings-out connected together, the melody itself appears
in canon in contrary motion, and in the sixth, third, second,
and ninth. The three concluding bars are of marvellous
ingenuity, for in them all four lines of the melody are heard
simultaneously in the different parts.

In freedom of movement the partitas on " Vom Himmel
hoch " are in no way inferior either to the " Musikalisches
Opfer," the "Kunst der Fuge," or even the thirty Clavier
Variations. Bach was assured of perfect success, even in
the most difficult problems; and he here gives fresh proof
that it was not the mere fascination of technical difficulties
to overcome that led him to adopt these elaborate forms
in his later works, but that his musical sense grew deeper,
and imperatively demanded new modes of utterance. These
partitas are full of passionate vitality and poetical feeling.
The heavenly hosts soar up and down, their lovely song
sounding out over the cradle of the Infant Christ, while the
multitude of the redeemed "join the sweet song with joyful
hearts." But the experiences of a fruitful life of sixty
years have interwoven themselves with the emotions which
possessed him in earlier years at the Christmas festival,
and which he embodied in undying creations in the
organ chorales, in the Christmas Oratorio, the Magnificat,
and other works, and mingle with the feeling which in his
early youth had inspired him to produce those forms of art
which he was destined to ennoble for ever. The work has
an element of solemn thankfulness, like the gaze of an old
man who watches his grandchildren standing round their
Christmas tree, and is reminded of his own childhood.

If we found, as a characteristic feature of Bach's vocal

church music, that his genius, after traversing the whole range of art, should at last find its goal in the chorale cantata, it is no less important to notice the way in which he cultivated the organ chorale until the end of his life. His art described a mighty orbit, returning to the point from which it originally started. Handel's course of development is that of a mighty river, resting only when it reaches the great world-ocean. Bach, after traversing all the heights and depths of life, finds his ultimate repose in the peace of home. He does not throw himself into the world, but absorbs it into his own individuality. This subjective character may be traced in his music in all his periods, but it is even stronger in the last period of his life than during the years of his fullest prime. The organ chorale is, of all the forms employed by Bach, the most subjective, and it is that which he used most freely. His devotion to it was proved a few days before his death. The last composition which he undertook, with the help of Altnikol—for his sight was gone—was an elaboration of an early organ chorale "Wenn wir in höchsten Nöthen sein." To the end he consecrated the highest powers of his life to a form, of which the very essence is the joy of praising and praying to God in the congregation. Bach felt, like Augustine, that "Thou hast created us for Thyself, and our heart is unquiet till it finds repose in Thee."

VI.

BACH'S PRIVATE FRIENDSHIPS AND PUPILS; HIS GENERAL CULTURE.—BLINDNESS AND DEATH.

ALL that has been written as to Bach's life, from the year 1723, bears principally on the various aspects of his official position and his relations to the public generally at Leipzig. It has not been possible hitherto to discuss his position during all this time with regard to the musical world at large, nor his domestic life and his personal characteristics as developed in it.

Bach never saw Italy, that Eldorado of the German

musician ; indeed, he never crossed the German frontier. Still, he inherited a taste for wandering, and he travelled from Leipzig a good deal, considering the times and circumstances, and thus contributed himself to extend his fame as an artist.[416] He was still Capellmeister at Cöthen when he settled at Leipzig, and in the same year was appointed "outdoor" Capellmeister at Weissenfels. These offices required the person who held them to provide compositions for the use of the respective Courts when called upon to do so, and to present himself from time to time in person. A curious fate presided over Bach's connection with Weissenfels; it has left scarcely a trace to posterity. Not a single composition can be pointed to as written by Bach for the Court of Duke Christian, after his first dedicating a cantata to him from Weimar in 1716; all we know is that this same cantata was subsequently used again for a Court festival at Weissenfels.[417] From this we may be allowed to suppose that after Duke Christian's death in 1736 Bach's services were scarcely ever again claimed for any musical productions. His successor, Johann Adolph II., introduced a very economical régime, with a view to retrieving the fortunes of his family which was deeply in debt. He died in 1746, and with him this Saxon branch became extinct. Bach enjoyed the title of "*Hochfürstlich Weissenfelsische wirkliche Capellmeister*" till his death,[418] so it does not follow that he should have fulfilled any duties even during Johann Adolph's lifetime. However, he frequently visited the Court there between 1723 and 1736. He himself mentions incidentally that he had to quit Leipzig once or twice between 1723 and 1725, *ob impedimenta legitima*; on one of these occasions he had gone to Dresden,[419] and on the second we may suppose he went

---

[416] Forkel is to a certain extent in error when he says (p. 48) : "If he had only chosen to travel he might have concentrated in himself the admiration of the world, as indeed even his enemies allowed." The "enemy" must have been Scheibe, but he makes the remark in a different sense. Crit. Mus., p. 62.

[417] See Vol. I., p. 566 ff.

[418] See "Nützliche Nachrichten von denen Bemühungen derer Gelehrten . . . in Leipzig." 1750, p. 680.

[419] See Vol. II., p. 220.

to Weissenfels, where he had lately been appointed.   In the band under his direction there, and which was not unknown to fame, were his father-in-law, Joh. Caspar Wülcken, and Adam Emanuel Weltig, godfather to his son Ph. Emanuel.

Rather more is known regarding Bach's doings as Capell-meister at Cöthen after his removal to Leipzig.   It is evident that after the death of his first wife Prince Leopold recovered his strong interest in music, and his second wife, the Princess Charlotte, seems herself to have had a love for it since Bach ventured to dedicate to her a birthday cantata, November 30, 1726.[420]   On the 12th September of that year she had presented the Prince with an heir, just as Bach had brought out the first partita of the Clavierübung as *Opus* I. This coincidence prompted him to copy out the partita with particular care, and offer it on the Crown Prince's cradle with a dedicatory poem; and this poem, which is un-doubtedly original, is strong evidence of the friendly and informal relations subsisting between Bach and the royal family.   The dedication runs as follows:

" To the Most Serene Prince and Lord | the Lord *Emanuel Ludwig* | Crown Prince of Anhalt, Duke of Saxony, Enger and Westphalia, Count of Ascania, Lord of Bernburg and Zerbst, &c., &c., &c. | these small musical first fruits are dedicated with the humblest devotion | by Johann Sebastian Bach."

The verses are to this effect:

Serene
   and Infant Prince,
      whom swaddling bands encumber
 Although thy princely glance argues maturer age,
Forgive me if I dare to wake thee from thy slumber,
 And humbly crave thy grace for this my playful page.
These first fruits of my lyre to thee I dare to bring,
 Thou Prince first born to feel thy royal mother's kiss,
Hoping that she, to thee, the lay may some time sing,
 Since, in the world, thou art a first fruit too, like this.
The wiseheads fain would scare new-comers with a warning,
 Because into the world we come with cries and tears,

---

[420] See Vol. II., p. 158.

As though they could foretell the evening from the morning,
And see thy future destiny beyond the veil of years.
But I will answer them—and say that as these chords
That round thy cradle swell are sweet and clear and pure;
So shall thy life flow brightly on, through all that earth affords
Of joy and harmony—calm, happy, and secure.
May I, most hopeful Prince, play for thy delectation
When all thy baby powers are increased a thousandfold ;[421]
For my own part I only pray for constant inspiration,
        And remain,
                most noble Prince,
                        Thy
                                humble servant,
                                        Bach.[422]

The Crown Prince Emanuel Ludwig, however, gave the master no chance of " playing for his delectation," for he died August 17, 1728, and Prince Leopold followed his only son to the grave in a very few months.   I have already spoken of the grand funeral ode composed by Bach for his patron and friend ; I have been unable to find any further records of his connection with the Court of Cöthen.

Bach had enjoyed a great reputation at Dresden from 1717, and had been well remembered there.   He certainly visited it frequently from Leipzig, and often took his eldest son with him.[423]   When, in 1733, Friedemann was appointed organist to the Sophienkirche at Dresden, and Bach himself, in 1736, had an appointment at Court there, his visits became more frequent; however, we have direct evidence of only four between 1723 and 1750.   The first of these was between 1723 and 1725, and from what Bach says of it incidentally we may infer that he went by a special command from the King.[424]

---

[421] In German *tausendfach*, supplying the rhyme to *Bach*.

[422] The existence of this autograph was not known to the world till February, 1879, when the possessor of it sent a description of it and a copy of the dedication and verses to the Magdeburg *Zeitung*.   It was subsequently copied into the *Berliner Fremdenblatt* for February 20, 1879.   The steps I then took to obtain a sight of the autograph failed of any result; I had no answer to my application, and I cannot, therefore, be responsible for the accuracy of the communication.   Any doubt, however—though under the circumstances justifiable—may, in my opinion, be allowed to vanish when we consider the form and purport of the documents, which seem to me a guarantee of their genuineness.

[423] Forkel, p. 48.   [424] See Vol. II., p. 220.

In 1731 the first performance of *Cleofide* was given, and this tempted him to Dresden; on July 7 of that year Johann Adolph Hasse and his wife Faustina arrived from Venice with an introduction to the Capellmeister, and his opera, in which Faustina played the principal part, was given for the first time September 13. This was a great event in Dresden, and indeed of supreme importance to the Italian opera in Germany. The enthusiasm for Hasse's music and Faustina's singing knew no limit; one reporter says that to praise this pair in worthy terms is as vain as to try to light a candle at the sun. Bach proposed to give what would in these days be called an organ recital in the Sophienkirche on the following day at three o'clock. It does not appear that any member of the Court honoured him by attending it; but the whole band—including Hasse no doubt —were present, and Bach's success among his fellow artists was great and complete. Even the public prints took notice of it, which is certainly significant considering the impression made by *Cleofide;* and a rhymester of the day spoke of the marvellous power of his "nimble fingers" as transcending that of Orpheus.

After Bach, in 1733, had dedicated the *Kyrie* and *Gloria* of the B minor mass to King August III., and presented it personally in Dresden, and then, three years later, after repeated applications, had obtained the style and title of *Hofcomponist,* he again performed there for a few days, December 1, 1736, from two till four in the afternoon on the new organ by Silbermann in the Frauenkirche. On this occasion the company did not consist exclusively of his band; many distinguished persons met to admire the master.[425]

Among these was Baron Hermann Carl von Kayserling, who, a few years later, came into closer contact with Bach, and who must, even at this time, have known him, and have been favourably disposed towards him. The patent conferring on Bach the coveted title was ready by

---

[425] Fürstenau, Zur Geschichte der Musik am Hofe zu Dresden. II., pp. 171 and 222.

November 19, and given to the Baron to hand on to Bach on November 28. Bach, however, had known beforehand of the contents of the document, and immediately prepared to set out for Dresden and express his thanks in person, otherwise he could not have given his performance on December 1, and Kayserling's position as intermediary shows that his interest in Bach was already an understood thing. In him, indeed, Bach found a wealthy patron of high rank and wide interests. Before coming to Dresden as ambassador from St. Petersburg, December 13, 1733, he had held the president's chair at the Imperial Academy of Sciences at St. Petersburg. King August III. raised him to the rank of Count, October 30, 1741, and he remained at Dresden till 1745. As a "great lover and connoisseur of music" he was fond of collecting round him all the most remarkable artists of the city. Pisendel, Weiss, and Friedemann Bach were admitted to his house, and musicians on their travels esteemed it an honour to be introduced there.[426] All these circumstances must have contributed to make Bach's connection with the artist world of Dresden both pleasant and intimate; and that it was so was a well-known fact, even in the years from 1727 to 1731, so that trustworthy and interesting reports as to the doings of the Dresden band reached Leipzig almost every day.[427] Pisendel, who, so early as 1709, had visited Bach in Weimar in the course of a journey from Anspach to Leipzig, devoted much attention to the *Viola pomposa* invented by Bach. He liked this instrument for accompaniments. When Franz Benda came once on a visit to Dresden, in 1738, music was carried on at Weiss's house from early in the afternoon till midnight; Benda and Pisendel themselves played no less than twenty-four violin soli, while Weiss, between these, played eight or ten sonatas on the lute.[428]

One of Pisendel's best scholars was John Gottlieb Graun, and even Bach had such confidence in him that when, in 1726, he was called away from Dresden to be Concert-

---

[426] Hiller, Lebensbeschreibungen, p. 45.—Fürstenau, op. cit. p. 222, note.

[427] Scheibe, Uber die musikalische Composition, prof. p. lix.

[428] Hiller, op. cit., p. 45.

meister to Duke Moritz Wilhelm, of Sax-Merseburg, he entrusted his son Wilhelm Friedemann to his teaching for a time.[429]   He was attracted to Zelenka, the worthy pupil of Fux, by his serious taste chiefly for church-music, and in this respect he no doubt set him above Hasse.   Friedemann had to copy out a *Magnificat* by Zelenka, for the use of the St. Thomas's singers.[430]   We know no details as to Bach's intercourse with other Dresden celebrities in art, such as Buffardin, Heinichen, Hebenstreit and Quantz, but his acquaintance with Hasse and his wife was founded on sincere and reciprocal admiration ; they visited Bach several times in Leipzig.[431]

Hamburg, the goal of Bach's musical pilgrimage from Lüneburg, and of which he retained a keen recollection from the year 1720, he visited in 1727, so far as we know for the last time.   Jacob Wilhelm Lustig, the son of an organist in Hamburg, a pupil of Mattheson and of Telemann, and himself subsequently an organist of mark at Gröningen, at that time heard him play.   The words in which he has recorded the fact are eloquent in their simplicity : "There he heard great musicians, nay, Herr Bach himself."   Everything that even great players could do appeared weak and inferior when compared with that one supreme ideal.

How Bach and Mattheson got on together at this time cannot be known ; Mattheson's feeling against him has already been spoken of elsewhere.   In 1731 he once more asked him to contribute an autobiographical notice to the "Ehrenpforte," and as Bach did not comply he omitted him altogether from that work, because "he had had an unreasonable objection to giving any accurate and systematic account of the incidents of his life."   Now, Handel and Keiser did just the same, but they were, nevertheless, admitted to that temple of honour.   Telemann, the friend of his youth—who, if he had not changed his mind, might four years before have been comfortably installed as cantor of St. Thomas's—did not pass Bach over in this way.   In

---

[429] Marpurg, Hist. Krit. Beyträge, I., p. 430.
[430] Still extant, score and parts, in the Library of the Thomasschule.
[431] Forkel, p. 48.

his musical periodical, "Der Getreue Musik-Meister," published in 1728, he included a beautiful canon in four parts, of the most elaborate character, composed by Bach at Hamburg in 1727, and dedicated to Dr. Hudemann. Lustig also made acquaintance with this canon, mastered it and solved it, and twelve years later Mattheson included this solution in his "Vollkommene Capellmeister." We saw, when speaking of the cantata "Phœbus and Pan," how Hudemann showed his appreciation of the honour done him.[432]

Bach also revisited his native province of Thuringia from Leipzig. His connection with the Court of Weimar was at an end after Duke Wilhelm Ernst, in a pedantic whim, had appointed Samuel Drese's son, a quite second-rate musician, to be Capellmeister, while Bach had every right to the place. It is not even probable that any relations existed between Bach and the Court of Weimar so long as that duke remained alive; however, on the accession of Duke Ernst August (1728-1748), they were renewed. This sovereign prince, who in many respects was singularly and radically unlike his uncle, seems, like his half-brother, Joh. Ernst, to have inherited his love of music from his father, in whose service Bach had been for a short time in 1703. He was a persevering violin player, often beginning in the morning before he was up, and seems to have taken much pleasure in Italian opera music, like Duke Christian of Weissenfels.[433] One of the many purposes which the cantata

[432] At the time when I wrote Vol. I., p. 632 (of the original German. A passage omitted by the author's desire from Vol. II., p. 21, of this translation), Bach's visit to Hamburg in 1727 had escaped my notice; but it is to be inferred from the passage in Marpurg, Krit. Briefe, II., p. 470, where we have an account by Lustig of his own life, and this autobiography is chronologically arranged. The younger Kunze was born in 1720, and Lustig was teaching him in 1724-5; then followed lessons in composition, which he learnt from his father and Telemann. In 1728 Lustig went to Gröningen, but he had previously heard Bach play in Hamburg, and, as it was in 1727 that Bach dedicated the above-mentioned canon to Hudemann, he must have been in Hamburg in that year, and have written the canon there. This is evident also from Mattheson, pp. 412-13; from Mizler, Mus. Bib. III., p. 482; and Marpurg, Abhandlung von der Fuge, Part II., p. 99 (Tab. XXXIII., fig. 2). Hilgenfeldt also printed the canon without the solution, as the last musical supplement to his work.

[433] See the notices borrowed from the memoirs of Baron von Pöllnitz in Beaulieu-Marconnay, Ernst August, Herzog von Sachsen-Weimar-Eisenach, Hirzel, Leipzig, 1872, pp. 143-4 and p. 104.

"Was mir behagt" must have served was the keeping of Ernst August's birthday. Bach's eldest son has recorded for us that this Duke was "attached by sincere affection to the artist," no less than Leopold of Cöthen and Christian of Weissenfels.

Erfurt also, one of the old gathering-places of the Bach family had great attractions for Bach as he advanced in years. A cousin of his, Joh. Christoph, son of Ægidius Bach, was the leading member of the town musicians of Erfurt when Sebastian once more sought him out in the time-honoured town.[434] This must have been after 1727. Adlung was at that time organist at the Prediger Kirche, an office which Johann Bach had held in his time. Adlung on this occasion made great friends with Sebastian Bach; he made many inquiries as to his early life, and begged him to play to him on the clavier, in all of which the great master showed the polite amiability which characterised him on such occasions.[435]

Bach must have made some other journeys about 1730 and in July, 1736. It was on the former occasion that he was so severely called to task by the Leipzig Council[436] for having neglected the proper formalities in asking leave. The latter journey immediately preceded his great quarrel with Ernesti.[437] We do not know whither he went on either of these occasions, but in the course of the quarrel we learn from Ernesti's memoranda that Bach must have been absent from Leipzig tolerably often, since Ernesti mentions how he was accustomed to supply his place in such cases.

In later years Bach, as might be expected, moved about less, and his liking for "a quiet and domestic life, and a constant and undisturbed devotion to his art,"[438] preponderated. He could scarcely make up his mind, perhaps, to his last great expedition, which, however, had the most

---

[434] See Vol. I., p. 27.

[435] Adlung, Anl. zur Mus. Gel., p. 691. He does not mention any date, but it must certainly have been after 1727, since it was not till the end of that year that Adlung came to Erfurt from Jena. Adlung says "Herr Bach came to see *us*," whence we may safely infer that he was intimate already with the Bachs of Erfurt.

[436] See Vol. II., p. 243.   [437] See ante, p. 6.   [438] Forkel, p. 48.

important results of any. In 1740 Emanuel Bach had been made Capellmusiker and accompanist to Frederick the Great, and as the most important members of his band—the two Grauns, Franz Benda, Quantz, Nichelmann, and probably Baron—were all personally acquainted with Bach, and some of them had been his pupils, the king must of course have frequently heard him spoken of. The tone in which this was done excited his wish to see and hear the great artist himself. Emanuel sent word of this to Leipzig, but his father did not feel inclined to take the hint. It was not till the King became more and more urgent that he could make up his mind to set out, in May, 1747. He took Friedemann with him, and so must have taken the route *via* Halle, and on Sunday, May 7, he reached Potsdam. It was the custom to give a State Concert every evening from seven to nine, in which the king himself performed as soloist on the flute.[439] Of all that now followed we have a detailed account from Emanuel and from Friedemann.[440] Just as the king was about to perform his flute solo, a list was brought to him of the various strangers who had that day arrived. With his flute still in one hand, he glanced through the paper; he turned to the assembled band saying, with some excitement: " Gentlemen, old Bach is come!" His flute was laid aside, and Bach sent for at once to come to the château. He had put up at Emanuel's house, and he was not even allowed time to put on his black Court-dress; he had to appear at once in his travelling costume, just as he was. Friedemann tells us that his father having apologised somewhat at length for the deficiencies in his dress, the king bade him make no excuses, and that then a conversation began between the king and the artist.[441] Frederick had a high opinion of

---

[439] Marpurg, Hist. Krit. Beyträg. I., p. 76.   [440] Forkel, p. 9.

[441] It may be considered an unsettled question whether in this narrative Friedemann has not given the reins to his imagination. Spener's Zeitung—which was the first to direct attention—reports the matter as follows:— " May 11, 1747. His Majesty was informed that Capellmeister Bach had arrived in Potsdam, and that he was in the king's antechamber, waiting his Majesty's gracious permission to enter, and hear the music. His Majesty at once commanded that he should be admitted."

Silbermann's pianofortes, and Bach himself had had some share in perfecting these instruments.[442] The king had several, and Bach was required to try them, and improvise upon them. On the following day Bach played the organ in the Church of the Holy Ghost, at Potsdam, before a crowded audience ; but the king does not seem to have been present. However, he commanded his presence at the château again in the evening, and desired to hear him play a six-part fugue, that he might learn to what a pitch the art of polyphonic treatment could be carried ; Bach was to choose his own theme, since every subject is not fitted for treatment in so many parts, and he won the king's complete approval by his performance.

From Potsdam he also went to Berlin, and visited the opera-house built there in 1741-3 by Knobelsdorf. Nothing was then being played there, however. For regular performances only Mondays and Fridays in December and January were appointed, and besides these March 27, as being the Queen Dowager's birthday.[443] But Bach was interested in any place dedicated to musical purposes. It seems almost fabulous when the historian of this wonderful man is obliged to mention one more of his many gifts ; but, it is nevertheless true that Bach's keen judgment had penetrated the mysteries of the conditions of building which were favourable to acoustics ; he detected everything that was advantageous or detrimental to musical effects in the opera-house at Berlin, and, without hearing a note of music in it, he saw at a glance all that others had learned by experience. He also pointed out to his companions, in the dining-room attached to the opera-house, an acoustic phenomenon which, as he supposed, the architect had probably not intended to produce. The form of the arches betrayed the secret to him. When a speaker stood in one

---

[442] See Vol. II., p. 46.

[443] See Marpurg, Hist. Krit. Beyträge. I., p. 75. Brachvogel relates, in his Geschichte des Königl. Theaters zu Berlin (Berlin, Janke, 1877), Vol. I., p. 129, that Bach played at a State Concert with Signora Astrua ; but, in point of fact, Astrua did not appear till August, 1747, in a *pastoral* performed at Charlottenburg. See Marpurg, op. cit., p. 82

corner of the gallery of the hall—which was longer than square—and whispered against the wall, another person, standing in the corner diagonally opposite, with his face to the wall, could hear what was said though no one else could. Bach detected this at a glance, and experiment proved him to be right. The authority who records this adds that Bach could calculate accurately how a great composition would sound in a given space.[444] It is not superfluous to insist on this, since many might suppose that the master was so wholly absorbed in his own world of music as to disregard the sensible and physical effect of his works.

Bach had won the admiration of the Court by his extempore performance, but he had not been fully satisfied with himself. The thema for the fugue proposed to him by the king pleased him so well that he pledged himself to use it for a more extended composition, and do himself the honour of having it engraved to offer to his majesty. The result of this project was the " Musikalisches Opfer," of which the merit, as a work of art, has been duly pointed out.[445] How eager he was to fulfil his promise and how highly, therefore, he must have valued the great king's approval, is proved by the haste with which the " Musikalisches Opfer " was completed. The dedication which he prefixed to it is worthy of consideration.

MOST GRACIOUS KING,

I herewith dedicate to your Majesty, with the deepest submission, a musical offering, of which the noblest portion is the work of your Majesty's illustrious hand. It is with reverential satisfaction that I now remember your Majesty's very special royal favour, when some time since, during my stay in Potsdam, your Majesty condescended to play the theme for a fugue to me on the clavier, and at the same time graciously commanded me to work it out then and there in the royal presence. It was my humble duty to obey your Majesty's command. But I immediately perceived that, for lack of due preparation, the performance was not so successful as so excellent a theme required. I accordingly determined, and at once set to work, to treat this really royal theme more perfectly, and then to make it known to the world. This undertaking I have now carried out to the best of my ability, and

---

[444] Forkel, p. 20.   [445] See ante, p. 191 ff.

it has no end in view but this very blameless one—to exalt—though in only a trifling matter, the fame of a Monarch whose greatness and power must be admired and respected by all, and particularly in music, as in all the other sciences of war and peace. I make so bold therefore, as to add this most humble petition—That your Majesty will condescend to grant this present little work a gracious reception and to continue to vouchsafe your gracious favours to

your Majesty's
most obedient humble servant,

LEIPZIG, *July* 7, 1747.   THE AUTHOR.

Through all the conventional phrases of devotion, we can see in this dedication a dignified self-reliance, arising from the feeling, not merely of having enjoyed the favour of a great king, but of having been appreciated by him as a truly great artist.

In the first instance, as was but natural, it was always Bach's eminence as an organ player which compelled the admiration of the world ; according to Telemann, even during his lifetime it won him the epithet of " The Great."[446] But after about 1720 his compositions seem to have become rapidly and widely known ; principally, it is true, his instrumental works, and chiefly those for the clavier and organ. His vocal compositions are but rarely mentioned. Mattheson alludes to some in 1716, and in 1725 he criticises the cantata " Ich hatte viel Bekümmerniss." The adjuvant or deputy in Voigt's " Gespräch von der Musik " boasts, in 1742, that he " already possesses three collections of church cantatas " by the most celebrated composers, as Telemann, Stölzel, Bach, Kegel, and several others.[447] The secular " Coffee " cantata seems to have reached Frankfort in 1739.[448] But, as a general rule, Bach's concerted vocal compositions were partly, no doubt, too difficult ; partly, too, he had failed to hit the sentiment of his time, which had found its ideal in Telemann. It is worth noting that Samuel Petri, who was a capital musician,

---

[446] See a Sonnet by Telemann on J. S. Bach in the " Neueröffnetes Historisches *Curiosit*äten-*Cabinet*. Dresden 1751, p. 13 ; reprinted by Marpurg, Historisch-Kritische Beyträge, I, p. 561.

[447] Gespräch von der *Musik*, zwischen einem Organisten und Adjuvanten. (Talk about music, between an organist and his deputy.)   Erfurt, 1742, p. 2.

[448] See Vol. II., p. 641.

besides being a pupil of Friedemann Bach's and a great admirer of Sebastian's instrumental works, never mentions him as a writer of cantatas. "In Telemann's time," he says, "several composers sought to distinguish themselves in the church style, as Stölzel, Kramer, and Römhild, who was Capellmeister to the last Duke of Sax-Merseburg, besides others whose talents were too moderate for them to compare with Telemann."[449]

It was, of course, inevitable that Bach's constantly growing fame in the outside world must react on his position in the town where he was settled; artists and lovers of music alike, illustrious and unknown, sought to establish relations with him from abroad, and made pilgrimages in person to the house in St. Thomas's Church-yard. Emanuel Bach speaks from his own knowledge when he writes in his autobiography: "No master of music would willingly pass through this town (Leipzig) without making my father's acquaintance and obtaining permission to play to him. My father's greatness in composition, and in organ and clavier playing, which was quite remarkable, was too well known for any musician of importance to neglect the opportunity of making that great man's acquaintance when it was in any way possible."[450]

Among the more illustrious lovers of music, and next to Count Sporck and Baron von Kayserling, Georg Bertuch holds a prominent place. Bertuch was born at Helmers-hausen, in Franconia; he studied in Jena, and there became acquainted with Nikolaus Bach, with whom he purposed making a journey into Italy. In 1693 he held a disputation in Kiel on a legal and musical treatise entitled *De eo quod justum est circa ludos scenicos operasque modernas* (Of the law concerning stage plays and modern operas), which was printed at Nuremberg in 1696. He subsequently entered on a military career and became a General and Governor of the fort of Aggershuys, in Norway.[451] He was so zealous in the pursuit of music that in 1738 he came before the

---

[449] Petri, Anleitung zur praktischen Musik, p. 99.
[450] Burney, Diary III., p. 201.   [451] Walther, Mus. Lex., p. 90.

public with twenty-four sonatas in all the major and minor keys. He seems to have sent a copy to Bach; at any rate, he wrote him a letter in which he extolled the German composers as superior to all others, appealing to Lotti for evidence since he, though esteeming his own countrymen for their talents, did not value them as composers, but was of opinion that the real composers were Germans.[452] We also learn—though not, it is true, from a perfectly trustworthy authority—that Bach was on intimate terms with a noble and wealthy family of Livland, with whose eldest son (who had studied in Leipzig) Emanuel Bach was to make a journey through France, Italy, and England; this plan, however, came to nothing, in consequence of Emanuel's appointment by the Crown Prince of Prussia.[453] In Bach's later life he was also on friendly terms with a Count von Würben, whose son seems to have studied in Leipzig in 1747.[454]

We must mention a few of the musicians who visited Leipzig to see Bach, Franz Benda, a Bohemian by birth, made acquaintance with him in 1734, on his way from Berlin to Bayreuth. Johann Christian Hertel, of Swabia, who at Weimar, in 1726, had taken part in the mourning ceremonial music which Duke Ernst August had had performed on the death of his wife, took the route through Leipzig to Dresden, visited Bach and persuaded him to play to him.[455] Johann Francisci, of Neusohl, in Upper Hungary, came to Leipzig, 1725, at the time of the Easter Fair, "and was so happy as to make the acquaintance of the famous Capellmeister Bach, and to derive benefit from his skill.[456] Balthasar Reimann, an admirable organist of Hirschberg in Schleswig, whose praises were often sung by his fellow

---

[452] Mizler, Mus. Bib., Vol. I., Part IV., p. 83.

[453] Rochlitz, Für Freunde der Tonkunst, Vol. IV., p. 185 (third edition). Rochlitz obtained his information from Doles, Emanuel Bach's friend. Was not this noble family that of Baron von Kayserling?

[454] In the collection of autographs belonging to Herr Ott-Usteri, of Zürich, there was in 1869 a receipt, dated Leipzig, Dec. 5, 1747, and signed *Joh. Sebast. Bach*, for the sum of 1 rthlr., 8 groschen, paid by the "Herr Grav von Werben" (*sic*) for some work for the clavier, the title of which is illegible.

[455] Hiller, Lebensbeschreibungen, pp. 44 and 156.

[456] Mattheson, Ehrenpforte, p. 79.

countryman, Daniel Stoppe, tells us that between 1729 and 1740 he travelled to Leipzig, at the expense of a noble patron, to hear the celebrated Joh. Sebastian Bach play. "This great artist received me amiably, and so enchanted me by his uncommon skill that I have never regretted the journey."[457] Georg Heinrich Ludwig Schwanenberger, violinist in the band of the Duke of Brunswick, seems to have stood in the most confidential intimacy with Bach's family.[458] He was in Leipzig in October, 1728, just when one of Bach's daughters was baptised; one of her godfathers was Johann Caspar Wülcken, and he not being able to be present, Schwanenberger stood as his proxy.

It is to the visit of an illustrious musician that we owe a fine canon written by Bach in the last year but one before his death. The master has surrounded it with ingenious Latin sentences, which remind us of the inscriptions in the "Musikalisches Opfer." The whole is as follows:—

" *Fa Mi, et Mi Fa est tota Musica*

Canon super Fa Mi, a 7. post Tempus Musicum.

Domin Possessor
Fidelis Amici Beatum Esse Recordari
tibi haud ignotum : itaque
Bonæ Artis Cultorem Habeas

Lipsiæ d. 1 Martii
1749.   *verum am Icum Tuum.*"

---

[457] Mattheson, op. cit., p. 292.
[458] See Chrysander, Jahrb. für Mus. Wissensch., Vol I., p. 285.

It is a canon in seven parts on a *Basso ostinato* f' a' b' e'. As these notes by the rules of solmisation represent the syllables *fa mi* twice repeated, inasmuch as the two middle notes belong to the sixth hexachord and the others to the fifth, it was possible for Bach to say that the canon was written on *fa mi* (or *mi fa*). Each of the parts of the canon enters a double bar (*tempus musicum*) after the foregoing part. We also observe in the inscription written over the *Basso ostinato,* and again in the second line of the dedicatory subscription—as an acrostic—the name of Faber (Schmidt), while the last line but one yields the name of Bach. The prominent letters I T in the last line indicate *Isenaco-Thuringum* (Eisenach in Thuringia). Who the individual may have been to whom Bach dedicated this work with its graceful arabesques can only be guessed. Balthasar Schmidt, of Nuremberg, may have been the man, the publisher of Sebastian and of Emanuel Bach's works, and himself a skilled musician. Still, the words of the dedication lead us to infer a long standing friendship, and there is no evidence that such had existed between Bach and Balthasar Schmidt. It was, more probably, Johann Schmidt, the organist at Zella St. Blasii, in Thuringia, who must have been of about the same age as Bach. In 1720 he had been the teacher of Johann Peter Kellner, who has recorded that he was justly famous for his remarkable skill.[459]   He probably is the same person as the organist Johann Ch. Schmidt who copied out a clavier prelude by Seb. Bach for his own use, November 9, 1713. If so, the connection between him and Bach was a very old one. It is true that this Johann Schmidt resigned his place as organist to his son Christian Jakob in 1746; but there is nothing to show that he died at that time, and when we reflect that it was in the last years of his life that Bach had two of his works engraved and published by J. G. Schübler, of Zella,[460] we have good ground for

---

[459] Marpurg, Hist. Krit. Beyträge, I., p. 441. A composition by him exists in the Library of the R. Inst. for Church Music at Berlin.

[460] This was probably Johann Wolfgang Georg Schübler, son of a gunstock maker, of Zella. There is a composition by Schübler in a MS. Vol. of Miscellanies in the Royal Library at Berlin (see Buxtehude, Orgel-Comp.,

assuming that these dealings with an unknown man in a small and out-of-the-way place (otherwise quite inexplicable) may have been due to the instrumentality of Johann Schmidt.

Of far more importance as to Bach's private life than these incidental meetings, however frequent, with musicians from outside, were the pupils who crowded round him from far and near. Of the Mühlhausen, Weimar, and Cöthen periods we have only mentioned Schubart, Vogler, Tobias Krebs, Ziegler, Schneider, and Bernhard Bach as among those who enjoyed Bach's instruction. It may be partly accidental that we do not know of a greater number; still, it is certain that it was not till he was in Leipzig that he was busiest as a teacher. That strong feeling of family coherence which always existed in the members of the great Bach clan prompted the younger men of the different branches to adopt Leipzig by preference not merely for musical but for general study, so soon as Sebastian was settled in that town. On May 7, 1732, Samuel Anton, the eldest son of Joh. Ludwig Bach of Meiningen, was entered on the books of the University there. He lived in Sebastian's house, and formed a friendship with Emanuel, who had already been a student for six months. Samuel Anton was a man of great and various talents; he pursued art with some success, and studied music with Sebastian's assistance to such good purpose that he afterwards rose to be Court organist at Meiningen.[461] A few years later Johann Ernst, the son of Bernhard Bach of Eisenach, came to the Thomas-schule, and afterwards studied law at the University. His relations with Sebastian as his pupil are attested by the copy made by him of twelve concertos by Vivaldi and adapted by S. Bach to the clavier. In the spring of 1739,

---

Vol. I., pref., p. IV., No. 10). Marpurg has given Bach's canon without the Latin text in his Abhandlung von der Fuge, Pt. II., Tab. XXXVII., Figs. 6 and 7, see, too, p. 67. I discovered it entire and perfect in a beautiful copy of the last century among the papers left by Grasnick, from which it was obtained for the Royal Library at Berlin. The analysis is given in the musical supplement to this Vol., No. 4.

[461] See Vol. I., p. 10, and the lists of the Leipzig University for 1732.

came also Johann Elias Bach, already at that time the well-paid Cantor of Schweinfurth, to matriculate as a student of theology, and to advance himself in music under Sebastian. I shall presently have occasion to show that he retained a grateful remembrance of his illustrious relative.[462]

In the list of those of his disciples who were not related to him by blood, Heinrich Nikolaus Gerber claims the first place.   He was born in 1702 at Wenigen-Ehrich in Schwarzburg ; had been sent to the Gymnasium at Mühlhausen, and there had often heard the gifted but degenerate Friedrich Bach.[463]   In 1721 he left Mühlhausen and came to Sondershausen, and in May, 1724, entered as *studiosus juris* at the University of Leipzig.   He purposed at the same time to pursue the art of music, and was wont to sign himself in these years : *litterarum liberalium studiosus ac musicæ cultor*.   His veneration for Bach was so great that for a year he could not find courage enough to ask him to teach him.   But there was at the time a musician named Wilde in Leipzig—the same, probably, who in 1741 was Kammermusiker to the Emperor at St. Petersburg—and who had made a name by the improvements he had effected in the construction of various instruments ; he constituted himself the intermediary, and took Gerber to Bach. " Bach received him, as a native of Schwarzburg, with particular kindness, and ever after called him his fellow-countryman.   He promised to give him the instruction he craved, and at once asked him if he had been diligent in playing fugues.   At the first lesson he set his *Inventiones* before him ; after he had studied these to Bach's satisfaction he gave him a series of suites, and then the *Temperirte Clavier*.   This Bach played through to him three times with his inimitable skill, and he accounted those the happiest hours of his life when Bach, under pretence of not being in the humour to teach, would sit down to his excellent instrument, and the hours seemed to be but minutes." Gerber left Leipzig in 1727, and only once returned there, about 1737, to see his beloved master.   In 1731 he was

---

[462] See Vol. I., p. 156, and the lists of 1734.   [463] See Vol. I., p. 141.

appointed Court organist at Sondershausen, and did his great teacher honour as an artist at once gifted and modest.[464]

Johann Tobias Krebs, who had been Bach's diligent and gifted pupil during the Weimar period, sent no less than three sons, one after another, to the Thomasschule. The second, also Johann Tobias, came there in 1729, aged thirteen. Bach's verdict, when he had examined him, was that " he had a fine strong voice and good method" (see ante, p. 66); but with him music seems gradually to have sunk into the background. In 1740 he left the school with honours, and by 1743 was *Magister philosophiæ* of the University, and subsequently rector or warden of the school at Grimma. The third son, Johann Carl, seems also to have devoted himself to the learned sciences, and quitted the school with honours in 1747.[465] The most distinguished musician of the three was Johann Ludwig, the eldest. He was born at Buttestädt, February 10, 1713; was at the Thomasschule from 1726 to 1735 ; and then studied for two years at the University. Bach was on particularly confidential terms with this favourite pupil, whose musical talents he admired while he esteemed his learning.[466] He is said to have remarked in joke, " He is the one only crab (Krebs) in this brook (Bach)."[467] He made him cembalist in the musical society,[468] and recommended him to Professor Gottsched as teacher to his wife,[469] and even took pleasure in his compositions.[470] When Krebs left the school, Bach gave him the following testimonial :

The bearer of this, Herr Johann Ludwig Krebs, has asked me, the undersigned, to assist him with a testimonial as to his performances on our foundation. As I have no reason to refuse him, and can say this much, that I am persuaded that I have brought him to be a musician

---

[464] Gerber, Lex. I., col. 490.
[465] Nützliche Nachrichten, &c. Leipzig, 1740, p. 67; 1746, p. 164; 1747, p. 289.
[466] Köhler, Historia scholarum Lipsiensium.
[467] J. F. Reichardt, Mus. Almanach. Berlin, 1796.
[468] Gerber, Lex. I., col. 756.
[469] See the biography prefixed to her poems, " Der Frau Luise A. V. Gottschedinn sämmtliche kleinere Gedichte." Leipzig, 1763.
[470] See Tonhalle, Organ für Musikfreunde. Scr. 1869, p. 831.

who has distinguished himself among us, in so far as that he is skilled on the clavier, violin, and lute, and not less in composition, so that he need not be ashamed to be heard, as will be found by experience. I therefore wish him God's help to gain him advancement, and give him, to this end, my best recommendation.

Leipzig, August 24, 1735.

JOHANN SEBASTIAN BACH.

Capellmeister and *Director Musicæ*.[471]

In April, 1737, Krebs became organist at Zwickau, and a few months later Linke, the organist of Schneeberg, wrote to a friend : "A short time since I had the honour to see and to hear Monsieur Krebs, the new organist of Zwickau, a very good organ and clavier player; I must confess that what this man does better than others as an organist is something remarkable, and he is the creation of Bach."[472] In April, 1744, Krebs was appointed organist to the Castle at Zeitz, where he and the younger Schemelli worked together,[473] and in 1750 he became Court organist at Altenburg, where he died in 1780. He was, beyond a doubt, Bach's most distinguished pupil on the organ, and in every way one of the greatest of those who survived the master. Vogler may have been his equal in playing, but as a composer was far below him.

A younger artist who had received his first training from Bach in Cöthen, and who, after an interval, once more became his disciple in Leipzig, was Johann Schneider. He competed with Vogler in 1730 for the post of organist to the church of St. Nicholas, and succeeded in winning the prize, as I have already mentioned.[474] Here I need only mention his name in order not to omit all reference to an excellent musician of whom a witness says, that his organ playing was in such good taste that, excepting only his master, Bach, there was no better to be heard in Leipzig.[475]

---

[471] From the archives of Zwickau. Text quoted by Dr. Herzog in the *Zwickauer Wochenblatt*, March 26, 1875.

[472] Voigt Gespräch von der Musik, p. 103.

[473] See ante, p. 109.

[474] See Vol. II., p. 262.

[475] Mizler, Mus. Bib. III., p. 532.

In 1732 Georg Friedrich Einicke came to Leipzig; born
in 1710 at Hohlstedt in Thüringia, where his father was
cantor and organist. He followed the academic course till
1737; in music he formed himself on Bach, though at
the same time he made further progress by means of
his intercourse with Scheibe. He won a name by his
compositions, and seems to have been kindly remembered
by his master. We find them still corresponding at the
time of Bach's death, when Einicke was cantor at
Frankenhausen.[476]

A crowd of talent had gathered round Bach between 1735
and 1745. Among them, however, there was not one pupil
from the Thomasschule, any more than among those who
came to him at any later period, and ultimately distinguished
themselves. After all the differences between Bach and
Ernesti this is easily intelligible, and is rendered quite clear
by the unfavourable position which, after these squabbles,
Bach held as cantor. His best pupils thenceforth were the
University students, or such men as had devoted themselves
exclusively to music as a profession. Johann Friedrich
Agricola of Dobitsch, born in 1720, matriculated May 29,
1738, studied jurisprudence, history, and philosophy, and at
the same time obtained from Bach a course of thorough instruction in playing and composition. Bach thought him
advanced enough to play the cembalo in the Musical Union,
of which he (Bach) must therefore still have been conductor
in 1738, and he also employed him as accompanist in church
music. Agricola's mother was related to Handel, and is said
to have corresponded with him; Agricola, indeed, bestowed
much attention on Handel's works, even in Leipzig, and this
again reveals to us the sincere recognition and sympathy
with which Bach always regarded his equally great contemporary. In the autumn of 1741 Agricola went to
Berlin, where he was soon acknowledged to be the best
organ player, but he there eagerly turned his attention to
the opera and to the Italian method of singing. In 1751 he
became Court composer, and after Graun's death, in 1759,

---

[476] Marpurg, Kritische Briefe. II., p. 461.—Mattheson, Sieben Gespräche
der Weisheit und Musik. Hamburg. 1751, p. 189 f.

Capellmeister to the king. He wrote both church and instrumental music, but particularly operas; and his excellent general culture also enabled him to be a successful author. The world owes to him and to Emanuel Bach the Necrology of Sebastian Bach, which was published in 1754 by Mizler, in his Musikalische Bibliothek ; and in his notes to Adlung's *Musica mechanica organœdi* he has preserved for us many valuable details concerning Bach. His translation of Tosi's " Introduction to the Art of Singing," with notes and explanations, may still be considered a classical authority. He died in 1774.[477]

In 1738 Johann Friedrich Doles also came to the University; he was born in 1716, at Steinbach, in Henneberg, and had been educated at Schmalkalden and at Schleusingen.[478] He succeeded Bach as cantor in 1755, but his bias was towards the sentimental, the operatic and the vacuously popular, and he was not the true son of his master. During his tenure of the place the use of Bach's works was gradually lost in Leipzig ; still, he attached some importance to the fact of his having been Bach's pupil,[479] and even during his master's lifetime he won friends and admirers by his pleasing talent. It was he, and not Bach, who had to write the occasional music, in 1744, for the anniversary of the newly founded Musical Union, and in the same year he became cantor at Freiburg. I shall have more to say presently of the events of his life.

A man of more serious bent, and of far more fertile talent, was Gottfried August Homilius, born 1712, at Rosenthal, on the frontier of Bohemia. He had finished his studies under Bach by 1742, for he was then organist to the

---

[477] Marpurg, Historisch-Kritische Beyträge, I., p. 148.—Burney, Diary III., p. 58. There is a list of Agricola's works in Gerber, Lex. I., col 17.

[478] These data I have derived from his Latin autobiography, which I found among the documents of the Consistory at Leipzig. The amusing scenes which are said to have occurred between Friedemann Bach and Doles, who lodged in Bach's house (see Bitter, Bach's Söhne II., p. 156), are founded in error, since at that time Friedemann had left Leipzig. He had been living n Dresden since 1733.

[479] See a prefatory note to his cantata, " Ich komme vor dein Angesicht." Leipzig, 1790.

Frauenkirche at Dresden; he was subsequently cantor of the Kreuzschule and director of church music in that capital, and he died in 1785. He was admired as an organist, but his chief fame rests on his vocal church music, and his are undoubtedly the most important works that exist in this style of the second half of the eighteenth century. Though hardly on a par with their aim and purpose, they include many passages in a really lofty and grand sacred style.[480]

A musician of quite a different type, again, was Johann Philipp Kirnberger, born in 1721, at Saalfeld, in Thüringia, and who was persuaded by Gerber to go to Bach, whose pupil he was from 1739 till 1741. He then went to Poland, whence he returned in 1751 to become Court musician to the Princess Amalia of Prussia, at Berlin, where he died in 1783. He was of no great mark as a composer, but an excellent teacher of composition; if he had had a wider course of general culture and a thoroughly disciplined mind, he would unquestionably have been the greatest theoretical musician of his time. His works, which down to the present century were almost exclusively used as the final authority in teaching composition, have been fully discussed in this book.

Rudolph Straube, of Trebnitz, on the Elster, was principally known as a performer on the clavier; he entered the University February 27, 1740, and in 1750 made a journey through Germany and to England.[481] Another player was Christoph Transchel of Braunsdorf, born 1721; he matriculated as student of theology and philosophy June 21, 1742, and soon became known as Bach's pupil and friend. He was in great repute as a teacher in Leipzig till 1755, and then, till his death in 1800, at Dresden; he was distinguished alike for the finish of his playing and his elegant general culture.[482] Finally, we must mention

---

[480] Forkel, p. 42. Gerber, Lex. I., col. 665.

[481] Lists of the University.—Adlung Anl., p. 722.—Gerber, Lex. II., col. 599.

[482] Lists of the University.—Gerber, Lex. II., col. 671, and N. Lex. IV., col. 382. Transchel wrote six Polonaises for the clavier, which Forkel could regard as the best in the world next to those by Friedemann Bach. A MS. Vol. of miscellanies in the Royal Library at Berlin contains a composition by him (see Buxtehude's organ works, Vol. I., preface, p. iv., No. 10).

Johann Theophilus Goldberg, who had been brought to Dresden while still very young by Baron von Kayserling; he is said to have been born at Königsberg.[483] Friedemann Bach was his first master;[484] subsequently, about 1741, his patron frequently took him with him to Leipzig to obtain instruction from Sebastian. His facility and skill on the clavier, to which he devoted himself with untiring zeal, soon became quite astonishing; indeed, we have a standard by which to judge him in the thirty variations composed for him by J. S. Bach at Kayserling's request. Kayserling's health was feeble and he suffered from sleepless nights, and at such times he liked to have his melancholy dispelled by soft and somewhat cheerful music. These variations seem perfectly adapted to this end, and Forkel tells us that he was never weary of hearing them, and recompensed Bach for his artistic offering with a snuff-box containing a hundred Louis d'or.[485] Goldberg afterwards entered the service of Count Brühl, as Kammermusicus; he died early. His was a whimsical and eccentric nature, much resembling that of Friedemann, as it would seem from concurrent testimony; there is no doubt that his talent for composition was not great; still, a grand prelude by him for the clavier, in C major, is a solid work besides being brilliant, which of course was to be expected.[486]

During the last years of his life, Altnikol, Kittel, and Müthel were the pupils to whom Bach devoted most of his teaching. Johann Christoph Altnikol, who in 1749 became Bach's son-in-law, lived in Leipzig till 1747, and assisted in the church performances.[487] An attempt made by Friedemann Bach to have him appointed in his own place when he gave it up and left Dresden, in 1746, was unsuc-

---

[483] Forkel, p. 43. Reichardt, Mus. Alm., 1796, under App. 10, says he was born at Dantzig.

[484] Fürstenau II., p. 222, note.

[485] Forkel, p. 51, also p. 43.

[486] MS. in the Royal Library at Berlin, where, too, there is a sacred cantata by him.

[487] He was paid six thalers "for having assisted in the two high churches in the *Chorus musicus* from Michaelmas, 1745, till May 19, 1747." Accounts of St. Thomas's Church for 1747—48, p. 54.

cessful;[488] in 1747 he became organist to St. Wenceslaus, at Naumburg, where he died in July, 1759, after doing good work.[489] Joh. Christian Kittel of Erfurt was one of Bach's latest pupils, for at the time of the master's death he was only eighteen, he may even then have been with him. From Leipzig he went to Langensalza, and in 1756 he was at Erfurt where, in process of time, he became organist to the Predigerkirche. Kittel was an excellent organ player and composer, and a favourite teacher; he taught a great number of the best organists of Thuringia, and, with pious reverence for his own great teacher, did his utmost to transmit the traditions of Bach's art and style. He died at an advanced age in 1809.[490]

Joh. Gottfried Müthel had enjoyed the advantage of Bach's teaching for a few weeks only when his master's weak sight and ill-health disabled him from teaching. Müthel had come from the Ducal Court at Schwerin, where, after Michaelmas, 1748, at the latest, he had held the post of Court organist as his brother's successor. The Duke was so much attached to the young artist (born in 1729 at Mölln) that, in May, 1750, he granted him a year's leave, with the continuance of his salary; that he might perfect his knowledge under Bach. An introduction from the Duke himself secured him a friendly reception, and the additional favour of a lodging in Bach's house. He also was a witness of the master's last illness and death, and then, in order to make up as far as possible for the loss to himself so far as teaching was concerned, he went to Naumburg to Altnikol, Bach's son-in-law, and he was still there on June 2, 1751. From Schwerin he went

---

[488] See a document quoted by Bitter, Bach's Söhne II., p. 356 and 171.

[489] Register of deaths of that church. See also Forkel, p. 43.

[490] I have not been able to ascertain the exact date of Kittel's move to Langensalza, but in February, 1752, he was married there to Dorothea Fröhmer; he was organist there at the church of St. Boniface and "teacher in the girls' school." His successor, who lived to be a very old man, said that he had not been content after a time to keep this post in the girls' school, for his love of composition and writing music often made him do this in school hours, and so brought him into collision with authorities. Finally, he gave up the post. (Communicated by Herr Kirchner Stein, of Langensalza.) See, too, Gerber Lex. I., col. 728, and N. Lex. III., col. 57.

in June, 1753, as organist, to Riga, where he died. Members of his family still live and flourish in Livonia. His talent for clavier and organ playing was remarkable and thoroughly developed. His compositions, which are not numerous, are a test of the highest executive skill.[491]

From all this it may be fully understood how widely, in every direction, Bach's fame extended, and how vital was the influence he exercised over art. Nor is the list of his pupils by any means exhausted; disciples crowded round him in many cases only to be able to call themselves his pupils to the world, and boys who had been at the school and learnt from him only in class with a score of others prided themselves on it. One of these was Christoph Nichelmann, of Treuenbrietzen, born 1717, afterwards Capellmeister to Frederick the Great. From 1730—33 he was first treble in the church, and learned the clavier from Friedemann Bach. Johann Peter Kellner, of Gräfenroda, born 1705, who had been introduced to Bach's works by Schmidt, the organist of Zella, and had been greatly inspired by them, publicly expressed his satisfaction at his good fortune in having enjoyed the acquaintance of this admirable man, and though he was not, strictly speaking, his pupil, he may be called his disciple.[492] Thomas Trier stood in the same relation to him; he was born in 1716, at Themar, studied theology at Leipzig, and in 1747 was also the director of the Telemann Musical Union. In 1750 he was a candidate for the post of cantor after Bach, but Harrer was preferred. In Zittau, in 1753, he beat all competitors, among them Friedemann and Emanuel Bach, Krebs and Altnikol, all four of them pupils of Bach's. He remained there as organist of the church till 1790, enjoying the reputation of being one of the best organists in all Saxony. Bach's recommendation had been the foundation of his fortunes. Gerlach, by the same influence, obtained the place of organist

---

[491] I have been able to confirm and extend the information concerning Müthel as given by Burney III., p. 268. Müthel's presence at Naumburg, June 2, 1751, is proved by an entry in the Register of baptisms of the church of St. Wenceslaus.

[492] Marpurg, Hist. Krit. Beyträge, I., pp. 431 and 439.

to the New Church at Leipzig, and Christian Gräbner the younger and Carl Hartwig referred to the instruction they had received under Bach when in 1733 they were candidates for the place of organist to the Sophienkirche at Dresden.[493] Johann Christoph Dorn seems to have obtained the post of organist at Torgau by a written testimonial from the famous master. This testimonial has been preserved, and is dictated by a gentle spirit of kindliness which reminds us of the worthy Heinrich Bach, of Arnstadt. It runs as follows :—

A representative of Mons. Johann Christoph Dorn, who is a diligent musician, has applied to me, the undersigned, to give him a testimonial as to his proficiency and knowledge of music. Since I find, from the examples he has given me, that he has acquired a considerable degree of proficiency on the clavier, as well as on other instruments, and is thus in a position to do good service to God and to the State, I have not refused his proper request, but, on the contrary, shall testify that as he grows older, with his good natural gifts, he bids fair to become a very skilful musician.

Leipzig, May 11, 1731.

Joh. Seb. Bach,

Hochf. Sächss. Weissenfl. Capellmeister und

Direct. Chori Musici Lipsiensis.

According to the old and universal custom, the pupils formed part of the family. Bach, like his forefathers, clung to the idea of a guild among musicians, and Müthel cannot have been the only scholar whom he admitted to live in his house. Speaking of his pupils has led us, as it were, into the midst of Bach's domestic life, and we may now see, as far as the means at hand admit, how this remarkable personage appeared as the head of a family. If we enquire into the ordinary circumstances of his life, irrespective of his position and doings as an artist, when we remember the seclusion in which a citizen's household lived at that time, and Bach's simple and domestic nature, it seems probable that it was quiet and unvaried enough. The persons chosen by Bach as sponsors for his numerous children, thus indicating a certain intimacy, were, for the most part,

---

[493] See Vol. II., p. 225.   Bitter, Bach's Söhne II., p. 159.

members of the better class of officials or respectable merchants, though we find among them two lawyers and teachers in the University. In his later years there seems to have been a warm intimacy between the Bachs and the family of a merchant named Bose, and we may also assume a constant intercourse, founded on personal regard, with Johann Christian Hoffmann, musical instrument maker to the Court (Hof-instrumentenmacher). Hoffmann had settled at Leipzig so early as 1725 (his house was in the Grimmai Steinweg), and he was always eager to co-operate with Bach, who took pleasure and interest in the improvement of musical instruments. For instance, he prepared several specimens of the *Viola pomposa*.[494] When he died, February 1, 1750, it was found that out of respect for Bach he had bequeathed to him an instrument of his own making.

We find but very few traces of his social intercourse with any of the literary magnates of the city, excepting with his colleagues in the school. He had come into contact with Gottsched on the occasion of the mourning ceremonial in honour of Queen Christiana Eberhardine. He is not likely, however, to have had any very warm sympathy with a man who was so emphatically antagonistic to the opera,[495] and Gottsched's attempts in the way of poetry he can hardly have found interesting. However, a connection was formed between the two houses for a time by Gottsched's selecting Krebs as his wife's musicmaster. Luise Adelgunde Victoria, who came to Leipzig as a bride in 1735, had, besides other remarkable gifts, a very great talent for music. She already played well on the clavier and lute, and now wished to learn composition ; she made such rapid progress as soon to be able to compose a suite and a cantata. Krebs himself was absolutely bewitched by his pupil, who was then about twenty years of age, and so late as 1740 he dedicated to her —writing from *Zwickau*—a cahier of six " Preambles," which he had engraved on copper by Balthasar Schmidt, of

---

[494] Hiller, Lebensbeschreibungen, p. 45, note.

[495] His friend Hudemann, of Hamburg, wrote a treatise against Gottsched in defence of the opera in 1732, see Mizler, Mus. Bib. II., 3, p. 120.

Nuremberg, and in a romantic set of verses expressed himself as the obliged person—

> Who having thought to guide and school your ear,
> When you but played, was quite content to hear.[496]

Gottsched's house became for a time a centre of musical meetings. Sylvius Leopold Weiss, who once came from Dresden to Leipzig, visited the gifted lady, heard and applauded her playing, and played to her himself; Gräfe dedicated to her the second volume of his odes, and even Mizler made himself agreeable to her in a dedication. It is probable, therefore, that Bach would have been at her house ; indeed, the admiration with which T. L. Pitschel speaks of Bach—in the Belustigungen des Verstandes und Witzes[497]—in 1741, would seem to prove that at this period he must have moved within the Gottsched circle, and sometimes have charmed it by his playing.

Bach also had formed a lasting friendship with another of the professors at the University, who was also very popular, though less famous than Gottsched. Johann Abraham Birnbaum was promoted to the degree of *Magister*, February 20, 1721, at the early age of nineteen, and qualified as an instructor on October 15 of the same year.[498]   Rhetoric was his principal branch of learning, and his lectures were eagerly frequented. There was in Leipzig a private debating society of which Birnbaum was a member, and in 1735 he published a volume of the discourses which he had delivered there, in pure and flowing, but somewhat pedantic German.[499]   He played the clavier elegantly, and his taste for music brought him into contact with Bach.   He lived in the Brühl, and died, unmarried, August 8, 1748.

Bach mentions his death in a letter to Elias Bach, dated November 2, 1748, in a way which leads us to infer that the

---

[496] A copy of this work is in the Royal Library at Berlin.

[497] (Johann Joachim Schwabe), Vol. I., Leipzig, 1741, pp. 499 and 501.

[498] Sicul, Leipziger Jahr-Geschichte, 1721. pp. 199 and 236.

[499] Leipziger Neue Zeitungen von gelehrten Sachen, 1735, p. 603. One of the speeches made by him in this society, "uber den Hohen Geist des erblassten Thomasius," was published before 1729. A copy of it exists in the Library at Wernigerode.

cousin had enquired for him, and the friendship between
Bach and Birnbaum was known to a wide circle.

In a periodical, published by Johann Adolph Scheibe,
under the title "Critische Musikus" (beginning March 5,
1737), on May 14, 1737, an anonymous letter was printed,
containing an attack upon Bach. He was not named, but
the identity was unmistakable. Scheibe subsequently
confessed that the letter was a got-up affair, and he himself
the author. In it Bach's extraordinary skill in playing the
organ and clavier were highly praised, but his compositions
were found fault with for their lack of natural grace and
pleasing character, for a turgid and confused style and an
extravagant display of learned art. The writer alluded
chiefly to his vocal part-music, and came to the conclusion
that Bach was in music what Lohenstein had been in
verse.[500] A year later Scheibe wrote again : " Bach's
church pieces are constantly more artificial and tedious, and
by no means so full of impressive conviction or of such
intellectual reflection as the works of Telemann and
Graun."[501] Nor was he the only one to hold this opinion,
as it is easy to believe from the taste of the time and the
false ideas then prevalent as to church music. Nevertheless,
the whole affair has an unpleasant aspect, not only by reason
of the exalted and almost unapproachable merit of the
person attacked, but more particularly from the tone in
which fault is found, and considering who it was that made
the attack. Scheibe was a young man of knowledge and
acumen, and a talented writer, but only a second rate
practical musician. Every one in Leipzig knew perfectly
well that his test performance, when he hoped to obtain the
post of organist at St. Nicholas's, had found no favour in
Bach's opinion ; and very unsatisfactory—though no doubt
exaggerated—rumours were rife on the subject. Scheibe
was ambitious and jealous ; he had "agitated" against
Bach ever since, and had stirred up, or, at any rate,

---

[500] Critischer Musikus, p. 62.
[501] Mattheson, Kern melodischer Wissenschaft, Hamburg, 1738. Appendix,
"Gültige Zeugnisse," &c., p. 10.

promoted, a tide of opinion, which, so early as 1731, had put Bach and his adherents on the defensive. 1 have, I think, made it clear in a former page that the character of Midas in the cantata " Der Streit zwischen Phöbus und Pan " was meant for Scheibe ;[502] and in this attack, made under safe cover, the world saw an act of undignified personal revenge.

Bach was more deeply offended than perhaps he ought to have been; but it occurred just at a time when he was already in a highly irritated mood, in consequence of his squabble with Ernesti. It would almost seem that he himself had at one time thought of taking up his pen against Scheibe. However, it was Birnbaum who stepped in ; he began, in January, 1738, by publishing an anonymous article, " Unparteiische Anmerkungen über eine bedenkliche Stelle in dem sechsten Stücke des critischen Musikus "—(" Impartial remarks on an important passage," &c.). When, two months after, Scheibe brought out an answer to it, he came forward in March, unmasked, with a categorical defence. He dedicated both his articles to Bach, the latter, which is by far the best, in a long introductory letter. In the first he tried to weaken the case as against Bach's method of composition, and this was a province of art with which he was not sufficiently familiar. Scheibe's retort is an impertinent pamphlet. All sorts of petty scandal, which he had procured from Leipzig, is to be found in it, mixed up with insinuations, misrepresentations, and invective, and he reaches the utmost limits of insolence when he asserts that Bach has no special breadth of view in those branches of knowledge which may be particularly required of a learned composer. " How," he asks, " can a man be faultless as a writer of music who has not sufficiently studied natural philosophy, so as to have investigated and become familiar with the forces of nature and of reason ? How can he have all the advantages which are indispensable to the cultivation of good taste who has hardly troubled himself at all with the critical study, the cultivation and the rules which are as necessary to music as they are to

---

[502] See Vol. II., p. 645.

oratory and poetry, so that without their aid it is hardly possible to write with feeling and expression." Such writing as this deserved to be thoroughly taken in hand, and Birnbaum dealt to Scheibe the measure that was due. He was himself a perfectly competent authority in all that related to rhetoric and poetry, and all that he replied to Scheibe's strictures from his own experience of Bach has every claim to our belief. But the matter has already been discussed.[503]

Scheibe was silenced for the time, and revenged himself only by a spiteful pasquinade flung at Bach under the form of a letter witten by one Cornelius in the " Critische Musikus " of April 2, 1739.[504] But in a second edition he could not refrain from reprinting his opponent's letters with annotations. He was conquered in the fight, not because the faults he attributed to Bach were in fact beyond proof, but by reason of the unbecoming manner in which he carried on the dispute. But it rained blows from all sides, and having brought the whole school of Bach down upon himself from far and wide, retribution haunted him throughout his life ; even in 1779 Kirnberger had a fling at him when an opportunity happened to offer.[505] And others, who would not withhold a due recognition of his talents and industry, still took care—like Mattheson and Marpurg—not to coincide in his verdict on Bach. Indeed, at a later period he himself seems to have arrived at the view that he had not taken the right tone towards this great man ; this is very evident from the preface to the second edition of the " Critische Musikus,[506] written in 1745.

Bach himself took an unusually lively personal interest in Birnbaum's different articles in this controversy. Scheibe pretended to know that the first of these papers had been distributed to his friends and acquaintances so early as January 8, 1738, "with no small pleasure." Bach's own

---

[503] See Vol. II., p. 238.

[504] See Schröter in Mizler, Mus. Bib. III., p. 235.

[505] Kunst des reinen Satzes, II., 3, p. 39.

[506] Containing all the controversy, pp. 833 to 1031.

answer was given—as he best could give it—by the publication of Part III. of the Clavierübung, of which Mizler
wrote: "This work is a sufficient answer to those who
venture to criticise the Herr Hofcompositeur's compositions."[507] However, when Scheibe, in this pasquinade
tried to show Bach in the light of a man who had never
given himself time to learn to write a letter of any length,
who had never attended to general culture, and rarely read
even musical essays or books, it was either heedless
detraction or a lie pure and simple. Bach, it is true, to
Mattheson's great vexation, had never given an autobiography to the Ehrenpforte, though repeatedly solicited;
but in other ways, so far as the practice of his art allowed
—and he very rightly made this the chief aim of his life—he
showed more interest in the literature of music than many
of his contemporaries. His library of books on music,
most of which at his death fell into the hands of Emanuel,
must have been by no means inconsiderable.[508] He frequently watched literary disputes with attentive interest.
When Sorge of Lobenstein (1745—1747) was publishing
the "Vorgemach der (antechamber to) Musikalischen
Composition," some persons expressed a doubt as to the
authorship; Telemann was supposed to have written it
while Sorge had only lent his name. Bach took much
interest in the matter, and, to Sorge's great distress,
expressed the same opinion, "that he had ploughed with
another man's heifer," and even after his death this unfavourable view was brought up against him.[509]

Bach's participation in an affair which heated the temper
of the musical world for a time in and after 1749, also gave
rise to a vehement war of words. Doles had gone to
Freiberg as cantor in 1744, and the *Rector* there, since 1747,
was Johann Gottlieb Biedermann, a man distinguished for
his learning. In 1748 he, as qualified to decide in such

---

[507] Mus. Bib. II., p. 156.
[508] Emanuel gave several of these "rare old books and dissertations on music"
to Burney. Diary III., p. 215.
[509] See Marpurg, Krit. Briefe I., p. 139.

matters, determined to have a *singspiel* performed in com-
memoration of the peace of Westphalia, concluded just a
century before. A blind poet, named Enderlein, wrote the
text, and his subject was " Germany made happy after a
long war by a general peace." Act I. " The miseries of the
thirty years' war." Act II. " The prospect of peace and
the hindrances to it." Act III. " Peace concluded."
Act IV. " Peace declared to the advantage and joy of all."
The music was by Doles, who, as Biedermann remarked in
a note to the printed text, had so done his work " that both
skilled and delicate ears would be charmed by it." The
piece was not an opera in the sense in which the word was
then used, but a vocal performance mixed up with spoken
dialogue ; such pieces were very commonly performed in the
schools of Saxony during the first half of the eighteenth
century, though their importance in the history of German
opera has hitherto been by no means fully appreciated.
The town council had a stage erected and encouraged
the project in every possible way. The performance took
place in the Kaufhaus on October 14, at four in the
afternoon, and was repeated on the following days.[510] The
audiences were very numerous, and flowed in from the
neighbouring towns and country, but the chief applause
was bestowed on the music. It may have been an annoyance
to Biedermann to see the cantor's importance and influence
among the scholars greatly increased by this circumstance,
and to feel that the success of music threatened the
interests of learning ; and it was even whispered that
various unpleasant details had occurred in calculating
the receipts and awarding the composer's honorarium.
In short, the constantly recurring feud between rector and
cantor broke out afresh, and this time Freiberg was the
scene of the struggle. Biedermann, in his next school
programme, May 12, 1749, expressed his irritation only too
emphatically ; the main idea of this document, printed in

---

[510] A copy of the printed text with an introductory note by Biedermann, two
sheets in folio, is preserved in the Library of the Freiberg Society of Antiquaries.
See also Beyträge zur Historie und Aufnahme des Theaters. Stuttgart, 1750,
p. 596.

Latin, and having for its text a passage from the Mostellaria
of Plautus (*Musice hercle agitis aetatem, ita ut vos decet*, Act
III., Sc. 2, v. 40), is that the over-much practice of music
is apt to lead the young astray into a life of dissipation,
and so far he is right and unanswerable; but when, with
the memory still fresh of the triumph achieved by music,
though he had been annoyed by it, he goes on to name
certain *mauvais sujets* who had devoted themselves to music,
when he refers to Horace—who classes musicians with
bayadères, quacks, and beggarly priests—and says that the
Christians of old excluded them from their pious meetings,
and only allowed them to take the sacrament once a year,
the whole musical community was justified in feeling itself
insulted; and this naturally was the issue. Those named
and those ignored alike fell upon Biedermann with equal
virulence; Mattheson alone wrote five articles against him.
Others again tried to take his part, and a vehement literary
war broke out which lasted till 1751. Biedermann had to
endure many unreasonable attacks as a punishment for his
want of tact. When Bach learnt what had been going on
at Freiberg, and saw Biedermann's programme, his old
wounds ached anew; however, he had lived through similar
experiences with his rector. He sent the document to
Schröter at Nordhausen, a member of the musical society,
begging him to review it and reply to it, as he could find no
one capable of doing it in Leipzig or the neighbourhood.
Schröter consented; he sent a review to Bach and left it to
him to get it printed in some periodical paper. It met
Bach's wishes, and, on December 10, 1749, he wrote to
Einicke in Frankenhausen, "Schröter's review is well done
and quite to my taste, and will shortly appear in print. . . .
Herr Mattheson's Mithridates had caused a very violent
commotion as has been told me on trustworthy testimony.
If yet some other Refutations should follow, as I suspect, I
make no doubt the author's ears will he purged and made
more apt to hear music." However, he handed over the
matter of the printing to another person, who took upon
himself to make certain alterations and additions, and to
add causticity to the tone of the document, which was

S

before very moderate and dignified. In the altered review Biedermann was given to understand that he was better versed in the writings of the heathen than in the word of God, and the article, quite without Schröter's consent, was entitled " Christian Judgments."

Schröter, however, was more touchy than he need have been as to the treatment his review had undergone, and he wrote a letter, April 9, 1750, which he desired Einicke to send on to Bach. On May 26, 1750, Bach wrote to Einicke "Pray make my compliments to Herr Schröter, till I am able to write to him, and I will then excuse myself with regard to the alterations in his review; though in fact I am not to blame in the matter at all; they are solely attributable to the person to whom I entrusted it to print." Schröter would not be satisfied with this and demanded among other things a public explanation from Bach. But death interfered to put an end to the matter.

The worthy Einicke, however, had got drawn into the squabble without any fault of his own. A partisan of Biedermann's supposed him to be the author of "Christian Judgments," speaking of him as a "certain Cantor of F. [rankenhausen] who had formerly been a miserable schoolmaster at H. [ohlstedt]; " and this prompted him to lay the whole facts before Mattheson.[511]

The review by Schröter was not, however, the only means of retaliation on Biedermann adopted by Bach. He once more took up the cantata " Der Streit zwischen Phöbus und Pan," which eighteen years previously he had composed as a satire upon those who attacked his music (see Vol. II., p. 473), and had it performed. It would seem that the performance was by one of the musical unions of the town, though Bach was no longer in direct connection with either of them. Johann Michael Schmidt, of Meiningen, had been studying in Leipzig since March 12, 1749, and he, a few years later, published a well-considered book, which was

---

[511] Mattheson, Sieben Gespräche, &c., Hamburg, 1751, p. 181. Adlung gives a full account of the matter, Anl. Mus. Gel., p. 70. See also Marpurg, Krit. Briefe, I., p. 253. Lindner, Zur Tonkunst, p. 64. Bitter has reprinted the " Christliche Beurtheilung," J. S. Bach, II., p. 340.

received with great approbation, entitled *Musico-Theologia*.[512] In this work Bach is frequently referred to with admiration, and in one place it is said that the chief aim of the composer should be to give an adequate representation of the state of feeling he wished to express, and the actions proceeding from them, and to hold the mirror up to nature. "The more nature was copied in his compositions the more pleasure he would give his hearers. From this theory of art sprang the Calendar of the months depicted in music, Bach's 'Gesprächspiel,' the Lyre, the Cuckoo, the Nightingale, the Posthorn, and others." These names evidently designate some cantatas of a gay, light character, which were popular at the time but are now lost. The "Gesprächspiel" can only have been a secular cantata by Bach; from the context it cannot possibly have been one of his dramatic occasional pieces. The choice, therefore, remains between the Coffee Cantata and "Phöbus und Pan." But, since the point under consideration is definite expression and imitation of nature, both of which are to be found in their widest sense in this cantata, we can hardly doubt that the latter is meant; and all the less because we actually have a text for it dated 1749; Michael Schmidt may, indeed, have sung in the performance, or, at any rate, have been present at it.

Moreover, this text contains a passage which clearly shows the aim and end of this performance. In the last recitative Picander had originally written :—

> "And now, Apollo, strike the lyre again,
> For nought is sweeter than thy soothing strain."

Here it runs as follows :—

> "Now strike the lyre with redoubled power,
> Storm like Hortensius, like Orbilius roar."

And again at the end :—

> "Now strike the lyre with redoubled power,
> Storm like Birolius, like Hortensius roar."

Now Orbilius, as is well known, is the schoolmaster in Horace,[513] and Birolius is an anagram serving to suggest the

---

[512] *MUSICO-THEOLOGIA*, oder Erbauliche Anwendung Musikalischer Wahrheiten; Bayreuth und Hof. 1754. See Marpurg Hist. Krit. Beil. I., p. 346.
[513] Ep. II., 1, lines 70, 71.

name of Biedermann. I think it possible also to identify
Hortensius. Quintus Hortensius was Cicero's only rival
in eloquence, both being regarded as models of Latin diction.
The man who revived the knowledge of these two orators
among the learned in Germany in the eighteenth century
was Ernesti, who had edited an edition of Cicero in 1737.
It was all the more obvious to dub him by the name of
Hortensius, because a name had been found in classic
literature to fit Biedermann. Thus the rector at Freiberg
and the rector at Leipzig were bracketed as the pair who
stood as the butt of Bach's satire in the cantata.[514] From
this it appears that Bach's resentment against Ernesti was
deeply rooted.

Biedermann meanwhile knew very well what were Bach's
feelings towards him. He said of one of the polemical
papers of which he wrongly suspected him to be the author,
that " the stupid lies proceeded from that foul Bach "—to
such amenities of language had the disputants descended.
After his *programme* it was certainly impossible to attack
Biedermann on the score of indifference to music ; but his
previous history was very well known in Leipzig through
the cantor Doles, and this showed the rector in an unfavourable light.

The eager vehemence displayed by the venerable
composer in upholding the honour and dignity of his
beloved art has something pathetic in it when we find him
singing its praises with enthusiasm in a cantata which, at
this time, he had performed on three occasions. This
is the cantata " O holder Tag, erwünschte Zeit,"
which was now refitted with a text exclusively in
praise of music. Here we find the words " Alas, beloved
muse of harmony, sweet as thy music is to many ears, yet

---

[514] Though Dehn asserts (op. cit. p. 479, note) that by Hortensius Bach
meant to designate a certain Gärtner who gave the Thomasschule scholars
too much to do with music ; but I know not on what this hypothesis rests.
Karl Christian Gärtner, who at a later date edited the Bremen documents was,
it is true, a native of Freiberg and he had lived for a time in Leipzig, but only
until 1745, nor is there anything to prove that he ever came into personal
contact with Bach.

art thou sad and standest pensive there; many there be
who scorn thy charms. Methinks I hear thee complaining
and saying, ' Be still, ye pipes and flutes, ye fail to please;
even I myself am weary of your tones; away with songs for
I am left alone.' But calm thyself, fair muse; thy glory is
not dead, nor altogether banished and despised." (See Vol.
II., p. 635 f.)

All these occurrences bear a two-fold significance; they
show us, in the first place, Bach's intelligent interest in
literary matters, and they also point to a strongly marked
characteristic of his nature. There was in him—it had already
often shown itself (see Vol. II., p. 648), a certain pugnacity,
or even contentiousness, which shows him to have had a
near affinity with the orthodox Lutherans, of the type,
for instance, of Eilmar, the pastor of Mühlhausen. And the
reader who has followed me in the analysis of Bach's
compositions must often have detected the traces of this
spirit in his works. I need only remind him here of the
cantatas " Christ lag in Todesbanden " and " Es erhub sich
ein Streit," and of the double chorus " Nun ist das Heil und
die Kraft." He stood apart from the orthodox, it is true, by
the deep personal fervency of his feelings and by a touching
and childlike simplicity that betrayed itself when they were
appealed to. He was a typical German; at once a hero
and a child, untamed and yet impressionable and tender;
most nearly akin to Luther among theologians. Even
the tenacity with which he fought for his rights, and
of which many instances have been given, was an essential
element in such a nature. He was irritable—but so is every
artist—and his masterful nature could break out in un-
governed wrath. The organist of St. Thomas's, either
Gräbner or Görner, was one day playing the organ at a
rehearsal and made some mistake. Bach snatched off his
wig in a rage, flung it at the criminal and thundered out
" He had better have been a cobbler."[515] It occasionally
happened that he would turn a recalcitrant scholar out of

---

[515] Hilgenfeldt, p. 172. I cannot trace the origin of the story; but
Hilgenfeldt was generally cautious enough not to accept any facts for which
he had not trustworthy authority.

the choir with no small commotion in the middle of service, and then in the evening dismiss him from the supper table with an equally high hand ; and as by these arbitrary proceedings he often sacrificed his dignity as a teacher, he very naturally sometimes found a difficulty in keeping the rout of boys in order. But these weak points could not diminish the high opinion in which he was held by all who knew well the honest depth and soundness of his character. His personal pupils bear witness to this, for all without exception regarded him with unbounded respect and devotion.[516]

Bach had a justifiably good opinion of himself, and this the Leipzig Council, among others, must more than once have had reason to know. Still, like all noble natures, he was devoid of conceit and full of human sympathy and consideration for others. His pupils had only to follow the example he set them of industry ; he never held them accountable for their lesser or greater natural gifts. Nor was praise invariably acceptable to him. Once when some one had spoken with enthusiasm of his wonderful skill on the organ he said with indifference " There is nothing very wonderful about it ; you have only to hit the right notes at the right moment and the instrument does the rest."[517] In the same way he was never known to hesitate or refuse to play out of affectation, and he was always ready and willing to perform alone or with others.

It was noted as one of his peculiarities that, though a master of improvisation, he never liked to begin with anything of his own ; he preferred to play at sight a composition put before him, and could then go off into an impromptu, as if he had needed the impetus from outside to stimulate the flow of his own invention. The evidence of this is interesting enough to be quoted at length. It is recorded by a certain theological student, T. L. Pitschel, who was studying at Leipzig about 1738, took the degree of Master in 1740, and died there in 1743, aged 27. He was

---

[516] Necrology, p. 173.

[517] This characteristic anecdote is from Köhler, *Historia Scholarum Lipsiensium.* Note to p. 94.

an ally of Gottsched's, and published in a paper which was the organ of the party (Belustigungen des Verstandes und Witzes) a letter to a friend "On frequenting public worship." In this he says: "You know that the famous man who in our town enjoys the greatest praise for his music and the admiration of all connoisseurs is never able to enchant his hearers with his own musicial combinations until he has played something already written, and so inspired his inventiveness"; and farther on: "That gifted man, of whom I have already spoken, always needs to play from the page something worse than his own ideas can ever be. And yet these good ideas of his result from those inferior ones."[518] And it was no doubt the same vein in his nature which made Bach prefer to find some impulse of occasion for his own artistic productions, as is constantly traceable, especially in his compositions for singing.

He also played music written by others from a genuine interest in seeing what they had done and could do, and in the same way he liked to hear others play their compositions. Things that particularly pleased him he would copy out, not only in his younger days when he was working at his own development, but at the time of his ripest maturity. Vocal works exist to this day in his handwriting, by Lotti, Caldara, Ludwig and Bernhard Bach, Handel, Telemann, and Keiser, and clavier pieces by Grigny, Dieupart, and even Hurlebusch. His collection of printed works, or of copies by other hands, was not a small one. Unfortunately they were so promptly dispersed by his sons at his death that a list of them was not even included in the inventory of his property. That his knowledge and interest extended to a remote past is proved by his having possessed Elias Ammerbach's *Orgel oder Instrument Tabulatur* of 1571, and Frescobaldi's *Fiori musicali* of 1635; and, as has been already said, he collected theoretical works on music.

When he spent a Sunday away from home he always followed the music of the service with particular attention.

---

[518] (Johann Joachim Schwabe). Belustigungen, &c., Vol. I., Leipzig, 1741, pp. 499 and 501.

If a fugue was introduced, and if one of his sons happened
to be with him, he would, as soon as he had heard the
thema, say beforehand what the composer ought to make of
it in the farther treatment, and what, if he could, he might
make of it. If it was worked out as he had sketched it, he
would nudge his son's elbow, and be quite delighted.[519]
Cause for blame, however, as may be supposed, more often
occurred than for satisfaction. Still, his sons have put it
upon record how lenient his verdicts always were ; that he
never allowed himself to speak in severe terms of the work
of a fellow artist, though to his scholars he thought it his
duty to speak the severest unqualified truth. Hurlebusch,
of Brunswick, a restless, conceited player, who was always
going from place to place, once introduced himself to Bach
at Leipzig, not to hear him play, but to be heard ; and Bach
obliged him in the matter with the utmost patience. On
leaving, Hurlebusch presented Bach's eldest sons with a
printed copy of his own collected works with an injunction
to study them diligently. The father knew full well that
both Friedemann and Emanuel Bach were far beyond such
things, but he only laughed quietly to himself, and was
perfectly friendly and polite to the donor. He was
particularly averse to seeing a fellow artist humiliated by a
comparison with his own superiority, and would never
willingly refer to the competition with Marchand, which had
attracted attention throughout Germany.

Even during his lifetime mythical anecdotes were rife
about him ; for instance, it was said that he would go into
a church dressed as a poor village schoolmaster and request
the organist to allow him to play, and then excite the
astonishment of the congregation and of the organist, who
declared it must be either Bach or the devil. He would
never listen to such stories if by chance they came to his
ears.[520]

He lived in music, in his downsitting and his uprising ;
a story, of which the main idea at any rate may be true, will

---

[519] Forkel, p. 46.
[520] Forkel, p. 45.

prove this. He had often met a certain troup of beggars in whose *crescendo* supplications he fancied he had detected a certain series of intervals. At first he made believe to be ready to give them something, but to find no money about him, then their cry reached a piercing pitch; then two or three times he gave them a very small alms, and the acuteness of their tones was somewhat qualified; finally he gave them a rather considerable sum which, to his great delight, resulted in a full resolution of the chord, and a complete and satisfactory close.[521]

Bach's nature was, above all, grave and earnest, and with all his politeness and consideration for his fellow men his demeanour was dignified and commanded respect. If we may trust the portraits which remain of him his appearance answered perfectly to this. To judge from them he must have been of a powerful, broad and stalwart build, with a full but vigorous and marked face, a wide brow, strongly arched eyebrows, and a stern or even sinister line between them. In the nose and mouth, on the contrary, we find an expression of easy humour; the eyes are keen and eager, but in his youth he was somewhat shortsighted.[522]

All his actions were based on a genuine piety which was not the outcome of any mental struggle, but inborn and natural; and he clung to the tenets of his fathers. He was fond of reading theological and edifying books, and his library included eighty-three volumes of that class at his death.[523] The authors represented sufficiently indicate his religious bent and views. Luther must be first mentioned,

---

[521] Reichardt, Mus. Alm., fols. L. 2 and 3. Berlin, 1796.

[522] Necrology, p. 167. There were four portraits of him in oil; two by Hausmann, the Court painter to the Duke of Saxony. One of these is at the Thomasschule at Leipzig, and it contains the canon presented to the Musical Union. (This is worked out in Hilgenfeldt, Mus. Supp., No. 3). The other portrait by Hausmann became the property of Emanuel Bach. A third oil portrait belonged to Kittel, and a fourth to the Princess Amalie; this is now in the Library at the Joachimsthal at Berlin.

[523] See, in Appendix B, XVI., the inventory of his property. I owe this interesting document to the industry and kindness of my friend Dr. Wustmann, of Leipzig, who discovered it among the legal archives of that circuit.

as Bach seems to have possessed his works in two editions.[524] The Table Talk and a volume of Sermons are also mentioned, separately. Most of the other works are by old Lutheran divines of the sixteenth and seventeenth centuries. Calovius, who appears in three folio volumes (born 1612, died at Wittenberg, 1686), was a truculent controversialist, and one of the most passionate champions of orthodoxy. Heinrich Müller (died in 1675), Professor and Superintendent at Rostock, was a man of softer mould; Bach possessed several of his works.[525] The *Schola Pietatis* of Johannes Gerhard, of Jena (died 1637), contains a treatise on the duties of the Christian, in five books; the learning, manly character and piety of its author must have recommended it strongly to Bach, who also possessed a well known work, " Die wahre Christenthum," by Gerhard's master and friend, Johann Arnd (died 1621, at Celle). Superintendent General August Pfeiffer again is well represented; he was an esteemed professor and preacher of Leipzig in the seventeenth century, and from 1681 was for several years Archdeacon of St. Thomas's. The three titles, "Evangelische Christenschule," " Anticalvinismus," and " Antimelancholicus " have a special interest, because they are also written in Anna Magdalena's " Clavier-Büchlein," of 1722. They were inserted there not by accident or for a fancy, but indicate his particular liking for the books, of which the purport was to be reflected in the contents of the little music book.

Besides these orthodox Lutheran works we also find some of a more mystical tendency. Among these it is particularly interesting to find the sermons of the Dominican Tauler, the direct product of mediæval mysticism. Spener's edition

---

[524] That in seven Vols. is the Wittenberg edition of 1539; that in eight the Jena edition of 1556. There is an error in the inventory—which, of course, I have printed exactly as I found it—as to the author of the " *Examen Concilii Tridentini*, which is attributed to Luther. It is by *Martinus Chemnitzius* (born 1522, died after 1568, at Rostock), and the two following works are no doubt by the same writer.

[525] The folio edition of " Evangelische Schluss Kett " was brought out at Frankfort, 1734, and Bach must have bought it late in life.

of 1703, quarto, can hardly be the one in Bach's possession, for, as that is valued only at four groschen, it must have been an old and much worn copy. The pietists are represented by a work of Spener and one by Franck which serves to prove that Bach, with all his old Lutheran feeling, was not a fanatical partisan of orthodoxy, but could take a lofty and impartial position (see Vol. I., p. 360). Johann Jakob Rambach, whose writings he liked greatly, was not, strictly speaking, of the pietist school.

Bach's knowledge of the Bible, as shown by his church cantatas, was evidently as extensive as his acquaintance with hymns. We see from his owning Bünting's *Itinerarium Sacræ Scripturæ* that he must have tried to realise the Bible history as vividly and as picturesquely as possible. In this Itinerary all the travels of the Patriarchs, Judges, Kings, Prophets, Princes and their peoples, of Joseph and the Virgin Mary, of the Wise Men from the east, Christ and His apostles were traced out and estimated in German miles ; it also contains a full description of all countries and towns mentioned in the Bible. Judge as we may the scientific value of such a work, it is at any rate an evidence that Bach did not regard his Bible merely as a repertory of texts for lyric verses, or even for dogmatic argument, but that he tried to make himself familiar with it in every sense. Another proof is his having owned Josephus's "History of the Jews."

At the time that the inventory was taken there was no religious poetry among the books, excepting the comprehensive collection in eight volumes made by Paul Wagner (see Vol. II., p. 278). Some of his heirs must, therefore, have already appropriated them. We find two series of fifty-two sermons, each by Neumeister, for the years 1721 and 1729, and there can be no doubt he must also have had Neumeister's sacred poems as well as those of Franck, Rambach, and Picander. But what else he may have had in this kind, or in secular literature, remains unknown.

When Bach moved, in 1723, to the cantor's house in St. Thomas's Church-yard, with his second wife, there went with him four children of his first marriage (see Vol. II., p. 8). By his second wife he had seven daughters and six sons, but only three daughters and three sons survived him. Of the rest three lived only a few days, the others their father laid in the grave at ages when they were beginning to understand something of life. Legendary lore has been busy with his family as well as with himself. He was said to have had an idiot son, David, who "having learnt music well, by his wild but most expressive and melancholy improvisations on the clavier, often drew tears from his hearers"; it was added that he died at the age of fourteen or fifteen.[526] This David never existed, nor did any child of Bach's die at that age;[527] it is possible that Gottfried Heinrich, the eldest of the second family, may have given rise to this fable. In Emanuel's opinion he had a great genius but it never developed. In the papers relating to Bach's property after his death he is spoken of as imbecile, and legally incapable of acting. He died February, 1763, at Naumburg, where he had been taken, it would seem, even before his father's death, by his brother-in-law, Altnikol.

Bach himself has told us of his happy home life, and of the little concerts he delighted in conducting with his sons, his wife, and his eldest daughter (see Vol. II., p. 254). He took conscientious care of the education of his children, and one main reason which decided his removal from Cöthen to Leipzig was the prospect of the better means of education offered by the University of that town. Wilhelm Friedemann, his favourite, was entered for matriculation as early as December 22, 1723, and he, as well as his younger brother Emanuel, had, according to the good custom of the time, the benefit of a complete course of academical education. It was not originally their father's intention that Emanuel should take up music as a profession, but when his great talent led to his doing so Bach was very well content, and

---

[526] Rochlitz, Für Freunde der Tonkunst. IV., p. 182 (3rd ed.). It has been copied from him even quite lately.

[527] See App. B., XV. The Necrology also mentions thirteen children of the second marriage. The genealogies never mention a son named David.

throughout his life he watched the musical proclivities of his sons with affectionate interest. He made their compositions known as he let them make his known,[528] published theirs and his own through the same publisher—Balthasar Schmidt, of Nuremberg—and copied out with his own hand anything by them that he particularly liked.[529] Friedemann's style was more nearly like his own than Emanuel's, and in his unbounded devotion to this eldest son he perhaps overlooked the fact that even during his own lifetime Friedemann risked becoming the mere caricature of himself. Emanuel's smaller and narrower forms are equally based on his father's work. For instance, his treatment of the first sonata movement in two sections, in which he was the precursor of Haydn, is founded on those preludes of the " Wohltemperirte Clavier " which are in two sections; and a still broader outline was offered by several of Sebastian's arias in which the first section does not close in the principal key. But even before Emanuel had brought out his well-known six clavier sonatas of 1742, Krebs had selected the same form for his " Preambles " of 1740. Emanuel's leaning towards what was popular, facile, and pleasing in style still farther diverted him from his father's road.

Bach spared no pains to smoothe his children's way through life; when Bernhard, the third son of the first family, was twenty years of age, and the post of organist to the Marienkirche at Mühlhausen fell vacant, Bach exerted himself to procure for his son the place which he himself had filled twenty-eight years previously. The letter he wrote to Mühlhausen on this occasion has been preserved :—

Most Noble and Most Learned Gentlemen, and particularly Most Worshipful *Senior* (of the Council), Most Esteemed Patron,

It has come to my knowledge that Herr Hetzehenn, organist to the town of Mühlhausen, died not long since in that town, and that

---

[528] Friedemann's Clavier Sonata of 1744 was to be had " 1, of the author in Dresden ; 2, of his father in Leipzig; and 3, of his brother in Berlin." While Sebastian's six three-part chorales " are to be had in Leipzig of Capellmeister Bach, of his sons in Berlin and Halle, and of the publisher in Zella."

[529] As Friedemann's Concerto for the Organ in D minor, which exists in his father's hand in the Royal Library at Berlin.

his place has not yet been filled up. Now, my younger son, Johann
Gottfried Bernhard Bach, has for some time made himself so skilful in
music that I undoubtedly consider him perfectly competent and capable
to compete for the vacant post of town organist. I therefore request
you, most noble gentlemen, with all reverence and submission, that you
will be pleased to vouchsafe to my son your invaluable intercession for
the obtaining of the post he applies for, and so to fulfil my desires and
make my son happy; so that I hereby once more, as before for former
favours, now again may find ample cause to assure you that I remain
with unalterable devotion,

Your Honours',

And particularly your most Worshipful Senior's,

Most Devoted Servant,

JOH. SEBAST. BACH.[530]

Formerly organist to the church *Divi Blas*, at Mülhausen.

Leipzig, May 2, 1735.

Addressed to the Most Noble and Learned Herr, Herr Tobia
Rothschieren, the Illustrious *Juris Consultus* and Honourable Member
as well as Most Worthy *Senior* of the Learned and Wise Council of the
Imperial and Free Town of Mülhausen, at Mülhausen.

Bach was not unsuccessful in reminding the Council of
their former goodwill to him.   Bernhard was elected,
but before long gave up the post to turn his attention
to learning.   He went to Jena, where Nikolaus Bach,
the worthy senior of the family, was living, and in 1738
was studying law there ; but in the following year he
was seized with a violent fever, which carried him off (May
27, 1739).[531]   There were now, besides Gottfried Heinrich,
only four sons left on which the father might found
his hopes.   He was still living when Johann Christoph
Friedrich (born 1732) was appointed, still quite young, to be
Kammermusicus to Count von Lippe, at Bückeburg.
Hoffmann, the instrument maker, having bequeathed to him
a clavier of his own making, Bach presented it to this son to
aid in fitting him out for this place.

In the now diminished home circle, Johann Christian
(born 1735) seems to have been the Benjamin of the family,

---

[530] The signature alone is autograph ; the seal is a rose and crown ;
preserved at Mülhausen.

[531] Walther, in a MS. addition to the Lexicon, gives May 30. This is an
error, as it is proved by the Jena register.

and to have enjoyed his father's particular affection. His talents were precocious, and his father gave him three claviers with pedals, all at once, so conspicuous a piece of partiality that after their father's death the children of the first marriage were prepared to dispute it.

Of the daughters, none married till Elizabeth Juliane Friederike (born 1726) married Altnikol, January 20, 1749. To enable the young people to set up a house in comfort, the father's assistance was again called in. The Council of Naumburg had in 1746 appealed to Bach's skill and knowledge with reference to the repairs of the organ of that town; since then the post of organist had become vacant. When Bach learnt this he immediately asked for it for Altnikol, without letting him know that he had done so. He urgently recommended him as his "former beloved scholar, who had already had an organ under his care for some time at Niederwiesa, and had competent knowledge both to play and manage it," who also "was exceptionally skilled in composition, in singing, and on the violin." Altnikol was accordingly chosen for the place July 30, 1748.[532] Bach's first grandchild, the issue of this marriage (born October 4, 1749), was named Johann Sebastian.

The only wedding which ever took place in his house was, of course, an event of great importance; we find traces of this in the second of two letters which he wrote at the end of 1748, to his cousin Elias Bach at Schweinfurth. These letters give us a glimpse of Bach's feelings as a householder, father of a family, and host.

Leipzig, October 6, 1748.

Most worshipful and respected cousin,

    I must try to say much in a few words, as time presses, though I am heartily thankful for God's grace and blessing on the abundant vintage and on the marriage now soon to take place. With the copy of the Prussian fugue that you ask for I cannot at present oblige you, for the edition is *justement* this day sold out, since only 100 were printed, most of which have been given *gratis* to good friends. But between this and the New Year's Fair a few more will be printed, and if my worthy cousin is still minded to have a copy you have only to

---

[532] Bach's letters on this occasion were published at length by Friedrich Brauer, in Euterpe (a musical paper), published by Merseburger, Leipzig, 1864, p. 41.

give me notice of an opportunity with the remittance of a thaler, and
it shall be forwarded at your desire. Finally, with salutations from us
all, I remain,

Your honour's devoted,

J. S. BACH.

P.S. My son in Berlin has now two male heirs; the first born about
the time when we, alas! suffered the Prussian invasion,[533] the other is
14 days old.

Addressed to Monsieur.

Monsieur J. E. Bach,

Chanteur et Inspecteur du Gymnase,

p. l'occasion.   a Schweinfourth.[534]

Elias had been in personal intimacy with Sebastian during
his student days in Leipzig, and was full of regard and
gratitude for him. He gave expression to these feelings in
a present which gave rise to another letter from Bach.

Leipzig, November 2, 1748.

Most worshipful and respected cousin,

That you and your dear wife are still well, I was assured by your
gratifying letter received yesterday with the splendid little cask of new
wine for which accept hereby my thanks, as due. It is, however, much
to be regretted that the little cask has suffered either from some jar in
the carriage of it or other accident, for after opening it in this place
for the usual inspection it was found almost a third part empty, and
according to the report of the inspector now contains no more than 6
kannen (quart or so); for indeed it is a pity that of so noble a gift of
God the smallest drop should have been wasted. However, for the
good gift I have received from my worthy cousin I am heartily obliged,
though I must *pro nunc* confess my inability, not being in a position to
take any worthy revenge (make a worthy return). However, *quod
differtur non affertur*, I hope to have an opportunity when I may in
some way repay my debt. It is much to be regretted that the distance
between our towns does not allow of our visiting each other in person;
else I would take the liberty of humbly inviting my respected cousin to
my daughter Liessgen's wedding, which is to take place in the next
month of January, 1749, to the new organist of Naumburg, Herr
Altnikol. But in consequence of the above-mentioned difficulty, and
also of the inconvenient season, I cannot allow myself to hope to see
you with us in person; I will only beg you, in your absence, to help
them with your Christian good wishes, wherewith I beg to recommend

---

[533] November 30, 1745.

[534] On a sheet quarto, only one page written on; the seal is almost broken
away. It belongs to Herr Schöne (Oberregierungsrath), of Berlin.

myself to my worthy cousin's remembrance, and with warmest greetings to you from all here,

I remain your honour's most devoted and
faithful cousin and servant to command,

JOH. SEB. BACH.

P.S. M. (agister) Birnbaum has been buried now six weeks.

P.M. (on the next page) Although my good cousin kindly offers to assist me in procuring the same liquor again, I must decline on account of the excessive expense here; for the freight was 16 gr., the delivery at the house 2 gr., the inspector, 2 gr., the town excise 5 gr. 3 pf., and the general excise 3 gr., so my good cousin may calculate that it costs me nearly 5 gr. a measure, which is somewhat too much for a present.

Addressed to

Monsieur
Monsieur J. E. Bach,
Chanteur et Inspector des Gymnasiastes de la
Ville Imperialle,
à Schweinfourth. [535]

Bach, it will be seen by these letters, was economical and exact; still, not to let this trait in his character preponderate unfairly, it must he remarked on the other hand that it was known to all that he gave a hearty welcome to every one, from far or near, who came to his house, that in consequence his house was hardly ever empty of visitors,[536] and without thrifty management it would have been impossible for him with his numerous family to keep up the comfortable and respectable style of housekeeping, simple as it was, which he so long enjoyed. The inventory of his property enables us fully to understand and appreciate this.[537]

Bach allowed himself a certain luxury in the matter of instruments; of claviers alone he had five—or six if we include the little spinett (spinettgen)—not counting the four he gave to his youngest son. Besides these he had a lute, two "lautenclaviere," a viol da gamba, and violins. violas, and violoncellos in such number that he could supply enough for any of the more simple kinds of concerted

---

[535] Two quarto pages written almost all over; the seal broken away. In the possession of Herr Schöne, of Berlin.

[536] Forkel, p. 45.

[537] See Appendix B., XVI.

music. The fittings of his house, too, from the moderate
stock of silver plate to the black leather chairs, and the
laborious master's writing table furnished with drawers,
give us the idea of modest but respectable ease. He even
laid by some little savings; and it is a trait of the old Bach
character—always ready to help any needy member of the
family—that part of this money was lent to relations.[588]

It was in such a home as this, piously submitting to the
common woes of humanity, and heartily and soberly enjoying
the pleasures of German family life, that Johann Sebastian
Bach lived and worked and awaited death. His vigorous
body enshrined, even to advanced age, a healthy, energetic,
and creative spirit. The only drawback was that a con-
genital weakness of the eyes was gradually but seriously
increased by his incessant toil, in his youth often carried
on through the night, and at last became serious disease.
In the winter of 1749-50 he decided on following the
advice of a friend and allowing an operation to be
performed by a famous English oculist then resident in
Leipzig; this was probably John Taylor, who had been
much resorted to in Berlin. This unfortunately failed, both
on a first and on a second trial, so that Bach was henceforth totally blind. Nor was this all. The medical treatment
associated with the operation had such bad effects that his
health, hitherto unfailing, was severely shaken. On July 18
he suddenly found his eyesight restored, and could bear
daylight; but this was life's parting greeting; a few hours
after he was stricken by apoplexy followed by high fever,
and he died on Tuesday, July 28, 1750, at a quarter to nine
in the evening.[589]

By his deathbed stood his wife and daughters, his youngest
son Christian, his son-in-law Altnikol, and his pupil Müthel.
He had been working with Altnikol only a few days before
his death. An organ chorale composed in a former time
was floating in his soul, ready as he was to die, and he
wanted to complete and perfect it. He dictated and Altnikol

---

[588] " Frau Krebsin " was his wife's sister.
[589] Necrology, p. 167. Spener's *Zeitung*, Aug. 6, 1750.

wrote. "Wenn wir in höchsten Nöthen sein" ("Lord, when we are in direct need") was the name he had originally given it; he now adapted the sentiment to another hymn and wrote above it "Vor deinen Thron tret ich hiemit" ("Before Thy throne with this I come"). Joh. Michael Schmidt, the young theologian, who admired Bach to his dying day, said afterwards that "all that the advocates of materialism could bring forward must collapse before this one example."[540]

The funeral took place on Friday, July 31, early in the morning, in the church of St. John's; as was usual when church or school officials were buried, the whole school followed him to the grave. Many bells, too, were generally tolled on such occasions. The 31st of July was the second day of public humiliation in the year. In the church, which, for twenty-seven years, Bach's mighty tones had so often filled, the preacher announced from the pulpit, "The very worthy and venerable Herr Johann Sebastian Bach, Hofcomponist to his Kingly Majesty of Poland and Electoral and Serene Highness of Saxony, Capellmeister to his highness the Prince of Anhalt, Cöthen, and Cantor to the school of St. Thomas's in town, having fallen calmly and blessedly asleep in God, in St. Thomas's Churchyard, his body has this day, according to christian usage, been consigned to the earth."[541] His grave was near the church; but when,

---

[540] *Musico-Theologia*, p. 197.

[541] The note of this announcement written across a quarto leaf I found in the library of the Historical Society at Leipzig. And below it are the words: "Announced again on the next day of humiliation after July 31, 1750," in explanation of which I may mention that at that time three days of repentance were held annually in Leipzig.

In the Register of deaths, Vol. XXVIII., fol. 292b, we find "1750, Friday, July 31, a man died aged 67, Herr Johann Sebastian Bach, Cantor of the Thomasschule, ♂ 4 K. (children)"—"fees 2 Thlr. 14 gr." The age is given wrong, and if the statement four children is correct, Heinrich must have been already removed to Naumburg. The costs which, when the whole school attended, commonly amounted to about 20 thlrs., are here reduced to 2 thlrs. 14 gr., as was always the case when church or school officials were buried; the charges were as follows: 12 gr. for alms, 6 gr. for the burying, 12 gr. to the registrar. 1 thlr. 8 gr. to the two gate keepers.

A note which exists in the Town Library at Leipzig is as follows: "A man, 67 years, Herr Johann Sebastian Bach, Capellmeister and Cantor to the school

within this century, the graveyard was removed farther from the church and the old site opened as a road-way, Bach's grave, with many others, was obliterated, and it is now no longer possible to determine the spot where his bones were laid to rest.[542]

The mourning for Bach was universal wherever there were true musicians and friends of music. The Musical Union of Leipzig did honour to his memory by performing a mourning ode as a cantata; and Telemann dedicated a feeling sonnet to his departed friend.[543] Bach's colleague, Magister Thomas Kriegel, also celebrated him in a short but warmly expressed eulogium.[544] The Town Council seem to have less appreciated the loss the city had experienced; in two sittings, on August 7 and 8, it was remarked satirically that, "the school needed a Cantor and not a Capellmeister," and that "Herr Bach had been a great musician, but not a schoolmaster."

Bach left no will. His property was legally valued, after his eldest sons had greatly impaired it by abstracting all the musical portion of it; then the widow and children agreed to a division. Anna Magdalena undertook the guardianship of those under age, and Johann Gottlieb Görner, who during Bach's lifetime had often dared to consider himself his rival, assisted her greatly in the distribution of the property. She also was allowed the payment of her husband's salary for the half year following on his death, till December 13.

The whole family then dispersed. Friedemann, who had represented Emanuel's interests as well as his own, re-

---

of St. Thomas's; died at the school and was buried, with a hearse, July 30, 1750." This also comes from the Registry Office. The hearse (*Leichenwagen*), in contradistinction to the *Leichenkutsche*, was used for grand funerals. If the date July 30 is not a slip of the pen it may perhaps imply that the body was conveyed to the mortuary of St. John's Churchyard on the previous (Thursday) evening.

[542] The Necrology gives an approximate idea of its original situation, p. 172. There is no clue in the registers of St. John's churchyard. It is possible, though not certain, that some pages of them have been lost. Herr Heinlein, however, in his work, Der Friedhof zu Leipzig, 1844, p. 202, believes that he saw a page in which Bach was mentioned, but it had become illegible.

[543] Necrology, p. 173, Neueröffnetes, Hist. *Curiosit*äten-*Cabinet*, 1751, p. 13.

[544] Nützliche Nachrichten, &c., 1750, p. 680.

turned to Halle, and Friedrich to Bückeburg. Heinrich
remained with Altnikol at Naumburg; Christian, aged 15,
was taken to Berlin for a time by his brother Emanuel.
These sons, all talented, some very remarkably gifted, and
with their great father's fame to support them, now tried
to make their way in the world without the aid of his
experience. It does not lie within the scope of this book to
trace their fortunes or criticise their work. But at any rate
they were so far successful that for at least one generation
more the name of Bach was a name of credit and glory in
the world of German art.

Anna Magdalena, left with three daughters, fell into
poverty. In 1752 she was receiving moneys from the town,
as she was in need, and had offered some musical relics for
sale. Whether the sons could not or would not help is not
known, but it is certain that her circumstances became
narrower, till at last she lived on public benevolence. She
died February 27, 1760, as an " alms woman," in a house in
the Hainstrasse. Her coffin was followed to the grave by
a quarter of the school, as was usual with quite poor
folks, and the place of her burial is unknown. The town
left the widow of one of its greatest sons—herself, too, an
artist—to perish thus.

The then surviving unmarried daughters lived to see a
day when their father's music was less and less remembered.
Katharina Dorothea died on January 14, 1774; Johanna
Carolina on August 18, 1781. It was only his youngest
child, Regina Johanna, who lived till Germany began once
more to value Sebastian Bach. She, too, lived in privation
and solitude, and it is to the credit of Rochlitz that, by
an appeal to the public, he at last secured her ease in the
evening of life. She died December 14, 1809, the last of all
the family.

Having followed the course of a great man's life to a
close, we will not dwell on the melancholy picture of the
ruin of all that he had constructed and the dispersal of all
he had held together. What under such circumstances is
lost is undoubtedly the least precious portion of what he
has created. It is true that Bach's creative spirit worked less

actively and fruitfully in the succeeding generation than has often been the case with a great genius. And it is especially in Bach's sons that we may mark the decay of that power which had culminated after several centuries of growth, and which utterly disappeared in their posterity. But, in truth, for nearly a century the whole German nation have entered into that inheritance ; it has recovered its connection with Bach, and, through him, with the almost forgotten centuries of its own musical history. The works of his creation—the highest outcome of an essentially national art, whose origin lies in the period of the Reformation—are like a precious seed which bursts the soil at last to be garnered in perennial sheaves. Henceforth it will not be possible that Bach should be forgotten so long as the German people exist. His resurrection, in the works of a later generation of artists, has already begun ; but we who are not of the mystic guild have our duty too, each in his degree, to labour that the spirit of the great man may be more widely understood and loved.

APPENDIX (A, TO VOL. III.)

1 (p. 39). **The B minor mass** exists entire, or in part, in three original MS. copies: the autograph complete score in the Berlin Library; the original parts of the *Kyrie* and *Gloria* in the library of the King of Saxony, at Dresden; the autograph score of the *Sanctus* in its first state in the Berlin Library. The parts belonging to the whole score and to the *Sanctus* are lost, as is the separate score of the *Kyrie* and *Gloria*. In the collective score these two numbers show some deviations from the parts preserved at Dresden, which proves that this complete score was written later than the Dresden parts. From the watermark, M A, it would have been about 1736 (see Vol. II., p. 697). As regards the date of the *Credo*, it is surprising to discover that it is written on the same paper as the cantata "Wir Danken dir Gott," and parts of the cantatas "Herr, deine Augen," and "Wer weiss, wie nahe" (see Vol. II., p. 702). On this we may base the hypothesis that it was composed in 1732, thus earlier than the *Kyrie* and *Gloria*. Against this, however, it may be said that in the *Agnus*, too, the same watermark seems to be traceable, though too faint for certainty. From this we might infer that the *Agnus* also was older than the *Kyrie*; but from the connection of the *Agnus* with the *Sanctus* through the *Osanna* this is highly improbable; in this instance the internal evidence seems to me to outweigh that of the watermark. In the first sketch, even the *Sanctus* is distinguished as an independent composition by the *J. J.* at the beginning, and at the end, *Fine SDG*. The theme of the fugue *Pleni sunt cœli* was at first written thus:—

ple - ni sunt cœ - li et ter-ra glo - - - - - ri - a . . tu - a

and in this form it is hastily noted down on the first page, as was usual with Bach when an idea occurred to him while he was working up another composition. But that this *Sanctus* was originally a Christmas piece is clear from the fact that the following lines are to be seen on the same page and written with the same ink as the rest of the sketch:—

(*sic*).

Ich freue . . mich in dir und heis-se dich will - kom - men, Mein
Mein lie - bes Je - su-lein, du hast dir vor - ge - nom - men,

Brü-der-lein zu sein, ach wie ein süs - ser Thon, wie freund-lich sieht er aus   der

gro - se   Got - tes-sohn.

In Thee is all my joy, of morning stars the brightest!
O Jesu, Lord of love, Thy holy word Thou plightest
My brother to be called: how gracious is the word!
How tenderly benign Thy glorious face, O Lord!

This is part of a Christmas hymn by Caspar Ziegler, with a little
known air, both of which Bach made use of for the third day of Christmas (St. John's day).   He has here noted down the melody, evidently
in order to return to it for the cantata which he intended to perform for
the first time on the same occasion as the *Sanctus*.   The watermark of
both is the half moon in the first half-sheet, the second being blank,
and Bach began to use such paper as this in 1735.   On the same page
as the above quoted, staves of music are written in Bach's hand, " *NB.*
Die *Partcyen* sind in Böhmen bey Graff *Sporck* " (" The parts are with
Count Sporck, in Bohemia ").   This Graff Sporck must undoubtedly
be the same as is spoken of at p. 43 of this Vol.; he died March 30,
1738, and his family was extinct, as he left no son; so, as Bach had sent
him the parts, the *Sanctus* must have been written for Christmas, 1737,
at latest.   We may, however, question whether in fact the score also
may not have been sent to him, and he have returned that only and retained the parts.   If this were the case—and it seems to me a
permissible suggestion—the *Sanctus* may have been written earlier.
Bach would hardly have composed it in 1736, as he was engaged in a
violent squabble with Ernesti and his choir, and so out of favour, and
certainly not in the humour to produce two new works for the same
festival, one of them on so grand a scale.   We are therefore thrown
back to Christmas, 1735.   From the watermark we cannot go farther
back than this; but there is another point in favour of this
year.   If we compare the closing chorus of the Easter oratorio
with the *Sanctus* we trace in them a remarkable relationship.   Both
are constructed in the form of the French *ouverture*, and each
has, in its two sections, similar proportions; in each there is a
movement in ⅜ time following one in common time, with the change
conducted in the same manner.   Still, no one can suppose that
the Easter oratorio chorus is the earlier.   On the contrary, it
rather seems like the outcome of a somewhat weary advance along
the road opened up in the *Sanctus*.   The Easter oratorio was probably composed in 1736 (see Vol. II., p. 714).

2 (pp. 73, 75). **This new and distinct watermark**

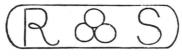

characterises the following cantatas :—

1. Ihr werdet weinen—Third Sunday after Easter.
2. Es ist euch gut, dass ich hingehe—Fourth Sunday after Easter.
3. Bisher habt ihr nichts gebeten—Fifth Sunday after Easter.
4. Auf Christi Himmelfahrt—Ascension Day.
5. Sie werden euch in den Bann thun (A minor)—Sunday after Ascension Day.
6. Wer mich liebet—Whitsunday.
7. Also hat Gott die Welt geliebt—Whitsun Monday.
8. Er rufet seine Schafe—Whitsun Tuesday.

These, as may be observed, form an unbroken series. At the top of the last page of No. 1 are the words *Dominica Quasimodogeniti. Concerto*, and below, a beginning of some music crossed out, seven bars long, of which this is the upper part :—

Whether this sketch was ever worked out is not known; if it was, the composition is undoubtedly lost. At any rate, Bach intended, with the music for the Third Sunday, also to compose a work for the First Sunday after Easter. Thus there would be missing only a cantata for the Second Sunday after Easter to complete a series from Easter to Trinity Sunday, and it will presently be shown that this cantata probably is extant. I regard these eight cantatas as composed consecutively, for one and the same year. Considering Bach's extensive use of writing materials, and the fact that paper with this watermark was never used by him, excepting in these cantatas and in a single MS., to be mentioned presently—so far as is known—considering, too, their natural connection, the contrary hypothesis hardly seems tenable. Besides, as to Nos. 6 and 7, we have yet other evidence. No. 6 is in two of its movements no more than a remodelled form of an older Whitsuntide cantata, beginning with the same words (see Vol. I., p. 512, and Vol. II., p. 688). On the back of the autograph score of that earlier composition we find the thema of the closing chorus of No. 7, and with it its first answer; thus Bach must have had recourse to the original Whitsuntide cantata to use parts of it for the new one, and while he was engaged in the work the theme of the fugue of No. 7 occurred to him, and he noted it down on the back of the sheet. These eight cantatas also exhibit a general affinity in form and structure which betrays their relationship, and especially we find one unusual instrument, the *Violoncello piccolo*, introduced into several of them. To which year are they to be assigned? The score of No. 4 directs the use of an organ obbligato as accompaniment to the duet. For this an independent Rückpositiv was indispensable, and we have seen (Vol. II., p. 282) that this was not constructed till 1730, so that No. 4, and consequently the whole series, was not composed before 1731. However, two cantatas exist, " Der Herr ist mein getreuer Hirt" for the Second Sunday after Easter, and " Ich liebe den Höchsten " for Whit Sunday, which must on good grounds be assigned to the year 1731 or 1732 (Vol. I., p. 699). Thus one of these years is thrown out of count. 1733 is equally out of the question, on account of the general mourning. Now, it is my opinion that it was only in specially exceptional cases that Bach wrote cantatas for the same Sundays in two successive years, and for this reason I believe this group cannot have been written before 1734.

But there is other evidence. Bach wrote a cantata, " Gott der Herr ist Sonn und Schild," for the Reformation Festival, and on the blank page of the fourth sheet of the autograph we find written at the top " *J. J. Doica Exaudi* (Sunday after Ascension Day) Sie werden euch in den Bann thun," and below it a very charming and peculiar beginning for five instruments, of which the first two lines are written in the violin clef, the two middle ones in alto, and the lowest in the bass. I believe the four upper instruments to have been for oboi (*d'amore* and *da caccia*). Above the lowest line that is filled, one is left empty for a bass voice; key A minor, common time. There are but seven bars in the fragment. On comparing this with No. 5 of this group it is plain that we have here the composer's first sketch of that cantata, so that if we could determine the date of the Reformation cantata we should obtain a trustworthy landmark. We have seen that Bach and the writers of his texts always had due regard to the general character of the Sunday or festival for which they were writing, and some to the purport of the text appointed for the sermon. There was no fixed and regular text for the Reformation Festival, one was chosen each year by the authorities. I have been so fortunate as to come upon a MS. list of the texts prescribed for this festival during Bach's residence at Leipzig. It is among the " Ephoralarchiv " of that town, "*ACTA* die Feyer des Reformations-Festes betr. (concerning the Festival of the Reformation) *Superintendur*, Leipzig, 1755." In 1723 the Gospel for the Sunday on which it falls, being the Twenty-third Sunday after Trinity ; 1724, Ps. xv., 1, 3 ; 1725, Heb. iii., 7, 14 ; 1726, Matt. xvi., 24, 26 ; 1727, Ps. lxxxv., 6, 8 ; 1728, Gospel, Twenty-third Sunday after Trinity; 1729, Titus ii., 14 ; 1730, Rev. xiv., 6, 8 ; 1731, Luke xiii., 6, 9 ; 1732, 2nd. Tim. i, 12 ; 1733, Is. li., 15, 16 ; 1734, Gospel, Nineteenth Sunday after Trinity ; 1735,

Ps. lxxx., 15, 20; 1736, Rev. iii., 1, 6; 1737, Rev. xiv., 6, 8; 1738, Rev. iii., 14, 18; 1739, Ps. xxxiii., 18; 1740, 2 Thes. ii., 10, 12; 1741, Rev. xiv., 6, 8; 1742, Rom. vi., 17, 18; 1743, Rev. iii., 10, 11; 1744, Is. lv., 10, 11; 1745, Gospel, Twentieth Sunday after Trinity; 1746, omitted; 1747, Rev. xiv., 6, 8; 1748, Is. xxvi., 9, 10; 1749, Is. xlv., 22, 25. Glancing through these texts, we see that the words of the cantata "Gott der Herr ist Sonn" only suits those for 1733, 1735, and 1739. The Reformation Festival had, no doubt, a very distinct poetical sentiment of its own, and when any special occasion took the precedence, as in 1730 and 1739, the years of Jubilee, it would be misleading to seek for any close connection between the sermon and the cantata. Thus the cantata "Ein feste Burg" (see Vol. II., p. 470) may very well have been connected with the sermon in 1730; still, it is possible that it was not written till 1739. But it is hardly possible that the cantata "Gott der Herr" should have been written in 1739, since— firstly, several portions of it have been worked into the A major and G major masses, and internal and external evidence alike concur in dating these in 1737-38; and secondly, the watermark of the original parts is found again in the original MS. of the music for Easter Monday, "Erfreut euch ihr Herzen," and for Easter Tuesday, "Ein Herz, das seinen Jesum," so that we must assume that these works were composed at about the same time. But in the parts of the Easter music we also find the mark M A, which is not to be met with in any other MS. by Bach of 1739. Thus we must fall back upon the years 1733 and 1735.

The above-mentioned sketch of No. 5 is on the fourth sheet of the Reformation Cantata; but the complete score fills altogether six sheets. Of these, 1, 2, 5, and 6 are alike in the size, quality, and watermark of the paper. Sheets 3 and 4 are different in size from the rest and from each other. It is plain that Bach, when proceeding to write the Reformation Cantata, used a few sheets of old paper which he had not used before, or used but little, and which fell under his hand. The contrary idea, that he should have sketched the first idea of No. 5 in the Reformation Cantata after the other was finished, is quite un- tenable, since it occurs in the middle of the score, and any one can see that Bach simply skipped over the page in question, because it was already partly used (there are other notes of musical themes upon it). Besides, the watermark in this sheet, though not very distinct, is recognisable by a practised eye as the same as that in the paper of the other eight cantatas in question. From this it would follow that the cantata for the Sunday after Ascension day was composed before the Reformation Cantata, and if so it cannot possibly have been written in 1733. For in 1733 Bach could not have composed this series, since there was no concerted music at all between Quinquagesima and the fourth Sunday after Trinity. The Reformation Cantata would thus have been written in 1735, and this leads us directly to the date of this series, which must also have been 1735.

With regard to No. 4, there is still a doubt, and we must once more refer to the Reformation Cantata. Sheets 1, 2, 5 and 6 of the score have the watermarks of a stag on one half sheet, and on the other

while in most of the parts we find this mark—

These marks recur in the following cantatas :—

(*a.*) Denn du wirst meine Seele—Easter Day.
(*b.*) Erfreut euch ihr Herzen—Easter Monday.
(*c.*) Ein Herz, das seinen Jesum—Easter Tuesday.
(*d.*) Gott fähret auf—Ascension Day.

And *a* and *d* have the same watermarks as the score of the Reformation Cantata ; and *b* and *c* that of the parts with the addition on the other half sheet of the figure of an eagle. It is evident that *a* and *d* must have been written nearly at the same time as the Reformation Cantata, and somewhat before it. But the paper on which the Reformation Cantata is written is of no less than four different kinds, showing that the economical composer was using up the remains of a former stock, particularly as the watermarks do not recur in any composition which can with certainty be dated later, excepting only a few scraps inserted into the parts of the St. John Passion for the third performance, probably in 1736. But if *a* and *d* do belong to the year 1735, we find that we have two cantatas by Bach for that year, a circumstance which must be considered as suspicious; and if I accept the hypothesis after mature deliberation, it is on the following grounds: Firstly, two cantatas were in fact needed for every Ascension day (see Vol. II., p. 193). Secondly, it was by no means unusual with the composers of that period to compose music for both the morning and evening services of the same day (see Vol. II., p. 270), and there can be no doubt that the impulse towards composition was very strong in Bach in 1735. Thirdly, if, in the absence of any alternative, we conclude that the cantatas *a* to *d* form a series, as 1 to 8 do, the fact that two of them, *a* and *c*, are remodellings of older works is an argument in favour of their having been written in this year, for it is impossible not to perceive that at this time Bach constantly had recourse to his earlier works ; 6 and 7, in the first series, are partly derived from Weimar compositions, while we know that the St. Luke Passion had been remodelled not long before, and reproduced probably in 1734. The Weimar cantata, " Komm du süsse Todesstunde," was also taken out again about this time, and the most probable hypothesis is that it was on February 2, 1735, for the paper of the score now extant is exactly like that of October 5, 1734 (a small eagle and HR ; see Vol. II., p. 708). The title indicates first the original purpose of the cantata, the sixteenth Sunday after Trinity, and below this, its subsequent use, *Festo Purificationis Mariae.* Finally, the date of the watermark in *a* and *d* is further supported by an organ part to Keiser's St. Mark Passion, prepared by Bach for his second performance of that work in Leipzig, the first having been in Weimar. Bach, having produced his own Passions in 1729, 1731, 1734, and 1736, the year 1735 remains open for Keiser's Passion. I must not omit to mention that among the parts of No. 8 a few leaves occur, which show them to be contemporaneous with the score of the Easter oratorio (see Vol. II., p. 715). From this we can only conclude that No. 8 was performed again at Whitsuntide, 1738, and that those portions of the copy that had been lost were then replaced.

Thus we have for the year 1735 a series of cantatas from Easter day till Whit Tuesday inclusive, and two for Ascension day. Only a cantata for the first Sunday after Easter is wanting, which was no doubt included by Bach, and if performed has been lost. That for the second Sunday after Easter has, I believe, survived in the composition " Ich bin ein guter Hirt." There is no difficulty as to the watermark, since it is the same as recurs in the scores of Nos. 2 and 3 (see below, note 3) and in musical character it has a marked affinity to the others. It must be further discussed in the next note.

3 (p. 91). **The Half Moon Watermark on the first half sheet** (the other being blank) is characteristic of the greater number of the cantatas of the last period of Bach's works. It occurs in the following :—

1. Ach Gott vom Himmel sieh darein.
2. Ach Gott, wie manches Herzeleid (A major).
3. Ach lieben Christen seid getrost.
4. Ach wie flüchtig, ach wie nichtig.
5. Aus tiefer Noth.
6. Bisher habt ihr nichts gebeten.
7. Bleib bei uns, denn es will Abend werden.
8. Christ unser Herr zum Jordan kam.
9. Christum wir sollen loben schon.
10. Das neugeborne Kindelein.
11. Du Friedefürst, Herr Jesu.
12. Erhalt uns Herr bei deinem Wort.
13. Es ist euch gut, das ich hingehe.
14. Gelobet seist du, Jesu Christ.
15. Herr Christ der einig Gottssohn.
16. Herr Gott dich loben alle wir.
17. Herr Jesu Christ wahr Mensch und Gott.

18. Ich bin ein guter Hirt.
19. Ich freue mich in dir.
20. Ich hab in Gottes Herz.
21. Jesu nun sei gepreiset.
22. Liebster Immanuel.
23. Mache dich mein Geist bereit.
24. Meinen Jesum lass ich nicht.
25. Meine Seele erhebet den Herren.
26. Mit Fried und Freud ich fahr dahin.
27. Nun komm, der Heiden Heiland (B minor).
28. Schmücke dich, o liebe Seele.
29. Was frag ich nach der Welt.
30. Was mein Gott will, das g'scheh.
31. Wo soll ich fliehen hin.

These are all chorale cantatas with the exception of Nos. 6, 7, 13, and 18. We can verify the date at which this paper was first used by Nos. 6 and 13, since in the original MSS. we find, besides the half moon, the watermark (see woodcut in note 2) which distinguishes the group immediately preceding: it is 1735; and further evidence is to be found in the connection between No. 7 and the Easter Oratorio (see Vol. II., p. 715) and between No. 19 and the *Sanctus* of the B minor Mass (see note 2). In No. 11 the text bears unmistakable reference to the war in which the country was then engaged, though it must also be admitted that the immediate suggestion was given by the Epistle for the day, which prophesies the dispersion of the Jews. Still the use of the hymn " Du Friedefürst " points to some contemporary event of a similar character. The introduction of an independent verse as a recitative is, however, conclusive. The text—as is always the case with Bach's later chorale cantatas—is mainly a paraphrase of some of the verses of a well known hymn. The alto aria is founded on the second verse, the tenor recitative on the third ; the fourth and fifth are omitted ; verse six is adapted for the terzett ; the seventh, which is the last, is simply treated as the closing chorale. But the words of the alto recitative immediately before this finale are quite independent of the hymn, and to this effect :—

> Let not Thy people bleed, O God,
> Too long beneath Thy rod !
> O Lord, who art the Lord of law and right,
> Thou know'st the adversary's wrath,
> His cruelty and lawless might.
> Put forth Thy strong and saving hand,
> Defend our terror-stricken land ;
> For Thou canst bid their raging cease,
> And keep us in abiding peace.

These words indicate some stress of war in Saxony itself, and in 1774, the first year of the second war with Schleswig, hostilities commenced with an incursion of the Prussian foe through the heart of Saxony. In 1745 Saxony suffered even more severely, but there was no twenty-fifth Sunday after Trinity—for which this cantata was written—so that 1744 is the latest year in which this watermark can be proved to have been used. In Nos. 21, 29, and 31 of this list we find among the sheets with the half moon others with the M A watermark, and these must therefore be ascribed to the earlier years of the period between 1735—44; not later probably than 1736. No. 29 is for the ninth Sunday after Trinity. In 1736 Bach was absent from Leipzig on the eighth and ninth Sundays after Trinity (July 22 and 29; see ante, p. 6), so this one at any rate must be assigned to 1735. So probably must No. 31, written for the nineteenth Sunday after Trinity; since at the end of 1736 Bach's quarrel with Ernesti was going on; and for the same reason No. 21, a New Year's cantata, is no doubt to be dated 1736.

In 29 we detect a third watermark, an eagle, but this occurs in such various forms and at such various periods as to be useless in chronological enquiries. I have, however, classed together the MSS. in which it appears exactly in the same form. These are :—

Jesu der du meine Seele ;
Wass Gott thut, das ist wohlgethan, G major—21st Sunday after Trinity ;
Allein zu dir, Herr Jesu Christ ;
Nimm von uns Herr ;

so that these cantatas might be supposed to belong, like No. 29, to the year 1735, but, as it happens, the twenty-first Sunday after Trinity in 1735 was the Reformation Festival, when " Gott, der ist Sonn und Schild " was most likely given; at any rate, not a regular Sunday cantata.

4 (p. 113). **The five hymn tunes, preserved to us by Joh. Ludwig Krebs,** are to be found in a MS. collection of pieces for the organ and harpsichord which was inherited from him by his successors in office at Altenburg, until they fell into the hands of Herr F. A. Roitzsch, of Leipzig, who has always authorised me to make full use of his treasures for my immediate purpose.

The melodies are set to the hymns " Hier lieg ich nun, mein Gott, zu deinen Füssen," " Das walt mein Gott, Gott Vater, Sohn," "Gott mein Herz dir Dank," " Meine Seele, lass es gehen," " Ich gnüge mich an meinem Stande." This book includes compositions by Buxtehude, Reinken, Böhm, Leyding, Walther, Kauffmann, Bach, and others, in no sort of order, and, though it cannot be directly proved, it is most likely Krebs selected and copied them while he was Bach's pupil at Leipzig.

He was at the Thomasschule till 1735, and a student at the University till 1737, and must have been familiar with Bach at the time when he was at work on the musical portion of Schemelli's hymn-book. These five melodies are not sketches but copies, and very hasty ones, for in three the air alone is given, and the bass even not indicated. But as the transcriber thought them worthy to be included in a book with works by the most illustrious masters, he must have esteemed them highly; in fact, they bear the stamp of a master-hand, and examination will show us that that hand is Bach's.

What leads us directly to the conclusion that Bach wrote them as addenda to the melodies for Schemelli is this : The hymn " Hier lieg ich nun o Herr (mein Gott) zu deinen Füssen," though it had been made popular by Freylinghausen's hymn-book, was not included in Schemelli's, while, on the other hand, it has the five penitential hymns attributed to Johann Arndt, " Hier lieg ich nun, o Vater aller Gnaden," set to the same tune. This hymn seems never to have become more extensively known ; it is not mentioned even by J. B. König. Neither it nor the fellow hymn in Freylinghausen seems to have had any original melody of its own; both are to be sung to that of " Der Tag ist hin, mein Jesu bei mir bleibe." But the words of " Hier lieg ich nun, o Vater aller Gnaden " are such as might well inspire Bach to set them to a tune of their own ; and in point of fact the air preserved by Krebs not only suits Freylinghausen's charming verses less well on the whole than it does Schemelli's, but in detail it is so admirably appropriate to this latter, and its fitness is so thoroughly characteristic of Bach, that in my opinion there is not the slightest doubt that it was actually composed for it. To facilitate comparison I have given both the texts in the musical supplement.

The case seems to be somewhat different with regard to the air to " Gott mein Herz dir Dank." The verses, which are by the Countess Amélie Juliane, a thanksgiving after partaking of the communion, is not to be found in Schemelli's hymn-book, but he has a morning hymn for a communicant, which seems to have been tolerably exactly imitated from it, " Gott sei Lob, der Tag ist kommen." But there was no proper melody for either of these, and the hymns themselves seem to have been included only occasionally. " Gott sei Lob " occurs in Part II. of the Arnstadt hymn-book of 1745 ; " Gott mein Herz " was known in Sondershausen through Heinrich N. Gerber's " Choralbuch." If Bach wanted to supply a melody for Schemelli's hymn-book it was obvious that he should make use of the original, which he probably had known in Thuringia, rather than of the imitated version ; and the air, though it suits both, is more perfectly suited to the former.

The words to the other melodies preserved by Krebs are all to be found in Schemelli's hymn-book. " Das walt mein Gott " had long had a proper tune ; " Meine Seele lass es gehen " is marked to be sung to the tune of " Herr ich habe missgehandelt," but it had also proper tunes, which are given by Dretzel and by König. The tunes given by Krebs are quite unlike these, and occur nowhere else. The hymn " Ich gnüge mich an meinem Stande " has no tune of its own. Dretzel, in compiling his collection "Des Evangelischen Zions Musicalische Harmonie" (probably 1731), found only the text in the hymn-books, and himself added a tune to it; but we find no reference to this in Schemelli, who enjoins that it shall be sung to the tune of "Wer nur den lieben Gott lässt walten"; but the metre of the last two lines does not perfectly agree, so the need of a proper melody must have been felt. It may be remembered that Bach had set a cantata by Picander beginning "Ich bin vergnügt" (see Vol. II., p. 443). Picander had evidently this hymn in his mind, as we see from the resemblance in feeling, as well as in several turns of phrase. Bach, therefore, must have had a special interest in the hymn given by Schemelli, and it is probably not by mere accident that the air wrote for it, like the cantata, is in E minor.

5 (p. 153). **The English Suites** are not known in autograph. But among the literary remains of Heinrich N. Gerber there are copies of four of them, those in A major, G minor, E minor, and D minor, which, after the death of Ernst Ludwig Gerber (the writer of the "Lexicon"), became the property of Hofrath André, and then of Herr Ruhl, music director at Frankfurt-am-Main. They are now in the possession of Dr. Erich Prieger, of Berlin, who kindly allowed me to make use of them. Gerber made these copies when he was studying at the University of Leipzig, and under Bach 1724—1727. This is evident from the superscription to the first suite: "L. [itterarum] L. [iberalium] S. [tudiosus]. a [c] M. [usicæ] C. [ultor]; and besides this the copies are, as to writing, paper, and ink, exactly similar to a figured bass written by Gerber to a sonata by Albinoni (see Vol. II., p. 293). He also copied eight other suites, including six of the French suites, at the same period and in the same style. This was of course the result of the teaching he obtained from Bach (see ante, p. 127). Though he copied only four he must have known of a fifth, at least; for he designates that in A major as the *first*, G minor as *second*, E minor as *fourth*, and D minor as *fifth*; thus either that in F major or that in A minor must have been already written. But it is probable that all six were by this time finished, since Bach wrote them to order all at about the same time, and in 1726 we find him already at work on another grand set of suites, the six Partitas of the "Clavierübung." The most important copy of the English set, next to that by Gerber, is one by Joh. Christian Bach, Sebastian's youngest son. The MS. is in the hands of Herr Arnold Mendelssohn, in Bonn. The title page of the G minor suite, which is in the same hand as all the copies, and apparently of the same date, is as follows: *pp* (*i.e., proprium*) *J. C. Bach*; and on the title page of the A major suite the owner has added, evidently at a later date: *pp Jean Chretien Bach*, and this title is also interesting from having the note: *fait pour les Anglois.* From this we may infer that there is some truth in Forkel's statement that Bach composed these suites for an illustrious Englishman. The copy is throughout very careful, but it is not possible to determine when it was

made. The writing is tolerably free and bold; if Christian Bach wrote them out at Leipzig in his father's lifetime it must have been in 1749 or 1750 at earliest, as he was born in 1735. The MS. is, however, no longer complete; the suite in F major is wanting.

6 (p. 155). **The Clavierübung (or Practice).** Only Part I. of this work has the date of publication on the title page, and the dates of the first appearance of the other parts has hitherto only been approximately known. However, as regards Part II. we find a note by J. G. Walther, written into his copy of the Lexicon, which passed from Gerber's library into that of the Gesellschaft 'der Musikfreunde' at Vienna, saying that " It was brought out for the Easter Fair of 1735 by Joh. Weigel, engraved on copper." Part III. is mentioned by Mizler (Mus. Bib., VII., Part I., p. 156) among "remarkable musical novelties." This volume of the Mus. Bib. came out in 1740; Part VI. of Vol. I. had appeared in 1738. Mizler would beyond a doubt have mentioned Bach's work as soon as he knew of it, so this assigns it to 1739 at the earliest. It is not impossible that it should have been as late as 1740, but not probable, because Mizler's book was certainly brought out at Easter 1740, and Bach's work could not have appeared earlier in that year. Mizler simply writes: " Here, too, Herr Capellmeister Bach has published Part III.," &c., and he would have noticed it more fully if he had seen it before it was given to the public. As to Part IV., which Bach himself did not designate as Part IV., but simply as " Clavier-übung," while in size and shape it also differs from the other three—thus much is certain as to its first publication: It was brought out in Nuremberg by Balthasar Schmidt, who also published, in 1742, the six Sonatas by Emmanuel Bach, dedicated to Frederick the Great. Now these are numbered 20 by the publisher, and the Variations by Sebastian Bach are numbered 16; these, then, must have been printed first. But how long before? Balthasar Schmidt printed a good deal in his time, considering his position. Thus, a concerto (M. Scheuenstuhl, in G minor) published by him in 1738 is No. 9, and in 1745 we already find him at No. 27 (Em. Bach's Concerto in D major). J. G. Walther, who watched the novelties in the music market with a keen eye, says in a MS. note to the Lexicon, that Em. Bach's six sonatas came out " circa 1743." From this we may infer that the sonatas were brought out, not by Easter, 1742, but towards the end of that year. Thus Seb. Bach's Variations may quite well have appeared for the Easter Fair, 1742. This would be certain if we were justified in attributing any great weight to the fact that in the statement as to the origin of the Variations the order for them is ascribed to " Graf" (Count) Kayserling. For his original title was only Freiherr or Baron, and the archives in Dresden show that it was August III. who raised him to the dignity of " Graf," Oct. 30, 1741. But this is not very trustworthy evidence, and we must be satisfied to decide that the Variations were published not later than 1742, and probably in that year.

7 (p. 181). **The Chromatic Fantasia and Fugue.** Among the papers of Herr Grasnick, of Berlin, who died in 1877, there was a MS. copy of this work in an unknown hand, dated December 6, 1730. The MS. consists of fourteen sheets of small oblong quarto, and was evidently put together expressly for this work, which almost fills it, the rest is written over with little inventions, which are evidently the attempts of a beginner. Notwithstanding numerous mistakes, made apparently by an unskilled copyist, in the absence of the autograph, this is by far the most reliable copy extant. Griepenkerl has added to his edition of the Chromatic Fantasia and Fugue (P. S. I., C. 4, No. 1—207) two variorum readings, the second of which has no independent value, while the first, which is derived from a MS. of the work by F. W. Rust, Capellmeister at Dessau, 1757, shows an earlier and possibly the original form of the work. The MS. of 1730 has already lost this form, so we are justified in dating the actual composition of the work at least ten years earlier. The accuracy of the form in which—as being probably the ultimate purpose of the author—Griepenkerl has edited the work, seems in more than one respect extremely open to suspicion. For wherever we find the older (or Rust's) form agree with the later (or Grasnick's) we must agree to acknowledge Bach's unaltered purpose, as a third remodelled form from his hand is most unlikely to have existed. Indeed, we have further support of this view in a MS. by Kittel, one of Bach's latest scholars, and of the Chromatic Fantasia only, by Müthel, his very last pupil. The exact *replica* of the earlier form was in Grasnick's bequest, and the later recension has for a long time been in the Royal Library at Berlin. Both agree, in all important points, with the MS. of 1730; the most conspicuous variant in the fantasia is in bar 49, at the beginning of the recitative, where, in opposition to Griepenkerl's reading, we find the following, which is now universally accepted, and seems in itself more justified :—

The fugue also shows some remarkable differences, as in bar 72. The upper part is :—

Griepenkerl follows Forkel's MS. In 1819, one year after Forkel's death, he published, through Peters, of Leipzig, a second edition of the Chromatic Fantasia and Fugue under the title " Neue Ausgabe mit einer Beźeichnung ihres wahren Vortrags, wie derselbe von J. S. Bach,

auf W. Friedemann Bach, von diesem auf Forkel und von Forkel auf
seine Schüler gekommen." (A new edition, with indications of the right
way of playing it, as it came from J. S. Bach, through W. F. Bach,
to Forkel, and from him to his pupils.) He also added a preface that
is well worth reading, on Bach's method of playing, as derived by
Forkel from Friedemann Bach, and so handed down to the present
time. Forkel, indeed, first obtained the Chromatic Fantasia and Fugue
in MS. from Friedemann Bach (see his work on J. S. Bach, p. 56). We
may therefore assume that all that we find as deviations from the most
trustworthy of Forkel's other MS. copies is also due to Friedemann
Bach, who, in the spasmodic vagaries of his genius, was not unfrequently deficient in reverence towards his father's great works.

8 (p. 191). **The " Musikalisches Opfer."** A perfect copy of
the original edition exists in the Amalien Library of the Joachimsthal
Gymnasium at Berlin. It has a special value as being the dedication
copy sent by Bach to Frederick the Great, who must have given it to
his sister. This copy proves two things. First, that under the title
" Musikalisches Opfer " Bach originally included only the three-part
simple fugue, six canons and the canon fugue, so that when he began
the work he was not fully determined as to its extent and character.
This dedication copy contains (*a*) three leaves of music and two with
the title and dedication. The paper is remarkably fine and thick, in
very large oblong folio, and the five leaves are bound in leather, with
gold tooling. The music consists of the three-part simple fugue and
one canon, in which the alto had the *Cantus firmus*, while the treble and
bass have counterpoint in canon. This canon is entitled *Canon perpetuus
super Thema Regium*, the fugue is called a *Ricercar*. (*b*) An upright
folio sheet of the same character as to the size and quality of the
paper, but only laid in, on account of its being cut the other way, and
the two inside pages have printed on them five canons and a *Fuga
canonica in Epidiapente*," with the title to the whole, " *Canones diversi
super Thema Regium*." All this is printed, but all the sheets have written
notes and additions. Besides the complimentary addresses given in
the text of this volume, which are inserted to the right of canons 4 and
5 on the upright folio sheet, we find on the blank first page of this sheet
the title " *Thematis Regii elaborationes canonicæ* " ; on the first page, also
blank, of the oblong folio, " *Regis Jussu Cantio Et Reliqua Canonica Arte
Resoluta*." This is the reason why the publishers of the later editions
put this sentence at the beginning of the whole work ; but this was not
Bach's latest intention, nor that it should be placed before the first
fugue and canon. The Latin sentences—or at any rate, the second of
them—evidently only occurred to him when the engraving was
finished, and as he was eager to dedicate and offer this copy, he had it
written in it. But the sense of it is not exact as applied to the contents
of the oblong folio volume, as he himself detected, and when he afterwards had a separate slip engraved and printed with these words, he

had it gummed on to the first page of the upright folio sheet where it is more appropriate, and the copies printed for sale have it in this place.

I have said that Bach was eager to forward this dedication copy. On the 7th and 8th of May, 1747, he played before Frederick the Great at Potsdam, and the printed dedication of the "Musikalisches Opfer" is dated July 7 of the same year. Thus the composition and engraving were got through in two months, and the engraving must have taken all the more time as the engraver did not live in Leipzig. On page eight, at the bottom—not, to be sure, of these particular sheets—but of those which contain the six-part Ricercar, we find " *J. G. Schübler sc.*," but the two works are so perfectly similar in workmanship, paper, and partly in size and shape, that the engraver of both was no doubt the same person. Schübler lived at Zella St. Blasii, near Suhl, and two weeks must be allowed for delays in sending backwards and forwards with proof corrections and specimen sheets, under the conditions of communication at that time. Under these circumstances the singularities of the appearance of the work are accounted for; they are those of an over hasty production, and evidences of hurry in engraving the music may be ascribed to the same causes; for instance, in the second canon on the upright folio sheets the letters *Th* (Thema) are wanting to the lowest stave, and in the fugue in canon there is no indication as to what instrument is to play the upper part of the canon.

All the rest of the music which is now included under the title "Musikalisches Opfer" does not, as we have seen, strictly speaking belong to it, but was composed by Bach afterwards and sent to the king without any formal dedication. This also may be divided into two portions. The six-part Ricercar and two canons attached to it compose a part or cahier of four leaves in oblong folio, separately played. The presentation copy of this, too, is in the Amalien library, but in unpretending guise, not bound or even stitched into a cover; the leaves are simply held together by a pin through the fold. The sonata, on the other hand, and the canon for flute, violin and bass, are engraved in upright folio—three sheets without either title or cover. These were specially preserved in the Amalien library, and seem to have been used; at any rate, in the continuo part there are corrections added in ink. It is hard to say why Bach should have had the shape of the paper altered.

As the whole collection now exists it is a strange conglomerate of pieces, wanting not only internal connection but external uniformity. The contents are fugues, canons, and sonatas. But the fugues, as well as the canons, are dispersed in the original edition; the canons are in no less than four separate groups, and, as regards their form, have no sort of arrangement. This confusion may have been fortuitous and annoying to the author himself, but after he had once started the publication was beyond remedy. Bach had 100 copies printed off in the first instance, and gave them away for the most part to friends.

These were exhausted by October 6, 1748, and on that day he wrote to his cousin, Elias Bach, of Schweinfurt, to have a few more copies printed off at once, and that each copy was to cost one thaler. Whether the trio was included in this order is doubtful since he only mentions the "Preussiche Fuge." The work afterwards came into the market, and in 1761 it was sold by Breitkopf for 1 thlr. 12 gr., as we see by his circular for Easter, 1761. But, according to the common custom at that time, it was also much copied, and as it was not a complete or inseparable whole each one transcribed only as much as he pleased, and in whatever order was most convenient. Complete copies in MS. must have been extremely rare, and I do not know of a single one now existing. Agricola copied the three-part simple fugue and three of the canons ; this MS. is in the Amalien-Bibliothek. Above the first canon he has written: "*Canone perp : sopra il soggetto dato dal Rè,*" and Kirnberger has used the same superscription in his "Kunst des reinen Satzes," II., 3, p. 45.

9 (p. 219). **Six Chorales for the Organ.** Rust was the first to point out (B.-G., XXV.,[2] p. V.) that the title of the original edition affords a ground for estimating the date of its publication ; his only error is that he limits it to 1747—1749. Friedemann Bach was established as organist at Halle by 1746 (see Chrysander, Jahrb. für Mus. Wissensch. Vol. II., p. 244), and it is possible the work may have been published even so late as 1750. Bach kept up business relations with Schübler till his death ; in the papers relating to his affairs and bequests we find, among "other necessary payments," paid to "Herr Schübler 2 thlr. 16 gr." This small sum could not relate to the "Kunst der Fuge"; besides, it is improbable on other grounds that Schübler should have engraved that work; but it may very well relate to the six chorales, and we may infer that these either were not published till 1750, or that some new copies were at that time printed off.

10 (p. 219). **The Variations on "Vom Himmel hoch."** The Necrology says, p. 173, "Bach delivered to the Society the chorale ' Vom Himmel hoch' completely worked out, and it was afterwards engraved on copper." From this the work cannot have been engraved until after Bach had presented it to the Society. As he was busy all through the summer of 1747, and even before that, the chorales cannot very well have appeared before 1748. This result cannot be reconciled with a certain remarkable circumstance. In 1745 Emmanuel Bach brought out, through Balthasar Schmidt, of Nuremberg, a clavier concerto with accompaniments in D major (see his autobiography in Burney III., p. 203), and this concerto is numbered 27 by the publisher. Seb. Bach's setting of the Christmas chorale is numbered 28, and therefore must have been brought out immediately after his son's work. Schmidt was just then much employed (see ante, note 6) ; but if the chorales were not published till after Bach had joined the Society, Schmidt would have published nothing for about three years, and that is incredible. It is

my opinion that these chorale settings were already engraved by 1746 at latest, and the statement that they were composed for the Society cannot, therefore, be accurate. Mizler knew in the spring of 1746 that Bach intended to join. Possibly Bach wished to enter the Society with a perfectly finished work, which would be, to a certain extent, beyond the reach of discussion, and so, as the work was already being engraved, postponed joining the Society for one reason or another. That this was in fact the real state of things stands almost confessed by the statement in the Necrology, which in such matters as these was certainly not written by either Emanuel Bach or Agricola, or any other musician. What can the words "completely worked out" (*Vollständig gearbeitet*) mean? It was not usual to lay unfinished works before the Society, and Bach was the last man to do such a thing. Or would any musician have spoken of such a work as "the chorale"? It is clear to my apprehension that the writer has misunderstood the information given him and distorted the facts. The statement, as he received it, may have been, "Bach worked out a chorale composition on 'Vom Himmel hoch,' and had it engraved on copper, and then laid the finished work before the Society."

END OF APPENDIX A.

APPENDIX B.

[In the German edition of this work Herr Spitta has printed at length a considerable number of curious and interesting extracts from the town, school, and church archives of Leipzig. They would, however, lose much of their value by being translated, as part of their interest arises from the quaint language in which they are couched. The translators have therefore exercised their discretion in selecting and abridging, and no documents have been given entire, excepting those which have some musical interest, or which either emanated from Bach himself or bear directly on his position and proceedings. A brief summary of each note is given for the reader's guidance.]

I.

To Vol. I., p. 2.

Count Günther's Letter was discovered in September, 1868, on a yellow and half mouldy sheet in the Archives of the Principality, at Sondershausen. The oldest document extant having any bearing on the Bachs, who may have been Sebastian's ancestors, may be printed here at length. It was to the friendly help of my late lamented colleague, Professor Th. Irmisch, that I owe my success in deciphering it.

" Günther, Count of Swarzburg, and Lord of Arnstet and Sundershussen :[1]—First our greeting to you, most worthy and learned and well-beloved. You have, no doubt, not forgotten that we have written to you in manifold ways, and have also let you know by word of mouth that our subjects of Gräfenrode, Hans Bach and Hans Abendroth, who are burdened with spiritual proceedings, originating from Mentz, and because of one Hans Schuler, of Vlfinau, a subject of your spiritual jurisdiction, have craved not to be refused help and justice from us, and from our officials ; or else, from your oversight as spiritual ordinary, in the place of our gracious Lord (Archbishop) of Mentz to penetrate to this place (to put themselves under our protection). And although as we have been informed you have written to Mentz about it with one and suitable offers, but still fruitlessly as regards relieving the burdens of our faithful subjects, and it is quite grievous to know that the poor folks are so undeservedly burdened. Well then—it is our gracious mind that you shall once more in regard of their destitution, and our command for the benefit of the poor folks, help them, and bring it about that they are relieved of their burdens. We will then take care that the Hans Schuler is duly dealt with. Help at once, and justice before

---

[1] Günther the XXXIX., " der Bremer," born 1455, died 1531 ; reigned from 1503.

us or our judges for our (men), and refuse not, but let all be done and carried out rapidly, or presently call them to appear before you in your court, as Ordinary presiding over justice and dues, to render and give up to the complainant so much as (what) is acknowledged so by you. You shall show yourself well disposed herein, and we will subscribe ourselves and acknowledge ourselves your debtor.

"Given on Friday (? it was the 23rd Feb.) before the feast of St. Matthias *anno Nono.*

" To the very worthy and learned Master Johan Somering, cathedral chaplain at Erfurt, our well-beloved."[2]

II.

To Vol. I., p. 26.

Johann Ernst Bach of Eisenach. It is no part of my plan to follow up the Bach family in all directions down to the generation of which Sebastian was a member. Hence, I can, in this place, mention only Bernhard Bach's only son, Johann Ernst, born September 1, 1722, died January 28, 1777. He studied at St. Thomas's school at Leipzig, somewhere about 1735, and left evidence in a copy of his own making of twelve Concertos by Vivaldi, which Sebastian Bach had arranged for the organ or cembalo that he had learned of his illustrious relation. He studied jurisprudence at the Leipzig University, and settled as a lawyer in his native town of Eisenach. But his musical skill was so great that he not only became his father's colleague as organist in 1748, and after his death held the same office for life, but in 1756 was even appointed Capellmeister of Sax Weimar with a salary of 400 thalers a year. That he took the greatest interest in the improvement of the band is proved by various " *Pro Memoria,*" in the archives of Weimar. He kept his residence and appointment in Eisenach all the same, and only went occasionally to Weimar, and so was, according to the expression of the time " out-door" (von Haus aus) Capellmeister. He wrote an intelligent and thoughtful preface to Adlung's book, "Von der Musikalischen Gelahrtheit." The esteem and respect he everywhere enjoyed were due, according to Gerber, to his admirable character. I have, in MS., copies of the period of his Mourning Ode on the death of his patron, the Duke Ernst August Constantin, and a Magnificat in German. The first named work is of smooth and tender character, but not grandiose; the Magnificat deals with massive choral movements, and artistic, though not always happy, contrapuntal combinations. Another Magnificat of a more pleasing character is the property of Herr A. Dörffel of Leipzig, as it would seem in the original autograph. Besides these the Royal Library at

---

[2] Sömmering was in 1507 Domherr or Canon of the church of St. Severus in Erfurt, and doctor of both branches of law, civil and ecclesiastical.

Berlin has two church cantatas by him, the 18th Psalm, and a Kyrie and Gloria on the Chorale, "Es woll uns Gott genädig sein," so arranged that the two first lines of the chorale are used for the Kyrie, and the rest for the Gloria. The whole composition shows a skilful musician, and is one of the best sacred pieces of that time, which, to be sure, was not in any way on the whole important in the history of art. Of his other compositions recently published, my knowledge is limited to a Fantasia and Fugue for Clavier in F major ("Alte Claviermusik" neu herausgegeben von E. Pauer. Leipzig, B. Senff. Ser. 2, part 3). Another fantasia, with Fugue in A minor, and a Sonata in A major, exist in MS. in the Royal Library at Berlin. The dates of his birth and death I have taken from a pedigree drawn up by his great grandson, Herr Bach of Eisenach.

III.

To Vol. I., p. 156.

Valentin Bach. I have already alluded to the sons of Valentin Bach, in referring to the connection which subsequently existed between Elias Bach and Sebastian. The pedigree here referred to mentions three more of his sons: Friedrich Adam, born September 5, 1752, died March 2, 1815; Johann Michael, born 1754; Simon Friedrich, born 1755, died May 2, 1799. It is however certain that this does not complete the list of the male members of the family of that time, as is proved by a testimonial which Elias Bach granted to one of his relations, and of which the original still exists in the possession of Fräulein Emmert. As it has a particular interest from a musical point of view I here give it at full length :—

"Whereas the representative of the said Johann Valentin Bach has asked me in becoming terms for a credible testimonial as to his conduct hitherto, I am in no way averse to doing so; on the contrary, can with truth confidently assure every one, be he whom he may, before whom this testimonial is laid that the above mentioned Johann Valentin Bach during his five years residence at the *Alumneum* of this place has always been found obedient, diligent, and faithful, and in music particularly has gone so far that he can sing well in discant, tenor, and bass parts,[3] and can also play well on the clavier and other instruments. Wherefore I do not hesitate hereby to give him my best recommendation to all, be they whom they may, who are patrons, lovers, and promoters of the noble art of music for the advancement of his praiseworthy purpose. Given at Schweinfurth, August 12, 1752.

"JOHANN ELIAS BACH,

"*Cant.* and *Alumn. Insp.*"

[Seal.]

But exactly who this young Valentin Bach may have been, I cannot say.

---

[3] Meaning, no doubt, he could read the different clefs.

IV.

To Vol. I., p. 258.

Specification of the Organ in the Marien-Kirche at Lubeck.

Friedrich Erhardt Niedt, Musikalische Handleitung II., 189 (Hamburg, 1721), says: "The organ in the Marien-Kirche at Lübeck has 54 stops.

Werk.

(1) Principal 16 ft. (2) Quintadena 16 ft. (3) Octava 8 ft. (4) Spitz-Flöte 8 ft. (5) Octava 4 ft. (6) Hohlflöte 4 ft. (7) Nasat 3 ft. (8) Rauschpfeiffe (mixture) 4 ranks. (9) Scharff (sharp mixture) 4 ranks. (10) Mixtura 15 ranks. (11) Trommete 16 ft. (12) Trommete 8 ft. (13) Zinke 8 ft.

Brust.

(1) Principal 16 ft. (2) Gedact 8 ft. (3) Octava 4 ft. (4) Hohlflöte 4 ft. (5) Sesquialtera 2 ranks. (6) Feld-Pfeiffe 2 ft. (7) Gemshorn 2 ft. (8) Sifflet 1½. (9) Mixtura 8 ranks. (10) Cimbel 3 ranks. (11) Krumhorn 8 ft. (12) Regal 8 ft.

Rück-Positiv.

(1) Principal 8 ft. (2) Bordun 16 ft. (3) Blockflöte 8 ft. (4) Sesquialtera 2 ranks. (5) Hohlflöte 8 ft. (6) Quintadena 8 ft. (7) Octava 4 ft. (8) Spiel-flöte 2 ft. (9) Mixtura 5 ranks. (10) Dulcian 16 ft. (11) Baarpfeiffe 8 ft. Trichter-Regal 8 ft. (This was of no new invention). (13) Vox humana. (14) Scharff (sharp mixture) 4 to 5 ranks.

Pedal.

(1) Principal 32 ft. (2) Sub-bass 16 ft. (3) Octava 8 ft. (4) Bauer-flöte 2 ft. (5) Mixtura 6 ranks. (6) Gross-Posaun 24 ft. (7) Posaune 16 ft. (8) Trommete 8 ft. (9) Principal 16 ft. (10) Gedact 8 ft. (11) Octava 4 ft. (12) Nachthorn 2 ft. (13) Dulcian 16 ft. (14) Krumhorn 8 ft. (15) Cornet 2 ft.

There were besides the Cimbel-Stern, two Trummeln, two Tremulants, and 16 bellows.

That No. 1 of the Brustwerk is an 8 ft. stop, and that a mistake was made in its title, was noticed by Jimmerthal in his before mentioned work, p. 6; and as to the Posaune stop on the pedal of "24 ft.," it is to be understood that the "32 ft. tone" began with the F and not with the C.

V.

To Vol. I., p. 336.

Documents from the archives of Mühlhausen relating to the post of organist in that town.

Bach's emoluments were fixed at—

85 gulden in money and his deputy paid.

3 malter of corn.

2 cords of wood, 1 beech and 1 oak or aspen.

6 loads of brushwood delivered at his door.

Dated June 15, 1707.

VI.

To Vol. I., p. 526 (referred to as V.)

A List of the Ducal Orchestra at Weimar between the years 1714 and 1716.

Private Secretary, Governor of the pages and bass singer, Gottfried Ephraim Theile (written in small) has his food at the Court.

Bassoon	Bernhard George Ulrich,
Cammer *fourier*[4] and trumpeter	Johann Christoph Heininger,
	has table allowances.
Castle Warden and Trumpeter	Johann Christian Biedermann,
	has table allowances.
Trumpeter	Johann Martin Fichtel,
	has table allowances.
Trumpeter	Johann Wendelin Eichenberg,
	has table allowances.
Trumpeter	Johann Georg Beumelburg,
	has table allowances.
Trumpeter	Conrad Landgraf.
Drummer	Andreas Nicol,
	is to have table allowances.
Court Capellmeister	Salomo Drese,
	has daily 1 loaf and 1 stoup of beer from the cellar.
Court Vice-Capellmeister	Drese.
Concertmeister and Court Organist	Johann Sebastian Bach.
Secretary and Tenor	Aiblinger.
Tenor and Court Cantor	Döbernitz.
Court Cantor and Bass (coll. quint.)	Alt.
Alto	Bernhardi.
Discantist (treble)	Weichard,
	also has free table.
Discantist	Gerrmann.
Chamber Musician (Cammer Musicus)	Johann Andreas Ehrbach.
Musician and Violinist	Eck.
Violinist and Musician	Johann Georg Hoffmann,
	lives in Jena, but when he is here he has his living at Court.
Court Secretary and Musician, also Violinist	} August Gottfried Denstedt.

---

[4] Intendant of the royal apartments.

Besides these there were six boys. This list is from that of Wilhelm Ernst's suite in the grand ducal archives at Weimar. The musicians named before the Capellmeister resided in the castle, which accounts for the order of the names. Generally—as in the list for 1726—the order of precedence gave the Capellmeiste the next place to the Governor of the pages, and after him came the ministers of country parishes. The trumpeters and drummers come after the under master of the school (sub-conrector) and the Master of the Mint; then follow the rest of the musicians "in order as they are engaged;" then the writers and copyists of the Consistory, and then, after a whole list of other persons almost at the end, the town and Court cantors and organists and the rest of the school officials. Bach, however, being at the same time concertmeister had a position not far below that of the Capellmeister. The *Stadt musicus*, town musician, at the time was Valentin Balzer.

I.

To Vol. II., p. 185.

A document referring to Bach's appointment as Cantor of St. Thomas's, Leipzig.

II.

To Vol. II., p. 186 (referred to as VI.)

May 5; 1723.

Herr Johann Sebastian Bach, hitherto Capellmeister to the Princely Court of Anhalt Cöthen, appeared in the Council-chamber, and *Dominus Consul Regens D. Lange* proposed that he should be chosen Cantor to the School of St. Thomas, as being the most capable candidate, and he was unanimously elected.

Ille. Humbly thanked them and pledged himself to fidelity and diligence.

Eodem. It was accordingly announced that he would be duly notified to that effect, so that he might be pleased to arrange for the ceremony of presentation and all else.

Ille. Thanked them for the notification, and would not fail to do all that was necessary.

Eodem. Notice of the selection they had made was given also to the pastor of the Church of St. Thomas, the *Licentiate* Weisen, who thanked them and wished them every blessing.

The Cantor of the Thomasschule's counterpart agreement:—

After their worships, the Council of this town of Leipzig, had accepted me to be Cantor of the School of St. Thomas, they required of me an agreement as to certain points, namely:—

1. That I should set a bright and good example to the boys by a sober and secluded life, attend school, diligently and faithfully instruct the boys.

2. And bring the music in the two chief churches of this town into good repute to the best of my ability.

3. Show all respect and obedience to their worships the Council, and defend and promote their honour and reputation to the utmost, and in all places, also if a member of the Council requires the boys for a musical performance unhesitatingly to obey, and besides this, never allow them to travel into the country for funerals or weddings without the fore-knowledge and consent of the burgomaster in office, and the governor of the school.

4. Give due obedience to the inspectors and governors of the school in all they command in the name of the Worshipful Council.

5. Admit no boys into the school who have not already the elements of music or who have no aptitude for being instructed therein, nor without the knowledge and leave of the inspectors and governor.

6. To the end that the churches may not be at unnecessary expense I should diligently instruct the boys not merely in vocal but in instrumental music.

7. To the end that good order may prevail in those churches I should so arrange the music that it may not last too long, and also in such wise as that it may not be operatic, but incite the hearers to devotion.

8. Supply good scholars to the New Church.

9. Treat the boys kindly and considerately, or, if they will not obey, punish such in moderation or report them to the authority.

10. Faithfully carry out instruction in the school and whatever else it is my duty to do.

11. And what I am unable to teach myself I am to cause to be taught by some other competent person without cost or help from their worships the Council, or from the school.

12. That I should not quit the town without leave from the burgomaster in office.

13. Should follow the funeral processions with the boys, as is customary, as often as possible.

14. And take no office under the University without the consent of their worships.

And to all this I hereby pledge myself, and faithfully to fulfil all this as is here set down, under pain of losing my place if I act against it, in witness of which I have signed this duplicate bond, and sealed it with my seal. Given in Leipzig, August 13, 1722.

Herr Johann Christian Bach signed and sealed the same. May 5, 1723.

Also Herr Gottlob Harrer (date missing).

This document, as will be seen, is merely the sketch for the bond; Bach's name is inserted wrongly.

III.

To Vol. II., p. 188.

Document relating to the dispute between the Council and Consistory.

IV.

Vol. II., p. 193, &c. (referred to as VII.)

Five memorials of Kuhnau's, addressed to the Town Council and to the University on the following dates: December 4, 1704; March 17, 1709; September 1, 1710; December 18, 1717; and May 29, 1720.

A. (Vol. II., p. 203).

The first is preserved among the archives of the Town Council of Leipzig (*Consistorialia*, Vol. X. *Varia*, 1619 till 1767, and reminds their worships that he had lately applied to them on the subject of the trumpets in the two principal churches which by long use had become worn out, bent, and useless; so that they had commissioned him to ask of Heinrich Pfeiffer, the gatekeeper of St. Thomas's, who is particularly skilled and experienced in the making of such instruments, the lowest price of a complete set of four, a *quart-posaune* (*i.e.*, a low trombone), tenor, alto and treble trombone, and how much he would allow for the old set of three.

He goes on to say that the price of such instruments has doubled within a few years; that he had laid Heinrich Pfeiffer's estimate and specification before their worships, and had humbly petitioned them to order a new set for all three churches. He then begs that to save expense a case may be made to hold six violins, which have to be carried to church, and that a Colochon (*Colascione* or Calichon) with a case may be provided as being an indispensable instrument which they are forced to borrow, not possessing one in either church, and mentions that Marcus Buchner is particularly " happy " in making them. This instrument was also known as the Italian lute, and Baron describes it as simply a bass viol lute.

He laments the diminution of numbers in the singers in the churches in consequence of their finding it more lucrative to sing in the opera, (see p. 205), and recommends to their worships' consideration certain details of arrangement, tending, as he hopes, to remedy the evil by placing more power in his hands, as he already had to appoint the hymns for all three churches (see p. 232).

The memorial is addressed to D. Joh. Alexander Christen, Governor of the School of St. Thomas, and burgomaster in office.

B. (p. 280).

In the next memorial he appeals to their " paternal care and interest in the wellbeing of the churches and schools " to consider certain points to which he proceeds to draw their attention as follows :—

1. The school violin is much broken, and so ill fitted for daily practice

that the small sum of 1 thlr. and a few groschen earned by following funerals and set aside for repairs is insufficient for its restoration.

2. A new regal is needed, the old one being constantly in need of repair; still they might do with it a little longer on the chance of such an instrument being for sale at a low price.

3. On the other hand, they are greatly in need of a good colochon both for school practice and for church use, and he again recommends Mark Buchner.

4. A sand hour-glass is much needed, and the sexton has been frequently asked to see to this, but it does not appear that he has applied for it.

5. A board with nails is needed on which to hang the violins (in the right choir) that they may not be laid on the floor.

6. Unless a new step is fitted in St. Nicholas' for the Stadtpfeiffer to stand on, one or another will chance to break his leg, or at least to sprain his foot.

7. It is much to be desired that a fund of not less than 300 thalers should be created, of which the interest should be employed to keep the two great clavicembalos (one in each church) in proper repair, since they have to be seen to each time there is a performance, and in the state they are in this costs six or seven thalers.

8 and 9 refer to the numbers of the choir, and 10 complains again of the increasing influence of the opera; this, he says, causes the greatest mischief, for the better students, as soon as they have acquired, at the cost of infinite pains to the cantor, sufficient practice, long to find themselves among the "*Operisten*," and he suggests finally that *stipendia* shall be given to certain musicians who shall supplement the efforts of the eight Stadtpfeiffer, and particularly to two good violinists and to a good bass singer since there is a difficulty (probably an impossibility) in supplying such a voice from among the scholars.

C. (p. 214).

refers to the services to be performed in the New Church of St. Paul.

D. (p. 203).

has not much interest for the English reader. He complains of the injury done to the boys' voices by the perambulations and funerals.

E. (p. 208).

is the specification of various plans by which the church music of Leipzig may be improved. The document is in the Town Library at Leipzig. In consequence of there being no regular organist, and the music in the Neue Kirche being performed by young students, chiefly from the Thomasschule, the music had degenerated and become operatic in character, which naturally scandalised those members of the congregation who appreciated and loved the true style of church music. The organ also had suffered much injury at the hands of inexperienced players who did not understand how to remedy the effects of change of weather, &c. Kuhnau therefore suggests that a regular organist should be appointed, who should also undertake to direct the music, and to manage the choir; and that he should be made to serve three churches in rotation. He concludes by giving suggestions as to the details of payment of the organist and the choir. The document is dated Leipzig, the 29th of May, 1720.

V., VI., & VII.

are of no interest to the English reader.

VIII.

To Vol. II., p. 282.

Supplement to the account of the Thomaskirche from Candlemas, 1747, to Candlemas, 1748.

"Notice is hereby given that, since the organ in the Thomaskirche has for a long time been almost useless by reason of the great quantity of dust and dirt, and in order that it may not fall still further into decay, the following contract has been duly and carefully drawn up and concluded between Herr D. Gottfried Lange, Privy Councillor of War to the King of Poland and Grand Duke of Saxony, Burgomaster of this town, and appointed overseer of the church of St. Thomas, of the one part, and H. Johann Scheibe, organ builder in this town, of the other part, to this effect:—

1.

The said organ-builder, Johann Scheibe, promises to repair thoroughly and make good with glue and leather all the injuries done to the organ in the Thomaskirche through the great heat of last summer, and from other causes.

2.

As the said organ, and more especially all the pipes contained in it, are full of dust, so that most of them do not speak, the organ-builder, Scheibe, shall be bound, during their renovation, to take entirely to pieces all the pipes throughout, all the stops to which they belong, and, not only to cleanse them thoroughly from dust and dirt, but also to repair whatever injuries they may have sustained, and to put them back in their proper places.

3.

All the mouthpieces and tongues in the reed work: as the *Bass Posaune*, the *Bass Trumpet*, and in the *Rückpositiv*, the *Trumpet* and the *Krumhorn*, and also in the *Brustpositiv*, the two reed-stops, are to be cleansed and repaired with saltpetre and zinc, also anything that is damaged is to be put right.

4.

H. Scheibe promises to open all the wind-chests in the organ, so

III.

that the dust and dirt can be thoroughly removed from the valves, and
also to guard against such damage for the future.

5.
He will also renew the case wherever the iron and brass-work has
parted, and also

6.
Will put the two-manual couplers into repair.

7.
He promises to voice all the pipes afresh, and to tune them, as also
to tune the whole organ, together in good harmony and right pitch, and
to make the intonation even throughout. He is also to manage the
work so that some of the more necessary stops can be used at every
service during the repairs.

8.
Finally, after the work is finished, anything that may be still found
defective at the trial and examination of the renovated and repaired
organ, Herr Scheibe promises to correct and improve at once without
further question, and without demanding payment above what has been
agreed. And he hereby binds himself to be responsible according to
the best of his power for good and honest work in this organ.

9.
Herr Scheibe provides all the materials required for the work above
described and for the thorough repair of the organ, paying all the work-
men employed by him, and promises hereby to bring the whole
instrument into a state to be played upon, and to deliver it over
between the present date and next Michaelmas. On the other hand,
the Herr Overseer, Herr Lange, Privy Councillor of War, and Burgomaster, shall allow the necessary scaffolding to be put up in front of the
organ by the carpenters, for the pipes to be laid on during the repair
and renovation of the organ, and to prevent damage to the instrument,
which scaffold is to be taken away by the carpenters after the work is
completed.

For all and each of the points specified in this contract, the Herr
overseer of the Thomaskirche shall give to Scheibe, the organ-builder,
the sum of

Two hundred Thalers,

to be paid in instalments out of the funds of the church.

As the contracting parties of both parts now present are in earnest
in will and intention, and they both promise to fulfil this contract
in all points, for the more certain fulfilment of the contract it is made
out in duplicate, and signed and sealed by both contracting parties,
Leipzig, June 28, 1747.

Lange's contract above is sealed and also bears the date of June 23.
The Council's order for the repair was given on June 26. Scheibe

received his payment in six instalments ; the last on November 4, 1747.

IX.

To Vol. II., p. 519.

The injunction commanding the first performance of the St. John Passion in the church of St. Nicholas.

X.

1. Vol. II., p. 506.

The text has no interest for the English reader.

2. Vol. II., p. 627. Title :—

Drama | *Per Musica,* | Welches | Bey dem Allerhöchsten | *Crönungs-Feste* | des | Aller-Durchlauchtigsten und Gross- | mächtigsten | *Augusti III.* | Königs in Pohlen und Churfür- | sten zu Sachsen | in unter-thänigster Ehrfurcht aufgeführet wurde | in dem | *Collegio Musico* | durch | *J. S. B.* | Leipzig, dem Janr. 1734. | Gedruckt bey Bernhard Christoph Breitkopf.

The personages are *Valour, Justice, Clemency* and *Pallas.*

The text is of no interest to the English reader.

3. Vol. II., p. 630. Title :—

Drama | *Per Musica,* | Welches | Bey dem Allerhöchsten | *Geburths-Feste* | Der | Allerdurchlauchtigsten und Grossmäch- | tigsten | *Königin in Pohlen* | und | *Churfürstin zu Sachsen* | in unterthänigster Ehrfurcht | aufgeführet wurde | in dem | *Collegio Musico* | Durch | *J. S. B.* | Leipzig, dem 8 December, 1733. | Gedruckt bey Bernhard Christoph Breitkopf.

Personages : *Irene, Bellona, Pallas, Fama.*

4. Vol. II., p. 263. Title :—

" Als die von E. Hoch-Edlen und Hoch-Weisen Rath der Stadt Leipzig umgebauete und eingerichtete Schule zu S. Thomae den 5. Jun. durch etliche Reden eingeweyhet wurde, ward folgende *CANTATA* dabey verfertiget und aufgeführet von Joh. Sebastian Bach, Fürstl. Sächs. Weissenfels. Capellmeister, und besagter Schulen Cantore, und *M.* Johann Heinrich Winckler, *Collega* IV.

" Leipzig, gedruckt Bernhard Christoph Breitkopf."

XI.

To Vol. III., p. 11.

ACTA, concerning the appointment of the Prefects in the School of St. Thomas, in this town, 1736. (In the archives of the Town Council, Leipzig.)

Magnifici.

Most Noble, Illustrious, Learned and Worshipful Gentlemen and Patrons.[5]

August 12, 1736.

May it please your worships graciously to allow me to represent to you that, whereas according to your worships' ordering of the School of St. Thomas, it pertains (is the duty of) to the Cantor to choose from among the scholars those whom he considers fit and able to be Prefects, and in electing them to have regard, not only to the voice that it be good and clear, but also to see that the Prefects, and especially the one who leads the first Choir, shall be able to undertake the direction of the Musical Choir in the absence or illness of the Cantor ; and whereas this rule has been hitherto observed by the Cantors without the concurrence of the Rectors : yet and notwithstanding, the present Rector, M. Johann Aug. Ernesti, has lately endeavoured, without my knowledge and approval, to assume the appointment of the Prefect in the first Choir, so that he recently appointed Krause, the Prefect of the second Choir, to be the Prefect of the first Choir, and refuses to withdraw in spite of all my civil remonstrances. Since I cannot suffer this to pass, being against the aforesaid order and traditional usage of the school, and to the prejudice of my successors and to the injury of the Musical Choir, I now present to your Worships my most dutiful petition, graciously to decide this difference between the Rector and myself in my office ; and because this presumption on the part of the Rector to the appointing of the Prefects might lead to strife and to the prejudice of the scholars, I pray that in your great benevolence and care for the School of St. Thomas you will direct the Rector, M. Ernesti, to leave for the future, as hitherto, and according to the order and usage of the school, the appointment of Prefects to myself alone, and thus graciously protect me in my office.

Trusting to your Worships' most gracious indulgence, and abiding in the most dutiful respect,

I am yours, &c.,

Most obediently,

J. S. BACH.

August 13, 1736.

Though only yesterday I in a most respectful memorial troubled your Worships, because of the great indignity done to me by Herr Rector Ernesti, through his attempted encroachment on the function hitherto assigned to myself of Cantor and of Director of the Musical Choir in the St. Thomas School here, by his interference in the appointment of the Prefect, and prayed for your Worships' gracious protection : yet I find myself under the necessity of again most humbly bringing to

---

[5] The original is lavish in the reiteration of titles and attributes, which are here omitted.

your Worships' notice that, although I had already informed the said Herr Rector Ernesti that I had complained to your Worships, and that I expected your decided judgment on the matter, he nevertheless, regardless of the respect due to your Honourable Council, again presumed to let all the scholars know that none should under pain of relegation and castigation dare to sing or conduct the usual motett in place of Krause, who is, as I stated in my most dutiful memorial of yesterday, unfit for the direction of a musical choir, and whom he wishes to force upon me as Prefect of the first Choir. Hence it came then that in the Nicolai Church at the afternoon service yesterday to my great humiliation and dejection not a single scholar would undertake to lead the singing, much less to conduct the motett, for fear of being punished. Indeed, the service would thereby have been interrupted had not most fortunately these duties been undertaken by an old scholar of St. Thomas's, of the name of Krebs, at my request. I represented in my late most humble memorial that the appointment of the Prefect does not, according to the rules and usage of the school, pertain to the Rector; he has moreover by his mode of action greatly vexed and offended against me in my official position, and thus weakened and indeed tried to deprive me of the full authority over the scholars in all matters of church and other music which I ought to have, and which authority was also conferred on me by your most Honourable Council on my accession to office. It is hence to be feared that were such high-handed proceedings to continue the services would be interfered with, and the music of the Church greatly deteriorate, while the school itself would in a short time be so injured that it would take many years to restore it to the same degree of efficiency in which it has hitherto been. Therefore I once more submit to your Worships my most dutiful and earnest supplication, since officially I cannot pass the matter over, that you will stringently admonish the Rector, since discipline is endangered, that he will hereafter not molest me in my office, nor hinder the scholars in their obedience to me by his unjust warnings and by threats of severe punishment, but rather that he will see to it, as is his duty, that the school and Musical Choir shall be improved rather than deteriorated. I hope for your gracious indulgence and protection in my office, and abiding in the most profound respect,

I am, &c.,

J. S. BACH.

Fol. 5. P.M.

The full and true history of the matter regarding the scholar Krause, whom the Rector wishes to force upon me as first Prefect, is as follows : Said Krause had so long as a year ago so bad a reputation on account of his disorderly life and his consequent debts, that a council meeting was held, which emphatically intimated to him that, although he had on account of his dissolute life well deserved to be forthwith expelled from the school, yet, in consideration of his needy circumstances (for he had himself owned to have contracted debts to the amount of twenty thalers), and on his promising amendment, they were willing to try him for another quarter when, according as his behaviour was improved or not, he would be informed whether he was to be retained or removed. Now, the Rector has always shown a special predilection for him, Krause, and verbally begged me to make him a Prefect, but I remonstrated that he was not fitted for it, whereupon the Rector replied that I might nevertheless do so, since it might enable Krause to free himself of his debts, and so the school be spared a constantly increasing scandal, especially as his time would soon be out, and he would thus be got rid of with a good grace. I therefore, willing to do the Rector a pleasure, made Krause a Prefect in the New Church, where the scholars have nothing else to sing but chorales and motetts, and have nothing to do with other concerted music, which is managed by the organist himself, for I considered that his school years had expired all but one, and it was not to be expected that he would ever come to conduct either the first or second Choirs. Subsequently however the Prefect of the first Choir, by name Nagel, from Nürnberg, complained at the singing at the last New Year that owing to weakness of constitution he should not be able to continue with it; it therefore became necessary to make a change out of the usual course of time in the arrangement of the Prefects, and to shift the second Prefect into the first Choir, and of necessity to receive the oft-named Krause into the second Choir. He, however, made various mistakes in beating the time, as I have been told by the Herr Con-Rector, who undertook the inspection of the second Choir, and upon enquiry concerning these mistakes all the scholars laid the blame wholly and solely on the Prefect on account of his faulty beating of the time. Moreover, I myself at a recent singing lesson took occasion to test his conducting of the time, when he acquitted himself so badly that he could not even give the accurate beat in the two chief modes of time, namely, the equal or common time, and the unequal or triple time,' but made triple into common time, and *vice versâ*, as all the scholars will readily confirm. Being, therefore, fully convinced of his incapacity, I could not possibly trust him as Prefect of the first Choir, particularly as the sacred music which is performed by the first Choir, and which is mostly of my own composition, is incomparably more difficult and intricate than that which is done by the second Choir, these sing only on festivals and in choosing their music I am mainly guided by the ability of those who are to render it. And although further circumstances might be mentioned which would still more prove the incapacity of Krause, yet I think the grounds already adduced sufficiently show my complaints to your Honourable Council to be justified, and to call for an early remedy without delay.

Leipzig, 15th August, 1736.[6]   JOH. SEB. BACH.

---

[6] Autograph throughout.

Ernesti's reply, dated August 17, 1736. He denies Bach's assertion that the appointment of the Prefects had always lain with the Cantor, who only selected such scholars as he deemed fit for the post, and then presented them to the Rector for appointment. He further asserts Krause to have been dismissed not from incapacity but out of spite to himself, since he, Ernesti, had some time previously sent Krause to the Cantor with the request that he would appoint him Prefect, and since Krause's dismissal was due to this inadequate cause, he, Ernesti, had interdicted it. After a while Bach had consented to reinstate Krause, but on various pretexts had deferred doing so. Thereupon Ernesti informs Bach that unless he forthwith reinstates Krause he shall do so himself on the next Sunday, but receives no answer. Ernesti then informs the scholars that none were to attempt, on pain of severe penalties, to undertake the post of the Prefect he had appointed. Bach, however, when he finds Krause still acting as Prefect, expels him again without ceremony. Ernesti then refers the matter to the Superintendent, who promises enquiry, and meanwhile directs that Ernesti's Prefects are to retain their places. Bach replies that he does not care, and when the Prefects had gone to their places at the afternoon service "he with much shouting and noise again drove Krause from the choir and directed the scholar Claus to take the place of Prefect, who did so, but excused himself to me while yet in the Church. And in the evening he drove the other Prefect away from the (supper) table because he had obeyed me." Ernesti declares Bach's assertions and complaints to be unfounded, and begs the Council not to entertain his complaints, but to admonish him to obedience and to attend to his duties with greater diligence. For he ascribes the unfortunate dereliction of duty on the part of Krause to Bach's neglect in not undertaking the direction of certain musical performances himself, but leaving it entirely in the hands of Krause. He concludes by begging the Council to support him in his office as Rector.

August 20, 1736.

Your Worships will call to your gracious remembrance that I was under the necessity of bringing to your notice the disorders which occurred this day week in the performance of public service in consequence of the arrangements made by the Rector of the Thomasschule here, M. Ernesti. To-day, both forenoon and afternoon, the same things occurred again, and I was obliged, in order to avoid a great commotion in the Church and disturbance of the service, to direct the motett myself, and to get a student to lead the singing. And as matters are likely to become worse in the course of time, and I shall scarcely be able to maintain my authority in future with the scholars placed under me without the effectual interference of your Worships, my noble Patrons, and should therefore not be responsible were further and perhaps irreparable disorders to arise, I cannot avoid respectfully representing this to your Worships with the most dutiful prayer that your Worships will be pleased to restrain the Rector without delay, and that you will, by accelerating the final resolution for which I have prayed, and according to your zeal for the common weal, prevent, as is to be apprehended, further public offences in the Church, disorders in the school, diminution of my authority with the scholars requisite in my office, and other serious consequences.

J. S. BACH.

February 12, 1737.

The Rector of the St. Thomas School here, Herr *M.* J. A. Ernesti, has lately presumed to force upon me, against my will, an unfit individual as Prefect of the first Choir which is composed of the scholars of the said school, and as I neither could nor would accept him, the said *M.* Ernesti forbade all the scholars that none, except his own arbitrarily appointed Prefect, should, under pain of relegation, either lead the singing of the motett or direct it. It was thus effected that on the following Sunday at the afternoon service not a single scholar would undertake to lead the singing nor direct the motett, out of fear of the threatened punishment, and indeed the service would have been interrupted had I not persuaded a student, who was able, to undertake these duties. By this proceeding on the part of the Rector I have not only been greatly injured and molested in my office, but have also been deprived of the respect due to me by the scholars, and thus been lowered in my position towards them. And yet, according to the orders passed by your honourable Council with regard to the St. Thomas School, cap. 14, s. 4, it pertains to me to choose the Prefecti of the Choirs without the concurrence of the H. Rector, an order which has hitherto been continuously observed both by myself and by my predecessors; and this has its reasonable grounds, since the Prefecti, according to the said school order, have to fill my, the Cantor's, place, and to conduct, as I cannot be present at the same time in all the Churches; and as I have the special care and supervision of the first Choir I must know best who is most suited to me. Therefore, secondly, the prohibition of the Rector issued to the scholars that none should sing under another Prefect, is most unjust, seeing that nothing effectual can be achieved if the scholars are prevented from obeying me in all matters pertaining to the singing. In order, therefore, that these doings may have no ill result, I have the strongest grounds for moving in the matter, and am compelled in this difficulty to apply to your Honours. My most humble petition, therefore, is that you will protect me in my office, and strictly enjoin the H. Rector, M. Ernesti, that he will no longer molest me in the same, that he will abstain in future from choosing Prefecti without my knowledge or consent, and from forbidding the boys to obey me in regard to the singing, that you will further be pleased to instruct the Superintendent or one of the clergy of St. Thomas's Church, without unbecoming restriction, to enjoin the school children to again render me the respect and obedience due to me, and so enable me for the future to fulfil the duties of my post. As I now trust by this, my not unreasonable petition, to obtain the protection and aid of your Worships, so I remain as before with continual respect,

Your most obedient, &c.,

J. S. BACH.

August 21, 1737.

Your Magnificences, &c., will graciously call to mind how I, under date February 12, of the present year, complained to your Honours of the Rector of the St. Thomas School, M. J. A. Ernesti, concerning his interference in my office, and also his prohibition to the scholars of obedience to me, and the consequent humiliation to me, in regard whereof I humbly craved your aid and protection. Since then, it is true, your honourable Council has sent me a decree, copy of which is enclosed under A; but, on the one hand, satisfaction is not done to me, thereby, for the humiliation inflicted on me by the said Rector, and, on the other hand, I am seriously aggrieved thereby. For as the Rector publicly and in open Church, and also in the presence of the entire first class, threatened all the scholars with relegation and loss of the caution (money ?) if any should be disposed to obey my orders, wherefore I not unreasonably demand that my honour be re-established; so and in like manner the above-named decree of the Council is based upon a school order made in 1723, which differs materially from the old school orders in many points, and tends greatly to my prejudice as well in the exercise of my office and in regard to the accruing perquisites, while it has never been actually in force; for, when at one time the promulgation thereof was to be proceeded with, the late Rector, Ernesti, declared himself against, to the effect that it should be, in the first place, sent in to the honourable Consistorium, whose decision thereon was to be awaited. But the ratification has, so far as I know, not yet ensued, and I cannot therefore acknowledge a new school order so prejudicial to me, especially as the amount of my perquisites was therein to be much reduced, and the old order must still continue in force.

The aforesaid decree of the Council, based as it is on this new order, cannot therefore remedy the matter. More especially impracticable is that part of it which declares that it shall not be competent for me to suspend a scholar who has once been appointed to a function, much less to remove him therefrom. For cases occur where a change has forthwith to be made, and where a detailed enquiry in a minor matter of mere discipline or other school affair cannot be undertaken. Such changes do in all lesser schools belong to the province of the

Cantor, as it would be impossible to control the youths if they knew that one could not at once deal with them, and in other respects too, it would be hopeless to fulfil the duties of one's office satisfactorily. Your Honours have required to be informed on this matter, and I herewith again make my most humble petition: that your Worships will protect me in the exercise of my office and ensure me the needful respect; that you will prohibit all undue interference on the part of the Rector, *M.* Ernesti; also to restore my honour with the scholars, which has, through the instrumentality of the said Rector, been wounded; and that you will give the necessary instructions to defend me against the new school order so far as it militates against me, and prevents me from the due performance of my duties. For the aid thus to be granted to me I shall as ever, remain with profound respect,

Yours, &c.,

J. S. BACH.

prs. 29 Oct., 1737.
Praes. d. 13 Dec., 1737.

Most Noble, Most Mighty King and Prince,
Most Gracious Sovereign,

That your Majesty has been most graciously pleased to confer on me the title of composer to your Majesty will command my most humble gratitude through life. As therefore I claim for myself in most humble confidence the protection of your Majesty, so I now venture most respectfully to beg for the same on account of my present oppressors. My predecessors, the Cantors in the St. Thomas School here, have always, and according to the traditional usage of the school, possessed the right to appoint the Prefecti in the Musical Choirs, and that for the well-founded reason that they, more than any others, were in a position to know which individual was the most capable, and this prerogative I have enjoyed for a considerable time and without question from anyone. Nevertheless, the present Rector, *M.* Johann August Ernesti, has lately been bold enough to fill up a Prefecture without my concurrence, and that with an individual with very little knowledge of music. And when I became aware of his incompetence, and felt under the necessity of making a change on account of the consequent disorder in the music, and appointed in his place a more skilful person, the said Rector, Ernesti, not only directly opposed me, but also, to my greatest affront and humiliation, forbade all the assembled scholars, under pain of "baculation," to render me obedience in my arrangements. Now, although I have endeavoured to maintain my well founded prerogative before the magistrate here in the enclosure A, and have also implored the Royal Consistory here for satisfaction (enclosure B) for the injury done me, yet from the latter I have received nothing at all, and from the former only the instructions herewith enclosed under C. Since now, most gracious King and Sovereign, the Council here completely deprive me of the right I have hitherto enjoyed, as shown by the enclosure, and in doing so rest themselves on a new school order made in the year 1723, which I do not regard as binding on me, principally because if it is to be lawful it has never been confirmed by the Consistorium. Therefore I now, in most humble submission, appeal to your Majesty—

1. To command the Council here to see that I am not molested in my *jure quæsito ratione* of appointing the *Præfecti Chori Musici*, and therein protect me ; and

2. To be pleased to direct the Consistorium of this place to require an apology from the Rector Ernesti for the indignity done to me, and also to charge without reserve the Superintendent, Dr. Deyling, to instruct the entire school (*coetus*), that all the boys of the school shall show me the customary and due respect and obedience. This most exalted Royal Favour I anticipate with undying gratitude, and remain in lowliest submission,

Your Majesty's
Most submissive and most dutiful,

Leipzig, 18 Oct., 1737.   J. S. BACH.

To the Most Noble, Most Mighty Prince and Sovereign, Friedrich August, King of Poland, &c. &c.

XII.*

(Ante, p. 118.)

Rules and Instructions for Playing
Thorough-bass or Accompaniment in Four Parts,
made for
his Scholars in music
by
Herr Johann Sebastian Bach,
of Leipzig,
Royal Court Composer and Capellmeister,
also Director of the Music and Cantor of the Thomasschule,
1738.[7]

Signatures.	6	43	76	7	98	9	6 5	65 43	b7	4 3	⊤	5b	Without Signature.	8
Middle Parts.	3	5	3	3	3	3	3	8	3	♉	2	3		5
Additional Parts.	3 8 6	8	8 3 5 8	5	5	—	—	5 5b	—	6	6			3

* The translators take this opportunity of gratefully acknowledging valuable assistance given by Mr. W. S. Rockstro in preparing this portion of the appendix for publication.

[7] The title is in the handwriting of Johann Peter Kellner, which is also noticeable here and there, further on, in corrections and additions.

Short Instructions for what is called Thorough-bass.

The signatures which occur in Thorough-bass are chiefly the following nine—viz., 2, 3, 4, 5♭, 5, 6, 7, 8, 9.

These are divided into consonances and dissonances. Four of them are consonances—viz., 3, 5, 6, 8.

These again are divided into perfect and imperfect.

The perfect consonances are : [8] the fifth and octave, and the imperfect are the third and sixth.

The remaining five are dissonances—viz., 2, 4, 5♭, 7, 9.

When no number or signature stands over the bass note, the chord consisting of 3, 5 and 8 is to be played.

The fifth and eighth must not, however, be taken in such a manner that either lies uppermost twice running, otherwise the result will be consecutive fifths or octaves, the greatest error in music.

N.B.—They are to be taken *vice versâ*.

Sometimes also a 3, 5, or 8 is found above a note ; this generally means that the chord is to be taken in such a manner that the 3, 5, or 8 shall be the topmost note.

Here follows a list of the signatures with which the third may be taken,

$$
\begin{array}{ll}
\text{With a} & 7 \\
& 6 \\
& 5\ 6 \\
& 6\ 5 \\
& \left.\begin{array}{l} 6 \\ 5 \end{array}\right\} \\
& \left.\begin{array}{l} 6 \\ 5♭ \end{array}\right\} \\
& \left.\begin{array}{l} 7 \\ 5 \end{array}\right\} \quad \text{the third is taken.} \\
& \left.\begin{array}{l} ♭7 \\ 5♭ \end{array}\right\} \\
& \left.\begin{array}{l} 8 \\ 7 \end{array}\right\} \\
& \left.\begin{array}{l} 8 \\ 6 \end{array}\right\} \\
& \left.\begin{array}{l} 9\ 8 \\ 7\ 6 \end{array}\right\}
\end{array}
$$

N.B.—For those who cannot remember this rule, it is only necessary to keep this much in mind ; whenever 6 or 7 occur, whether alone or with other figures, the 3 may be taken.

Except in the case of $\frac{6}{4}$, resolved into $\frac{3}{5}$ when an 8 is to be played, as will be seen presently.

With $\begin{array}{c} 7 \\ 4 \\ 2 \end{array}$ nothing else is played.

---

[8] In the original there is a note of interrogation instead of the colon.

Here follow such signatures as are resolved always into the common chord.

With 9 8, 3 and 5
„ 4 3, 5 „ 8
„ $\begin{Bmatrix} 6\ 5 \\ 4\ 3 \end{Bmatrix}$ 8 „ „ } are played.
„ $\begin{Bmatrix} 9\ 8 \\ 4\ 3 \end{Bmatrix}$ 5 „ „

N.B.—If the rule cannot be remembered, keep the following in mind: such notes of the chord as are absent from the resolution are to be played with the preceding signature.

Here follow those signatures which must each be committed to memory by itself.

With $\frac{4}{2}$ the 6 is taken.

With $\frac{4}{3}$ the 6 is also taken.

With $\flat 7$ when a $\sharp$ stands above the bass as well, the 3 and 5 are taken.

With $5\flat$ the 6 is taken.

A $\sharp$ or $\natural$ indicates that the third is to be major, and a $\flat$ that it is to be minor.

The 4 3, 5$\flat$, $\frac{6}{5}$, 7 and 9

(1) must in an ordinary way be already in the previous chord.

(2) must remain in the same part.

(3) must be resolved by descending one degree.

ELEMENTARY INSTRUCTION IN FIGURED-BASS.

CAP. I.

OF THE ETYMOLOGY.

The word *Bassus* is derived from the Greek βάσις, which signifies the root or foundation of a thing. Others derive it from the old Latin word *bassus*, signifying *profundus*, deep. By the word taken alone is understood the lowest part in music, or any bass part that produces a deep note, whether this note be sung or played upon a bass viol, bassoon, trombone, or the like.

By the term Figured or General-Bass, however, is understood a bass that is played on the organ or clavier with both hands in such a way that all or most of the parts in the music are played *generaliter* or simultaneously, or in general terms, together. It is also called *Bassus Continuus*, or with the Italian termination, *Basso continuo*, because it continues throughout the piece, even when the other parts pause now and then, although at the present day this Bass itself frequently pauses, especially in works of great ingenuity of construction.

Cap. II.

DEFINITION OF THE TERM.

Figured-bass is the whole foundation of the music, and is played with both hands in such a manner that the left hand plays the notes written down, while the right adds in consonances or dissonances, the result being an agreeable harmony to the glory of God and justifiable gratification of the senses; for the sole end and aim of general-bass, like that of all music, should be nothing else than God's glory and pleasant recreations. Where this object is not kept in view there can be no true music, but an infernal scraping and bawling.

Cap. III.

OF THE CLEF-SIGNATURES IN USE IN FIGURED-BASS.

All kinds of these clef-signatures are found in figured bass, such as discant, alto, tenor, &c. I will give a list of those most generally in use. (1.) The French violin clef, written on the first line thus: indicating the note g′. (2.) The German violin clef is written on the second line with the same sign: . (3.) The treble or soprano clef is the sign for that class of singers, and is written on the lowest line thus: indicating the note c′. (4.) The ordinary alto clef is written on the middle line thus: indicating the same note. (5.) The tenor, on the fourth line indicating the same note. (6.) The ordinary bass clef on the fourth line (sic) indicates the f.[9] (7.) More generally it may be observed that the sign indicates the once-marked g′ wherever it occurs. The sign is the once-marked c′. This

N.B.—When higher clefs than these occur in figured-bass they are called *Bassetgen*.

---

[9] In the MS. "the once-marked f′."

[10] This partially incorrect form of the bass clef is retained throughout the work by the writer. From this point onwards it has been corrected by me. It always indicates the f.

Cap. IV.

OF TIME OR MEASUREMENT.

Of this much need not here be said, for it is presupposed that a person wishing to learn figured-bass will not only have learnt the notes but also the intervals before doing so, whether by previous practice of music or from some other cause, and also the differences of time. For no one can inculcate a knowledge of time all at once. This must, however, be noticed, that in the present day one single kind of time is indicated in two ways, thus: $\overline{\underline{}}$, the second way being used by the French in pieces that are to be played quickly or briskly, and the Germans adopting it from the French. But the Germans and Italians abide for the most part by the first method, and adopt a slow time. If the piece is to be played fast the composer expressly adds *Allegro* or *Presto* to it; if slowly, the pace is indicated by the word *Adagio* or *Lento*.

Cap. V.

OF THE HARMONIC TRIAD.

The harmonic triad belongs properly to the subject of composition, but as figured-bass is a beginning of composition, and may even, because of the arrangement of consonances and dissonances, be called an extemporaneous composition, made by the person who plays the figured bass, the subject of the triad may be fitly mentioned in this place. Now if a person who desires to learn the subject can make good progress in this subject, and can impress it upon his memory, he may be sure that he has already mastered a great part of the entire art. The harmonic triad is a combination of the third and fifth which is placed above a bass note, and it may be constructed on all the notes, and both in the major and the minor—

 [11]

And so on through all the notes. This is called *Radix harmonica*, because all harmony springs from it. And this harmonic triad is either simple or full (*simplex* or *aucta*). (1.) The simple root (*Radix simplex*) is the simple triad, properly so-called, and consists only of the three notes, as shown in the example. (2.) *Radix auctor* or the increased or full triad has the octaves added in, as may be seen here:—

---

[11] This set of examples exactly agrees with the MS., notwithstanding the want of connection in the case of the fifth, and the wrong signature in either the sixth or seventh triad.

Cap. VI.

SUNDRY RULES FOR PLAYING FROM FIGURED-BASS IN FOUR PARTS THROUGHOUT.

Regula I.

The written bass is to be played with the left hand alone, but it may play the other parts, too, together with the right hand, whether they are indicated or not.

Regula II.

The third may be played with most of the figured notes, when it is not prevented by a second or a fourth expressly indicated.

Regula III.

Two fifths or two octaves must not occur next one another, for this is not only a fault but it sounds wrong. To avoid this there is an old rule, that the hands must always go against one another, so that when the left goes up the right must go down, and when the right goes up the left must go down.

Regula IV.

The best way to avoid and get rid of two fifths or octaves is to take the sixth in and so to effect an alternation.

Cap. VII.

HOW TO PLAY WHEN NO FIGURES ARE WRITTEN ABOVE THE BASS.

When nothing stands written above the bass, none but consonances, especially the third, fifth, and eighth are to be played; for example, in the case of a bass of this kind :—

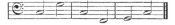

the consonances would be played in the right hand, as follows :—

But it is not necessary to remain bound down to one kind of treatment, but the lowest part may be made the uppermost part or the treble. Then the bass just given could be also played in this way :—

The inner part when placed uppermost gives another variety, and yet the notes are of the same kind :—

But that it may be seen how, when fifths and octaves follow one another, they do not fit together, but sound wrong, although they are perfect consonances, the following example is given :—

Cap. VIII.

Rules for the figures which stand above the notes.

Regula I.

The sign ♯ when it stands above a note betokens the major third, and those sharps which stand at the beginning of the bass part hold good for the treble also. For example, when such a ♯ stands above A the major third—*i.e.*, C♯—must be played, and so also the ♯ is indicated in the case of C where, if it were absent, it would be necessary to play C. And the case is the same with the ♭, namely, when the ♭ stands above the note the minor third is to be taken, and this rule must be strictly observed.

Regula II.

Thus, in short, all that is marked ♯ is to be in the major, and all that is marked ♭ in the minor.

Regula III.

When the number six stands above a note, it betokens the interval of the sixth, that is, I must count from the bass or from the note over which the figure stands and strike the sixth key. With this may be played either the third or the doubled sixth, and sometimes the octave, especially when a note follows immediately with the indication $\frac{6}{5}$; *e.g.*—

Regula IV.

When the fifth and sixth follow one another the fifth must be pre-pared—*i.e.*, must be in the previous chord—the third and octave are struck together with the bass and the sixth played afterwards, but if, on the contrary, the sixth comes before the fifth, none of this holds good, but it is to be played as written—*i.e.*, the 8 3 6 are taken with the bass and the fifth afterwards, the sixth may be doubled and only the 3 taken with it—*e.g.*—

REGULA V.

When 5 and 6 stand above a note, the fifth must be in the chord before, and the 3 and 6 must be added with the bass—*e.g.*—

REGULA VI.

When the fourth and the third stand together, the fourth must always be prepared, and the third struck afterwards; the fifth and octave are to be played simultaneously with the bass, whether they are indicated by figures or not; the term "preparation" signifies that a note is played in the treble part by the right hand, and then remains held by the right hand over the next following figured bass note.

----

[12] The slur is wanting in the MS.
[14] The slurs wanting in the MS.

[13] In the MS. $\flat$ 5 6.
[15] The slurs wanting in the MS.

Regula VII.

When the second and fourth are indicated over a note ($\frac{4}{2}$) the sixth is generally taken too, although not indicated. The notes in the chord of $\frac{6}{4}$ are always struck afresh when the bass note is held from the preceding chord, and the $\frac{6}{4}$ is resolved by means of the chord of $\frac{6}{5}$ when the bass descends a semitone, as may be seen by the following example—

Regula VIII.

When the false (imperfect) fifth ($\flat$ 5) is indicated, it must always be prepared; the 3 and 6, whether indicated or not, must be played together with the bass as seen in the following example—

Where such closing phrases (*Cadentz Clauseln*) as $\begin{smallmatrix}7&6&5\\3&4&4&3\end{smallmatrix}$ or $\begin{smallmatrix}7&6&5\\ \sharp4&4&\sharp\end{smallmatrix}$ occur, they are called Syncopations, because they are, as it were, bound and intricate in their character; sometimes, too, they are indicated simply by 3-4-4-3, but yet played in full, as below :—

Where passages of rapid notes following one another occur, as they frequently do in figured-bass, it is not necessary to play chords to every note, but only in minims or crotchets; the other bass notes are

---

[16] The third chord in the right hand, and the slurs, are wanting in the MS.
[17] Figuring in the MS. $\begin{smallmatrix}6\\5\flat\\\flat\end{smallmatrix}$. The slur from g'—g' is wanting.

called passing-notes because they slide, as it were, from one principal
note to the other—

CAP. IX.

REGULA I.

When the seventh stands alone, it must be prepared, and the 3 and
5, or 3 and 8, or frequently, too, the three doubled, are to be added with
the bass—

REGULA II.

When the seventh and sixth come one after the other, the seventh
must be prepared, and then either the 3, the 8, or the doubled 3 added
with the bass, and finally the sixth, either major or minor, must be
played afterwards—

---

[18] In the MS. the right hand has the chord g'.
b'
d'

[19] In the MS. the bass is

[20] The dots after the two notes in the inner parts are wanting.

REGULA III.

When the ninth and octave come together, the ninth must be pre-pared, the octave played after the bass, and the 3 and 5 played with the bass.

REGULA IV.

When the ninth and seventh are followed by the octave and sixth $\left(\begin{smallmatrix}9&8\\7&6\end{smallmatrix}\right)$ the $\frac{9}{7}$ must be prepared, and the 3 taken with the bass, the $\frac{8}{6}$ being played afterwards.

REGULA V.

Sometimes there also occur the figures $\left(\begin{smallmatrix}11&10\\9&8\end{smallmatrix}\right)$; in this case the $\frac{11}{9}$ must be prepared, the 5 taken with the bass, and the $\frac{10}{8}$ played after-wards. Those which remain cannot be well explained in words, but may be gathered from the last example.

But in order that what has hitherto been said may be impressed on the mind as completely as possible, we subjoin verbal and musical examples.

CAP. X.

EXEMPLUM I.

When no number stands over a note, nothing but the simple chord of 3, 5, and 8 is to be played, but this must be carefully observed, that always when the right hand descends, the left hand must go up, and when the left hand goes down, the right must ascend. This is called *motus* [21] *contrarius*, and in this way it is possible to avoid many con-secutive fifths and octaves—

[21] In the MS. *modus.*
[22] B in the left hand.

Exemplum II.

When the figure 4 stands above a note it must be prepared in the preceding chord, the 5 and 8 are then added, and lastly the 4 is resolved into 3—

Exemplum III.

When the figures 7 6 stand over a note, the seventh must be prepared in the preceding chord, and the 3 and 5, or the 3 and 8, or sometimes the doubled 3, are added with the bass, and the prepared seventh is resolved into the sixth—

---

[23] The chord is ⸾ in the right hand, and the figuring is $\frac{6}{5}$.

[24] Figuring ♭6.   [25] Figuring ♭$\frac{6}{5}$.

[26] c″ in the upper part.   [27] *Sic*, imperfect and incorrect.

EXEMPLUM IV.

When 9 8 stands over a note, the ninth must be prepared in the preceding chord, the 3 and 5 taken in the bass, and then the 9 resolved into 8—

EXEMPLUM V.

When $\frac{11}{9}$ $\frac{10}{8}$ or $\frac{9}{4}$ $\frac{8}{3}$ stand over a note, the $\frac{11}{9}$ or $\frac{9}{4}$ must be prepared, the 5 added in the bass, and then the discord resolved into $\frac{10}{8}$ or $\frac{8}{3}$. For the 9 is equivalent to the 2 and the 10 to the 3; the 11 to the 4 and the 12 to the 5—

---

[28] g′ in the alto part.　　　[29] *Sic.*　　　[30] *Sic.*
[31] No B flat in the bass.

Exemplum VI.

When $\frac{6}{4}$, or $\frac{4}{2}$, or 2 or 4 stand over a note, the bass must be held from the preceding chord, and the $\frac{4}{2}$ taken in the right hand, and resolved generally into $\frac{6}{5}$, if the bass descends a semitone or a whole tone—

Exemplum VII.

When 6 and 5 stand side by side over a note they are to be played one after the other, and either the 8 played with the bass or the 3 or the 6 doubled; but if one stands above the other, the 3 is to be added and played together with them.

---

[32] Figuring ♭7.   [33] *Sic.*

EXEMPLUM VIII.

When in the bass part there occurs the note that forms the third of the opening chord, the 6 must always be played to it, whether indicated or not, from which it follows that if a cadence leads into another key, the above will hold good of some other note—*e.g.*—

Starting from the C, the 6 must always be played above the E, and starting from A, the 6 must start above C—

[34] c′ in the alto.   [35] g′ in the tenor.

The following examples will throw more light on the subject—

38 g' in the alto.
39 The third chord is wanting in the right hand.
40 The ♭ not before, but above the bass note.
41 *Sic.*   42 *Sic.*   43 Only half a bar.   44 d' in the tenor.

49 d′ in the tenor.

50 The sharp before g′ is wanting.

51 Should be—

52 f′ ♯ in the tenor.

53 Figuring 56.

[56] *Sic.*

[57] This does not agree with the figuring, but might be corrected by reversing the order of the inner parts as they now stand, and making them crotchets,

[58] Inner parts $\frac{f\sharp}{d}$

[59] *Sic.*

11.

12.

---

60 The bass is certainly wrong. It is probably—

61 a♮ in the upper part is wanting.   62 *Sic.*   63 *Sic.*

[64] The g′ in the tenor, required by the figuring, is wanting.

[65] The f in the bass ought to be d. The sharp in the figuring thus loses its significance, but should probably be placed over the last crotchet.

[66] In the middle part, c″ alone, a crotchet.

15.

---

⁶⁷ *Sic.*   ⁶⁸ The a in the bass is wanting.   ⁶⁹ *Sic.*
⁷⁰ The figure 6 stands incorrectly above the a.

16.

[71] Probably intended for—   [72] The d' in the tenor is wanting.

[73] f' ♯ in the tenor.   [74] The last chord is wanting in the right hand.
[75] *Sic*   [76] *Sic.*   [77] *Sic.*

RULES FOR PLAYING EN QUATRE (IN GROUPS OF FOUR NOTES).

1. Consecutive descending passages with 6 indicated.

For the first set marked with 6, the sixth may be doubled, but for every alternate group the octave is to be taken, and continued to the end.

2. Consecutive ascending passages with 6 indicated.

The octave may be taken for the first set, but the sixth must be doubled in the alternate groups.

3. Consecutive passages with 5, 6.

The player must begin quite high up with the right hand, and proceed *per motum*[78] *contrarium* ; the octave is to be taken with the sixth.

4.

The 6 may be doubled, or the 8 may be added in.

N.B.—The 3 must always lie at the top.

5. Consecutive passages with 7, 6. N.B.—Dissonances are never to be doubled.

---

[78] MS., *Modum.*

The 5 may be taken with the 7, and the 8 with the following 6; the 6 may also be doubled. In cases where the 5 cannot be played with the 7, the 8 may be taken.

6. Passages with 7 to be resolved into 3. In playing this kind of *En quatre* the 5 or 8 may be taken with the 7.

7. The 7th which is resolved into the 3rd in such a manner that the 3rd taken with the 7th itself forms a new 7th, continuing in this way to the end.

---

[79] This example partly anticipates what is coming afterwards, probably only by an error of the transcriber.

With the first 7 the 5 or 8 may be taken, but if the 5 is taken with the first 7, the 8 must be taken with the next, and *vice versâ*.

8. The $\frac{6}{5}$ resolved into the 3. This kind is in four parts of itself.

The 8 must be taken with the preceding 6, for if the 6 were doubled the result would be consecutive fifths; the same holds good of the following examples.

9. The chord of 5♭ can be applied to the same passage as that in the foregoing examples.

10. The 4. 3.

This chord $\frac{6}{5}$ is brought in to assist in rendering many other different signatures, especially those which are consecutive, besides those with 4, 3, and they may be worked out with cognate phases (*Clausulæ cognatæ*).

11. The 9 resolved into 8 can also be well continued by means of the $\frac{6}{5}$.

12. The $\frac{9}{4}$, $\frac{8}{3}$ may be continued by the $\frac{6}{5}$.

[80] In bars 12-15, the sharps are wanting, both in the bass part and in the figuring.

[81] The figures on the fifth quaver are $\frac{9}{4}$
$\frac{}{5}$

[82] The figures over the first quaver are $\frac{9}{4}$.
$\frac{}{5}$

[83] The figures over the fifth quaver are $\frac{9}{4}$.
$\frac{}{5}$

Instead of the perfect 5th the 5♭ may be taken, as shown above, and in this way the $\frac{9}{4}, \frac{8}{3}$ can be brought in each by itself or both together.

13. The $\frac{4}{2}$ resolved into 6.

14. The $\frac{4}{2}$ may be brought in in still another way.

THE MOST USUAL CLAUSULÆ FINALES (CLOSING CADENCES).

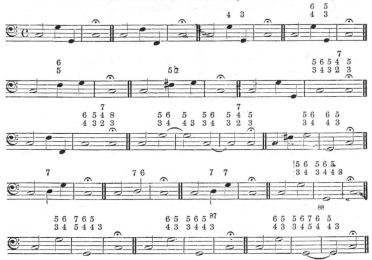

XIII.

(Ante, p. 118.)

Some most necessary rules from the *General Basso di J. S. B.*

(From Anna Magdalena Bach's Clavier book of 1725.)

The Scales. The scale with the greater third—*i.e.*, the major scale, is: (1.) *tonus*; (2.) a whole tone; (3.) a whole; (4.) a half; (5.) a whole; (6.) a half tone; (7.) a whole tone; (8.) a whole tone. The scale with the lesser third—*i.e.*, the minor scale, is: *tonus*; (2.) a whole tone; (3.) a half; (4.) a whole; (6.) a half; (7.) a whole; (8) a whole tone; from whence comes the following rule—

The 2nd is great in both scales; the 4th always smaller, the 5th and 8th are perfect, and as is the 3rd so are also the 6th and 7th.

The chord consists of 3 notes, namely, the 3rd, lesser or greater, the 5th and 8th, or, for instance, the chord of C is C E G.

On the next three pages are written the following rules in Bach' own hand:

Several rules of figured-bass.

1. Each chief note has a chord, either its own or borrowed.

2. The proper chord of a fundamental note consists of the 3, 5, and 8. N.B. Of these three *species* (*sic*) none can change except the 3, which may be great or small, according to whether the scale is major or minor.

---

[87] Figuring $_4$.   [88] Figuring $\frac{7}{4}$

3. A borrowed chord is one which consists of *species* other than the ordinary ones, being placed over a fundamental note, as for instance,

6 6 6 5 7 9
4, 3, 5, 4, 5, 7, &c.
2 6 3 8 3 3

4. A ♯ or ♭ alone over a note shows that the third is to be major in the case of a ♯ and minor in the case of a ♭, the other two *species* remaining the same.

5. A 5 alone, as also an 8, betokens the full chord.

6. A 6 alone may be filled up in three ways. 1st, with the 3 and 8; 2nd, with the doubled 3; and 3rd, with the doubled 6 and the 3. N.B.—Where 6 *major* and 3 *minor* occur together over a note, the sixth may not be doubled, because it would sound wrong; but the 8 and 3 must be played instead.

7. 2 over a note is accompanied with a doubled fifth, and sometimes also with 4 and 5 together; not seldom also—[here Bach seems to have intended to add something, for which he left an empty space in the book].

8. The ordinary 4, especially when followed by a 3, is accompanied with the 5 and 8, but if there is a stroke through it the 2 and 6 are played with it.

9. The 7 is accompanied in three ways: 1st, with the 3 and 5; 2nd, with the 3 and 8; and 3rd, with the doubled 3.

10. The 9 appears to have a similarity to the 2, and indeed by itself it is the 2 doubled, but it is accompanied in quite a different way— viz.: by the 3 and 5; instead of the 5 the 6 is put sometimes, but very rarely.

11. The $\frac{4}{2}$ takes the 6 as well, and sometimes the 5th in its place.

12. With the $\frac{5}{4}$ the 8 is taken, and the 4 resolves into the 3.

13. With the $\frac{6}{5}$ the 3 is taken, whether it be major or minor.

14. With the $\frac{7}{5}$ the 3 is taken.

15. With the $\frac{9}{7}$ the 3 is taken.

The other points which ought to be remembered are better conveyed by word of mouth than in writing.

XIV.

(Ante p. 133.)

Joh. Phil. Kirnberger's Elucidations of the third part of the " Clavierübung."[89]

Analysis

of several modulations and transpositions which occur in Herr Joh. Seb. Bach's hymns.

---

[89] Compare Kunst des reinen Satzes II., 1, p. 49.

On page 30 of Bach's collection of hymns, occurs the hymns: Dies sind die heil. 10 Gebot.

This hymn is in the Mixolydian mode, that is, G major with F natural instead of F sharp. In this mode it is possible to modulate into F, which neither suits the Lydian mode (our F) nor the Ionic (our C major) because their leading notes are only a semitone below the tonic instead of a whole tone: thus, in C major not B flat, but B is the leading note, and in F major not E flat, but E.

From the 25th to the 26th bars he modulates into F major and remains in that key until the 36th bar.

Note.—Ordinarily in a major mode, whether Ionic or Lydian, modulation is effected into the key of the fifth above with the greater third, as from C major to G major and from F major to C major.

In the Mixolydian mode (our G major) modulation cannot be effected from the chief key, G major, to its fifth above, D major, but must go into D minor, because F in the Mixolydian mode is the proper third from D.

The modulation into D minor takes place in this hymn from bars 39 and 40.

Note.—As the Mixolydian mode has no semitone below the tonic for a leading note, and consequently no major chord of the dominant, by means of which a closing cadence might be made; it has to close by going from the chord of the sub-dominant to that of the tonic, as—

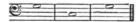

The modulation to D minor on page 35 (bars 1—19), in the Mixolydian mode, occurs in other places also, and the close is made by leading from C in the bass part to the tonic G.

The hymn, *Wir gläuben all an einen Gott*, on page 37, is in the Strict Doric mode, D minor, in which the major sixth B is essential, and the minor sixth B flat is allowed.

On page 39 this hymn is found in the same mode, but transposed into E; and in order to keep to the mode there is a ♯ before C, so that just as B was the major sixth from D, so C♯ is the major sixth from E, notwithstanding that ordinarily F♯ alone is in the signature of the key of E minor.

The chorale which follows this, *Vater unser im Himmelreich* is also in the Doric mode transposed to E, and to be known by the C♯ in the signature.

On page 46 is found this same hymn in its proper place in D without B flat—*i.e.*, with the major sixth B.

The hymn on page 47, *Christ unser Herr zum Jordan kam*, is also in the Doric mode, but transposed a note lower into C, as may be seen in the signature at the beginning. Now ordinarily in C minor there is a ♭ prefixed to B, E, and A; here, however, A natural is the essential major sixth, and A with the sign ♭ written before, as ♭A, is the permissible minor sixth from the key-note.

And on page 50 this same chorale is set in the Doric mode in its proper key of D. It closes at the end not on the key-note, but in its dominant chord of A with the greater third, C♯—*i.e.*, A major.

The hymn *Aus tiefer Noth schrei ich zu dir*, etc., on p. 51, is in the Phrygian mode, in the key of E with the lesser third, or E minor.

Note.—This mode differs from the other two minor modes, the Doric and Æolic, in that its second from the key-note is a semitone, as E to F; whereas in the Doric, the interval D to E, and in the Æolic the interval A to B, are whole tones.

The last two keys, as D minor and A minor, differ from one another in its being possible in the Doric mode to modulate into E minor, because this E has the lesser third belonging to the minor triad, and the perfect fifth—*i.e.*, E G B.

From A minor, the Æolian mode, it is not possible to modulate into B, since B has no perfect fifth.

In the Doric mode it is not possible to modulate by a semitone higher into E♭ major, nor is it possible to modulate from the Æolic mode by a semitone higher into B♭ major, but it is possible in the Phrygian mode to modulate from E to F major.

This same chorale is set on page 54 in this particular mode, but it is transposed a whole tone higher, being in F♯ instead of E.

The Phrygian mode may be recognised by the signature, for usually the minor mode of this key has both F♯ and G♯ marked in the signature; here, however, the second of the scale is G, F♯ bearing the same relation to it that E bears to F.

The hymn *Jesus Christus unser Heiland*, on page 56, is also in the Doric mode. On page 60 the same chorale is transposed into F.

Note.—The Doric mode may be recognised in the signature, since there is no ♭ before D, D being the essential major sixth from F; if, however, D with the flat written before it occurs, it is the permissible minor sixth from the key-note.

XV.

(Ante, p. 268).

This note contains a complete list not only of Bach's children by his second wife, but of their Godparents. The translators have abridged it.

1. *Christiane Sophie Henriette*, born in the summer of 1723; died June 29, 1726.

2. *Gottfried Heinrich*, baptised February 27, 1724. His Godmother was Frau Regina Maria, wife of Herr Johann H. Ernesti, Rector of the Thomasschule. He was buried at Naumburg, Feb. 12, 1763.

3. *Christian Gottlieb*, baptised April 14, 1725; died September 21, 1728.

4. *Elisabeth Juliane Friederike*, baptised April 5, 1726. The date of her death is unknown.

5. *Ernestus Andreas*, baptised October 30, 1727 ; died November 1, 1727.
6. *Regine Johanna*, baptised October 10, 1728. Her Godmothers were Anna Magdalena, "the well-beloved daughter" of Ernesti, and another of his daughters stood proxy for the other Godmother. She died April 25, 1733.
7. *Christiane Benedicta*, baptised January 1, 1730 ; died January 4, 1730.
8. *Christiane Dorothea*, baptised March 18, 1731. One of her Godmothers was Frau Christiana Dorothea, wife of J. C. Hebenstreit, Conrector of the School. She died August 30 or 31, 1732.
9. *Johann Christoph Friedrich*, baptised June 23, 1732 ; died January 26, 1795.
10. *Johann August Abraham*, baptised November 5, 1733. The younger Ernesti was one of his Godfathers, and Abraham Krügel, *Tertius* of the school, was the other. His Godmother was Frau Elisabeth Charitas, wife of Gessner, the new Rector. He died November 6, 1733.
11. *Johann Christian*, baptised September 7, 1735. The younger Ernesti, now Rector of the Thomasschule was one of his Godfathers. He died at the beginning of January, 1782.
12. *Johanna Caroline*, baptised October 30, 1737 ; died August 18, 1781.
13. *Regine Susanna*, baptised February 22, 1742 ; died December 14, 1809.

XVI.

(Ante, p. 273.)

Specification of the property belonging to and left by Herr Johann Sebastian Bach, deceased July 28, 1750, late Cantor to the school of St. Thomas, in Leipzig. (From archives preserved at Leipzig).

CAP. I.

	Thlr.	Gr.	Pf.
A share in a mine known as Ursula Erbstolln at Little Voigtsberg . . . . . . Worth	60	0	0

CAP. II.
In hard cash.

(a) in Gold	112	18	0

(b) in silver money.

(α) In specie, thalers, gulden and half gulden . . .	119	0	0
β In medals, tokens, &c.	25	20	0

CAP. III.
Assets to Credit.

A bond of Frau. Krebs	58	0	0
,, ,, Unruh	4	0	0
,, ,, Haase	3	0	0
Total	65	0	0

CAP. IV.

Found as cash in hand	36	0	0

Out of which some of the *Debitores passivi*, specified under †, Chap. I. and II., fols. a and b, were paid.

CAP. V.   In silver plate and other objects of value.

		Thlr.	Gr.	Pf.
1 pair of candlesticks, 32 loth,[90] at 12 gr.		16	0	0
1 ditto ditto, 27 loth, at 12 gr.		13	12	0
6 cups alike, 63 loth, at 11 gr.		28	7	0
1 ditto smaller, 10 loth, at 12 gr.		5	0	0
1 ditto pierced, 12 loth, at 13 gr.		6	12	0
1 ditto still smaller, 10 loth, at 11 gr.		4	14	0
1 tankard and cover, 28 loth, at 13 gr.		15	4	0
1 large coffee pot, 32 loth, at 13 gr.		19	12	0
1 ditto smaller, 20 loth, at 13 gr.		10	20	0
1 large tea pot, 28 loth, at 13 gr.		15	4	0
1 sugar basin and spoon, 26 loth, at 12 gr.		13	0	0
1 ditto smaller, 14 loth, at 12 gr.		7	0	0
1 snuff box and spoon, 12 loth, at 16 gr.		8	0	0
1 ditto, engraved, 8 loth, at 16 gr.		5	8	0
1 ditto, inlaid		1	8	0
2 salt cellars, 11 loth, at 12 gr.		5	12	0
1 coffee waiter, 11 loth, at 12 gr.		5	12	0
½-dozen knives, forks, and spoons, in a case, 48 loth, at 12 gr.		24	0	0
1 case of knives and spoons, 9 loth, at 10 gr.		3	18	0
1 gold ring		2	0	0
1 ditto		1	12	0
1 snuff box of Agate, set in gold		40	0	0
Total		251	11	0

CAP. VI.   In instruments.

	Thlr.	Gr.	Pf.
1 complete (*fournirt*) clavier, which, if possible, the family will keep	80	0	0
1 clavesin (*sic*)	50	0	0
1 ditto	50	0	0
1 ditto	50	0	0
1 ditto, smaller	20	0	0
1 lute-harpsichord	30	0	0
1 ditto	30	0	0
1 violin by Stainer	8	0	0
1 ordinary violin	2	0	0
1 ditto piccolo	1	8	0
1 viola	5	0	0
1 ditto	5	0	0
1 ditto	0	16	0
1 small bass viol	6	0	0
1 violoncello	6	0	0
1 ditto	0	16	0
1 viola da gamba	3	0	
1 lute	21	0	0
1 little spinett	3	0	0
Total	371	16	0

[90] A *loth* weight is about half-an-ounce.

Cap. VII.

In white metal.

	Thlr.	Gr.	Pf.
1 large dish	1	8	0
1 ditto smaller	0	16	0
1 ditto .	0	16	0
1 ditto smaller	0	8	0
1 ditto .	0	8	0
1 small dish	0	6	0
1 ditto .	0	6	0
1 ditto still smaller	0	4	0
1 ditto	0	4	0
1 ditto .	0	4	0
1 washing basin .	0	8	0
2 dozen plates, each ¾-lb., at 4 gr.	3	0	0
4 jugs with metal fittings .	1	8	0
Total	9	0	0

Cap. VIII.

In copper and pinchbeck.

	Thlr.	Gr.	Pf.
2 dish covers with iron fittings .	3	0	0
3 pairs pinchbeck candlesticks	2	0	0
1 pinchbeck coffee pot.	0	16	0
1 ditto smaller .	0	16	0
1 ditto still smaller	0	6	0
1 pinchbeck coffee tray	0	16	0
1 copper kettle .	0	8	0
1 ditto smaller .	0	8	0
Total	7	22	0

Cap. IX.

Clothes and personal sundries.

	Thlr.	Gr.	Pf.
1 silver court sword .	12	0	0
1 stick, silver mount .	1	8	0
1 pair silver shoe buckles .	0	16	0
1 coat of *Gros du Tour* (silk), somewhat worn	8	0	0
1 mourning cloak of *Drap des Dames* .	5	0	0
1 cloth coat .	6	0	0
Total	33	0	0

Cap. X.

At the wash.

11 surplices .

CAP. XI.

House furniture.

	Thlr.	Gr.	Pf.
1 chest of drawers	14	0	0
1 linen press	2	0	0
1 clothes press	2	0	0
1 dozen black leather chairs	2	0	0
½-dozen leather chairs	2	0	0
1 writing table with drawers	3	0	0
6 tables	2	0	0
7 wooden bedsteads	2	8	0
Total	29	8	0

CAP. XII.

In theological books.
In folio.

Calovius, works, 3 vols.	2	0	0
Luther, Opera, 7 vols.	5	0	0
Idem liber, 8 vols.	4	0	0
Ej. Tischreden (Table talk)	0	16	0
Ej. Examen Conc. Trid.	0	16	0
Ej. Comment. über den Psalm 3ter Theil	0	16	0
Ej. Hauss-Postille (family sermons) , ...	1	0	0
Müller, Schluss Kette	1	0	0
Tauler, Predigten (sermons)	0	4	0
Scheubler, Gold-Grube (gold diggings) 11 parts, 2 vols. .	1	8	0
Pintingius, Reise Buch der Heil. Schrifft (Bünting, Itinerary of the Scriptures)	0	8	0
Olearius, Haupt Schlüssel (master key to the Scriptures) 3 vols.	2	0	0
Josephus, Geschichte der Jüden (history)	2	0	0

In quarto.

Pfeiffer, Apostolische Christen-Schule	1	0	0
Ej. Evangelische Schatzkammer (treasury) . . .	0	16	0
Pfeiffer, Ehe Schule	0	4	0
Ej. Evangelischer Augapffel (Apple of the Eye) . . .	0	16	0
Ej. Kern und Safft der Heil S. (Core and Sap of Sacred Scripture)	1	0	0
Müller, Predigten über den Schaden Josephs . . .	0	16	0
Ej. Schluss Kette	1	0	0
Ej. Atheismus	0	4	0
Ej. Judaismus	0	16	0
Stenger, Postille	1	0	0
Ej. Grundveste der Augspurg, Conf. (Ground of the Augsburg Conf.)	0	16	0
Geyer, Zeit und Ewigkeit (Time and Eternity) . . .	0	16	0
Carried forward	29	4	0

	Thlr.	Gr.	Pf.
Brought forward	29	4	0
Rambach, Betrachtung (Reflections)	1	0	0
Ej. Betrachtung über den Rath Gottes (Reflections on the Councils of God)	0	16	0
Luther, Hauss Postille	0	16	0
Frober, Psalm	0	4	0
Unterschiedene Predigten (various sermons) . . .	0	4	0
Adam, Güldener Augapffel (Golden Apple of the Eye) .	0	4	0
Meiffart, Erinnerung (Reminiscences)	0	4	0
Heinisch, Offenbahrung Joh. (On the Revelation of St. John)	0	4	0
Jauckler, Richtschnur der Christl. Lehre (Clue to Christian Doctrine)	0	1	0

In octavo.

	Thlr.	Gr.	Pf.
Franck, Hauss Postilla	0	8	0
Pfeiffer, Evangelische Christen Schule . . .	0	8	0
Ej. Anti-Calvin	0	8	0
Ej. Christenthum	0	8	0
Ej. Anti-Melancholicus	0	8	0
Rambach, Betrachtung über die Thränen Jesu (On the Tears of Jesus)	0	8	0
Müller, Liebes Flamme (Flame of Love)	0	8	0
Ej. Erquickstunden (Hours of Refreshment) . . .	0	8	0
Ej. Rath Gottes (God's Councils)	0	4	0
Ej. Lutherus defensus	0	8	0
Gerhard, *Schola Pietatis*, 5 vols.	0	12	0
Neümeister, Tisch des Herrn (The Lord's Table) . .	0	8	0
Ej. Lehre von der Heil Tauffe (Doctrine of Holy Baptism)	0	8	0
Spener, Eyfer wider das Pabstthum (Zeal against the Papacy)	0	8	0
Hunn, Reinigkeit der Glaubens Lehre (Purity of Faith and Doctrine)	0	4	0
Kling, Warnung vor Abfall von der Luther. Relig. (Warning against the Decay of the Lutheran Religion) . . .	0	4	0
Arnd, Wahres Christenthum	0	8	0
Wagner, Leipziger Gesangbuch, 8 vols.	1	0	0
Total	38	17	0

Recapitulation.

	Thlr.	Gr.	Pf.
Fol. 1 *a*, Cap. I., one share	60	0	0
„ 1 *a*, „ II., in cash	—	—	—
a, in gold	112	18	0
„ 1 *a*, „ „ *b*, in silver money	—	—	—
a, in thalers, gulden, and half-gulden .	119	0	0
„ 1 *b*, „ „ β, in other pieces	25	20	0
„ 1 *b*, „ III., in outstanding assets	65	0	0
Carried forward	382	14	0

	Thlr.	Gr.	Pf.
Brought forward	382	14	0
Fol. 2 *a*, Cap. IV., in cash in hand, out of which some of the debts entered under fol. 8, *a* and *b* † Cap. I. and II. are paid .	36	0	0
,, 2 *a* and *b*, Cap. V., in silver-plate and other valuables	251	11	0
,, 3 *a*, Cap. VI., in instruments	371	16	0
,, 3 *b*, ,, VII., in white metal	9	0	0
,, 3 *b* and 4*a*, Cap. VIII., in copper and pinchbeck . .	7	22	0
,, 4 *a*, Cap. IX., in clothes and personal sundries . .	32	0	0
,, 4 *b*, ,, X., at the wash, 11 surplices . . .	—	—	—
,, 4 *b*, ,, XI., in house furniture	29	8	0
,, 5 *a* and *b*, 6 *a* and *b*, Cap. XII., in theological books .	38	17	0
Total	1158	16	0

†

Debita passiva.

According to their bills, some of which were paid out of the money specified in Cap. IV., of fol 2.

CAP. I.

	Thlr.	Gr.	Pf.
(As per bills)	143	21	6

CAP. II.

Other necessary expenses.

In necessary matters	1	8	0
To Herr Schübler	2	16	0
To the maid	4	0	0
For taxing (the property)	1	0	0
Total	9	0	0

Recapitulation.

Fol. 8, *a* and *b*, Cap. I., in payment of bills	143	21	6
Fol. 8, *b*, Cap. II., in other expenses	9	0	0
Total	152	21	6

Anna Magdalena Bach, widow.

D. Friedrich Heinrich Graff, as *curator* (representing her interests).

Catharina Dorothea Bach.

Wilhelm Friedemann Bach, for myself and for Carl Emanuel Bach, my brother, and as representing my sister above named.

Gottfried Heinrich Bach.

Gottlob Sigismund Hesemann, as representing the above, G. H. Bach.

Elisabeth Juliana Friderica Altnikol (born Bach).

Johann Christoph Altnikol, as the husband and representative of my wife Elisabeth Juliana Friderica (born Bach).

Johann Gottlieb Görner, as guardian in their father's stead, of
Johann Christoph Friedrich Bach;
Johann Christian Bach ;
Johanna Carolina Bach;
Regina Susanna Bach.

THE deed of appointment of guardians sets forth that, whereas
"The Worshipful Gentleman, Herr Johann Sebastian Bach, late
Cantor of the School of St. Thomas, at Leipzig, had fallen asleep in
the Lord, on July 28, 1750, and had left three children of his first
marriage, namely :—
Herr Wilhelm Friedemann Bach;
Herr Carl Philipp Emanuel Bach; and
Jungfrau Catharina Dorothea Bach;
and no less than six children of his marriage with his present widow,
Dame Anna Magdalena (born Wülcke), namely :—
Herr Gottfried Heinrich Bach.
Dame Elisabeth Juliana Friderica (married to Altnikol) ;
Herr Johann Christoph Friedrich Bach ;
Jungfrau Johanna Carolina Bach ; and
Jungfrau Regina Susanna Bach;
of which the four last are still under age, and has left his property to
be divided among his said widow and heirs.   Herr Johann Gottlieb
Görner, *Director Musices* at the University of Leipzig, is appointed
guardian of the four children under age, and with Herr Gottlob
Sigismund Hesemann *L. L. Studiosus*, as representative of Herr
Gottfried H. Bach, who is imbecile."

I.

All the heirs (each being named) and the guardians and
representatives of those who are legally incapable, having read through
the specification of the property left by their father, each and all
declare it to be correct and satisfactory.

2.

With regard to the share mentioned in Cap. I. of the Specification,
the heirs are all agreed that it shall remain in a common fund and put
into the charge and keeping of the widow, who shall take her own third
part, leaving the rest to be equally divided among the children.

3.

The cash in gold and silver moneys, specified in Cap. II., *a* and
b, is distributed equally in kind among the heirs, the widow's portion
of one-third amounting to 77 thlrs. 6 gr., and that of each child to 17
thlrs. 4 gr.

4.

The coins enumerated in Cap. II. β. were also divided *in natura* among them by lot; the widow's share amounting to 8 thlrs. 14 gr. 8 pf., and that of each child to 1 thlr. 21 gr. 11 pf.   Some of the pieces were probably curious, and may have had a value above that of the bullion.

5.

Of the outstanding assets, specified in Cap. III., the widow Bach takes her sister's bond of 58 thlrs., and as her share of it amounts to 19 thlrs. 8 gr., she has paid the remaining 38 thlrs. 16 gr. to the children in cash, namely, to each 4 thlrs. 7 gr. 1 pf.; but they, with the permission of their lawfully appointed guardians, have given it back to the widow, and ceded the bond to her in such a way that she can dispose of it according to her pleasure, as her own property; and the widow has given to them a receipt for the same in proper form.

As regards the bonds of Unruh and Haase, these persons are not to be found, and the widow is, therefore, left in possession of the papers.

6.

The ready money in hand has been spent in part payment of outstanding debts, for which see Section 14.

7.

In the interest, and with the consent of all concerned, the agate snuff box, mounted in gold, is for the present withdrawn from among the valuables specified in Cap. V., and valued at 40 thlrs., partly because it is a piece of property fit only for the collector and connoisseur, and partly because it is too valuable to be assigned by lot to either of the children, and until a purchaser shall be found it is left in care of the widow. (All the rest of the things are allotted according to the valuation of Herr Berthold, the goldsmith, in such a way as that the widow, having a pair of candlesticks, the larger coffee pot, the tea pot, two of the snuff boxes, the pierced cup, and the coffee waiter, acquires the value of 72 thlrs.; and the children, each, sundry articles to the sum of 15 thlrs. 15 gr. 11 pf. Altnikol's wife became the possessor of the tankard with the lid, and the eldest son and daughter each had a gold ring.)

8.

The instruments specified under Cap. VI. (as they cannot be divided, and as no purchaser offers) are also set aside, with the hope that they may be sold before Easter. The widow is meanwhile to have the care and use of them, and when each may be sold is to keep her third of the purchase money and divide the other two-thirds among the nine children. But because Herr Joh. Christian Bach, the youngest son of the deceased, had received from his father during his lifetime three claviers with pedal, these have not been included in the specification, since he declares them to have been given to him as a present, and has brought witnesses to that effect, the widow and Herr Altnikol and Herr Hesemann, having known of it. The guardian, however, finds something suspicious in the matter, as do also the children of the first marriage, but they refrain from urging their objections, and, on the contrary, the widow, the other heirs and their representatives acknowledge and admit the gift.

9.

The white metal, copper, and pinchbeck goods, enumerated in Caps. VII. and VIII., have by common consent been exempted from taxation, and after the deduction of one-third, amounting to 5 thlrs. 15 gr. 4 pf., each child takes a share of 1 thlr. 6 gr.

10.

The silk coat, the mourning cloak, the shoe buckles, and the stick have also been exempted from taxation, and the widow having taken her share of the 5 thlrs., children take each 1 thlr. 2 gr. 8 pf. The silver sword, belonging to the court accoutrements, was taken by the eldest son, Herr Friedemann, who paid for it; and the 6 thlrs. paid for the cloth coat, which also belonged to the court accoutrements, and which was previously left to Gottfried Heinrich Bach, was divided among the five sons, the share of each being 1 thlr. 4 gr. 9 pf.

11.

The linen of the deceased is, with the unanimous consent of the seniors, divided among the children under age.

12.

The furniture is also by common consent taken at the specified valuation, and the widow takes 9 thlrs. 18 gr. 8 pf., and each child 2 thlrs. 4 gr. 1 pf.

13.

The books are allotted according to the valuation; the widow's share is 12 thlrs. 21 gr. 8 pf., each child's 2 thlrs. 20 gr. 10 pf.

14.

Finally, the debts enumerated under † Cap. I. and II. as amounting to 152 thlrs. 21 gr. 6 pf., having been found perfectly correct after the sum of 36 thlrs., specified as cash in hand in Cap. IV., has been deducted, there still remains a balance of debt of 116 thlrs. 21 gr. 6 pf. The widow, therefore, pays for her third part 38 thlrs. 23 gr. 2 pf., and each child 8 thlrs. 15 gr. 10 pf., which is deducted from their respective shares of the inheritance. And the widow and children and their representatives agree to defray the cost and charges of their father's funeral.

15.

Mem.—Whereas Herr Görner is appointed to represent the children under age only so far as the division and distribution of the estate is concerned, and the widow is, irrespective of that, their sole and only guardian; the guardian is to be responsible for the joint division of the property in accordance with the foregoing statement.

Leipzig, Nov. 11, 1750.

Signed by all the family and representatives.

(The accounts of each child by lot, payment, and purchase are given at full length in the German edition, where the curious reader will find two petitions from Dame Anna Magdalena Bach, widow, to the Rector and Patrons of the University; the first, dated October 17, 1750, begging that, whereas her husband, J. S. Bach, had died on July 28, having four children under age, they would be pleased to appoint a *tutor* or guardian immediately for the protection of the interests of these children; and the second, dated October 21, 1750, craving that since she is fully determined not to marry again, but to take upon herself the general guardianship of the children, they will confirm her in this, and appoint Herr Görner to represent her and them in the matter of the division of her late husband's estate.

The last document quoted is a petition on the part of Johann Christoph Friedrich Bach that the Council would confirm him in the possession of the instrument left to his father by J. C. Hoffmann, for which, at the same time, he deposits a receipt).

MUSICAL SUPPLEMENT

ORGAN CHORALE.
«Warum betrübst du dich, mein Herz.»

Joh. Christoph Bach.

* The «d» is wanting in the MS.

FUGUE.

Supplement II. (Vol. I. p. 427).

Tomaso Albinoni.

Supplement III. (Vol. I. p. 431).

SONATA

by

JOHANN ADAM REINKEN.

Allegro.

Allemande.
Allegro.

Courante.

Sarabande.

Gigue.
Presto.

The two clavier pieces mentioned in Vol. II. p. 39.

I.
Applicatio.

Joh. Seb. Bach.

II.
Praeambulum.

Joh. Seb. Bach.

PRAELUDIUM.

Joh. Seb. Bach.

SONATA.
For Violin and Bass
by
T. ALBINONI.
The figured bass accompaniment by Heinrich Nikol.Gerber,
Corrected throughout by Sebastian Bach.

1 · Gerber; originally thus:

2) Gerber: 3) Gerber:

Allegro.

Adagio.

Allegro.

7) Gerber: 8) Gerber: 9) Gerber: 10) Gerber:

First altered
by Bach to:

11) Gerber:

Supplement VII. (Vol. II. p. 551).

Final Chorale of Part I. of the Matthew Passion
in its original form.

Supplement VIIIᵃ (Vol. III. p. 109, and Vol. I. p. 594).

CHORALE
"Gelobet seist du Jesu Christ."
Arranged by Sebastian Bach for accompanying the congregation.

Supplement VIII.^b (Vol. III. p. 113).

SIX HYMNS.

Apparently composed by Sebastian Bach.

I.

Hier lieg ich nun, o Va _ ter al _ ler Gna _ den, vor
(Hier lieg ich nun, mein Gott, zu dei _ nen Fü _ ssen, ach

dei _ nem Thron mit Sünden _ last be _ la _ den, mein ei _ gen Herz schilt
la _ sse mich der süssen Huld ge _ nie _ ssen, mit welcher du die

mich ins An _ ge _ sicht, doch schrei ich noch: Ach Gott, ver _ stoss mich nicht!
Dei _ nen oft er _ quickst, und ih _ nen Licht, Trost, Freud und Kraft zuschickst.)

II.

Das walt mein Gott, Gott Va _ ter, Sohn, und heilger Geist, der mich erschaffen

hat, mir Leib und Seel gegeben, im Mutterleib das Leben, ge_sund ohn allem Schad.

III.

Gott, mein Herz dir Dank zu _ sen_det, weil mit Wohlthun die _ ser Tag
An _ ge _ fan _ gen und vol _ len_det, so dass ich mit Jauchzen sag:

Ich bin al _ ler Sün _ den los, ru he sanft in Je _ su Schooss,

ich bin Je _ su Braut heut worden, steh in sei _ nem Lie _ bes _ or _ den.

IV.

Mei_ne See_le, lass es ge _ hen, wie es in der Welt jetzt geht.
Mei_ne See_le, lass es ste _ hen, wie es je _ tzo geht und steht.

Lieb_ste See_le, hal _ te stil _ le, den _ ke, dass es Got _ tes Wil_le.

V.

Ich gnü_ge mich an meinem Stande,
Und acht es gar für kei_ne Schande,

in den der Höchste mich ge _ setzt,
bin ich nicht je_dem gleich ge_ schätzt.

Ich darf so we_nig mei_nen Schö_pfer anklagen als der Thon den Töpfer.

VI.

Wa _ rum be_trübst du dich und
Du sorgst,wie will es doch noch

beu_gest dich zur
end _ lich mit dir

Er _ den,mein
wer _ den, und

sehr geplag_ter Geist,mein ab_ge_mat_ter Sinn.
fährest ü _ ber Welt und ü _ berHim_mel hin.

Wirst du dich nicht recht fest in

Got_tes Wil_len grün_den,kannst du in E _ wigkeit nicht wahre Ru _ he fin_den.

Supplement IX. (Vol. III. p. 239).

Solution of a seven-part Canon by Bach above a ground bass (Basso ostinato).

INDEX.

III.

ERRATA.

VOL. I.

Page 35, line 6 from bottom, for " Cembalo " read " Harpsichord."

,, 43, line 19, for " Gospel " read " Gospels."

,, 49, bottom line, for " Gospel " read " Gospels."

,, 164, line 14, omit comma.

,, 165, for three bottom lines, read " Of his sacred melodies, which were composed partly . . . . . and partly to his own verses, that."

,, 166, line 22, for " Cantata " read " Cantate."

,, 186, line 4 of note, for " Lüneberg " read " Lüneburg."

,, 190, bottom line of note 15, for " that year " read " 1870."

,, 208, line 5, for " Manier " read " mannerism."

,, 249, note 89, at end add " 6."

,, 251, line 8, for " *manieren* " read " mannerisms."

,, 296, note 125, for " Bach Soc." read " B. G."

,, 328, line 12, for " turned " read " turned up."

,, 351, note 24, for " B. S." read " B. G."

,, 399, note 81, after " Cah. 8." insert " (247)."

,, 515, line 19, for " Zachaus " read " Zachau."

,, 521, line 2 from bottom, for " Zachaus " read " Zachau."

,, 526, note 235, for " App. B. V." read " App. B. VI. (Vol. III., p. 300)."

,, 537, note 248, for " Brocke " read " Brockes."

,, 640, for lines 6—7, read " has only a figured-bass accompaniment, one has a single instrument concertante, and one is accompanied," &c.

VOL. II.

Page 9, note 17, for " Siculs " read " Sicul."

,, 11, line 1, for " Brock's " read " Brockes'."

,, 80, line 4, for " C minor " read " C major."

,, 82, line 8 from bottom, for " in augmentation " read " as a double fugue."

,, 100, note 142, last line, for " D major " read " G major."

,, 161, line 18, for " minor " read " major."

,, 172, at end of note 247, add " (200)."

,, 186, note 13, for " App. B. VI." read " App. B. II. (Vol. III., p. 301)."

,, 200, omit note 40.

,, 203, for note 43 read " App. B. IV. D."

,, 205, for note 45 read " App. B. IV. A."

,, 208, for note 50 read " App. B. IV. E."

Page 214, for note 59 read " App. B. IV. C."

   ,,   232, note 86, for " see App. B. VII." read " given, in an abridged form, in App. B. IV. A."

   ,,   280, for note 159 read " App. B. IV. B."

   ,,   293, note 195, last line but two, for " supplement I." read " supplement VI."

   ,,   344, line 26, for " Brocke " read " Brockes."

   ,,   345, line 19, for " Brocke's " read " Brockes'."

   ,,   348, line 10, for " Brocke " read " Brockes."

   ,,   405, line 21, for " der " read " dir."

   ,,   415, line 9, for the " rhythm only " read " the rhythm alone being identical with that of the theme."

   ,,   418, line 14, for " *Schalmei* " read " *schalmeien.*"

   ,,   426, line 19, for " Brocke's " read " Brockes' "

   ,,   468, for note 527 read " ante, p. 357."

   ,,   536, line 7, for " Enter not into judgment " read " Herr, gehe nicht ins Gericht."

   ,,   551, note 634, for " No. 3 " read " No. VII."

   ,,   633, note 785, for " note " read " ante."

   ,,   671, in the second musical example (line 6) the first of the group of four semiquavers in the lower part should be an F sharp, not a tied E natural.

   ,,   698, line 18, for " note 3 of Vol. III." read " note 3 of App. A. to Vol. III."

   ,,   702, line 6, for " sie " read " sei."

   ,,   702, line 8, for " Sündenkneckt " read " Sündenknecht."

   ,,   715, line 32, for " sie " read " sei."

   ,,   717, line 7, for " Academy for Singing " read " Singakademie."

VOL. III.

Page 11, after note 7 insert " and will be found in an abridged form in App. B. (to Vol. III.), No. I."

   ,,   109, note 151, line 4, for (4 A.) read (VIII. A.)

   ,,   113, note 161, line 2, for (4 B.) read (VIII. B.)

   ,,   133, note 214, for " App. B. XII." read " App. B. XIV."

   ,,   239, note 459, last line, for " No. 4 " read " No. IX."